French politics
and society

French politics and society

ALISTAIR COLE

PRENTICE HALL

LONDON   NEW YORK   TORONTO   SYDNEY   TOKYO
SINGAPORE   MADRID   MEXICO CITY   MUNICH   PARIS

First published 1998 by
Prentice Hall Europe
Campus 400, Maylands Avenue
Hemel Hempstead
Hertfordshire, HP2 7EZ
A division of
Simon & Schuster International Group

Typeset in 9.5/12pt Sabon
by Dorwyn Ltd, Rowlands Castle, Hants

Printed and bound in Great Britain by
Hartnolls Limited, Bodmin, Cornwall

Library of Congress Cataloging-in-Publication Data

Cole, Alistair, 1959–
    French politics and society / Alistair Cole.
      p.   cm.
    Includes bibliographical references and index.
    ISBN 0-13-433954-1 (pbk. : alk. paper)
      1. France–Politics and government–1945– 2. France–
    Social conditions–1945– I. Title.
    JN2594.2.C63   1998
    306.2'0944-dc21   97-3710
                                                       CIP

British Library Cataloguing in Publication Data

A catalogue record for this book is available from
the British Library

ISBN: 0–13–433954–1 (pbk)

1 2 3 4 5   02 01 00 99 98

Contents

Preface

French Politics and Society aspires to be a student text with a difference. It is aimed primarily at undergraduates studying French politics in a wide range of possible courses and degree schemes in further and higher education. It also endeavours to attract postgraduate students and professional researchers into French and European politics working in several disciplines, notably political science, European studies, history and sociology.

French Politics and Society attempts to be fairly comprehensive in its scope, bringing together various fields of discussion within one text. While drawing upon examples from all stages of French history, the book stresses in particular the importance of the modifications to the French polity which have occurred since 1981. The central underlying theme of the book is that there has been a weakening of 'French exceptionalism' throughout the 1980s and 1990s, as a result of both internal and external pressures upon the French political system . This has had an impact upon the nation's political institutions (Part II), its representative forces (Part III) and its role in Europe (Part IV). Put simply, France was a country rather less different from its European neighbours in 1995 than in 1981. The various pressures at work will become apparent when reading the individual chapters. The underlying intellectual rationale for the book is to provide an overview of this process, as it affects various aspects of the French polity, with special attention being paid to developments since the early 1980s.

Most chapters are concerned primarily with the French Fifth Republic (1958–). As it approaches its fortieth anniversary, the Fifth Republic can boast to be the second longest surviving political regime in post-revolutionary French history. In terms of this most basic measurement, the regime must be considered a success. Its longevity has rested upon a combination of political stability, institutional adaptability and democratic legitimacy that has provided a just equilibrium. Its credibility is testified by the fact that no serious political party contests the underlying legitimacy of the regime, as opposed to particular features of it.

The case for the Fifth Republic has been abundantly argued throughout its existence. For apologists, the French Fifth Republic is a stable political system superimposed upon a dynamic society. It has restored political stability from the chronic precariousness of the post-war Fourth Republic. The regime has proved

Map 1 French regions and departments

flexible and adaptable. The alternation in power between right and left in 1981, and the repeated experiences of 'cohabitation' (1986–8, 1993–5) have proved that the political regime has the capacity to withstand systemic pressures that many had predicted would hasten its demise. Measured in terms of its political performance, the regime has considerable achievements to its credit. It has presided over a strengthening of France's international prestige and economic prowess. France has been a key member state of the European Union since its creation in the late 1950s, exercising a political weight beyond its numerical and economic significance. The regime can take some credit for the transformation of the French economy from an overwhelmingly rural, small-scale enterprise into a dynamic, high-technology outfit. French society itself has followed suit, moving

away from a rural, small town community into a modern, urban and sophisticated populace.

Set against this, more pessimistic observers have noted a new crisis of confidence,
if not in France's political institutions, then at least in the politicians exercising the
highest political offices. The spate of political corruption scandals throughout the
1980s and 1990s has revived a deeply rooted anti-political streak within French
political culture. The feeling that *ils sont tous pourris* ('they're all corrupt') recalled
similar Poujadist sentiments of the 1950s during the twilight years of the Fourth
Republic. The distance between a centralised Parisian élite and the mass of the
population appears as great as ever. Such sentiments provide the background
against which latent traditions of political and social intolerance have resurfaced.
The combined issues of race relations, security and national preference have assumed a renewed importance, to the extent of harming France's international
reputation as the country of the rights of man.

This book draws upon disparate sources of inspiration. Rather than enumerate
these in detail, I should like to thank the numerous people who have contributed
directly or indirectly to the publication of the book. Clare Grist of Prentice Hall
demanded exacting standards, a tradition to which her successor Ruth Pratten
remained faithful. This was all in a good cause. Tim Stenhouse is warmly thanked
for his contribution to Chapter 14, which is mainly his. The comments made by the
anonymous readers were invaluable, helping me to improve the final product. I
thank them – whoever they are! The writing-up stage of this book coincided with
my living in France, conducting research for an ESRC project on French regional
and local governance. Unattributed comments in Chapters 7, 8 and 12 came from
several of the numerous interviews conducted in the course of 1994–5 in connec-
tion with this project. I should also like to thank Peter John (University of South-
ampton) for his stimulating insights, as well as Patrick Le Galès, Joseph Fontaine
and Erik Neveu (Institute of Political Studies, Rennes) and Gérard Marcou (University of Lille 2) for correcting certain of my misconceived ideas about contemporary
France. Finally, I should like to thank the MA students who followed my course,
'End of the French Exception' at Bradford University. Their perceptive criticisms
forced me to abandon certain cherished themes, and to modify others.

Alistair Cole

Abbreviations

CAP	Common Agricultural Policy
CDF	Charbonnages de France
CDS	Centre des démocrates sociaux
CERES	Centre de recherches et d'études socialistes
CES	Comité économique et social
CESR	Comité économique et social régional
CFDT	Confédération française démocratique du travail
CGPME	Confédération générale des petites et moyennes entreprises
CGT	Confédération générale du travail
CMP	Commission mixte paritaire
CNESOM	Conférence nationale des élus socialistes originaires du Maghreb
CNPF	Conseil national du patronat français
CPSU	Communist Party of the Soviet Union
CSA	Conseil supérieur de l'audiovisuel
DATAR	Délégation à l'aménagement du territoire et à l'action régionale
DDE	Direction départmentale d'équipement
DGD	Dotation générale de la décentralisation
DGE	Dotation générale d'équipement
DIV	Délégation interministérielle à la ville
EC	European Community
ECSC	European Coal and Steel Community
Edf	Electricité de France
EEC	European Economic Community
EMS	European monetary system
EMU	Economic and monetary union
ENA	Ecole nationale d'Administration
EU	European Union
EURATOM	European Atomic Energy Agency
FD	Force démocrate
FEN	Fédération de l'éducation nationale
FIS	Front islamique du salut
FN	Front national

FNLC	Front national pour la libération de la Corse
FNSEA	Fédération nationale des syndicats des exploitants agricoles
FO	Force ouvrière
FSU	Fédération syndicale unitaire
GATT	General Agreement on Tariffs and Trade
Gdf	Gaz de France
GDP	Gross domestic product
GRECE	Groupements de recherches et d'études pour la civilisation européenne
LO	Lutte ouvrière
Mdc	Mouvement des citoyens
MPF	Mouvement pour la France
MRG	Mouvement des radicaux de gauche
MRP	Mouvement républicain populaire
MSI	Movimento Sociale Italiano
NATO	North Atlantic Treaty Organisation
ONI	Office national d'immigration
PCF	Parti communiste français
PR	Parti républicain
PS	Parti socialiste
PSU	Parti socialiste unifié
RI	Républicains indépendants
RPF	Rassemblement du peuple français
RPR	Rassemblement pour la république
SFIO	Section française de l'internationale ouvrière
SGCI	Secrétariat général du comité interministériel
SNES	Syndicat national de l'enseignement secondaire
SNI	Syndicat national des instituteurs
SOFRES	Société française des enquêtes par sondage
SPD	Sozialedemokratische Partei Deutschlands
TGV	Train à grande vitesse
TPG	Trésorier-Payeur général
UDF	Union pour la démocratie française
UDR	Union des démocrates pour la république
UIMM	Union des industries métallurgiques et minières
UK	United Kindgom
UNR	Union pour la nouvelle république
UPA	Union patronale des artisans
US	United States of America
USSR	Union of Soviet Socialist Republics
WEU	West European Union

Part I

The making of modern France

Chapter 1

The making of modern France

1.1 Introduction and objectives

This introductory chapter places the evolution of the French polity in its broad historical perspective up until 1958. The chapter provides an overview of French political history, with particular emphasis on the role of the state in building a French identity and upon the legacy of the French Revolution and its aftermath. As a result of multiple social, economic and ideological cleavages; and of territorial, linguistic and religious identities, the problem of political legitimacy is revealed as essential throughout most of French history. Chapter 1 also highlights various sources of historical continuity between the pre-revolutionary monarchy (known as the *ancien régime*) and the post-revolutionary order, and puts into context the impact of political divisions upon the operation of French society.

By comparison with most of its European neighbours, such as Germany, Italy and the Netherlands, France is an old country. Modern France can trace its lineage back at least to the Capetian monarchy of the tenth century; Italy and Germany were only unified as independent national states in 1861 and 1870 respectively. But its relative age must not disguise the fact that the modern French nation is in certain respects an artificial creation. There was no natural empathy between the various provinces which came to form France. In the pre-revolutionary period, many provinces of France shared no natural common cultural or linguistic ties, but co-existed in a more or less autonomous manner, with a large degree of autonomy from the central government in Paris. Small rural communities throughout France were suspicious of all outside authorities, and lived a largely self-sufficient autarkic existence. The preponderance of agriculture in the French economy suggested why features of this social model survived until the early twentieth century. Identity was rooted in locality, or town, rather than the nation. The fact that French nationhood was imposed upon unwilling provinces (such as Normandy, Brittany, Acquitaine, Burgundy and Provence) by a succession of French kings, and later by the revolution, served to reinforce this point. A city as French as Lille only became part of the nation in the late seventeenth century; Nice in the nineteenth century.

France was overwhelmingly a rural nation. Even in the pre-revolutionary period, there were marked regional variations in the economic prosperity of the peasantry, and in the political freedoms exercised by subjects. In certain regions of France, forms of traditional local self-government had existed for centuries; whereas in other areas, subjects were deprived of any political rights and tightly controlled by a zealous aristocracy. Regional differences were themselves linked to varying kinship and economic structures in different parts of the country.

In domestic terms, pre-revolutionary French history had usually appeared to turn around the attempts made by the central government in Paris to impose its will upon existing provinces, to conquer new regions and to extend the orbit of its competence. The attempt to impose central control was a constant feature of the pre-revolutionary French monarchs, most notably of Louis xiv (1648–1715), whose chief minister Colbert endeavoured (with mixed success) to expand the competence of the state into the economic sphere, as well as to impose a measure of political uniformity upon the provincial nobles.

1.2 The *ancien régime*

Political historians dwell correctly on the importance of 1789 and the French Revolution as the fundamental reference point in French history. But many of the predominant traits of the French political tradition are older than the revolution, rooted in the *ancien régime*, as the pre-revolutionary monarchy is known. The main historical legacy of the *ancien régime* was to have created a central institution in the form of the monarchy, which was able to impose a degree of authority upon the powerful feudal aristocratic landowners, and other particularistic interests (such as the church). In a number of key spheres, the revolution built upon the centralising pretensions of the old absolutist monarchy:

- The origins of state economic interventionism lay with the *ancien régime*, although efforts at state-sponsored commercial and industrial development met with limited success. France remained a feudal society until the revolution.
- French monarchs named officials (*intendants*) in each of the kingdom's provinces to administer the essential functions of the state: public order, the raising of finances, and the levying of troops for military adventures abroad. In practice, these officials were constrained to bargain with powerful vested interests, including the nobility and the clergy. The creation of the prefect by Napoleon represented a far more systematic application of the principle of central state direction.
- French kings claimed their legitimacy from divine right: they were answerable to God alone. They were supported in this claim by the Catholic Church, which thus derived its power from its role as an ideological legitimising agency for the *ancien régime*, as well as from the vast wealth it had accumulated. This undivided form of political legitimacy was echoed later by the revolution, with its insistence on the general interest.

The heyday of the old monarchy was in the late seventeenth and early eighteenth centuries, when, under the influence of Louis XIV, France became the dominant power in Europe. The palace of Versailles remains until this day a testament to the glory of the old French monarchy. But throughout the course of the eighteenth century, the monarchy became steadily less effective and more corrupt, its authority challenged by the rising bourgeoisie in the towns, by the state's incapacity to control the feudal nobility, and by its diminishing international prestige.

1.3 The French Revolution: the making of modern France

The statist tradition in France certainly preceded the revolution, but the case must not be overstated. The French Revolution, with its civil wars and its crushing of the power of the aristocracy and the clergy, created the conditions for the emergence of France as a genuinely unified post-feudal nation. The French Revolution was thus the fundamental reference point in the development of the French nation-state.

- The revolution abolished the absolutist monarchy, which claimed to rule by divine right, and replaced it with a republic committed to the values of freedom, equality and brotherhood (*liberté, égalité et fraternité*). In spite of the restoration of the monarchical or imperial forms of government in 1815, 1830 and 1852, the republic became firmly embedded in French political consciousness as the natural revolutionary form of government. It was durably re-established after 1875, although the republican form of government continued to be contested by powerful political forces until the aftermath of the Second World War.
- The French revolutionary settlement also satisfied the mass of the peasantry. It achieved this notably by the sale of lands confiscated from the church and nobility, which created a class of prosperous small landowners indebted to the revolution. Loyalty was further assured by the abolition of feudal labour obligations to the aristocracy. The revolution thus transformed the peasantry into one of the mainstays of support against any return to the pre-revolutionary social order, even after the monarchy had been restored in 1815. The conservatism and loyalty of the peasantry underpinned the stability of the republic as a form of government after 1870.
- The revolution crushed the political and economic power of the old landed aristocracy; more than anything else, this facilitated the creation of a more uniform centralised state, begun under the revolution, but greatly refined under Napoleon. The key foundations of modern republican France might be traced to a curious synthesis of the parliamentary regime (*régime d'assemblée*), the revolutionary tradition, and the authoritarian centralising institutions created or consolidated by Napoleon.

The Napoleonic legacy continues to shape many of the institutions of contemporary France. These include (or included until recently) the following:

- Administrative uniformity throughout France, notably by the division of the country into departments, cantons and communes, each with the same legal responsibilities. Administrative acts were to be judged by a system of administrative courts, separate from the judicial system.
- Central control over territorial administration and local government: the prefect was created as the representative of the central government in each department; the mayor was first and foremost an official of central government.
- A high measure of state interventionism in social mores by means of the civil code, a detailed regulation of family and property relations, and codes of moral conduct.
- A professional bureaucracy, conceived of as an élite to serve the state, create order and enforce uniformity. The creation of the *école polytechnique* in 1804 was intended to train an élite dedicated to state service.

The emergence of a strong central state during the revolutionary and Napoleonic periods was accompanied by a gradual but ruthless suppression of all linguistic and regional identities; the progress of the idea of nation thus became largely synonymous with that of the state itself. It is in this sense that modern France might be considered to be an artificial or a state-led creation.

1.4 The French Revolution: a divisive heritage

The legacy of the French Revolution itself was highly divisive. This divisive heritage can be illustrated in relation to three spheres: the conflict between the church and anti-clerical movements; the legacy of political violence and the revolutionary tradition; and the lack of consensus over the form of government.

The Catholic Church, anti-clericalism and the republican state

The most divisive legacy bequeathed by the French Revolution related to the bitter dispute between the Catholic Church, the anti-clerical republican movement, and the French state. The close association of the Catholic Church with the *ancien régime* made it into an obvious target for the revolution. The church condemned the revolution of 1789 as godless; in turn, the revolution led a fierce attack on the privileges enjoyed by the Catholic Church under the monarchy, notably by confiscating church lands and redistributing them to the peasantry. Church and state reached a new compromise under Napoleon's concordat of 1801, but they remained ideological rivals. The concordat recognised Catholicism as the religion of 'the great majority of French people', although Protestantism and Judaism were also tolerated religions. When the monarchy was restored in 1815, the church recovered much of its former political influence, but by then it was probably too late. To be republican became synonymous with an anti-clerical stance; to be a practising Catholic automatically signified opposition to the notion of restoring a godless, secular republic. The church also became associated with defence of a hierarchical, conservative, pre-revolutionary social order.

Once the republic had been restored in 1870, it was natural that the ideological battle between church and state should recommence. This took two forms. First, there was an attack by the republicans on the continuing existence of powerful schools run by the Catholic Church; these schools were suspected by republicans of perverting the nation's schoolchildren with the anti-republican ethos of Catholicism. Second, the period from 1870 onwards was characterised by an uneven, but fierce ideological battle between the Catholic Church and the republic, culminating in the separation of church and state in 1905, and the renewed *de facto* opposition of the church to the republic until the aftermath of the Vichy regime of 1940–4.

One of the principal battlegrounds between church and state was in the sphere of education. The state's response to perceived clerical influence was to create its own echelon of republican primary schools. In the Ferry laws of 1879–86, the republican state created a secular rival to the powerful church schools, which aimed to reproduce republican values (Wright, 1987). The conflict between church and state schools has remained imbued in French consciousness ever since. The ideological conflict between church and state (fanned by the Dreyfus affair of 1899–1905) culminated in 1905, when the republic decreed the separation of church and state, which had been tied since Napoleon's concordat of 1801. Catholicism was no longer recognised as the official state religion; priests were removed from the state payroll, and many church lands were again confiscated. Henceforth, the republic was to be a secular one.

Until the First World War, religion was more important than social class in explaining political divisions within France. A party such as the Radical Party, which was fiercely anti-clerical, was automatically placed on the left of the political spectrum, in spite of its basic social and economic conservatism. And Catholics were automatically considered to be on the right, even when they declared themselves to be socially progressive. This situation only gradually changed with the rise of the Socialist and Communist Parties in the 1930s and the breakthrough of the politics of class and nationalism. Catholics became fully reconciled with the republic as a result of their participation in the wartime resistance, despite the official role performed by the church during the Vichy regime. The formation of a progressive Christian-democratic party in 1944 – the MRP – symbolised the final rallying of the Catholics to the republic. While the MRP started out as a left-of-centre party imbued with reformist notions of social Catholicism, it became transformed into a recognisably conservative party, under the pressure of its conservative, Catholic electorate. As the church schools example illustrates, vestiges of the clerical–anti-clerical conflict remain today, and a practising Catholic is far more likely than a declared atheist to support a right-wing party (Michelat and Simon, 1977).

The revolutionary tradition

The second sphere in which the revolution left a distinctive legacy was in the creation of an ill-defined revolutionary tradition, perhaps better expressed as a revolutionary myth, which spawned its own antibody in the form of a powerful counter-revolutionary movement. The upheavals of 1789–99 were not unique: there were further revolutionary outbreaks on a smaller scale in 1830, 1848 and 1871, as well as various abortive attempts. There developed a disposition towards the use of violence and street protest to achieve political ends: relatively small groups of conspirators might succeed in toppling a regime, as occurred in the uprising of 1830. As the levers of power were so centralised in Paris, the capital became the theatre for countless confrontations, which then extended to the provinces (the pattern has not disappeared). In the nineteenth century, French people turned against each other with great ferocity: to take one example, the Paris Commune of 1871 was crushed with 20,000 deaths.

The revolutionary tradition was itself highly ambiguous. It could mean either the tradition bequeathed by the French Revolution (which included a moderate Girondin phase, as well as the more violent and messianic Jacobin phase), or else a commitment to using revolutionary means to seize power, a more specific connotation which would exclude most moderate republicans. One powerful strand in the French revolutionary tradition became legitimised which was extremist, authoritarian and potentially violent, rather than committed to compromise. And yet the prevailing republican strand hardly fitted this description; by the early twentieth century, republicanism became synonymous with preservation of the existing social order. The aspirations of moderate republicans were largely satisfied with the consolidation of the Third Republic after 1875; these men became transformed into conservative apologists of the existing political, social and economic order. With the consolidation of the Third Republic, the mantle of revolutionary challenge to the status quo shifted from republicans to anarcho-syndicalists, to Marxist socialists and (after 1920) to communists (Ridley, 1970; Tiersky, 1974; Kriegel, 1985). For several generations, the PCF successfully articulated the aspirations of alienated industrial workers, and maintained a revolutionary tradition in French politics.

The existence of a revolutionary tradition on the political left was matched on the right by the preservation of a powerful anti-democratic strand in French politics, embodied by monarchist or bonapartist political forces throughout the nineteenth century: such forces held the ascendancy for most of the period 1815–70, especially from 1815 to 1830, and from 1852 to 1870 (Rémond, 1982). They occupied a marginal place for most of the Third Republic, but were recognisable as part of the conservative anti-Dreyfus coalition at the turn of the century. During the twentieth century, the counter-revolutionary current found expression in the anti-parliamentary leagues of the inter-war years and later in the visceral hostility to republicanism by the wartime Vichy regime (Paxton, 1973). Some would contend that J.-M. Le Pen's Front national is the latest manifestation of a counter-revolutionary strain in French politics.

The form of government

The correct form of government was closely linked to the church–state dispute and the republican/anti-republican division. Throughout the 150 years following 1789, there was a basic lack of consensus in relation to the organisation of the political system, as there was, indeed, in relation to the organisation of society as a whole. Since 1789, France has experienced three periods of monarchy, five republics, two spells of imperial rule and the reactionary wartime Vichy state (see Table 1.1).

Most transitions from one regime to another involved violence or the threat of violence. In comparative terms, the real comparison ought perhaps to be drawn not between France and Britain (the model of a relatively peaceful evolutionary transition, if we except Ireland), but between Britain and the major continental European states – France, Germany, Italy – all of which experienced periods of intense political instability and disruption before achieving the status of relatively stable liberal democracies during the post-1945 period. Excepting the brief wartime Vichy regime, the republican form of government finally prevailed after periods of monarchical and imperial rule. And yet there remained a basic lack of consensus in relation to the political regime throughout most of the Third and Fourth Republics; this damaged the legitimacy of both regimes. The contrast afforded later by the Fifth Republic was salutary.

1.5 The Third Republic, 1870–1940

The Third Republic – which lasted for seventy years – was France's longest-lasting post-revolutionary regime. A number of prominent features came to be associated with the operation of the political system, features which arguably reflected the divided state of French society throughout this period. France was a highly fragmented society, a society in which there was no natural majority for any particular course of action. The major sources of cleavage revolved around tensions between Paris and the provinces; the enduring influence of regional and local identities; the conflict between church and state; republicanism and challenges to the republic; and the politics of social class and industrialisation.

As remarked above, there was a lack of consensus in relation to the political system, which reflected the divided ideological and social make-up of French

Table 1.1 Post-revolutionary political regimes

Years	Period	Regime type
1789–1815	Revolutionary/Napoleonic period	Monarchy/Republic/Empire
1815–30	Restored Bourbons	Monarchy
1830–48	July Monarchy	Monarchy
1848–52	Second Republic	Republic
1852–70	Second Empire	Empire
1870–1940	Third Republic	Republic
1940–4	Vichy	Dictatorship
1944–58	Fourth Republic	Republic
1958–	Fifth Republic	Republic

society. The most powerful source of division was that which pitted devout Catholics, who detested what they considered as the godless republic, against anti-clerical republicans, determined to defend the republican form of government against threats from monarchists and anti-republican clergy. This divergence between republican anti-clericals and Catholic anti-republicans dominated the first 30 years of the Third Republic, until the republicans definitively established control during the Dreyfus affair at the beginning of the twentieth century. During the inter-war period, the republic again came under powerful attack both from the left, in the form of the PCF, created in 1920 to support the Russian revolution and foster revolution in France; and in the 1930s, from the ultra-right-wing Leagues, who aimed to replace the democratic republic with a more authoritarian regime. The anti-democratic undercurrent in French politics finally triumphed under duress in March 1940, when the Third Republic voted full powers to Marshall Pétain, who negotiated an armistice with Hitler after Germany's invasion of France. It provided a brief parenthesis before a return to the established republican form of government at the liberation.

The Third Republic appeared on the surface as a fragile, parliamentary-dominated system. The principal characteristics of the Third Republic's political system bore scant reference to the constitutional provisions theoretically governing its operation. The constitution of the Third Republic was finally adopted in 1875 as a compromise between monarchists and republicans. Under pressure from the monarchist majority elected in 1871 at the end of the Franco-Prussian War, the 1875 constitution provided for a strong President, portrayed by the monarchists (who could not agree among themselves on who should be king) as a monarchical type of strong leader. The putative strong presidency was still-born as a result of the MacMahon crisis of 1876–7. President MacMahon's dissolution of the Chamber of Deputies in 1876 did not succeed in its objective of producing a subservient assembly; indeed, a more firmly republican majority was elected in the 1877 election, one determined to uphold the rights of parliament. This precedent enshrined parliamentary omnipotence, and disqualified presidential use of the weapon of dissolution (Thomson, 1969). By 1879 the republican forces had clearly established their ascendancy at all levels of government, with the result that the constitution of 1875 was never really applied as it had been intended.

Instead of being dominated by strong leaders, the Third Republic evolved into a political system dominated by a strong parliament, which ensured that – for the most part – governments remained weak and unstable. During its 70-year history there were 110 different cabinets: governmental instability was a sign that deputies were performing their duty as collective guarantors of the national interest, and as defenders of civil society against the state. The republican tradition was thus interpreted to suit the reality of France as a divided, localist, society with no natural majority for any particular course of action. On the rare occasions when the nation was divided into mutually hostile camps – 1876–7, 1902–6, 1936–7 – governments could take firm decisions and rely on *de facto* parliamentary coalitions, but such occasions were short lived. In the absence of cohesive political parties, deputies defended the interests of their constituents, upon whom their political survival depended.

The manner in which parliament itself was organised during the Third Republic reinforced the tendency for the legislature to act as a block on effective governmental action. The lower house, the Chamber of Deputies, was composed of around 500 deputies, who, for most of the period, each represented a single-member constituency. The upper house, the Senate, was composed of 300 senators, indirectly elected by electoral colleges within the departments, and consisted predominantly of local councillors. It was created to act as a conservative check on the Chamber. The Senate was overwhelmingly biased towards small town and rural France, at the expense of the more dynamic, urban areas. With its right to veto bills passed by the lower house, the Senate could be counted upon to frustrate any efforts to enact social reforms, levy income tax or generally disturb the interests of small town and rural France (Anderson, 1977). One such example occurred in 1912 when the Radicals finally pushed income tax through the Chamber, only to be vetoed by the Senate.

Throughout the Third Republic, political parties were weak and poorly organised. The existence of universal male suffrage meant that elections were fiercely and usually fairly contested. Yet the weakness of party structures reduced the election process to a myriad of local contests. As in the United States Congress, what passed for parties were clusters of individual deputies representing conflicting local interests, who refused to be bound to tight parliamentary discipline. The fundamental relationship was that maintained between a deputy and his local constituents, rather than with party. This was especially true of the parties of the centre and right, although the parties of the left were far more disciplined. Party labels were often virtually meaningless: in line with the verbal leftism of French political culture, conservative candidates often attached to themselves revolutionary-sounding titles, which they discarded as soon as they had been elected. Furthermore, the pattern of electoral alliances varied greatly in different parts of the country; and there was no guarantee of electoral alliances being respected at a national level.

The Radical Party during the early twentieth century symbolised the ambiguity of party: in the pro-clerical west of France, where the church was strong, the Radicals were primarily an anti-clerical party, and attracted support from Socialist voters against conservatives; in the south-west, by contrast, where the Socialists predominated, Radical candidates were supported by conservative opinion as the only safeguard against the election of Socialist candidates. Radical deputies thus owed their election to different electoral clienteles; it was scarcely surprising that they could not long be bound by party discipline at a national level. And the Radicals possessed more cohesion than most other parliamentary groupings of the centre and right.

The lack of a natural majority, the weakness of parties, the geographical diversity of France and the weight of localism meant that it was virtually unprecedented – outside of periods of war and national crisis – for governments to rely on the disciplined support of a majority of parliamentarians. Instead, deputies and senators jealously preserved what they deemed to be their rights, and ensured that the executive was kept in a position of weak subservience. The norm was that general elections would virtually never produce clear-cut majorities, upon which governments could be formed. Governments tended to be formed as temporary coalitions to solve one or two outstanding problems, but they usually fell apart once these problems were solved.

There are several reasons for the decline of the Third Republic in the inter-war period. First, certain social groups felt excluded altogether from the political system: this was notably the case for the new urban working class which developed with the industrialisation of the late nineteenth and early twentieth centuries. The Third Republic steadfastly avoided addressing the concerns of industrial workers, as it avoided those of urban society in general. Second, the challenges faced by and the demands placed upon the political system altered markedly after the First World War. During the period prior to 1914, the functions of government were relatively limited; in these circumstances, the shortcomings of the political system were tolerable, since national politics simply did not enter into most people's lives. French society – overwhelmingly rural – was largely self-sufficient and inward looking. But the political system became progressively less tolerable in the inter-war period, when international crises such as the depression and the rise of fascism demanded governments which could take far-sighted decisions.

The rise of extreme internal and external challenges to the regime during the 1920s and 1930s further weakened the Third Republic, leaving it vulnerable to Hitler's aggressive designs. The polarisation occasioned by the victory of the left-wing Popular Front coalition in the 1936 election fuelled a mood of defeatism and revenge on the political right, symbolised by the slogan 'rather Hitler than Blum'. The breakdown of internal cohesion coincided with a period of aggressive expansionism on behalf of European fascism. The Third Republic finally collapsed in March 1940, when the parliament elected to support the Popular Front in 1936 voted full powers to Marshall Pétain, who suspended the constitution and signed an armistice with Nazi Germany.

The Third Republic has been much maligned, and yet it is not difficult to construct a defence of its political system. The system survived longer than any other since the revolution, eventually succumbing to an external invasion. The impact of governmental crises in Paris was minimal on French society: up until 1914 at least, loyalty to locality outweighed any loyalty to the nation, and ministerial crises were 'other people's' business. The effects of political instability were often exaggerated: the powerful Napoleonic administration provided much continuity of policy, notwithstanding biannual changes of government. Moreover, individual ministers occupied their posts for long periods in spite of governmental instability: to take one example, between 1906 and 1932 Aristide Briand was Prime Minister on eleven occasions, and Foreign Minister in seventeen different governments.

Ultimately, the static political regime of the Third Republic reflected the static nature of French society. France remained a largely rural, inward-looking society, at least until the 1920s, within which social and geographical mobility was rare.

Only when there was a clear dysfunctioning in the 1930s between an immobile political system, a world-wide economic crisis and a chaotic international situation did the regime appear ill-adapted to assume its responsibilities.

1.6 Vichy and the French Resistance, 1940–4

The Vichy regime lasted from 1940 to 1944. The formal division of the French territory into two zones in 1940 – an occupied sector in the north, a free zone in the south – created the illusion of independence for the Vichy government, although Marshall Pétain's margins of manoeuvre were severely restricted. The German occupation of the previously free Vichy zone in November 1942 placed the regime in its proper perspective: that of a surrogate authoritarian, collaborationist state (Paxton, 1973). The collaborationism of the Vichy regime was incontestable; there is strong evidence that the French state inaugurated a programme of anti-Semitic arrests on its own initiative, in order to curry favour with the German authorities. The French police also co-operated with the system of forced labour introduced at the behest of the Germans, whereby young Frenchmen were sent to work in German arms factories.

The Vichy regime was, in reality, a personal dictatorship under Marshall Pétain which ruled thanks to the tolerance of the Nazis. The initial belief that Pétain had safeguarded French national sovereignty, and secured the best possible deal for France, conferred an aura of early legitimacy on the Marshall. The shortcomings of the Third Republic were blamed by many for the occupation of France; the clamour for more authoritarian government was a logical consequence of this. The ideological tenor of the Vichy regime was counter-revolutionary: in the discourse of Pétain's National Revolution, 'work, family and nation' replaced 'freedom, equality and brotherhood' as the ideological leitmotifs of the regime. France reverted to being an authoritarian political regime which idealised a hierarchical, corporatist society of the type the Marshall believed to have existed before the French Revolution. The anti-Semitism displayed by the Pétain regime derived in part from anxiety to please the Nazi overlords; but ideological justifications for anti-Semitism could also be derived from the ideology of the National Revolution itself (especially the emphasis placed on *intégrist* Catholicism). The experience of the wartime Vichy regime has remained a subject of fierce controversy in France ever since. This was demonstrated by the continuing debate over the nature and extent of wartime collaboration, by the spate of recent trials of war criminals such as Klaus Barbie and Paul Touvier, and by the controversy over former President Mitterrand's role as a minor civil servant of the Vichy regime.

Resistance to the Vichy regime and to German occupation took two forms: internal and external. The external resistance crystallised itself under the leadership of Charles de Gaulle, a young general in the French army who fled France upon the signing of the armistice. In June 1940, de Gaulle called upon Frenchmen everywhere to join his Free French Resistance army, based in London. De Gaulle came unquestioningly to lead the French Resistance; initially contested, his status as the key resistance chief was eventually recognised by the allies, and ultimately by the main internal resistance movements. The internal resistance consisted of various groups, divided to some extent along ideological lines, but united in its opposition to Vichy and to Nazi occupation. The main forces active in the internal resistance were Communists, Socialists and Christians.

Tensions between the two branches of the French Resistance were transparent. The internal resistance movement was dominated by the Communists, who were portrayed by de Gaulle as fighting an ideology (Nazism) rather than a country (Germany), leaving the external resistance fighters as the only true patriots. To some extent, the internal, Communist-dominated resistance dreamt of a new France; the Gaullist-led external resistance sought above all to restore the old France, with a satisfactorily reformed political system. While the internal resistance reasoned in terms of daily survival and was inclined to unrealistic dreams to stimulate the immediate resistance effort, the external resistance was more open to cultivating diplomatic contacts with the allies, to compromise and to concessions.

The evidence suggests that few Frenchmen were involved in acts of resistance, and that the imperatives of physical survival ensured a largely subjugated population until the liberation in 1944. The unification of the resistance forces under de Gaulle's control after the liberation of Paris most probably helped avoid any possibility of civil war (the Communists notably laid down their arms, in spite of their controlling large areas of France) and created a powerful coalition of forces anxious to rebuild and unify France. In August 1944, de Gaulle became the premier of a provisional government composed of the main resistance forces: the Communists, the Socialists, the Christian Democrats and de Gaulle himself. A new progressive dawn beckoned.

1.7 The Fourth Republic, 1944–58

The liberation of France in August 1944 swept away the Vichy regime, and inaugurated a new period of French history in a spirit of near-universal optimism. From highly auspicious beginnings, however, the Fourth Republic was rapidly faced by a crisis of legitimacy in its mission. The period 1944–6 revealed a lack of constitutional consensus, which seriously weakened the political legitimacy of the new Fourth Republic. There was agreement among most politicians that the form of government should be republican. No one – not even *integrist* Catholics – seriously contested this. In fact, the anti-democratic, anti-republican forces had been discredited by the Vichy regime. In addition, the pre-war parties of the centre and right were widely distrusted either for collaborating with the Vichy regime, or for failing to resist it (which, in immediate post-war eyes, amounted to the same thing). The strength of the left was revealed in the first three elections of the post-war period (October 1945, June 1946, November 1946), which witnessed major gains for the two left-wing parties – the SFIO and the PCF – and a breakthrough for the new Christian-democratic party, the MRP.

In a first constitutional referendum in October 1945, the overwhelming majority of the French population invested the provisional government with responsibility for drawing up a new constitution, rather than reverting to the 1875 charter. Although it was clear that people did not want a return to the Third Republic, it was much less obvious what type of regime was to replace it. There were, essentially, three different points of view within the provisional government:

- De Gaulle believed in a rationalised democratic system, similar to the eventual Fifth Republic: in broad terms, he advocated a strong President who would stand above the petty quarrels of party politicians and incarnate the unity of the French nation. The parties of the left and centre (the SFIO, the PCF and the MRP) suspected de Gaulle of preparing a system which might lead to dictatorship. Unable to agree with his partners, and vigorously opposed to any return to a parliamentary-dominated regime, de Gaulle resigned as premier in January 1946. The loss of the prestige of the resistance hero was a severe blow to the nascent Fourth Republic.

- The two main parties of the left – the SFIO and the PCF – also called for strong disciplined governments, but they argued that these would have to base their authority on a single, powerful parliamentary assembly. The left thereby re-iterated its belief in the Jacobin tradition of a single directing assembly, accepting few checks and balances to moderate the expression of the general will.

- The Christian-democratic MRP rejected de Gaulle's advocacy of strong personal leadership, but it was wary of the left as well. The MRP opted for a parliamentary system with checks and balances to prevent arbitrary executive rule, whether presidentially or parliamentarily inspired.

Once de Gaulle had resigned, the PCF and the SFIO (but not the MRP) proposed their version of the constitution for ratification in a referendum held in April 1946. In their draft constitution, the PCF and the SFIO proposed to abolish the second chamber – the Senate – and to create a monocameral parliamentary system. This was because the Senate, representing the interests of rural and small town rather than urban France, had consistently frustrated social reform during the Third Republic. The left's proposed constitution proved abortive; it was rejected in the April 1946 constitutional referendum, marking the first serious reversal of the post-war progression of the left, and a further severe setback to the new regime. Quite apart from the predictable opposition of de Gaulle, this projected constitution was also fiercely contested by all other significant parties, including the MRP. A majority of French people feared that a single-chamber parliamentary system would be equivalent to handing unrestrained power to the left-wing parties.

The constitution of the Fourth Republic was narrowly adopted in a third constitutional referendum in October 1946, with 9,500,000 votes for, 8,500,000 against, and 9,000,000 abstentions (Williams, 1964). The constitution-makers hoped that the 1946 constitution would encourage the development of strong cabinets, based on the support of a few large parties, and would thereby end the chronic division which had characterised the Third Republic. It aimed to emulate the British system of strong governments drawing their support from disciplined majorities in the lower chamber. But in fact the Fourth Republican constitution established a parliamentary regime which was not fundamentally dissimilar to that of the Third. The idea that stable progressive governments would replace the transient coalitions of the Third Republic actually had little solid constitutional foundation: it depended for its reality upon the continuing political co-operation of the main resistance parties. This was called into question in 1947.

The principal features of the political regime created by the 1946 constitution were those of a parliamentary democracy. The supremacy of parliament was re-affirmed in the October 1946 constitution in a more overt manner than in the constitution of 1875: in so doing it reasserted traditions of the absolute sovereignty of parliament which dated back to the French Revolution. The powers of the Senate, renamed the Council of the Republic, were limited: notably, it lost the power of veto over bills passed by the lower chamber, and its rights were limited to those of delay and consultation, somewhat like the British House of Lords. The President of the Republic remained largely a symbolic figurehead, as in the Third Republic. The subordination of the President was to be ensured by an indirect method of election by the two houses of parliament. Despite the affirmation of parliamentary supremacy, the rights of the executive were strengthened in certain respects: notably, through the complicated provisions allowing the Prime Minister to call for a dissolution of the Chamber of Deputies, which Edgar Faure used to good effect in 1955 (the first time a dissolution had occurred since 1876).

1.8 The decline and fall of the Fourth Republic

The Fourth Republic has traditionally been judged a failure in most respects. It lasted a mere twelve years, before it collapsed in the face of a military insurrection in Algeria.

The immediate legacy of the French Resistance had been to strengthen the parties of the left (Socialists and Communists) and to reconcile the Catholic community to republican values. The three great parties of the Resistance (the PCF, the SFIO and the MRP) had believed that if they remained united, France would have a stable political system based on a progressive left-wing majority. In fact, this presupposition was unfounded: in May 1947, the tripartite governing coalition collapsed when the Communists were expelled from government by the Socialist Minister of the Interior, Jules Moch. The PCF's departure was dictated by a combination of internal and external pressures. The role of the US government, which made it clear that the removal of Communists from government was an essential precondition for France receiving massive financial aid under the Marshall plan, was primordial (Johnson, 1981). In addition, the cold war began in earnest in 1947, as Stalin began to consolidate his grip on eastern Europe and as revelations of the nature of Stalinism began to filter through to the western democracies. The PCF reacted to its exclusion by declaring its fidelity to Moscow and reinforcing its control over a marginalised working class counter-culture. From 1947, almost until the collapse of the Fourth Republic in 1958, the Communist Party declared its total hostility to the regime.

The Fourth Republic also suffered after 1947 from the development of powerful new enemies on the right. The divisions of the left, the onset of the cold war in 1947 and the electorate's disillusion with the left-wing parties allowed the French right to recover a measure of influence. In 1947 the right found a new champion in General de Gaulle, who founded the Rassemblement du peuple français (RPF) as a movement dedicated to replacing the Fourth Republic with a more presidential-style regime. From 1947 to 1951, the RPF rivalled the Communist Party as France's best organised and most popular party. From 1947 onwards, the Fourth Republic was thus opposed by powerful enemies to its left (the PCF) and its right (the RPF). This forced the so-called centre parties (Socialists, Radicals, Christian Democrats and moderate Conservatives) into a series of 'third force' alliances from 1947–51, whose only rationale was to safeguard the Republic. There was little political cohesion in these defensive alliances, a factor which further weakened the authority of the French state.

After the breakdown of tripartism, political instability returned after 1947, of a type which recalled that of the old Third Republic. Despite the fact that the centre parties combined to defend the republic against its enemies, no party could resist manoeuvring to increase its influence in government. This led to the return of a pattern of governmental instability: from 1947 to 1958 governments lasted an average of some six months, just as they had done in the Third Republic. In the eyes of the French electorate, the Fourth Republic, which had never benefited from a broad consensus in its favour, became discredited by the selfish games played by its politicians. An example of the perceived cynicism of the politicians of the Fourth Republic came in 1951, when, faced with the prospect of a negative, anti-regime majority (PCF, RPF), the centre parties changed the electoral system in a way which deliberately discriminated against their rivals (Cole and Campbell, 1989).

As in the Third Republic, parliamentary supremacy came to be directly equated with weak executive government. Parliamentarians were extremely jealous to preserve their prerogatives, especially on the centre and right of the political spectrum. One consequence of this was a preference for rather uncharismatic, consensual personalities as premier, since strong leaders might attempt to limit the rights of parliament. When clearly exceptional leaders did emerge, with widespread support in the country – the best example being the Radical Pierre Mendès-France in 1954–5 – a majority of deputies rapidly crystallised in order to bring them down. This was pushing a distrust of strong leaders to the extreme.

The political system appeared out of step with what was happening in the country as a whole, which by the early 1950s was experiencing an unprecedented industrial take-off and social modernisation. One of the most telling critiques of the Fourth Republic was that, although France was modernising itself in a remarkable manner during the post-war period, this was occurring in spite of the lethargy of the central politicians. This accusation appears somewhat unjust, but it contributed towards the discredit of the regime.

The result of this governmental instability was that central government gradually lost the authority necessary to take tough decisions in a period of rapid international change and domestic overhaul. Given the renewed weakness of government, the problems that the Fourth Republic had to tackle were overwhelming. First, the task of post-war reconstruction was immense and demanded concerted, strong government, which appeared lacking due to the absence of effective political authority. In fact, this apparent inaction needs to be qualified. The introduction of elaborate planning mechanisms (the five-year plans) and the creation of the General Commissariat for Planning testified to a powerful impetus in favour of economic and social modernisation on behalf of the state. The point is that this state-led economic modernisation programme went ahead with little reference to a divided political élite.

Second, the post-war period was one of heightened international crisis, signalled by the movement towards the break-up of the French empire with the outbreak of the Indochinese rebellion in 1946, and the onset of the cold war in 1947. This dual problem paralysed French foreign policy throughout the Fourth Republic. France was gradually forced to accept that it was no longer a first-rank international player, that it could no longer sustain a far-flung empire, and that its interest lay in co-operating with others in Europe, and the Atlantic alliance. Due to the weakness of its political system, foreign policy crises had a devastating impact upon the domestic political situation within the Fourth Republic. There was a direct and obvious relationship between permanent government instability within France and the perception of weakness in the eyes of foreign governments. Furthermore, the inability of the central state to control the activities of its agents in the armed forces and the colonial administrations proved a tangible sign of its weakness, which, in a vicious circle, led to a further diminution of confidence in the capacity of the state to fulfil its functions.

The problem of decolonisation prevailed above all others. The retention of France's extensive empire had been one concession obtained by Marshall Pétain in the armistice agreement with Hitler. The country's post-war colonial headache began almost immediately after the end of the war, the most important conflicts being in Indochina, Tunisia, Morocco and Algeria. The first of these was in Indochina, where from 1946 to 1954, a bitter war was fought between the French army and the Vietnamese nationalists, with the French finally admitting defeat in 1954. The pride of the French army was severely wounded. The decision taken by the Mendès-France government to withdraw from Tunisia and Morocco in 1954 and 1955 added insult to injury; it was regarded by many army officers as another humiliation for the despised Fourth Republic.

The French army was determined that France should not cede in Algeria. Algeria was almost universally regarded as an integral part of France, even by most left-wing opinion. It had been a French colony since 1830, and was peopled by some 1,000,000 native French settlers, who were determined to resist demands for independence from predominantly Muslim Algerians. A nexus of political, cultural, economic and religious influences combined to make Algeria by far the most important of the colonial disputes faced by the Fourth Republic. Civil war and nationalist revolt raged in Algeria from November 1954 onwards. Successive attempts by French governments to promote greater autonomy without ceding independence proved fruitless. Indeed, any attempt to introduce even moderate reform was fiercely resisted by the colonial settlers in Algeria, secretly abetted by the armed forces. The civilian government in Paris became progressively less able to control the activities of the military, of the colonial administration, or of the native French settlers, with the effect that by early 1958 the authority of the Paris government had almost completely vanished. Orders made by government departments in Paris were openly defied by the army and the colonial administration in Algeria: the problem of decolonisation was thus intricately linked with that of the lack of political authority of the government in Paris. The *coup de grâce* for the Fourth Republic came in May 1958, when the French army sided with rioting French settlers in Algiers (the capital of Algeria), who organised themselves into a Committee of Public Safety and declared their autonomy from the Fourth Republic. The military authorities made it clear that their price for guaranteeing not to invade mainland France was a return of the wartime hero General de Gaulle to power. To all intents and purposes, the Fourth Republic was dead.

The achievements of the Fourth Republic were for long overlooked. They need to be reiterated, in order to set in context the regime's generally negative image. During the first fifteen years of the post-war period, France moved away from being a stalemate society, and entered a period of rapid socioeconomic and demographic change; more rapid, indeed, than that experienced in any other western European nation. The French state succeeded in managing change in spite of (or perhaps because of) the Fourth Republic's weak political institutions. There is a strong argument that political weakness left the administration free to fill the vacuum left by the feuding party élites.

There was a rapid economic upturn: economic growth soon reached an average of 6 per cent per annum after 1950, helped by the effects of Marshall aid and, it has been argued, by active state interventionism in economic management in the form of a series of five-year plans. The seeds of the French economic miracle were sown in the Fourth Republic. Economic development had a radical impact on the nature of French society. There was a vast movement of population away from the land into the new urban areas. For the first time, France became a predominantly urban country, with a modern economy. The country also experienced a demographic explosion, in the form of a post-war baby-boom. In 1939 France's population was barely 40 million; by the end of the 1950s it had reached 50 million. On balance this economic and social modernisation made the old cleavages based on religion and class less acute. The accelerated pace of secularisation in the post-war period, and the formation of the Christian-democratic MRP also lessened the traditional importance of the clerical/anti-clerical cleavage.

The Fourth Republic could point to its own political achievements. The most notable of these lay in the sphere of European policy. The main initiatives culminating in the Treaty of Rome in 1957 were of French or Franco-German inspiration:

the European Coal and Steel Community of 1951, the abortive European Army of 1954, the Treaty of Rome of 1957. The complexity of French European policy was revealed by the proposed European Defence Community (the 'European Army'), first forwarded by premier René Pleven in 1951, as a means of providing a European safeguard over German rearmament. Although a French initiative, the European Defence Community treaty was finally defeated by the French National Assembly in 1954, due to a bitter legacy of anti-Germanism across the political spectrum.

Despite this powerful anti-German sentiment, the principal driving force of closer post-war European integration was that of Franco-German reconciliation, personified by far-sighted French and German statesmen, such as Robert Schuman, Jean Monnet and Konrad Adenauer. The European Economic Community was created in 1957 on the basis of a new Franco-German partnership, symbolising not only reconciliation between the two nations, but also cold-headed assessments of national interest on either side: the Franco-German axis has underpinned the Community and latterly the European Union ever since. From a French perspective, the EEC itself was often envisaged as a corset to prevent Germany from dominating the continent. The choice of European co-operation, at the same time realistic and idealistic, was made by visionary statesmen during the Fourth Republic, a choice which was badly shaken in the 1960s during de Gaulle's Fifth Republic.

As far as the effectiveness of the political system *per se* was concerned, the conclusion must be a globally negative one. Excessive parliamentary domination led to a return to the pattern of unstable governments, just as in the Third Republic. The most pressing issues of the 1950s – with the exception of Europe – found no real response from French governments because there was a power vacuum. Where progress was made in post-war France, it came about largely as a result of the professionalism of its bureaucracy, rather than of its politicians. The weakness of the political system damaged France's international reputation during this period. For these various reasons, the restoration of effective government was a key priority for the constitution-makers of 1958.

1.9 Conclusion and summary

A number of salient themes emerge from this brief overview of French history until 1958. The first relates to the crucial role performed by the state in building modern French identity and in imposing cohesion upon a divided society. This process began during the *ancien régime*, advanced during the French Revolution and Napoleonic periods, and consolidated itself in stages thereafter. The state justified its universal mission in terms of the general will, as French kings had previously evoked divine right in support of their rule. However important in terms of building a political identity, and however revealing of a particularly centralising state tradition, the role of the state should not be overstressed. Throughout the nineteenth century, an ambitious state co-existed alongside a largely self-sufficient society. The French nation remained extremely diverse prior to the Second World War. French remained a minority language in many French regions until the twentieth century.

The problem of political legitimacy was a consequence of the divisive legacy of the French Revolution. Disagreement over fundamental features of the political system pitted republicans against monarchists, Catholics against anti-clericals and later, nationalists against internationalists. As a result of multiple social, economic and ideological divisions, the problem of political legitimacy was a genuine problem throughout most of the period preceding the Fifth Republic (1958). The impact of such divisions should not be exaggerated. Throughout the nineteenth century, political conflicts were often limited to competition between rival Paris-based élites, with French society remaining relatively unaffected. This testified to a more pervasive division between Paris and the provinces, a recurrent feature of French political history inherent in the nature of the state-building process itself. Despite the persistence of a revolutionary political discourse, the capacity of the political system to deliver peace and prosperity only appeared seriously threatened during the 1930s, and again after 1947.

Indicative bibliography

Anderson, R.D. (1977) *France 1870–1914*, Routledge and Kegan Paul, London.

Courtier, P. (1994) *La Quatrième République*, PUF, Paris.

Elgey, G. (1993) *Histoire de la 4e République*, Fayard, Paris.

Hazareesingh, S. (1994) *Political Traditions in Modern France*, Oxford University Press, Oxford.

Larkin, M. (1988) *France since the Popular Front: Government and people, 1936–1986*, Clarendon Press, Oxford.

MacMillan, J. (1985) *Dreyfus to De Gaulle: Politics and society in France 1889–1969*, Edward Arnold, London.

Paxton, R. (1973) *La France de Vichy: 1940–1944*, Seuil, Paris.

Shennan, A. (1993) *De Gaulle*, Longman, London.

Thomson, D. (1969) *Democracy in France since 1870*, Oxford University Press, Oxford.

Williams, P.M. (1964) *Crisis and Compromise: Politics in the Fourth Republic*, Longman, London.

Chapter 2

France since 1958

2.1 Introduction and objectives

Chapter 2 considers the evolution of France's political system during the Fifth Republic (1958–96). It demonstrates how, unlike most of its predecessors, the political regime has proved capable not only of assuring political stability, but also of adapting to changing political, social, economic and international circumstances. The chapter narrates, in a fairly detailed manner, the main features of the Fifth Republic, analysing the broad development of the Fifth Republic by paying particular attention to the terms in office of the five French Presidents since 1958. Many issues signalled for attention here are also developed in more detail in later chapters.

The events surrounding the creation of the Fifth Republic had their origins in the Algerian crisis, which had sapped the energy of the Fourth Republic since November 1954 (Horne, 1977). On 13 May 1958, rebellious military officers, backed by rioting European settlers, finally overthrew the legal government in Algiers. The conspirators threatened to extend the rebellion to mainland France, unless General de Gaulle was called upon to lead the nation's affairs. To reinforce their point, French paratroopers invaded Corsica on 28 May 1958; plans were openly advanced for a military movement on Paris itself. The conspirators relied on the discredit of the Fourth Republic in the eyes of French public opinion, the complicity of the military high command and the support of powerful sections of the bureaucracy and the political élite. De Gaulle carefully cultivated his position as a potential saviour. Under threat of military invasion and possible civil war, the National Assembly invested Charles de Gaulle as the last premier of the Fourth Republic on 1 June 1958. De Gaulle immediately suspended the constitution of the Fourth Republic, and was granted authority to draw up a new constitution, which was overwhelmingly ratified by constitutional referendum in September 1958. General Charles de Gaulle became the Fifth Republic's first President in January 1959.

The allegation of an illegal seizure of power, made by Mendès-France, Mitterrand and others, deserves attention; de Gaulle's investiture took place against the backdrop of a possible military *coup d'état*. Yet we must recognise that powerful forces within the old Fourth Republic aided de Gaulle's accession. The fact that de Gaulle was invited to form a government by the incumbent President, Réné Coty, underlined that even men who swore by respect for the republican tradition were anxious to avoid the prospect of civil unrest and political collapse and turned to de Gaulle. Others who called for de Gaulle to lead a transitional government included the Socialist leader, Guy Mollet.

2.2 De Gaulle's Republic

The related problems of Algeria and the consolidation of de Gaulle's authority dominated French politics from 1958 to 1962. Propelled to power to maintain Algeria in French hands, General de Gaulle came to accept the case for Algerian independence. The bulk of Muslim opinion in Algeria supported independence; moreover, France's anti-imperialist discourse rested uneasily alongside the French colonial presence in Algeria. Algerian independence formed an integral part of France's new foreign policy under de Gaulle. The prospect of Algerian independence fulfilled domestic political functions as well. De Gaulle was determined to reduce the weight of entrenched interests preventing the state from representing national unity: no interest was more powerful than the military, which had brought the Fourth Republic to its knees. De Gaulle's change of direction over Algeria was met with fury by military commanders and French settlers in Algiers. Their responses included several attempts to assassinate de Gaulle, and a further military rising in Algiers in 1961.

In order to understand the subsequent development of the Fifth Republic, it is essential to grasp why de Gaulle was able to impose his authority between 1958 and 1962. The various actors involved in the crisis of May–June 1958 each assumed that de Gaulle could be moulded to their own designs. A majority of deputies considered that de Gaulle's return to power was far preferable to the threat of a military invasion of mainland France, but they firmly believed that he could be controlled once the immediate crisis over Algeria had passed. The French army and the settlers both believed that de Gaulle would never cede independence to Algeria. Subsequent events revealed that each was misguided. By granting Algerian independence, and by severely repressing attempts to reassert the army's power, de Gaulle crushed the political power of the military in French politics. By introducing direct election of the President in 1962, de Gaulle inflicted a severe political defeat on the parliamentarians nostalgic for the Fourth Republic.

The means by which de Gaulle imposed his authority was that of the referendum: with dubious constitutional legality, he called referendums on four occasions between 1958 and 1962 to appeal directly to the French electorate, above the heads of the parties and other intermediary institutions. The transitional political circumstances of the period 1958–62 enabled de Gaulle to rule in a manner which opponents castigated as personal rule (*pouvoir personnel*). By governing in such a largely personal manner, de Gaulle created the bases for the emergence of the presidency as the most powerful institution in the new regime (see Chapter 4).

As Machin (in Hall *et al.*, 1994) points out: 'Until 1962, the Algerian war proved to be a substitute for a presidential majority.' With the resolution of the Algerian conflict in April 1962, after the electorate's ratification of the Evian agreements, the historic mission which many had conferred on de Gaulle had been fulfilled. There was no longer any reason to retain his services: the old political class of the Fourth Republic was determined to regain the political initiative, and to stop short de Gaulle's attempt to create strong presidential leadership. De Gaulle recognised this; indeed, he provoked a conflict with the old parties, first by dismissing his premier Michel Debré in April 1962, and second by organising a referendum to introduce the direct election of the French President. Both initiatives were of doubtful constitutional validity; the October 1962 referendum in particular appeared to transgress the rules for calling referendums established by the 1958 constitution. The new Constitutional Council recognised this fact after the referendum, but declared itself incapable of altering the electorate's favourable verdict on de Gaulle's proposed reform. The October 1962 referendum was followed by the Fifth Republic's second parliamentary elections, held in November 1962, provoked by President de Gaulle's dissolution of the National Assembly elected in 1958. Gaullist control was further strengthened when an overall pro-Gaullist (UNR and RI) majority was elected to support President de Gaulle. The events of October–November 1962 thus reinforced the model of the strong presidency which commentators for long considered an integral part of the Fifth Republic.

The October 1962 constitutional referendum on the direct election of the presidency was of fundamental importance for the future development of the Fifth Republic: the directly elected President could now boast a popular legitimacy at least equal to that of the National Assembly. Direct election would give the President the necessary popular legitimacy to be able to ensure that other institutions fell into line with presidential wishes. Invigorated by a direct bond with the French people, the presidency was to act as the key element of legitimacy underpinning the Fifth Republic's political system. This presidential reading of the Fifth Republic held sway largely unchallenged until 1986. The emergence of a strong presidential leadership provided a focus around which other features of the emerging political system became organised. Paradoxically, however, by subjecting the President to direct election, de Gaulle succeeded in politicising the presidency, subjecting the office to fierce political competition, rather than protecting the institution from partisan rivalries.

The period spanning from June 1958 to November 1962 was of fundamental importance in understanding the future evolution of the regime. In key areas of policy, the standard was set not only for the remaining years of de Gaulle's presidency, but for those of his successors as President as well. By any comparative measurement, de Gaulle must rank as the most important President of the French Fifth Republic, as well as one of Europe's leading statesmen during the post-war period. Among the many aspects of de Gaulle's legacy, we should mention: the creation of a strong presidency, the realignment of the French party system, the resolution of the Algerian conflict, the adoption of a more independent foreign policy, the consolidation of the Franco-German alliance at the heart of the European Community, and the fostering of a new spirit of national self-confidence and economic prosperity.

At the heart of Gaullism lay a certain idea of France, with clear implications for how the political system should be organised (Lacouture, 1991; Shennan, 1993). De Gaulle's patriotic, even nationalistic beliefs required a form of republican government sufficiently strong to enable France to regain international respect, after the divisions of the Fourth Republic. In de Gaulle's terminology, this was a precondition for France 'being herself'. Since his Bayeux speech of 1946, de Gaulle had consistently advocated a strong presidency, able to represent the interests of the whole French nation, above what he portrayed as the particularistic interests represented by political parties. The first aspect of Gaullism was thus a reformed political system based on a strengthened executive, embodied by a strong President. The presidency lay at the core of the political system; all other features depended upon presidential impulsion, initiative or approval. In marked contrast to the Fourth Republic, the Fifth witnessed a return to political stability: during the period from 1958 to May 1995, there were four Presidents of the Republic, presiding over fifteen Prime Ministers and governments. While this measure of stability might appear imperfect by comparison with other European political systems, it represented marked progress by comparison with the Fourth Republic. Renewed political stability was based partly upon the strengthening of executive government in the Fifth Republic's constitution. It was also incumbent upon changes in the French party system. Whatever his intentions in introducing the direct election of the President, de Gaulle's 1962 reform stimulated a bipolarisation of political competition between left- and right-wing coalitions (see Chapter 9).

A second key feature of Gaullism lay in the sphere of foreign policy. At the heart of de Gaulle's foreign policy lay a belief in greater national independence and a determination that France should be recognised as a great power. The decision to produce an independent French nuclear deterrent, the attempt to reassert French national sovereignty within a 'Europe of the Nation-States', and the efforts to adopt a more independent, pro-Third World policy with respect to France's former colonies in Africa and elsewhere, all testfied to de Gaulle's obsession with protecting the 'rank of France' as a great power (Howorth, in Hall *et al.* 1994). The basis of the French exception in foreign and security policy stemmed from this period. In practice, this involved adopting greater independence from the Atlantic alliance and the United States, and a courting of the countries of eastern Europe. The most spectacular initiatives undertaken managed to fascinate and irritate France's allies at the same time. This was the case in 1966, when de Gaulle announced that France was withdrawing from the integrated military command structure of NATO, the military alliance between the USA and the main western European countries. National independence was also evoked to justify de Gaulle's announcement in 1961 that France would build its own independent nuclear deterrent, rather than buy missiles from the Americans.

The counterpart to greater independence from the USA was an attempt to strengthen France's role within Europe. This took two forms. First, de Gaulle attempted to strengthen the Paris/Bonn axis as the driving force of the EEC. In 1963 a Franco-German co-operation treaty was a clear step in this direction (Kolodziej, 1990). The other aspect of European policy was to promote France's interests at the expense of those of the United Kingdom, regarded as an American trojan horse within Europe (Portelli, 1994). De Gaulle's vision of a dominant France within Europe depended upon frustrating the UK's desire to join the EC. De Gaulle vetoed UK entry to the Community on two occasions, in 1963 and 1967. Finally, a number of rather eccentric French foreign policy initiatives in Africa, China and South America underlined de Gaulle's intention that France should recover a greater international influence.

The third aspect of Gaullism was the arrival of a period of economic prosperity, after the lean years of the late 1940s and 1950s. In fact, to attribute the economic take-off to de Gaulle is unfair to the Fourth Republic, which put into place the mechanisms for economic revival, but the figures were flattering for the French economy. French growth rates outpaced those of every EC country during the eleven years of de Gaulle's rule. Economic growth averaged 5.8 per cent in France during the period 1958–69, against 4.8 per cent in Germany, 4 per cent in the United States and 2.7 per cent in the United Kingdom (Albertini, 1978).

2.3 May 1968: the Fifth Republic in crisis

The Gaullist period is incomplete without an analysis of May 1968, which almost overthrew not only de Gaulle but the Fifth Republic itself (Hanley and Kerr, 1989). The three great domestic achievements of the Gaullist regime were claimed by apologists to be political stability, social consensus and economic growth. In each of these spheres, however, there existed reasons for dissatisfaction. The counterpart to political stability was the domination exercised by the Gaullist party at all levels of the state: the accusation that de Gaulle had presided over the creation of the Gaullist state (l'Etat-UNR) rang increasingly true with important sections of public opinion, as well as with non-Gaullist politicians. This was particularly marked within the civil service, where some argued that an American-style 'spoils system' had been created, with only trusted Gaullists nominated to the top administrative positions.

The 1958 constitution might have produced a form of political stability, but the opinion was widespread that this stability equated with stagnation or, worse, authoritarian government. Since 1965 de Gaulle had lost the vestiges of supra-partisan grandeur with which he had surrounded his rule, to become rather like any other political leader. Direct election of the presidency aggravated de Gaulle's problems: he had been re-elected in 1965, but only after being forced to a second ballot which had heralded the revival of the left-wing opposition (see Appendices 3 and 4). In 1967 the pro-Gaullist coalition (UNR and Giscard d'Estaing's RI) scraped to a one-seat overall majority over the combined forces of the left and the opposition centrists. The political edifice constructed by de Gaulle appeared far from being invincible almost one decade after his accession to power.

The Gaullist claim prior to May 1968 to have created social consensus was revealed to be artificial by the May events. Economic growth had been real enough, but its fruits had been unequally distributed among different social classes. Above all, however, the events of May 1968 reflected the spirit of the age, the outburst of one generation (the baby-boomers) against the social and political values embodied by the ruling élites. The radical protest movement was not confined to France; similar movements occurred across western Europe. France of the 1960s was a more open society than its predecessors, more receptive to influences from abroad. Nowhere in Europe did these protest movements overthrow existing political institutions. In France, the events of May 1968 seriously damaged de Gaulle's authority and were followed by his retirement one year later; but 1969 also witnessed the peaceful transition of power to President Pompidou and the strengthening of the Fifth Republic.

The protest movement of May 1968 was in reality a series of movements reflecting rather different concerns, but sharing a sense of frustration with the existing order and an ill-defined expectation of change . The May 1968 events were initially a generational phenomenon; only later did they acquire obvious class overtones. When analysing the events, it is essential to distinguish between two separate movements: the student uprising and the outbreak of mass strikes among French workers. The student events began on 3 May 1968, when police forcibly ejected protesting students from the Sorbonne. The brutal manner in which the students were treated by police sparked off a wave of public sympathy. From 3 May onwards, confrontations between students and police became regular incidents; the student protest did not die down until mid-June 1968. Of greater importance, student activism acted as the catalyst for the outbreak of a series of spontaneous strikes among workers: by mid-May, over 10 million French workers were on strike, with the country at a standstill. The motives behind these strikes were confused. They usually combined quantitative and qualitative demands: workers demanded a salary increase, but they also demanded more power within the firm, and expressed a sense of dissatisfaction at the authoritarian, Taylorian organisation of the workplace.

The May movement reached its apogee in the confusing events of 24–30 May 1968, when there appeared to be a vacuum of power amid rumours of de Gaulle's flight from the country. Thereafter the radical protest movement died down, and the conservative reaction set in. The turning point occurred on 30 May 1968, when de Gaulle returned from Germany, announced the dissolution of the National Assembly and called fresh general elections. A vast pro-Gaullist demonstration on the Champs-Elysées symbolically celebrated the turning of the tide. In the ensuing National Assembly election of June 1968, a landslide Gaullist victory was registered; this symbolised the reaction of the provinces against Parisian radicals and a humbling of the left-wing opposition parties. The evidence from the counter-revolution of June 1968 suggested that more French people were appalled at the disorder manifested in May than were supportive of the new demands formulated by the students and certain groups of workers.

The movement of May 1968 became a reference point, almost an ideology, for various new social groups created, or expanded, by post-war social change. Representatives of these new social groups called into question traditional moral values, replacing them with calls for liberty, autonomy, the right to difference, and anti-authoritarianism. It is difficult to avoid the conclusion that the various original movements to which May 1968 gave birth have all been absorbed by the existing institutions of French society. The movements inspired by them served mainly to place new issues on the political agenda. Many of the demands formulated by activists in the 1960s found themselves in party programmes during the 1970s. Pacifist, ecologist, regionalist, feminist, extreme-left and other 'alternative' groups assumed considerable importance during the 1970s. The election of the socialist François Mitterrand as President symbolised the hopes of these various radical movements. The crisis experienced by governmental socialism during the 1980s was in part also the crisis of ideals inspired by May 1968. Since the mid-1980s, even successful social movements, such as the Greens, have been anxious to distinguish themselves from the legacy of that time.

The short-term outcome of May–June 1968 was a victory for the Party of Order over the Party of Movement. On a political level, de Gaulle survived for only one more year, and never fully recovered the public esteem he had enjoyed prior to May 1968. The real Gaullist victor of the events of May and June was premier Georges Pompidou, who, in contrast to de Gaulle, retained his calm throughout the crisis and organised the Gaullist electoral victory. His barely veiled intention of succeeding de Gaulle as President hastened his dismissal as premier in June 1968. However, Pompidou's performance meant that he was henceforth a credible successor waiting in the wings. For the first time, it appeared as if a vote against de Gaulle would not bring down the Fifth Republic. This helped explain the French electorate's rejection of de Gaulle's ill-fated referendum of April 1969.

The 1969 presidential election was caused by de Gaulle's resignation in April 1969, provoked by the electorate's rejection of his referendum on the dual, complicated and unrelated issues of the reform of the Senate and the creation of regional authorities. In the referendum of April 1969, a small majority of those voting refrained from supporting de Gaulle, thereby immediately precipitating the General's resignation. The events of May 1968, and the subsequent evolution of the Fifth Republic, revealed that even a leader as prestigious as General de Gaulle could not retain the confidence of the French people indefinitely.

2.4 Georges Pompidou: the acceptable face of Gaullism?

After de Gaulle's resignation, the Gaullist UDR immediately rallied behind Pompidou, whose election as President in 1969 helped to legitimise the transition to the post-de Gaulle phase of the Fifth Republic (Roussel, 1984; Muron, 1994). The apparent ease of the succession was important for the regime, but misleading politically. This became clear in the early 1970s. Pompidou's political authority was fiercely contested not only by the left-wing opposition, but also from within his presidential majority. Having been the architect of the Gaullist landslide of June 1968, it would have been politically inadmissible for Pompidou to have dissolved the National Assembly upon his election as President, thereby electing a majority on his name. But the problems encountered by Pompidou with his own parliamentary majority pointed to the frailty of the Gaullist coalition in the absence of de Gaulle. They also suggested that a President's political authority is only really established when a parliamentary majority has been elected to support his action as President.

Whatever his personal qualities, Pompidou did not possess de Gaulle's historic stature. From 1969 to 1974, President Pompidou's principal political problem rested with his parliamentary majority. The fractious nature of the Gaullist party post-de Gaulle constrained Pompidou to exercise a far closer supervision over the operation of the majority than had ever been necessary for de Gaulle (Charlot, 1970). This strengthened the belief that historic Gaullism had died with de Gaulle. Pompidou's majority was beset with contradictions. Historic Gaullists suspected Pompidou on account of his political past (the fact that he was not involved in the Gaullist resistance). Conservative Gaullists were suspicious of Pompidou's nomination of the reforming Chaban-Delmas as Prime Minister in 1969, a nomination deemed politically necessary by Pompidou to reassure orthodox Gaullists (with Chaban-Delmas a pure representative of resistance Gaullism). In addition to an independent-minded premier, and pressures from within the Gaullist party, President Pompidou had to contend with the political pretensions of Valéry Giscard d'Estaing, the leader of the Independent Republicans, the most important non-Gaullist formation within the presidential majority. Giscard d'Estaing was bitterly opposed by leading Gaullists, who rightly suspected him of wanting to strengthen his party at their expense.

The style which Georges Pompidou brought to the presidency was markedly different from that of de Gaulle. Whereas General de Gaulle was personally austere and withdrawn, Georges Pompidou brought a more relaxed attitude to the Elysée palace. While de Gaulle had been shaped by his Catholicism, his experience in the armed forces and the French Resistance, Pompidou, with his past experience in banking and industry, was far more open to French business interests. In his presidential practice, Pompidou was more openly interventionist than de Gaulle. This manifested itself in several ways: a closer supervision over the ruling (but fractious) Gaullist party; a more open intervention in election campaigns and candidate selection; a closer supervision over key aspects of domestic policy (notably industrial and urban policy), as well as continuing suzerainty over foreign policy. Presidential supremacy was recalled under Pompidou on several occasions, the most spectacular being his sacking of premier Chaban-Delmas in 1972 only days after the latter had received an overwhelming vote of confidence from the National Assembly.

Pompidou's more interventionist style concealed a weaker political source of legitimacy. The 1973 National Assembly elections gave the first hints of the UDR's declining popularity with public opinion, a tendency which became fully apparent during the 1974 presidential election. Finally, ill-health and death prevented Pompidou from exercising his full seven-year presidential term, and reduced the President to being a pained spectator during the last twelve months of his life. The decline in Pompidou's physical capacities during the last year of his presidency, combined with the presence of a weak Prime Minister at Matignon (Messmer) led to accusations of a power vacuum, and of an undue influence being exerted by covert presidential advisers in the Elysée palace (notably Marie-France Garaud and Pierre Juillet). The whiff of scandal and corruption also lay close to the surface, notably in relation to property development in Paris.

The relationship between Pompidou and his first premier, Chaban-Delmas, testifies to the complexity of the relationship between President and Prime Minister in the Fifth Republic. Whereas Pompidou was unashamedly a British-style conservative, Chaban-Delmas almost qualified as being a left-Gaullist. As premier, Chaban-Delmas baptised his government programme under the slogan of the New Society. The reformist tone of Chaban-Delmas' premiership rested uneasily alongside Pompidou's conservatism. Ultimately, Pompidou's will prevailed, but for a long time Chaban-Delmas acted as a role model of a strong premier backed by influential advisers (such as Jacques Delors) who held sway over key aspects of domestic policy. The contradictions inherent in Chaban-Delmas' premiership encouraged Pompidou to rid himself of his first Prime Minister in 1972, and replace him with the lack-lustre, orthodox and conservative Pierre Messmer.

In important spheres of policy, the record of the Pompidou presidency was shaped by the legacy of de Gaulle's eleven-year rule, although there were departures from the Gaullist heritage as well. The main elements of continuity with Gaullism lay in the sphere of foreign policy and interventionist economic management. The onset of economic recession after the first oil crisis of 1973 became fully apparent only during Giscard d'Estaing's presidency: France continued to enjoy rates of economic growth superior to those of most of its European partners (Flockton and Kofman, 1989). The major policy evolution with respect to de Gaulle lay in the field of European policy. President Pompidou was far less enthusiastic than his predecessor about the Franco-German axis, although he was constrained to recognise its importance. Franco-German relations were soured somewhat by the difficult personal relations existing between Pompidou and the German Chancellors, Brandt and Schmidt. By contrast, Pompidou maintained a good personal relationship with the British Prime Minister, Edward Heath: one of the key decisions of his presidency was to remove de Gaulle's veto on British entry to the EC. A more sympathetic attitude towards the UK was combined with a more conciliatory tone towards the USA. Pompidou made it clear, however, that there could be no question of France rejoining the integrated military command structure of NATO, reaffirming the weight of the Gaullist legacy in this sphere.

The left-wing opposition was transformed during Pompidou's presidency. The 1969 presidential election had represented the nadir of the French left: the official Socialist candidate polled barely more than 5 per cent, trailing well behind the

Communist, J. Duclos (21 per cent). In July 1969 the old SFIO finally transformed itself into the new Socialist Party (PS), which began to revive in the 1970 local and 1971 municipal elections (Bell and Criddle, 1988). In June 1971, at the congress of Epinay, François Mitterrand, the former united left presidential candidate in 1965, captured control of the new party with the help of allies from the old SFIO. Mitterrand finally defeated Mollet, the former SFIO leader, who had remained consistently hostile to presidentialism and the Fifth Republic. Under Mitterrand's leadership, the PS committed itself to forming an alliance with the PCF. To achieve this alliance, Mitterrand agreed to the PCF's demand for a common programme of government, a detailed policy manifesto signed by the two parties. This committed the left to radical structural reforms, involving extensive nationalisation, decentralisation and increased workers' rights. Mitterrand was convinced that in order to become electable, the PS had to attract Communist voters (as a credible new radical party) as well as centre voters (as the only alternative to Gaullism). In June 1972 the PS, PCF and MRG signed the common programme of government. With the common programme, the left alliance seemed the only credible alternative to the governing coalition. The left alliance made significant gains at the 1973 National Assembly elections, although insufficient to challenge the presidential majority.

With the benefit of hindsight, it is clear that historic Gaullism died with de Gaulle. The piteous performance of Chaban-Delmas in the 1974 presidential election rang the death-knell of resistance Gaullism; Chirac's RPR was a different type of organisation altogether (Chapter 10). The 1974 presidential election ratified the declining fortunes of historic Gaullism: the UDR candidate Chaban-Delmas obtained 15.5 per cent, as against 32 per cent for his conservative rival, Giscard d'Estaing, and a strong showing for the united left candidate, Mitterrand (42 per cent). Pompidou's greatest symbolic achievement as President was to have facilitated the peaceful transition to the post-Gaullist period, while preserving the Fifth Republic. Associated with this, the second President ensured continuity with de Gaulle's legacy in most policy areas, while modifying their contentious aspects in a manner generally beneficial to France.

2.5 Valéry Giscard d'Estaing: the aristocracy in power, 1974–81

The narrow election of Valéry Giscard d'Estaing as the third President of the Fifth Republic (with 50.8 per cent, as against 49.2 per cent for Mitterrand) marked a watershed in the evolution of the regime. For the first time, control over the key institution escaped the powerful Gaullist party; deprived of its control over patronage, and its monopoly of the most powerful office, the UDR collapsed. Its disintegration was aggravated by the manoeuvres of Jacques Chirac, who led a group of 43 rebellious UDR deputies in support of Giscard d'Estaing from the first ballot of the presidential election.

As was the case with Pompidou, Giscard d'Estaing's initial choice of Prime Minister was heavily influenced by the conditions of his election. Giscard d'Estaing nominated Chirac as Prime Minister as a reward for his assistance during the presidential election. The new President calculated that appointing Chirac would assure him of the UDR's support, however reluctant, while at the same time allowing him to dismantle the 'UDR-state'. But Chirac remained a Gaullist, refused to be treated as Giscard d'Estaing's stooge and resigned from office in August 1976. He then took control of the UDR, rebaptised it Rassemblement pour la république (RPR) in December 1976 and concentrated on restoring the party's fortunes at the President's expense. Chirac was replaced as Prime Minister in August 1976 by Raymond Barre, a university professor with no formal party affiliation, who governed France until the 1981 presidential election. The internecine rivalries of the French right throughout Giscard d'Estaing's presidency were of fundamental importance in understanding why the Socialist Mitterrand eventually secured election in May 1981. In accordance with the pattern established for the first two Presidents, in the ensuing section several key aspects of Giscard d'Estaing's presidency will be signposted, before being pursued in more detail in subsequent chapters.

The public face presented by Giscard d'Estaing was that of a liberal reformer, determined to modernise the French economy and society. This optimistic portrayal was outlined in detail in his 1976 work, *La Démocratie française*. The President declared himself in favour of an 'advanced liberal society', a synthesis between a dynamic and open capitalist economy, and a society rejecting all forms of social exclusion, and relying on the participation of all social groups. Capitalism was portrayed as the ideal system for promoting consensus between social classes: it was important to reform capitalism, not to replace it, as was argued by the united left alliance. For supporters, Giscard d'Estaing's formulation provided a decent, humane and reformist vision. For critics, however, these platitudes bore little relationship to the reality of spiralling unemployment, inflation and economic crisis.

Whichever interpretation we make, Giscard d'Estaing lacked the means for his political ambitions. From the outset, the political foundations of the third President's rule were fragile (Duverger, 1977). Elected by the narrowest of majorities, Giscard d'Estaing's firm supporters comprised a small minority of the pro-presidential coalition. Throughout his presidency, but especially after 1976, President Giscard d'Estaing was unable to rely upon a disciplined parliamentary coalition to back his governments: essential measures had to be pushed through by relying on the use of restrictive articles of the 1958 constitution designed to favour the executive over parliament (notably article 49, clause 3). The fact that Barre's government (1976–81) was able to govern with only minor inconvenience, however, testified to the strength of the executive's position as deliberately established by the 1958 constitution.

During his 1974 presidential campaign, Giscard d'Estaing promised change with continuity, and without risk. In the course of the first two years of his presidency, the third President introduced several reforms tending to liberalise French society, and to modify the operation of its political system (Frears, 1981). After 1976, this mild reformist spirit was replaced by a cautious social and economic conservatism. The predominance of conservative Gaullists within the presidential majority limited the social reforms that could be enacted in the months following his election. It was indicative that the key reforms of 1974–5 (abortion, divorce, reform of the Constitutional Council) depended upon the votes of left-wing deputies for their enactment. The hostility of the President's conservative supporters dampened his reformist ambitions from 1975 onwards. Several announced reform projects were never introduced, such as decentralisation, the reform of the judicial system and a modification of state controls over the media.

The onset of severe economic problems after the oil crisis of 1973 greatly reduced the room for manoeuvre available to French governments, as to those elsewhere. The need to manage the economy as effectively as possible became by far the most important issue governments had to face. After an ill-advised economic relaunch under Chirac, premier Barre launched a series of tough anti-inflation plans, aimed at bringing under control France's traditionally lax attitude towards inflation, if necessary at the expense of increasing unemployment. On a comparative European level, the economic policies pursued by Barre's governments were similar to those being carried out by governments of comparable nations across Europe, whether controlled by conservatives, social democrats or socialists. This did not prevent the deflationary economic policy from being much maligned within France, especially by the Socialist–Communist opposition, but also to some extent by the Gaullist RPR.

Political commentators initially discerned a move towards a more openly presidential practice during Giscard d'Estaing's period in office. The fount of legitimacy was held to stem from the directly elected President. Giscard d'Estaing established a new precedent by addressing 'directive letters' to his Prime Ministers, outlining their duties for the following six months. There was little doubt that 1974–6 represented an interventionist phase of the French presidency. The principle of presidential initiative (Charlot, 1983a) was pushed further under Giscard d'Estaing than either of his predecessors; no sphere of policy was excluded from the possibility of presidential involvement. Examples often cited included the President's decree that the tempo of the national anthem should be speeded up in official meetings; the decision to intervene to halt the construction of a new motorway on the Paris left bank; and the decision to replace the Prefect of Paris with a directly elected Mayor (Frears, 1981). This latter policy badly backfired when Chirac, by now a bitter rival, defeated the President's own candidate for the prestigious post of the Mayor of Paris in 1977. Whereas Pompidou had taken a keen interest in industrial policy, Giscard d'Estaing preoccupied himself with aspects of social and financial policy that previous Presidents had been content to leave to the Prime Minister and the competent ministers (Wright, 1989). In reality, the appearance of hyper-presidential activism under Giscard d'Estaing disguised the fact that the political foundations of the third President's power were weaker than those of either of his predecessors. The more spectacular presidential interventions occurred during the early phase of his presidency, notably while he could still rely upon the support of the Gaullist premier Chirac.

From 1976 onwards, Giscard d'Estaing turned his attention to more traditional presidential interests: foreign policy, European affairs and defence. In foreign policy matters, he appeared often as the least Gaullist President of the Fifth Republic. This was the case, for instance, when he called into question de Gaulle's commitment to the nuclear doctrine of 'the weak's defence against the strong', and moved closer to NATO's rival doctrine of 'flexible response' (Howorth, in Hall *et al.* 1990). In other spheres, President Giscard d'Estaing displayed a greater continuity of policy with his predecessors. One such area lay in the sphere of European policy and Franco-German relations. Distancing himself from the UK, President Giscard d'Estaing established a close relationship with Chancellor Schmidt of West Germany. The fruits of this renewed period of Franco-German collaboration were widely recognised: the creation of the European Council in 1974 provided a regular forum for the heads of EC states to meet and take politically contentious decisions; the establishment of the European monetary system in 1979 provided a mechanism for closer European economic and monetary co-operation which proved of lasting worth.

Whatever the reality of his power, President Giscard d'Estaing disseminated an image of regal omnipotence, consistent with his aristocratic past. This occasionally led to a self-portrayal which bordered on the arrogant. His personal upbringing inculcated in Giscard d'Estaing the belief that he was destined for the highest political offices. His behaviour while in office led the third President to overestimate the strength of his position, especially after the left had failed to win the 1978 National Assembly election, subsequent to the breakdown of the united left alliance in 1977 (Bell and Criddle, 1988). His dealings with African heads of state appeared tantamount to excessive peddling of influence. His acceptance of a gift of diamonds from Colonel Bokassa, the self-styled Emperor of the Central African Republic, was particularly ill-advised: Bokassa had been implicated in serious abuses of human rights. As the 1981 presidential election approached, Giscard d'Estaing was so convinced of forthcoming electoral victory that he scarcely bothered campaigning for re-election. This attitude contributed to his unexpected defeat against Mitterrand in May 1981.

The historical importance of the third presidency lay in its symbolic function of assuring the transition to the post-Gaullist phase of the Fifth Republic, at a time when a majority of the French were not prepared to envisage a full-blown left-wing alternative. But, viewed as a whole, Giscard d'Estaing appeared more constrained than any other President of the Fifth Republic, a victim both of the onset of economic crisis, and of the weak political foundations underpinning his magistracy.

2.6 François Mitterrand, 1981–8: the chameleon

François Mitterrand's election as President in May 1981 was the catalyst for a series of important changes in the political operation of the Fifth Republic. Its political institutions experienced a double evolution during the 1980s under Mitterrand's aegis: the first alternation in power between right and left in 1981; the first 'cohabitation' between left and right in 1986. The transfer of power from right to left in 1981 legitimised the Fifth Republic in two important senses. It proved that the regime could withstand the democratic alternation in power, the key measurement of any liberal democracy; it also represented the final rallying of the left to the presidential institutions created by de Gaulle. The advent of cohabitation in 1986 was equally significant, since the regime did not collapse under the pressure of competing political forces controlling the presidency and the National Assembly. Instead, for the first time, the 1958 constitution was actually applied as it was written: the President presided, but the government governed.

The powerful presidency created by de Gaulle between 1958 and 1969, and consolidated by his successors, was initially strengthened further by Mitterrand's election in 1981. By dissolving the conservative-dominated National Assembly immediately after his election, and securing the election of an absolute Socialist majority, Mitterrand was able to secure a more complete control over the main institutions of political power than had been enjoyed by his two immediate predecessors. During the period 1981–6, Mitterrand mastered not only the presidency, but also the National Assembly, as well as the leadership of the presidential party (Cole, 1993a). No President since de Gaulle had been able to claim as much.

The early years of Mitterrand's presidency were characterised by a high degree of presidential interventionism (Cole, 1994a). As personally representative of *le changement*, Mitterrand symbolised the arrival of a new political order, and was involved in many of the principal policy decisions of the early period in office. It was President Mitterrand himself, for example, who insisted that the government maintain its electoral commitments with respect to the nationalisation programme of 1982, rather than moderate its provisions. Presidential interventionism was particularly marked during the early reformist years of the Mauroy premiership, 1981–4, but gradually Mitterrand intervened less frequently in matters of domestic politics. His most critical arbitration occurred in March 1983, when the French President opted that France should remain within the European Monetary System, at the expense of abandoning the Socialist government's Keynesian attempt to reflate the French economy.

Mitterrand was elected as President in 1981 committed to a break with capitalism. He was re-elected in 1988 advocating the merits of consensus, national unity and the modernisation of capitalism. The victorious Socialist candidate of 1981 was forced to water down, or to abandon, the main precepts of his presidential platform within two or three years. The first two years of Mitterrand's presidency stand out as a period of reformist effort unprecedented in scope at least since the post-war tripartite government of 1946–7. The reforms undertaken by Pierre Mauroy's government combined 'classical' quantitative left-wing policies in the sphere of social, economic and industrial policy with 'qualitative' reforms in other areas (notably decentralisation, enhanced workers' rights and various liberal civil rights measures). The main reforms enacted included the nationalisation of leading industrial groups and banks, the decentralisation measures and the accomplishment of wide-ranging welfare reforms (partly financed by redistributive taxation measures).

Certain reforms were transient; the effects of others became only slowly apparent. The decentralisation reforms of 1982–3 proved a case in point. The transfer of major policy responsibilities to the 96 departmental councils, and the direct election of the 22 regional assemblies had a major long-term impact whose effects are becoming clear only today (Lorrain, 1993). Other measures had unintended consequences, notably in the sphere of industrial policy and economic management (Machin and Wright, 1985; Ross *et al.*, 1987). Mitterrand came to office as a champion of the people of the left. In the French context this meant alliance with the Communist Party, Keynesian reflationist economic policies, nationalisation and support for traditional industrial sectors. By 1984 a complete reverse had taken place: a definite abandon of reflation in March 1983, for the *franc fort*; a drastic industrial modernisation programme, which virtually shut down the coal and ship-building industries; and the beginnings of a partial privatisation programme. These policy reversals indicated that governments do not act in isolation, especially in the economic sphere: the combined pressures of the international economy, spiralling trade and budget deficits, a sharp increase in inflation and diplomatic pressures from EC partners all constrained the French Socialists to change course. Mitterrand's salvation lay in the fact that the fourth President was sufficiently adaptable as a political leader to make a virtue out of necessity.

From 1984 onwards, Mitterrand's attentions were increasingly focused on issues of foreign policy, defence and, above all, Europe. In appraising Mitterrand's foreign policy, Stanley Hoffmann concluded that it was 'Gaullism by any other name' (Hoffmann, in Ross *et al.*, 1987). In key areas of foreign policy, Mitterrand was more faithful to the model of national independence promoted by General de Gaulle than his immediate predecessor had been: his acceptance of the strategic doctrines underpinning the French independent nuclear deterrent was a case in point. The importance placed by Mitterrand on bilateral Franco-German relations also recalled that of de Gaulle some twenty years earlier. The parallel with de Gaulle should not be overplayed, however. The Euromissile crisis of 1982–3 revealed Mitterrand as a stauncher supporter of the Atlantic cause than past French Presidents and current allies, far less prone to idealism in relation to the Soviet Bloc countries. In European policy, in symbolic and substantive terms, Mitterrand's Europe was far more integrationist than that espoused by de Gaulle (Lemaire-Prosche, 1990; Drake, in Raymond, 1994). From 1984 onwards, Mitterrand concentrated upon portraying himself as a great European statesman, with a coherent vision of Europe's future. Mitterrand was more genuinely convinced of the merits of a unified Europe than any of his predecessors, and proved more willing than them to sacrifice elements of national sovereignty in the interests of European integration.

As the Mitterrand presidency progressed, the fourth President withdrew from the intricacies of domestic policy. This process preceded the 1986–8 cohabitation, but expressed itself most fully during this episode. By calling upon Chirac, the leader of the victorious RPR–UDF coalition, to form a government in March 1986, President Mitterrand respected the democratic logic that the clear victors of the most recent general election should be entrusted with the responsibility of governing the nation. Any other outcome would have been undemocratic, although there was considerable speculation about Mitterrand's possible choices at the time, with the strongest alternative possibility being that the President might nominate an apolitical technocrat as premier. In the event, presidential supremacy disappeared once the President was faced by a determined Prime Minister armed with a parliamentary majority.

During the 1986–8 cohabitation, Chirac's RPR–UDF coalition engaged in a radical programme of economic liberalism, combined with a strong dose of social and political conservatism, with obvious overtones of Margaret Thatcher in the UK and Ronald Reagan in the United States (Tuppen, 1988). Despite the popularity of certain measures (such as privatisations), in its haste to reform French society Chirac's government misread the state of French opinion, and created the impression of a government governing in the interests of one social class. This was symbolised by the ill-considered and unpopular decision to abolish the wealth tax introduced by Mitterrand in 1982. Moreover, Chirac's mixture of economic liberalism and political conservatism failed in its central declared objective of reducing unemployment. Faced with the accumulated political mistakes of Chirac's government, and his own clever political positioning, President Mitterrand's popularity began to recover sharply.

Mitterrand discovered a new role during the 1986–8 cohabitation: that of 'arbiter-president'. The government was to be encouraged to govern, but as the arbiter of the nation, according to article 5 of the 1958 constitution, Mitterrand reserved for himself the right to criticise government policies by speaking in the name of the 'French people'. This new stance worked: Mitterrand was easily re-elected against a divided right-wing challenge in the 1988 presidential election (Gaffney, 1989a).

2.7 Mitterrand's second term, 1988–95

How Mitterrand won in 1988 was obvious: he attracted the support of a vital fraction of the centre-right electorate alienated by Chirac and unprepossessed by the other conservative challenger, Barre. And yet why Mitterrand stood was more difficult to discern. His 1988 presidential platform contained no firm proposals in the sphere of domestic policy, limiting itself to justifications of past presidential actions. Mitterrand was more ambitious in respect of Europe, which the incumbent President made a leitmotif of his second presidential mandate. Mitterrand's European mission, which appeared to triumph with the adoption of the Maastricht Treaty in December 1991, consisted of a steadfast vision of closer European integration, for which the French President deserved much credit or blame, depending upon one's viewpoint. At the same time, the political and diplomatic weight of the French President was diminished after the historic event of German unification in 1990, which altered the balance of European power in favour of Germany.

The pattern of presidential interventionism during Mitterrand's first mandate was curiously reversed during his second term. Whereas he had been highly active after his election as President in 1981, he was content, or at least constrained, to allow his fourth premier, Michel Rocard, a relatively free hand in domestic policy making from 1988 to 1991. Rocard's enforced resignation in May 1991 temporarily recalled Mitterrand's pre-eminence as President, but it was a move from which he never fully recovered, not least because it was misunderstood by public opinion. Indeed, under the premiership of Rocard's successor, Edith Cresson, President Mitterrand was forced to intervene more than he would ideally have liked, both in order to support publicly his beleaguered Prime Minister, and to ensure that her policy choices were not adopted.

The succession of Prime Ministers during Mitterrand's second term increased public disquiet with the lack of a sense of purpose displayed by the Socialist governments. The economic policy of the strong franc, pursued vigorously by Socialist and centre-right administrations after 1983, appeared to deprive governments of much leeway in conducting policy elsewhere, especially if this involved raising public expenditure. The inability of either centre-right or Socialist governments to master unemployment in particular had a devastating effect upon their electoral fortunes. This was revealed with alacrity in the 1993 National Assembly elections, at which the ruling Socialists were reduced to under 20 per cent and 67 seats (see Appendix 2 for full details). Combined with their perceived inability to master the economy, the Socialists suffered from a series of damaging corruption scandals, which did much to demolish their prior claim to moral superiority over the right. There was no incident as serious as the Bokassa diamonds affair to implicate Mitterrand personally, but the belief was widespread that men close to the President had been engaged in dubious activities that were not sanctioned. The tragic suicide in May 1993 of Pierre Bérégovoy, Mitterrand's sixth Prime Minister, appeared to many to symbolise the moral bankruptcy of the Socialists, destined to an extended period in the desert.

The advent of the Balladur government in March 1993 testified to the diminishing political returns of Mitterrand's extended period in office. In the final period of his presidency, Mitterrand's bargaining power appeared far weaker than at any other time of his tenure, including during the first cohabitation of 1986–8. This was partly because he was an obvious non-contender for a third presidential term, and partly because the Socialists' electoral humiliation of March 1993 removed any real illusions of grandeur. In domestic policy, Mitterrand had little visible input during the second period of cohabitation (March 1993–April 1995); his role was reduced to that of a moral gatekeeper, whom no one really trusted. Mitterrand attempted to reinvent the role of the arbiter-president that had served him so well during the first cohabitation, but with much less effect. Presidential influence continued to manifest itself in relation to foreign policy, most notably with regard to Mitterrand's refusal to agree to renewed nuclear testing in the South Pacific, and in his continuing attachment to certain symbols of Gaullist nuclear policy that even RPR military advisers considered outdated.

Mitterrand shaped the Fifth Republic more than any other President apart from de Gaulle. In key respects, the legacy of Mitterrand involved the deconstruction of the 'French exception', both domestically and on the international stage. France was a country rather less different from its European neighbours in 1995 than in 1981. Mitterrand's main achievements were in those spheres where his action had been least expected: he promoted European integration beyond the limits agreed by former French Presidents; he contributed under pressure towards the modernisation of French industry and financial capitalism; he de-ideologised the left and reconciled it to the market economy. The fact that these real achievements bore only a tenuous relationship to his 110 propositions of 1981 bears testament to the limited room for manoeuvre of national political leaderships in an increasingly interdependent and global age.

The second episode of cohabitation was played out against a background of fratricidal rivalry within the Gaullo-conservative camp, in the form of presidential competition between premier Edouard Balladur and Chirac, leader of the RPR. The division of the French right into two or three families is not new: in 1981 and 1988 right-wing divisions facilitated Mitterrand's victory. The original feature of the 1995 presidential campaign stemmed from the fact that both Chirac and Balladur came from the ranks of the neo-Gaullist RPR movement. This created an enormous dilemma for RPR deputies, especially until February 1995, when Balladur appeared the most likely victor. The fact that most RPR deputies supported Chirac even when his cause appeared forlorn is testament to the hold he exercised over the RPR, a movement he had built up since 1976 (Knapp, 1994).

Balladur's nomination as Prime Minister in March 1993 formed part of an unwritten agreement between the two men: for Balladur the premiership, for Chirac the presidency. This understanding was rapidly undermined by the 'Balladur effect': consistently high opinion poll ratings led Balladur to envisage the presidential mantle for himself. The exercise of the French premiership is believed by its practitioners to be a launching pad for presidential success, but this traditional adage was contradicted by the results of the first ballot, which left Balladur trailing in third place (18.54 per cent), behind the Socialist Jospin (23.3 per cent) and the Gaullist Chirac (20.8 per cent). The election of Jacques Chirac as the Fifth President of the Fifth Republic (by 52.7 per cent, against 47.3 per cent for Jospin) witnessed the recovery of the Elysée for Gaullism after a period of 21 years in the wilderness. A new chapter in the history of the Fifth Republic had begun.

2.8 President Chirac, 1995– : awaiting judgement

It is too early to judge the presidency of Jacques Chirac. Early developments suggested that an analogous evolution to that experienced by Mitterrand was being imposed on Chirac. Initially responsive to his first-round electoral clientele, President Chirac attempted to navigate a delicate path between the various contradictory promises that he had made during the election campaign. Forced to choose between opposing economic policies by the pressure of financial markets – as Mitterrand had been in 1982 – Chirac made a strong commitment in October 1995 to preparing France to participate in the single European currency, imposing the package of economic austerity measures this choice required. The government reshuffle of November 1995 ended the first reformist phase of the Chirac presidency, a shorter phase than the corresponding state of grace of the Mitterrand presidency (1981–2).

In terms of his positioning as an international statesman, early evidence suggested that President Chirac consciously attempted to imitate historic Gaullism, without having the means to impose Gaullist-style policies. Chirac's decision in June 1995 that France would resume unilateral nuclear testing in the South Pacific recalled earlier manifestations of French exceptionalism, as did the new President's refusal to bow to external pressures to cancel the decision. To the extent that Chirac chose a highly symbolic aspect of foreign policy to make his mark, this represented a sign of continuity with past Presidents. In other respects, President Chirac made his mark where least expected. In spite of the nuclear testing decision, this was notably the case in foreign and defence policy: that a Gaullist President should announce the end of conscription, the slashing of defence budgets and the partial reintegration of France into NATO marked a bolder break with the Gaullist legacy than any moves attempted by Chirac's three predecessors. The implications of these audacious moves are considered in Chapter 16.

2.9 Conclusion and summary

The election of a Gaullist President in 1995 was a fitting tribute to the longevity and adaptability of the Fifth Republic. Except for the far-right FN, each of France's major political parties has participated in governmental office since 1958. The Fifth Republic is France's second longest surviving post-revolutionary regime. It has attracted a degree of élite and popular support which sets it apart from other post-revolutionary French regimes. While initially shaped in the image of its creator, de Gaulle, the Fifth Republic demonstrated its capacity to resist becoming a personalist regime: subsequent chapters reveal how the Gaullist heritage has been surpassed in a range of sectors, as well as remaining steadfast in others.

Certain early observers predicted that the regime was destined to disappear with the departure of its founder. This did not transpire. The transition to a post-Gaullist phase occurred gradually: presaged by Pompidou's curtailed presidency of 1969–74, it was consolidated with the election of Giscard d'Estaing as the first non-Gaullist President in 1974. The final legitimisation of the Fifth Republic came in 1981, with the election of the Socialist Mitterrand as President. Approaching its fortieth anniversary, the Fifth Republic has thus demonstrated its longevity. Its adaptability was also fully illustrated in the course of the 1980s. The alternation in power between left and right in 1981 was followed in 1986 by the first experience of cohabitation, an experience repeated in 1993. Henceforth, the alternation in power of rival left- and right-wing parties, or coalitions, has become a banal occurrence.

Moving away from institutions, the period since 1958 has been one of relative prosperity (at least compared with other comparable nations), of a strengthening of French influence within Europe and internationally, and of economic and social modernisation. While an optimistic interpretation is favoured by certain commentators, others are less sanguine, pointing to the rise of the far right, a sense of ongoing economic crisis, diminishing confidence in politicians and widespread corruption to tarnish the reputation of the regime. The evidence presented in the ensuing chapters might support either interpretation. It is a measure of how far the Fifth Republic has imposed itself in popular consciousness, however, that contemporary disputes are centred around particular policies, or political practices, rather than overt challenges to the legitimacy of the political regime.

Indicative bibliography

Cole, A. (1994) *François Mitterrand: A study in political leadership*, Routledge, London.

Dreyfus, F.-G. (1982) *De Gaulle et le Gaullisme: essai d'interpretation*, PUF, Paris.

Duhamel, A. (1980) *La République giscardienne*, Grasset, Paris.

Duverger, M. (1977) *L'Echec au roi*, Albin Michel, Paris.

Frears, J. (1981) *France in the Giscard Presidency*, Allen and Unwin, London.

Hayward, J. (1993) *De Gaulle to Mitterrand: Presidential power in France*, France, # Hurst, London.

Horne, A. (1977) *A Savage War of Peace: Algeria, 1954–62*, Macmillan, London.

Lacouture, J. (1965) *De Gaulle*, Seuil, Paris.

Roussel, E. (1984) *Georges Pompidou*, Lattès, Paris.

Wright, V. (ed.) (1979) *Conflict and Consensus in France*, Frank Cass, London.

French political culture: myths and realities

3.1 Introduction and objectives

Chapter 3 introduces the reader to various interpretations of the French polity: namely, those based on the revolutionary tradition, subcultural identities, centre–periphery relations, and patterns of authority. Concentrating upon some of the most influential French, American and British studies, the chapter aims to demonstrate that traditional portrayals of French political culture are in need of revision. In conjunction with Chapters 1 and 2, this chapter aims to promote a broad understanding of the complexity and depth of French political culture. This exercise is an indispensable preliminary to the wider context of institutional development engaged in Part II.

3.2 Political culture in France: the traditional reading

As developed in much of the literature, French political culture is highly ambiguous. The cultural portrayals of France have a tendency to vary depending upon the cultural preconceptions of the observer. American observers, for instance, have provided some of the most stimulating insights into French culture, but these are not generally those highlighted by French analysts, in part because of different normative standpoints adopted (for instance, the definition of what constitutes civic behaviour). Furthermore, there is a very real difficulty in measuring cultural attitudes, especially in the period preceding the advent of opinion polls. This imparts a descriptive, impressionistic character to much of the early literature on political culture, especially textbook representations. To this extent, the notion of political culture can be misleading, since it disseminates potentially false images of modern and contemporary France.

At various stages in recent history, political culture has been advanced to explain a range of rather different obstacles to the smooth functioning of the French polity. Those studies undertaken before or immediately after the creation of the Fifth

Republic looked for cultural causes of French political instability. The prevailing idea present in texts written in the 1950s and 1960s was that France had been prevented from becoming a 'modern' or 'stable' country on account of its uneven historical development and its idiosyncratic national character. As Safran (1991, p. 44) points out: 'American social scientists pointed to France's reluctance to marry her century – to the habit of ideological thinking, the prevalence of class distrust, the tendency to excoriate the political establishment, the absence of civic minded-ness and an underdeveloped ethos of participation.'

Even though France eventually developed democratic political institutions, and an advanced socio-economic infrastructure, certain analysts continued to refer to France as a 'delinquent' society, one marked by tax evasion, alcoholism, un-disciplined motorists and a general lack of civic behaviour (Pitts, 1981). These 'delinquent' traits raised the question of the 'governability' of the French. As Hoffmann (1994) points out, 'most of these uncivic cultural traits no longer stand up to serious scrutiny'.

As formulated by classic political culture theorists such as Almond and Verba in *The Civic Culture* (1963), the notion of political culture has had difficulties in explaining political and socioeconomic change. In the French context, the cultural norms detected in the 1950s and 1960s often appear ill-designed to describe the France of the 1990s. The above remark applies even more forcefully to cultural stereotypes derived from the nineteenth century or earlier. The cultural perceptions developed when France was a static, economically inward-looking society are likely to be of limited assistance when attempting to assess how French politics and society have mutated under the impact of the dramatic economic, social, political and demographic changes of the post-war period. For political culture to be a meaningful concept, it has to transcend the cultural representations present at any one point in time. It also has to admit the importance of sub-cultures, either in addition to or against a prevailing national culture.

Traditional perceptions of French political culture have been shaped above all by two innovative surveys: *In Search of France*, edited by Stanley Hoffmann (1965), and *The Stalled Society* (*La Société bloquée*), by Michel Crozier (1970). Common to both Hoffmann's 'static society' and Crozier's 'stalled society' lay the idea that the French nation was afflicted by numerous blockages, which prevented a normal democratic functioning of its polity. These blockages included a habit for overly ideological and abstract thinking (induced by France's Cartesian education sys-tem), the persistence of class rivalries, a penchant for uncivic behaviour, a deeply ingrained anti-political strain within public opinion, a distrust of those in auth-ority, an inability to compromise or to conduct civilised face-to-face negotiations, and a weak sense of political efficacy, leading to a low level of participation in voluntary organisations such as political parties and pressure groups. Such cultural portrayals partly influenced élite behaviour. This was true of General de Gaulle himself, for whom the French were an unruly bunch of individualists who could never agree on anything, and who needed firm leadership to overcome their dis-unity. The belief that French society was archaic and conservative, and that only the state represented the general will of the people, was a powerful motivational force behind the state-led 'modernisation' drive from the late 1940s onwards. Given these cultural barriers, modernisation could only be carried out by a neutral, innovative and interventionist state.

In *In Search of France* Hoffmann contends, among other arguments, that relations between state and civil society are far more closed and less pluralistic in France than in the Anglo-Saxon countries. In Hoffman's opinion, French political culture combined extreme individualism and authoritarianism. On account of their individualism, French people were reluctant to participate in voluntary associations, such as political parties and interest groups. When they did join groups, such groups were weak, fragmented and ill-disposed to compromise. In order to resolve inevitable disputes, they appealed for arbitration to the state. This provided the impetus for the development of a powerful bureaucracy, to arbitrate disputes. There was a weak bargaining culture of negotiation between the competing groups themselves, and between groups and the state. In a critique of this portrayal, Vincent Wright (1989) demonstrates that relationships between pressure groups and the state were far more subtle than implied by Hoffmann.

Perhaps the most widely diffused exposé of the pessimistic appraisal of French culture was that provided by Michel Crozier, in two highly influential books, *The Stalled Society* and *The Bureaucratic Phenomenon* (Crozier, 1970, 1963) . The essence of Crozier's thesis was that the French were afraid of 'face to face contact' and were 'unable to cooperate'. In order to resolve disputes, individuals appealed systematically to those in positions of higher authority, especially representatives of the state, rather than attempting to negotiate, bargain or compromise among each other. This induced an exaggerated sense of hierarchy, but at the same time created the conditions for rebellion against this authority if unwelcome arbitrations were made. Thus French political culture combined a measure of routine authoritarianism with sporadic rebellions against authority. Underpinning Crozier's analysis is the belief that French people are torn between submissive subordination to the state, and insurrectional outbursts against it. In normal circumstances, such cultural traits normally produce a bureaucratic defensive mentality and a lack of initiative.

Appraisals of French political culture have long been overshadowed by the work of Hoffmann and Crozier. At best, they described aspects of French society at a particular stage of historical development. Even if we accept their initial premises, which are difficult to substantiate or disprove, it could be argued that French society has moved on since then. Critics of Crozier's thesis in particular have pointed to the development of voluntary groups and new forms of collective action, which point to a culture of negotiation and compromise. For Mendras (1989), for instance, Crozier's viewpoint is inadequate in analysing contemporary France. The opposition between Us and Them depicted by Crozier no longer accurately represents the structure of French society, or the norm to be adopted towards authority. The creation of new social groups during the post–war period (labelled rather schematically as the 'new middle classes'), which insist upon a bargaining model of authority, and whose values are broadly post-materialist, has weakened the authority patterns evoked by Crozier. These developments are eloquently summarised by Gaffney (in Gaffney and Kolinsky, 1991, p. 18), who refers to a convergence of lifestyles, aspirations and social outlook, an assumed growing political consensus, a developing urbanisation, salaraisation and tertiarisation, and the importance of a diffuse cultural liberalism as symbolising the cultural identity of the new France. These themes will be developed in more detail in Chapter 13.

3.3 Traits of French political culture

There have been numerous conflicting portrayals of the content of French political culture. These are often inherently contradictory. The traditional portrayal of French political culture pointed to the persistence of cleavages inherited from the French Revolution. The divisions occasioned by disputes over church, state and nation remained pertinent 150 years later; even today, they continue to provide the backdrop to many assessments of contemporary France. In their analysis of political culture, for example, Hanley *et al.* (1984, p. 109) emphasise the legacy of the French Revolution, the special status of Paris in French history, the slow rate of industrialisation, the role of the church and anti-clericalism, the closed relationship between state and civil society, and nationalism as 'the constants of French political culture'. Generally, the traditional portrayal of French political culture has emphasised the revolutionary tradition, the role of the state as an instrument of national unity, a tendency for uncivic behaviour and various characteristics attributed to France's status as a Catholic country. These variables are undoubtedly of critical importance in understanding the evolution of French history, but they present a rather static portrait of contemporary France. This is misleading, since it underplays the possibility that cultural attitudes might be altered by social, economic and political change.

A revolutionary tradition?

Republicanism in France traditionally declared its belief in the legitimacy of the revolutionary tradition. This tradition can have several meanings. At its most basic, it involved support for the French Revolution, avowed even by conservative republicans during the nineteenth century. For more radical republicans, the revolutionary tradition signified that French citizens had the right to overturn an unjust government, if its institutions affronted the ideals of the republic and democracy. For the left during the early twentieth century, the revolutionary tradition involved a commitment to provide a social and economic counterpart to the political revolution of 1789: in other words, to replace capitalism with socialism, as 1789 had eventually replaced the monarchy with the republic. This interpretation of the revolutionary tradition strongly characterised the activities of the French Communist Party during the inter-war years. A fourth version of the revolutionary tradition was that promulgated by the central state itself, channelled through the national education system. The revolutionary tradition was a justification for the actions of republicans in overturning monarchist governments during the eighteenth and nineteenth centuries. French children in state schools are saturated with the feats of their republican ancestors; an official revolutionary, republican tradition was inculcated by an interventionist state. Republican regimes have claimed the French Revolution of 1789 as the foundation of their own legitimacy: reference to the 1789 Declaration of the Rights of Man and Citizen in the preliminary of the 1958 constitution is a good example of this.

We must not overlook the fact that the French Revolution initially produced a divided political culture in France: for or against the republic, the church, the lay state. Whereas the French Revolution came to be accepted by most of the political élite, left and right continue to argue over whether or not the 1848 revolution and the Paris commune of 1871 were justified expressions of rebellion against unjust authority. The French revolutionary tradition is neither monolithic nor accepted by everybody. The official celebrations of the bicentenary of the French Revolution in 1989 were marred by counter-demonstrations by those contesting the legitimacy of events two centuries previously: Le Pen's Front national represented a powerful counter-revolutionary force on this occasion.

What remains of this revolutionary tradition in contemporary France? Until recently the main left-wing parties (the PCF and the PS) continued to refer to the French revolutionary tradition as a justification for their political activity. For the Communist Party, the notion of revolution formed an indelible element in the party's own political culture, however shallow that commitment revealed itself to be in May 1968. In practice, ever since its creation in 1920, the PCF has fought elections like any other party and has eschewed any serious attempt at revolutionary upheaval, even when circumstances appeared propitious, such as in 1944 or 1968. Despite its opposition to the 'personal power' that it accuses the presidential system of promoting, the PCF has in reality accepted working within the institutions of the Fifth Republic, rather than attempting to bring about a revolution. For the Socialist Party, it was sufficient that the Communist Party claimed a revolutionary heritage for it to define its own mission in terms of a revolutionary transformation of society. Invigorated by their own myths, the Socialists attempted to portray their victory in 1981 as being more a change of regime than a mere change of government. Such deception did not last for long. The failure of the Socialists' radical reform programme of 1981–2 destroyed many remaining illusions: it took a left-wing government finally to bury the revolutionary tradition.

On a slightly less exalted level, the French 'revolutionary tradition' has been invoked to explain the propensity of French citizens to take their protests to the streets. It does appear that certain social groups – such as farmers, fishermen and lorry drivers – have used the tactics associated with past 'revolutionaries' to forward their own corporate demands. But this is scarcely indicative of their desire to overthrow existing society. Henceforth, street demonstrations from unsatisfied social groups are open attempts to press for concessions, rather than mythical insurrections aimed at overthrowing the government. Student demonstrations in 1986, 1990 and 1995 were indicative of this new public spirit. Unlike their counterparts in May 1968, the young demonstrators never called into question the government's right to govern.

Whatever its historical significance, the revolutionary tradition has become a somewhat mythical aspect of French democracy. It is unclear what it signifies today, apart from a rather bland attachment to the slogans of the French Revolution. The disappearance of the political discourse of revolution, in association with the ideological discredit of Marxism, has been a further gauge of the weakening of the French exception.

Provincialism and the state

A celebration of provincialism has been noted by several observers as a defining feature of French political culture. This is the counterpart of an excessively centralised state apparatus and a concentration of politico-administrative power in Paris. Provincial distrust of the state and of Paris is certainly deeply embedded. This might be interpreted in terms of the process of state building in France, which took place by means of the incorporation and the suppression of regional identities. *La France profonde* has always distrusted the centralising and corrupting influence of Paris.

In all traditional, pre-1968 accounts of French political culture, emphasis was also laid on the importance of the central state as a cohesive idea holding together French society. As surveyed in Chapter 1, modern France was created as an extension of the central state. This process had begun under the *ancien régime*, as the monarchy attempted to impose its control over feudal barons. The process of state building was considerably strengthened by the revolution, which smashed the autonomous power of the aristocracy and imposed the will of Paris on the provinces. After the revolutionary upheavals of 1789–99, Napoleon provided a further impetus towards the creation of the centralised nation-state: the Emperor relied on autocratic personal rule, backed by unrivalled control over military force, to impose a powerful and efficient type of state machinery, key features of which have remained unaltered until the present. A highly organised and regimented bureaucracy (selected by means of a centralised and élitist system of national education) was the key legacy of the Napoleonic period . Throughout the one hundred years following the revolution, the central state attempted to ensure the lasting subordination of unruly provinces to its rule.

The nomination of central state representatives (prefects) in France's 96 departments was a testament to the state's centralising mission. But this affirmation of central authority went alongside a reality of regional variation. Research from various disciplines – and at various stages of French history – has revealed a rich provincial diversity subsisting beneath an officially regimented system. Sociologists have emphasised the diverse patterns of kinship and family structure, as well as varying types of authority structure in different French regions (Todd, 1988; Le

Bras, 1995). Linguists have revealed the survival of regional dialects in spite of efforts to subordinate them in the nineteenth century. Social historians and geographers have insisted upon the importance of territorial identities in explaining lasting regional political allegiances. Political scientists, finally, have illustrated how the state machinery (the prefectures, notably) has functioned in specific manners in different parts of the country. This reaffirms that provincial diversity is the counterpart to centralisation. Indeed, the traditional strength of the French state might be directly related to the endless variety of regional variations that public policymakers have to consider. This accounts in part for the highly codified nature of the French legal system, since regional variation was so strong across the nation that the state had to take positive action to affirm the revolutionary principle of equality.

Challenges to the French state have come in several directions: from the European Union and the process of European integration (Chapter 15), from decentralisation and the emergence of the regions (Chapter 8), from developments in the education system, from the globalising pressures of the international economy and from developments in public policy. Certain of these developments appear to have run against the grain of a highly *dirigiste* economic tradition. The French state is far from omnipotent. However, the importance of the state as a reference point of national identity remains more marked in France than in most other European nations, alongside a tradition of central state innovative action and a particular conception of public service which relies heavily on affirmative state action. Whether this conception of the neutral state can survive the process of European integration is open to doubt.

An uncivic nation?

Critical observers have diagnosed French political culture as being responsible for a weak sense of civic responsibility. This is typified by a deeply ingrained antipoliticism, and a pervasive distrust of politicians. That there exists a deep distrust of most politicians might be verified even by occasional visitors to France. This might be explained in terms of political culture, but other explanations are equally valid, notably those relating to political performance. Anti-political sentiments within the French electorate are particularly marked when the political and economic systems are not performing as effectively as they should be, such as during the Fourth Republic, or since the mid-1980s. It is important not to take such developments in isolation: strong anti-political sentiments within public opinion have not been limited to France, but have been a more general phenomenon throughout western Europe and the United States. Indeed, by many comparative measurements (such as the degree of electoral participation), France is a model of civic pride. Moreover, while politicians in general might be subject to criticism, one's own representative is usually spared excessive opprobrium. This is revealed by the rate of re-election of sitting mayors in the six-yearly municipal elections, even in circumstances of mayors being involved in criminal trials, as in the 1995 contest.

A low level of political participation and a excessive penchant for individualism were classically highlighted as evidence of *incivisme*. This is difficult to substantiate. It sits uneasily with the proliferation of voluntary associations during the post-war period; the fact is that one-half of French people claimed to belong to voluntary associations in the mid-1980s, a figure comparable with other European countries (cf. Chapter 12). Levels of participation in elections, where even municipal contests can attract three-quarters of registered voters to cast a ballot, are among the highest in Europe. As measured by participation rates, the French electorate would appear to have a preference for two types of election – the municipal and the presidential. The presidential election involves a direct communion with a supra-partisan leader; the municipal contest allows close contact with a recognised local spokesperson.

The suspicion of *incivisme* went alongside the absence of the regular alternations in power between social reformist and moderate conservative parties, of the type diagnosed in Britain, the Federal Republic of Germany and the USA. In the political circumstances of post-war France (the unstable coalitions of the Fourth Republic, giving way to a right-wing monopoly from 1958 to 1981), political discourse assumed a radical edge, a counterpart to a lack of face-to-face contact between political groups themselves. A tradition of ideological political reasoning appears well documented, especially on the left of French politics. There are several sound historical reasons why such a pattern should have prevailed for so long. The importance of ideology as a means of political competition can be related to the late development of an industrial working class, to the rivalry between the two left-wing parties, or to the Cartesian structure of the French education system. But it is clear that classic ideological frameworks of reference are in decline. The experience of the left in government after 1981 has discredited overtly ideological solutions to problems of public policy for the foreseeable future. The collapse of the Berlin Wall had a critical effect upon what remained of traditional ideological frames of reference.

There is little firm evidence of a stronger incidence of anti-civic attitudes in France than in comparable democracies. Safran (1994) points to the alleged French tendency for tax dodging as evidence to underline the lack of a civic culture in France. This is disingenuous. While no one might like paying tax, the high incidence of French tax evasion is more likely to reflect the structure of the taxation system than anti-civic attitudes. Viewed as a whole, the Fifth Republic appears to be a regime enjoying a high degree of political legitimacy. The acceptance by public opinion, and by the main political formations, of the fundamental precepts of the regime is an unprecedented development in republican France. Neither the Third Republic (1870–1940) nor the Fourth Republic (1944–58) could boast such an underlying consensus. While political choices divide French élites, the republican form of government is less contested in contemporary France than at any period since 1789. Catholics have become fully reconciled to the regime, even more so than during the short-lived Fourth Republic (Donegani, 1982). Republicanism has become banal, losing its mobilising force, but no longer inspiring intense hatred

(Kriegel, 1992). Even Jean-Marie Le Pen, while courting with the symbols of counter-revolution, and openly contesting 1789, is careful to portray himself as a republican.

A Catholic identity?

Certain cultural attributes have been attributed to France's heritage as a Catholic nation. A distinction must be drawn here between the cultural legacy of Catholicism and its impact upon political culture. In social terms, practising Catholicism appears to be in decline in France, as elsewhere in Europe, although France remains an overwhelmingly Catholic country in nominal terms. In terms of political culture, France has never been a culturally homogeneous Catholic society. Indeed, the divisive and bitter struggle between Catholicism and anti-clericalism helped to shape contemporary political identities.

In political terms, the heritage of Catholic anti-republicanism retarded the emergence of a modern Christian-democratic movement as a federating force of conservatism. The rallying of the Catholic Church to the republic during the 1890s did not represent a fundamental compromise with the theological foundations of Roman Catholicism, which continued to refute the legitimacy of the republican form of government until after the Second World War. Catholics excluded themselves from the republic until the emergence of French Christian democracy, in the form of the MRP (Mouvement républicain populaire) and its participation in the postwar progressive tripartite alliance. The failure of French Christian democracy in the Fourth Republic stemmed in part from its ambiguous political message: MRP voters were far more conservative than its progressively minded leaders, who espoused social Catholicism and class solidarity. It also suffered from being a regime party of the Fourth Republic, with the ultimate discredit that this implied. Even before the fall of the Fourth Republic, organised political Catholicism had to cope with the emergence of Gaullism as an alternative, pro-Catholic, federating force of French conservatism.

The influence of Catholicism might best be understood in subcultural terms: the existence of a powerful Catholic political subculture undoubtedly had a structuring effect on the political behaviour of France's most dedicated Catholics, rather similar to that exercised by the Communist Party over the industrial working class. This subculture was particularly present in the French countryside, especially in certain regions: Brittany, Normandy, Vendée, Alsace-Lorraine. The weakening of this subculture has been closely tied to the decline of rural France and the process of urbanisation, accelerated in the post-war period. In fact, as early as 1943, doubts were cast on the real incidence of religious practice and belief among a majority of French citizens (Mendras and Cole, 1991). The decreased incidence of religious belief, and the diminishing saliency of religious-based political cleavages, have reduced the differentiation between pious Catholics and other members of French society.

Traces of religious identification remain, however. More than any other issue, the defence of 'free' schools continues to mobilise Catholic opinion (and conservative opinion generally) in defence of its corporate identity. Deeply rooted in French history, this issue has an instrumental appeal that mobilises middle-class parents primarily in defence of the quality of education received by their children, rather than in terms of evangelisation. Religious identification also has a marked impact upon voting behaviour. Michelat and Simon's (1977) classic study revealed that voting patterns were closely associated with the degree of religious identity and practice. Regularly practising Catholics consistently supported right-wing parties; the strongest support for the left came from those professing no religion. This cleavage remained the most important indicator of voting choice in the second round of the 1995 presidential election (Le Monde, 1995b). While religious identity continues to matter at the margins, most French citizens are neither pious Catholics nor firm anti-clerical non-believers. The weakening of the significance of religious affiliation and partisan behaviour is another indication of France becoming rather less of a European exception.

An evolving regime

The Fifth Republic has managed to restore a measure of political stability generally unknown to past French regimes. It has also revealed itself to be more flexible than its critics contended. There is little doubt that the model of the French presidency established by de Gaulle and imitated by his successors has diminished the traditional republican distrust of strong leaders. The legendary figure of Napoleon III, the self-styled French emperor who ruled from 1852–1870 after subverting the short-lived Second Republic (1848–52), has faded into a distant collective past. Direct election has consolidated the authority of the President of the Republic as the *de facto* head of the executive, although the experience of two 'cohabitations' tempers this conclusion. Until 1981, while the left (the PS and the PCF) continued to regard the principle of 'presidential power' and personal rule as illegitimate, many political commentators asked whether the institutions of the Fifth Republic were in fact consensual. Mitterrand's election as the first Socialist President of the Republic in 1981 and his exercise of full presidential powers were primordial in this respect. They confirmed that the Socialist left now accepted the legitimacy of the presidential institution. For most of the period since 1958, the presidency has acted as the linchpin of the political system, although the presidential practice of successive Presidents has varied even outside of periods of cohabitation. The two experiences of cohabitation reveal the flexibility of the Fifth Republic's political system, and its capacity to adapt to changing circumstances.

The image of a French nation reconciled with its political system needs to be tempered. Older cultural representations have resurfaced in the discourse of the flourishing far-right movement: the distrust of representative democracy, the corruption of existing political élites, the moral decadence of modernity and the rejection of outsiders (in the form of immigrants) all have their roots in past representations of French culture. This underlines the fact that French culture – including French political culture – has always been multifaceted.

The weakening of subcultures?

The multifaceted nature of French culture is reinforced by the importance of subcultures, which exercise a far tighter influence over their members than a more diffuse national culture can possibly achieve. In several instances, analysis of subcultures has proved fruitful in explaining the persistence or otherwise of political phenomena. Subcultural analysis is essential for understanding the role of industrial workers in the politics of the French Communist Party and the trade union movement, as I shall illustrate below. The use of subculture might also prove useful in appraising the social organisation of France's immigrant communities, notwithstanding state-led efforts at 'integration' which go beyond those attempted in most other European countries. The weakening of subcultures has reduced differentiation between social groups and strengthened individualism, without necessarily increasing integration into a unified national culture.

The weakening of the proletarian subculture is of inestimable importance in understanding the decline of the Communist Party. Throughout the Fourth Republic, the PCF acted as a counter-community, in opposition to the rest of French society, in some senses a mirror image of the Catholic Church (Kriegel, 1985). The party was a highly organised community, which offered its members the emotional satisfaction of belonging to a cohesive, well-organised counter-society, with its own norms, duties and satisfactions. At its height, the PCF was a genuine tribune of the industrial working class, articulating the demands of alienated workers which other parties were incapable of articulating. The PCF's obsession with *ouvrièrisme* reflected its own position within the political system. Most of the party's electoral support came from industrial workers. With its conquest of the CGT in 1947, the PCF was the only party which could lay a genuine claim to be able to organise the working class politically. Communist Party cells proliferated in industries throughout France, especially in the larger factories, the mines and the docks. The role of the Renault factory at Boulogne Billancourt in the Paris 'red belt' was of particular symbolic importance. The decline of this tightly organized and cohesive subculture began in earnest in the 1960s, but it has accelerated greatly since the 1970s. The diminishing importance of traditional manufacturing industry, the enfeebling of class solidarity, the rise of unemployment and the breakdown of a specifically proletarian lifestyle and identity have all contributed to weakening the Communist subculture.

Somewhat like industrial workers, today's immigrant communities have adopted many of the characteristics of defensive subcultures, against which the racist Front national has targeted its political appeal. The interaction of leading subcultures with overall society can have a dynamic effect on both. The breakdown of specific subcultures increases the fluidity associated with the prevailing values within wider French society, such as individualism. Evidence suggests also that the integrative character of subcultures can be lost once they no longer control their members. Is it any coincidence that the Front national has prospered in former working-class bastions controlled by the Communist Party, today polarised between the remnants of an indigenous proletariat and a high presence in the local population of second-generation immigrant families?

3.4 Conclusion and summary

Traditional portrayals of French political culture contain grains of truth, but should be treated with caution. France in the mid-1990s is above all a pluralistic society which contains a broad range of political orientations and cultural practices within its midst. Social and political change has been pronounced throughout the post-war period. With the weakening of traditional structures of power, there has been a move towards a greater autonomy in all strata of society, a move facilitated by the weakening of the influence of traditional institutions such as the church, the state, political parties, the military and the extended family (Mendras and Cole, 1991). The birth of new social classes during the post-war period has been accompanied by a transformation of attitudes towards hierarchy and authority. Crozier's stalemate society no longer corresponds to an accurate portrayal of contemporary France. Although it failed as a political movement in the short term, the longer-term cultural significance of May 1968 should not be underestimated. The egalitarian, anti-hierarchical ethos present in that movement has had a profound impact upon French attitudes towards hierarchy and authority. In relation to patterns of authority, as well as key aspects of public policy, observers have discovered a weakening of the French 'exception'. France has become a European society similar in most respects to its neighbours; this is eminently more important than its cultural specificities, which nonetheless continue to provide a sense of national identity that gives the French a distinctive place among Europeans.

Indicative bibliography

Berstein, S., J.-F. Sirinelli and J.-P. Rioux (1994) 'La Culture politique en France depuis de Gaulle', *Vingtième siècle*, no. 44.

Crozier, M. (1963) *Le Phénomène bureaucratique*, Seuil, Paris.

Crozier, M. (1970) *La Société bloquée*, Seuil, Paris.

Gaffney, J. and E. Kolinsky (eds.) (1991) *Political Culture in France and Germany: A contemporary perspective*, Routledge, London.

Kriegel, B. (1992) 'L' Idée républicaine', *Revue politique et parlementaire*, vol. 94, no. 962.

Revue politique et parlementaire (1992) 'Les Valeurs de la république', *Revue politique et Parlementaire*, vol. 94, no. 962.

Rousellier, N. (1994) 'La Ligne de fuite: l'idée d'Europe dans la culture politique française', *Vingtième siècle*, no. 44.

Part II

Institutions and power

Chapter 4

An evolving constitution

4.1 Introduction and objectives

Chapter 4 analyses the constitution of the Fifth Republic. The formal provisions of the 1958 constitution are explained in some detail, as is the interpretation of these provisions made by the various political actors involved, both at the moment of its elaboration and in the subsequent four decades. In this manner, Chapter 4 attempts to combine an exercise in constitutional analysis with an appreciation of the behavioural realities underlying the 1958 constitutional settlement and its aftermath. After considering the evolving character of the 1958 constitution, and the modalities and motivations of constitutional reform, an attempt is made to place the French regime in comparative context.

It was explained in Chapter 2 how the Fourth Republic finally collapsed in May 1958, under the combined pressures of the conflict in Algeria, the deliquescence of the French state and the manoeuvres of a handful of conspirators. General de Gaulle was formally invested as the last premier of the Fourth Republic on 3 June 1958, after which the National Assembly immediately voted to suspend its sitting and invested a constitutional commission with authority to draw up a new constitution. Not for the first time in French history, the threat of force led to the drawing up of a new constitution under constrained circumstances.

In order to calm traditional republican fears of strong leaders, de Gaulle made it clear that he was 'not going to begin the life of a dictator at 68 years old'. De Gaulle's political and constitutional views were given their fullest expression in a speech at Bayeux in June 1946, in which he outlined his opposition to the proposed constitution of the Fourth Republic. In this speech, he resented what he considered to be artificial divisions provoked by petty politicians, political parties and self-serving pressure groups, which detracted from the overriding imperative of restoring French greatness. A strong sense of national identity thereby underpinned de Gaulle's constitutional preferences: the Fourth Republic must be a form of government sufficiently strong to enhance France's international prestige, and to allow France to re-enter the group of 'first-rank' nations. This patriotic imperative underpinned de Gaulle's Fourth Republican crusade for a stronger executive, notably in his role as leader of the RPF from 1947 to 1951.

That de Gaulle chose to be elected as President, rather than as premier, in December 1958 revealed his preference for a strong, but democratic and republican presidential leadership, one capable of subordinating those intermediary institutions such as parliament, parties and pressure groups. The political circumstances of 1958 were scarcely propitious to an overt defence of presidentialism: de Gaulle's return to power had provoked fear among his opponents of a return to personal rule of the type which had ended past republican experiences. In order to dispel such fears, and to rally the old politicians in support of the new regime, de Gaulle accepted that the new constitution should be drawn up by a constitutional commission. This was composed not only of Gaullists loyal to the General, but also of several representatives of the old parties of the Fourth Republic. It was chaired by Michel Debré, one of de Gaulle's closest lieutenants. Although de Gaulle and Debré did not share exactly the same constitutional views, they were both convinced of the need to restore strong executive authority (Andrews and Hoffmann, 1981).

4.2 The 1958 constitution

To some extent, the reality of the 1958 constitution was in the eye of the beholder. All involved agreed that it was a necessary compromise between efficiency, so lacking in the previous republics, and democracy, a requirement of the French republican tradition. Those involved in drawing up the constitution invoked different criteria for supporting it: for Debré, it created a British-style system of rationalised parliamentary government; for the Socialist leader Mollet, the fundamental principle was that of government responsibility to parliament (the cornerstone of a genuinely parliamentary system); de Gaulle later made it plain that the constitution invested the President of the Republic with supreme authority. Such ambiguity reflected the haste with which the constitution had been drawn up, as well as the conflicting objectives of its authors (Duhamel and Parodi, 1988). This also explained why the constitutional consensus broke down almost as soon as the constitution had been overwhelmingly ratified by referendum in September 1958.

The complexity and, indeed, inconsistency of the 1958 constitution precludes an exhaustive commentary. Subsequent chapters will refer where necessary to constitutional provisions relevant to particular institutions and situations; this chapter will limit itself to an overview of the major constitutional provisions regulating the executive and legislative branches of government, before considering how certain key aspects of the constitution have evolved since 1958 and, finally, attempting to categorise the type of political regime established by the Fifth Republic's constitution.

The constitution of 1958 (see Table 4.1) was arguably a compromise between two guiding, rather contradictory principles: the need for strong executive leadership (whether of the presidential or prime ministerial variety), and the principle of a

Table 4.1 Ten selected articles of the 1958 constitution

Article	Feature	Comments
5	The President is arbiter of the constitution.	Open to several interpretations.
8	The President names the Prime Minister.	No mention is made of dismissal.
11	The President can call a referendum on matters 'relating to the nation's economic and social policy, and public services', and on 'the organisation of public authorities'.	This excludes constitutional change (article 89).
12	The President can dissolve the National Assembly.	Only once every twelve months.
16	The President can assume 'emergency' powers, by suspending the constituion for a six-month period.	President alone determines conditions for this. Parliament sits as of right.
20	'The government shall determine and conduct the policy of the nation' and 'it shall be responsible to parliament'.	
21	The Prime Minister 'shall direct the operation of the government'.	
34	Parliament is concerned with 'matters of law'. 'Matters of regulation' are the government's responsibility alone.	Constitutional limits to parliamentary sovereignty.
38	Government can request parliament for authority to rule by decree in those policy sectors falling within the normal legislative domain.	Speeds up the policy process. Avoids parliamentary blocking tactics.
49 (clause 3)	'The Prime Minister may, after deliberation by the Council of Ministers, pledge the government's responsibility on the vote of a text. The text shall be considered as adopted unless a motion of censure is carried.'	This clause forces deputies to support a particular bill, or else to bring down the government. It has mainly been used to prop up minority governments, and those with small majorities.

government responsible to an elected parliament. The creation of a pure presidential system of the US type was explicitly rejected by the constitution-makers in
1958: however 'presidential' de Gaulle's intentions might appear in retrospect, the
General was anxious to exorcise suspicions that he was intent on inaugurating a
political regime based on personal rule. The 1958 constitution did greatly
strengthen the prerogatives of the President of the Republic, but it was also guided
by the principle of governmental responsibility to parliament, the canon of a parliamentary system, and contained references to the separation of powers. Michel
Debré openly looked to the British parliamentary system, with a strong premier
supported by stable cohesive majorities, as a model to imitate. This conception was
shared to some extent by the representatives of Fourth Republic parties, who feared
that a strong President would subvert republican democracy.

The 1958 constitution established a curious hybrid regime, immediately labelled
by most commentators as a dyarchy, or a twin-headed executive. It appeared to
create two powerful executive figures, the President of the Republic and the Prime
Minister. Whether the latter or the former was invested with executive authority
depended somewhat upon how the constitution was read. In fact, the constitution
seemed in many places contradictory. It could be open to a presidential and a prime
ministerial interpretation.

Certain articles in the constitution appeared to lend themselves to a presidential
reading. Article 5 proclaims that 'The President of the Republic shall watch to see
that the Constitution is respected. He shall ensure by his arbitrage the regular
functioning of the public authorities, as well as the continuity of the State'. The
crucial word here is 'arbitrage': it could be interpreted in a weak sense as the
President being an ultimate referee in times of crisis, but in normal circumstances
remaining above politics. But it could also be interpreted in a strong sense: that the
role of the President was to give direction to government action. It was interpreted
in the latter sense by de Gaulle, who used this article to justify the extension of
presidential authority after 1958. That this was possible bore witness to the strong
element of personal rule during the early formative years of the Fifth Republic. De
Gaulle envisaged his action as that of a positive arbiter, deciding what was in the
best interests of France.

In addition to traditional presidential powers under previous French republics,
the President was invested with a series of new powers whose application did not
require a prime ministerial counter-signature (Wright, in Hayward, 1993). The
most important of these were as follows:

- The right to dissolve the National Assembly, after consultation with the premier
  (article 12).
- The right to call a referendum on issues not involving constitutional change
  (article 11), or as the final stage of a constutional amendment (article 89).
- The right to nominate (but not to dismiss) the Prime Minister (article 8). Article
  8 also stipulates that the President nominates and dismisses ministers 'on the
  proposal of the premier'.

■ The right, under article 16, to declare a state of emergency should circumstances require it. These circumstances were to be diagnosed by the President alone.
■ The right to address written messages to the two houses of the French parliament (article 18).

All other presidential powers required a prime ministerial counter-signature, which, in terms of constitutional theory, curtailed their autonomous manipulation by the President. The constitution definitely strengthened the role of the President, who had occupied a relatively minor position in the Third and Fourth Republics. Despite this, most observers argued that, on a strict reading of the constitution, power was vested in the hands of the Prime Minister and government, rather than the President. Two articles of the 1958 constitution clearly stipulated that the Prime Minister, although named by the President, was the head of the executive in his or her own right:

■ Article 20 asserts that 'the government shall determine and conduct the policy of the nation' and that 'it shall be responsible to parliament'.
■ Article 21 stipulates that 'The Prime Minister shall direct the operation of the government'.

The Fifth Republic thus appeared to have an executive with two heads, the President and the Prime Minister. This potentially conflictual situation probably required either the President or the Prime Minister to assume a leading role. Developments after 1958 illustrated without any ambiguity that de Gaulle conceived of the presidency as the ultimate source of legitimacy within the political system. The presidential interpretation of the Fifth Republic prevailed, with somewhat varying rhythms and emphases, until the onset of cohabitation in 1986. The principal features of the relationship between French Presidents and their Prime Ministers are considered in Chapter 5.

A subjugated parliament

During the Third and Fourth Republics, a number of features had combined to create apparently omnipotent parliaments and to make governments unstable. The first of these was a belief, ultimately derived from the French Revolution, in the supremacy of the elected assembly as against the executive. This formed a powerful part of the French republican tradition. A second feature was a fear of strong leaders, predicated upon the tendency of 'great men' to subvert the institutions of the republic. During the Third and Fourth Republics, this had usually meant that mediocre politicians were selected as premiers, by zealous parliamentarians determined to retain their own prerogatives. In periods of crisis, the republican state had turned to 'great men', such as Georges Clemenceau during the First World War; and yet it had rid itself of their services once normal circumstances had returned. The institutional consequence of this was to strengthen the negative capacity of parliament to unmake governments. Third, the fragmented nature of political representation and the weakness of French political parties also contributed to the illusion of parliamentary omnipotence.

The supremacy of parliament during the Third and Fourth Republics was more apparent than real, but for the first time in French republican history the 1958 constitution placed written limits on the exercise of parliamentary sovereignty. All parties concerned in the constitutional committee agreed, albeit for different reasons, on the need to prevent a return of the political instability that had bedevilled the Fourth Republic. The Gaullists in particular were determined to restrain the power of the French parliament, with the result that the 1958 constitution greatly strengthened the executive branch of government, and drastically curbed the prerogatives of parliament. This was achieved notably via articles 34, 38 and 49 of the 1958 constitution. These articles, along with other restrictive clauses, are considered in Chapter 6.

4.3 The evolving constitution

The constitution of the Fifth Republic is not a static institution. In accordance with French political traditions, the constitution has been periodically reshaped to suit the perceived interests of incumbent leaders; or else emphasis has shifted from certain key aspects of the constitution to others. Interpretations of the constitution have varied between Presidents; indeed, the same Presidents have emphasised rather different constitutional conceptions at different stages of their presidencies. The evolutionary nature of the French constitution might be illustrated by considering the following themes: the mode of presidential election; the creation of new institutions; the falling into disuse of previously active institutions, and the adoption, or promise, of constitutional reform.

The mode of presidential election

In the 1958 constitution, the mode of electing the President of the Republic changed from an indirect parliamentary election to a system based on an electoral college of about 80,000 *notables*. De Gaulle recognised that, given the distrust of direct election among the traditional political élites, and their fear of personal rule, direct presidential election was simply not on the political agenda in 1958. These 'grand electors' were mainly local councillors serving in France's 36,000 communes. The social and geographical basis of the electoral college was over-representative of small town and rural France at the expense of the cities. Although de Gaulle had been overwhelmingly elected as the first President of the Republic in December 1958, he had reason to fear a far closer contest in the election scheduled for 1965. The electoral college had become a refuge for nostalgics of the Fourth Republic and other opponents of the General, who were particularly strong in the Senate and in local government, both key constituents of the electoral college.

During the Third and Fourth Republics, the President had been a relatively minor political figure, whose subordinate status formed one of the canons of republican political culture. The presidency's inferior status stemmed from the fear of strong leaders noted above, and from past experience of strong presidential rule in France. In 1851, Louis Napoleon was directly elected to become President of the Second Republic; one year later, the bonapartist President declared himself an Emperor and dissolved the short-lived regime. Distrust of the direct presidential election was a sign of republican pedigree. And yet it was difficult to defend the parliamentary mode of election which, in 1953, had required thirteen separate ballots before a majority of parliamentarians finally opted for Coty (Williams, 1964).

In order to build the prestige of the presidency on more solid foundations (and to secure his own political survival after 1965), de Gaulle successfully called a referendum in October 1962 on the direct election of the President of the Republic. Henceforth the prestige of the presidency was established on firmer institutional foundations which survived the passing of General de Gaulle in 1969, and which were broadly accepted by his successors as President. The result of direct election, and of the prestige of de Gaulle, was to tilt the institutional balance in favour of the President.

The creation of new institutions

The 1958 constitution created several new political institutions: the most important of these were the Constitutional Council, loosely modelled on the American supreme court; and the Economic and Social Council.

The Constitutional Council was intended to give substance to the reference to the separation of powers in the 1958 constitution. The function of the Council is to rule on the constitutionality of proposed government legislation, and to require governments to redraft bills where necessary. Its nine members are appointed in equal measure by the President of the Republic, the President of the National Assembly and the President of the Senate (Cicchillo, 1990). Members serve for nine years. Its current President, Roland Dumas, was appointed by outgoing President Mitterrand in 1995.

The early history of the Constitutional Council was hardly auspicious. De Gaulle openly mocked the institution. The Council itself lacked sufficient confidence to challenge the executive, even when the executive branch blatantly transgressed the constitution. In 1962, for instance, the Council proclaimed its inability to nullify the result of the referendum on the direct election of the President, because it had already taken place. Notwithstanding its timid beginnings, the Constitutional Council has grown steadily in prestige. This was partly as a result of President Giscard d'Estaing's reform in 1974, which extended access to the Council to include any total of 60 parliamentarians. In practice, this meant that opposition parties were able to refer contentious legislation for adjudication to the Council. In a series of judgments in the course of the 1980s and 1990s, the Court revealed its real political muscle, constraining governments to review nationalisation programmes (1982), redraw constituency boundaries (1986), revise the constitution to permit ratification of the Maastricht Treaty (1992) and abandon certain contentious articles of an anti-terrorist law (1996). In 1990 President Mitterrand attempted to extend access still further to include individual citizens, but ran up against the opposition of the Senate. Against the trend running in favour of the Council since 1974, President Chirac's constitutional reform of July 1995 limited the possibilities open to the Constitutional Council to oppose presidential initiatives, notably those taking the form of referendums under article 11 (see below).

The other novel institution created by the 1958 constitution was the Economic and Social Council (CES). The CES is an advisory body composed of representatives of business and labour interests, and a range of voluntary associations. It must be consulted by government before each new legislative proposal (*projet de loi*) is presented to parliament. Its action is relayed by the existence of 22 regional economic and social councils (CESRs) in France's regions. Although these are only advisory bodies, members affirm the importance of these regional insitutions in two domains: as a neutral meeting place for representatives of business and labour interests; and as a forum permitting reflection on matters of mutual interest to decision-makers. While there is little evidence of the CES or the CESRs having a direct input on policy making, their indirect influence must not be excluded. Other bodies whose creation was envisaged in the 1958 constitution have remained stillborn, or have had an ephemeral existence. This was the case for the High Court of Justice, whose reality was purely theoretical until it was briefly activated by Mitterrand in 1992, before being definitively forgotten in 1993.

The referendum provides an example of a mechanism formalised in the 1958 constitution, which has had varying fortunes since then. During the early period of regime consolidation (1958–62), General de Gaulle repeatedly used referendums to impose his authority on parliament, the political parties and the nation. The referendum was a device to impose de Gaulle's *de facto* executive authority to fill what might otherwise have proved a power vacuum. De Gaulle valued the referendum insofar as it initiated a personal relationship between the providential ruler and the nation, bypassing the intermediaries of party, parliament and pressure groups. De Gaulle's success in these early referendums established his presidential ascendancy more solidly than the ambiguous constitution of 1958, and helped to legitimise and stabilise the new regime.

The October 1962 referendum on direct election of the President was of crucial importance, for it helped to provide the necessary peacetime legitimacy for the presidentialisation of the regime which had occurred during the Algerian emergency. This fundamental change was highly controversial, however: not only was de Gaulle's manner of calling the referendum unconstitutional (see below), but this final result was approved by less than a majority of the overall electorate (62 per cent of voters, 46 per cent of registered voters). De Gaulle finally quit in April 1969 after the electorate refused to support his proposed constitutional reform of the Senate and the regions. The failure of the General's political blackmail provided a salutary lesson to his successors. With the departure of de Gaulle, and above all the manner of his departure, the referendum fell out of favour with French Presidents.

Although Presidents Pompidou and Mitterrand both held referendums, they were careful not to hedge their future survival on the results of these contests. And neither President felt confident enough to misinterpret the constitution in the manner chosen by General de Gaulle. The diminishing use of the referendum also reflected its limited efficacy as a weapon of presidential control: in 1972, President Pompidou's referendum on the accession of the UK, Ireland, Denmark and Norway to the EC was widely portrayed as a political manoeuvre designed to restore the President's falling fortunes: the high level of abstention (46 per cent) ruined the presidential effect. The referendum organised by Mitterrand on the New Caledonia agreements of 1988 was far less controversial. But it singularly failed to mobilise French voters to participate; on this occasion abstentions reached 65 per cent. The most recent attempted use of the referendum as a presidential tool – Mitterrand's referendum on the ratification of the Maastricht Treaty in September 1992 – so nearly backfired that the President was unable to claim the hoped-for political credit. The margin of approval (51/49) was far too close. The referendum has revealed itself to be a double-edged political tool, especially when relied upon to manufacture artificial political consensus.

These precedents did not deter President Chirac from extending the scope of the referendum almost immediately after his election. Under the terms of the constitutional amendment of July 1995, under article 11 the President can now call a referendum on any 'reform relating to the nation's economic and social policy, and public services'. This is in addition to referendums on issues relating to 'the organisation of public authorities' (Dely, 1995). Parliament has to be consulted before any referendum, but its debate is not binding upon the President. President Chirac's commitment to using the referendum as a tool of presidential authority reveals the continuing temptation of France's leaders to resort to this device to communicate directly with the French electorate.

4.4 Constitutional amendments

From a strictly judicial point of view, there are two manners in which the constitution can be amended, both contained in article 89 of the 1958 constitution:

- *The parliamentary road*. Upon proposal of the government, the constitution can be amended by a majority in both houses of the French parliament voting an identical amendment, followed by the ratification of three-fifths of Congress, as the joint meeting of both houses at the palace of Versailles is known. The 1958 constitution has been amended successfully in this manner on seven occasions, the most recent being the addition in July 1995 of a new article in order to create a single parliamentary session of nine months, and the modification of article 11 to extend the referendum. Another example occurred in June 1992, when a new article was added to the 1958 constitution in order to enable ratification of the Maastricht Treaty.

■ *The constitutional referendum.* According to article 89, the constitution might also be amended by a referendum, after an identical motion has been passed by both houses of parliament. This was the procedure which ought to have been complied with by General de Gaulle in the referendum on direct election of the President in 1962. Instead the General chose to invoke article 11 to justify his decision to call a referendum. Under the terms of article 11, the President is entitled to call a referendum without requiring a preliminary parliamentary vote, but this does not include a constitutional amendment. Article 11 was manifestly not suitable in the October 1962 referendum on direct election, which not only involved a major constitutional amendment, but also consolidated the presidentialist orientation of the regime. There was, perhaps, no better example than this of the Fifth Republic's political system depending upon the balance of power between rival political forces. No subsequent President would dare to treat the constitution in as cavalier a manner as de Gaulle in 1962.

Apart from instances of actual amendment, there have been several abortive efforts to amend the constitution. One of the most cited is that undertaken by President Pompidou in 1973 to reduce the presidential mandate to five years; this measure was approved by both houses of parliament in identical terms, and yet the President refrained either from calling a referendum or from convoking a joint session of Congress. Two reforms of the constitution were successfully engineered by President Giscard d'Estaing: the 1974 amendment allowing 60 parliamentarians to refer any bill to the constitutional council; and a 1976 amendment introducing the requirement for putative presidential candidates to obtain 500 signatures from public office holders before being able to stand for the presidency.

Throughout his term in office, President Mitterrand held forth the prospect of various reforms to ameliorate the 1958 constitution, which he had once described as a 'permanent coup d'état'. However, no significant constitutional reform was enacted during the course of his fourteen-year tenure. In 1984 Mitterrand inaugurated the amendment procedure under article 89 of the constitution in order to facilitate the calling of referendums. This proposal was rejected by the conservative-dominated Senate. In 1990 he failed in his attempt to extend the possibility of appeal to the Constitutional Council to ordinary citizens; once again, the Senate rejected the presidential proposal. In November 1992, Mitterrand called for substantial constitutional reform and set up the Vedel Commission to produce proposals to this effect. Among the reforms proposed by the Vedel Commission were: the reduction of the presidential mandate from seven to six years; a reform of the constitutional articles severely curtailing parliamentary authority, notably article 49, clause 3; the possibility for ordinary citizens to appeal to the Constitutional Council; and the reform of article 16, the emergency powers clause. President Mitterrand's proposals occurred at the twilight of his long presidency, when the possibility of their ratification was the most remote. They came too late, of course, to affect the conduct of his presidential mandate, despite the fact that he had promised constitutional reform in his 1981 and 1988 campaign addresses. They were quietly buried by the successor government of Edouard Balladur.

4.5 What type of political system is the Fifth Republic?

Constitutions are drawn up at specific moments in history. Almost inevitably, they reflect social conditions prevailing at particular points in a nation's history. The American constitution for instance, refers to a social and economic system which has been largely superseded. One measure of the success of a constitution lies in its adaptability to changing circumstances. By this measurement, the American written constitution and the British unwritten constitution have both fared relatively well. The sanctity of the American constitution has had no equivalent in French history. In keeping with tradition, the 1958 constitution was partially shaped by the conditions surrounding its elaboration. It refers, for example, to the French Community as a political union linking metropolitan France and its overseas colonies, although the decolonisation of French African states from 1958 to 1962 meant that this institution was still-born.

The political system created by the constitution of the Fifth Republic was a constitutional hybrid, containing recognisable elements of a presidential system, as well as those commonly associated with a parliamentary model. The constitution-makers specifically rejected a presidential system along the lines of the American model, but there was a marked evolution away from the (theoretical) parliamentary omnipotence which had characterised the Third and Fourth Republics. Probably the most significant feature of the constitution was its strengthening of the executive branch of government, by severely curtailing the rights of parliament, to such an extent that practices of executive manipulation became commonplace.

In order to gauge the confused reality of the constitutional system established in 1958, it is useful to portray it in a comparative perspective. The French Fifth Republic, *as established by the 1958 constitution*, lies somewhere between the two liberal-democratic poles of the American presidential system and the British parliamentary model. The kinship with the American system is obvious, though limited. The most obvious similarity between the two systems, aside from direct election introduced in 1962, relates to the irresponsibility and irremovability of both Presidents. Neither the American nor the French President can be ousted by a rebellious cabal in parliament, in stark contrast to the French premier during the Fourth Republic, or the Italian Prime Minister today. The differences between the constitutional positions of the two Presidents, however, are more significant than their similarities. Whereas the French system introduces a strict system of direct election, the US system is based on an electoral college, where the leading candidate takes the totality of college votes in each state. The French President's power of dissolution accords the head of state a formidable power of leverage over the elected assembly, in a manner quite alien to the American system of government, where the function of Congress is to check the exercise of executive power. The reference to the separation of powers in the French constitution bears little relationship to the spirit of the American constitution; in the French instance, the 'separation of powers' meant that certain policy spheres were to be removed from the competence of parliament; whereas in the spirit of the American constitution, the 'separation of powers' indicates the possibility for branches of government to check and balance each other, thereby ensuring a system of limited and divided government.

The prospect offered by the 1958 constitution of a direct relationship between the President and the nation is the antithesis of the interest intermediation and bargaining model underpinning the American federalist constitution: the referendum, in particular, stands out as a powerful presidential weapon even on a strict reading of the 1958 constitution. The American President's constitutional status as the chief executive, combining the functions of head of state and head of government, does not apply to the French President: on a strict reading, the 1958 constitution clearly vests executive authority with the Prime Minister.

The kinship with the British system of government is, on a strict constitutional reading, more apparent than with the American system. The constitution provides for a government responsible to parliament; a government which, as an ultimate sanction, can be revoked by parliament. Indeed, the restrictive clauses of the 1958 constitution were intended artificially to manufacture political stability, by allowing even minority governments to survive; the modelling on the British system was obvious (Frears and Morris, 1992).

4.6 Conclusion and summary

Ever since the French Revolution, the process of constitution building has usually involved a struggle for power between two or more opposing political groups. Reflecting a given balance of power at their inception, the longevity of French constitutions has depended either upon their non-implementation (as with the 1792 and 1875 constitutions), or upon their ability to gain broad public acceptance. Unlike in the United States, constitutions in France have not been sacrosanct symbols of a nation's identity and unity, as much as historical signposts indicating political crisis and exceptional circumstances. As Gaffney (1991, p. 14) points out, 'each of France's post-revolutionary regimes has sought a legitimation and consequential stability after its establishment which would transcend the exceptional circumstances of its creation'. The Fifth Republic is no exception in this respect.

Insofar as public allegiance in its favour is a broad measurement of legitimacy, the 1958 constitution (especially as modified by the 1962 reform introducing the direct election of the President) has proved its worth. It has been in operation for almost 40 years. No serious political force contests the Fifth Republic. Along with its ambiguity, the chief characteristic of the 1958 constitution is its flexibility. The existence of a written constitution has not prevented the regime from evolving in accordance with the evolution of democratic opinion in the nation at large. In the course of the 1980s, the Fifth Republic experienced its first real alternation in power between left and right in 1981, and the first 'cohabitation' from 1986 to 1988 between a President of the Republic and a National Assembly of different political persuasions. Rather than confirming a 'presidential' or a 'prime minis-terial' model of executive authority, the constitution leaves open various possible interpretations, consistent with the balance of political forces in the nation at large. It is clear that the 'presidential' reading prevalent throughout most of the Fifth Republic owed more to the political evolution of the regime than to the provisions of the 1958 constitution.

Indicative bibliography

Avril, P. (1992) *Le Conseil constitutionnel*, Montchrestien, Paris.

Cicchillo, R. (1990). 'The Conseil constitutionnel and judicial review', *Tocqueville Review*, vol. 12.

Cohen-Tangui, L. (1990), 'From one revolution to the next: the late rise of constitutionalism in France', *Tocqueville Review*, vol. 12.

Duhamel, O. and J.-L. Parodi (eds.) (1988) *La Constitution de la cinquième république*, Presses de la FNSP, Paris.

Frears, J. and P. Morris (1992) 'La Britannicité de la Ve République', *Espoir*, no. 85.

Maus, D. (ed.) (1992) *Les Grands Textes de la pratique institutionnelle de la cinquième république*, Documentation française, Paris.

Maus, D. *et al.* (ed.) (1992) *L'Ecriture de la constitution de 1958: actes du colloque du 30ème anniversaire*, Economica, Paris.

Stone, A. (1992) 'Where judicial politics are legislative politics: the French Constitutional Council', *West European Politics*, vol. 15, no. 3.

Chapter 5

Presidents and Prime Ministers

5.1 Introduction and objectives

The study of Presidents and Prime Ministers forms part of the staple diet of comparative politics. Along with the American President or the British Prime Minister, the French presidency has become one of the key political offices in western liberal democracies. The focus of Chapter 5 is rather broader than a simple description of the powers of the President, however. Rather than being concerned primarily with whether the Fifth Republic is a presidential or a prime ministerial system, it is hoped to demonstrate in this chapter that the French governmental system consists of a dynamic and changing set of relationships, rather than a static set of institutional positions. The reality of presidential power in France (or in the United States) cannot be discovered merely by reading the constitution. It involves observing Presidents in action, evaluating the resources at their disposal at any one time, as well as the constraints which weigh on their action, charting their relations with other influential decision-makers (at home and abroad), and realistically appraising the opportunity structure which conditions their action.

From a liberal-democratic perspective, Presidents and Prime Ministers are the most obviously recognisable political leaders. What sets the French case apart from others is the existence of two powerful political leaders recognised in the 1958 constitution, in the form of the President of the Republic and the Prime Minister. As illustrated in Chapter 4, the Fifth Republic is an evolving constitutional and political reality which fits neatly into neither of the traditional presidential or prime ministerial models of executive power. The study of political leadership in the Fifth Republic has, understandably, concentrated upon the figure of the President of the Republic, a testament to the model of the strong presidency created by President de Gaulle from 1958 to 1969, and imitated by his successors. After the repeated experiences of 'cohabitation' (1986–8, 1993–5), the focus of leadership politics in France is no longer exclusively presidential. In fact, the role of the French Prime Minister tended to be overlooked and underplayed during the prolonged period of presidential ascendancy (1958–86) (Elgie, 1993).

5.2 Political leadership in the French republican tradition

During the 150 years following the French Revolution, a fear of strong leaders was an essential part of the French republican tradition. This was because the 'Great Man' had transgressed the norms of democratic republicanism on more than one occasion. The example of Louis Napoleon (1848–70) became the model to avoid for republicans. Once the republican form of government had become durably established in 1875–6, the Third Republican élite was convinced of the need to safeguard against the threat of strong leaders. Thus defined, the republican tradition precluded strong political leadership, except in periods of crisis, when saviours were briefly resorted to as figures of national salvation. The collapse of the Third Republic in 1940, followed by the personalist excesses of the wartime Vichy regime, confirmed the worst fears of republicans. An authoritarian cult of the personality was fostered around Marshall Pétain, whose special qualities were contrasted with the alleged decadence of the previous parliamentary system. With the return of democracy, in the form of the Fourth Republic, there was a renewed reaction against unquestioning obedience to authoritarian leaders. Whatever the intentions of its founding fathers, the Fourth Republic was a parliamentary-centred regime characterised by weak, fleeting governmental coalitions. During the Fourth Republic, as in the Third, parliamentary supremacy came to be directly equated with weak executive government.

The appropriate form of political leadership was strongly contested throughout the Fourth Republic (1946–58). The post-war provisional government (1944–6) was headed by the wartime resistance hero, General Charles de Gaulle. De Gaulle believed in a rationalised democratic system, similar to the eventual Fifth Republic: broadly speaking, he advocated a strong President who would stand above what he considered to be the petty quarrels of party politicians, and incarnate the unity of the French nation. The General attributed France's collapse in 1940 at least in part to the degeneracy of its parliamentary system. De Gaulle's advocacy of strong personal leadership revived the traditional republican fears of strong leaders. The parties of the post-war left (Socialists, Communists and Christian-democrats) suspected de Gaulle of preparing a system which might lead to dictatorship. They advocated instead different variations on the parliamentary theme. The presidential system posited by de Gaulle in his Bayeux speech of November 1946 remained the unwritten alternative to the parliamentary regime of the Fourth Republic throughout its existence.

Through a combination of rare personal stature, skilful crisis management, the deliquescence of the Fourth Republic and the scheming of his followers, de Gaulle returned to a position of political leadership as a result of the Algerian rebellion, leading to the collapse of the Fourth Republic in May–June 1958. By rallying to de Gaulle, the French nation appeared to have reverted to the Great Man to resolve a crisis, as it had on several previous occasions in its history. In many respects, de Gaulle lay squarely within the tradition of the providential ruler, convinced as he was that he represented the unity of the nation above the squalid compromises made by politicians and political parties. But de Gaulle, the hero of the French Resistance, was far from being a leader who relied solely on personal power and the implicit threat of force. From the inception he enjoyed support from a majority of French people; this bestowed an element of personal legitimacy on de Gaulle which was quite separate from the process of constitution building engaged after June 1958. The 1958 constitution (Chapter 4) appeared to create two powerful executive figures, the President of the Republic and the Prime Minister. Whether the latter or the former was invested with executive authority depended somewhat upon how the constitution was read. Developments after 1958 illustrated without any ambiguity that de Gaulle conceived of the presidency as the ultimate source of legitimacy within the political system.

5.3 The French presidency

During the period 1958–86, there was little doubt that the presidency was the pinnacle of legitimacy giving coherence to the political system of the Fifth Republic. The strength of French presidency has lain partly in its combination of the monarchical trappings of power associated with the head of state, with the real executive authority conferred by direct election, and by the political precedent established by de Gaulle between 1958 and 1969. Any assessment of the contribution made by de Gaulle to the evolution of the Fifth Republic would provide proof, if proof were needed, that certain individuals leave their own unmistakable imprint upon history (Lacouture, 1991; Shennan, 1993). After an initial period of uncertainty and confusion, de Gaulle was able to impose his model of a strong presidency upon an initially hostile political class. This was possible as a result of several developments:

- The pressures created by the Algerian war and the lack of a serious alternative to his stewardship strengthened de Gaulle's position. The key national élites might have regarded de Gaulle with suspicion, but their imagined alternatives were far worse: civil war, military dictatorship or political anarchy.
- In the absense of a clear-cut parliamentary majority from 1958 to 1962, de Gaulle relied on a repeated use of referendums to consolidate his political authority: electors were invited to support de Gaulle, or hasten a return to chaos. The plebiscitary element in these early referendums was manifest.
- The sacking of premier Michel Debré in April 1962, followed by the October 1962 referendum establishing direct election of the President, consolidated a *de facto* evolution in favour of the President within the French executive.
- The emergence of the majoritarian presidential coalition in 1962 completed the process of presidential pre-eminence.

The existence of disciplined, pro-presidential coalitions controlling the National Assembly during the period 1962–86 was in stark contrast to the chaos of the Fourth Republic, where governments were short lived and multifarious. Presidential power was built upon propitious political circumstances, the balance of political forces, and the legacy of personal power moulded by de Gaulle and bequeathed to his successors. These political factors were of greater importance than any undisputed constitutional provisions. Political circumstances thus enabled de Gaulle to interpret the ambiguities in the 1958 constitution to his own advantage; by 1964 he was able to proclaim that 'the indivisible authority of the state is wholly confided to the President by the people who elected him and that there is no other authority, be it ministerial, civil, military, or judicial which is not conferred or maintained by him' (Wright, in Hayward, 1993).

The theme of presidentialism has dominated interpretations of the hybrid French executive. This has been misleading in several respects. It has tended to downplay (or ignore) the inputs of other actors, such as the Prime Minister, individual ministers, bureaucratic élites and interest groups. Moreover, it is clear that the pattern of political leadership in the Fifth Republic has not been static: encroaching presidentialism during the late 1960s, the 1970s and the early 1980s was replaced during the subsequent decade by a marked presidential withdrawal from the intricacies of domestic politics. Third, the notion of presidentialism imparts the impression that the President is consistently highly interventionist in all areas of policy. This has never been the case. Even during periods of presidential 'encroachment', notably under Pompidou, Giscard d'Estaing and early Mitterrand, large areas of policy making remained excluded from presidential interventionism or oversight.

Ever since de Gaulle's famous press conference of 1964, however, the 'principle of presidential initiative' (a phrase coined by Jean Charlot) has aptly described the underlying legitimacy of the Fifth Republic's political system, with the exception of the periods of cohabitation. Presidents have not only defined the broad parameters of governmental action; they have also reserved the right to intervene in any policy sphere. Except during periods of cohabitation, policy arbitration on exceptionally divisive issues has occurred at the Elysée (Thiebault, 1989). When conflicts have arisen between Presidents and their Prime Ministers, the former's views have invariably prevailed. The unpredictability of presidential interventions infuriated unsuspecting ministers as much under Chirac as they had under Mitterrand, Giscard d'Estaing, Pompidou and de Gaulle. Mitterrand's withdrawal of Savary's Education Bill in June 1984, without prior consultation or warning, proved a case in point.

It should not be assumed that all Presidents have been equally interventionist, nor that Presidents have been consistently interventionist; presidential practice has in fact varied with each incumbent, as well as at different stages of each presidency. It is clear that Presidents have chosen not to interfere in every aspect of detailed government policy, either because they do not possess the administrative resources or time to achieve this, or because of their personal political priorities. As a result of the powerful resources at their disposal, however, French Presidents have been able to choose the scope and nature of their intervention in domestic politics. Each President has had a rather different appreciation of what this entails. Each has paid a special attention to spheres of action, such as culture and architecture, which are likely to enhance his personal standing with posterity. Each has also claimed primary, if not exclusive, responsibility in matters of foreign policy, defence and European affairs. Presidents are not the only actors in determining French policy in these arenas, but they are the most important.

Under Giscard d'Estaing and Mitterrand, presidential involvement in domestic political priorities was stronger at the early stages of the presidential mandate. The primary mission of the Chirac (1974–6) and Mauroy (1981–4) governments was to transform the President's electoral programme into legislation, and prime ministerial activity was supervised closely by the President. This has less obviously been the case for President Chirac, who has favoured the classic presidential domain of intervention: foreign policy, defence and European affairs. Intervention by Chirac in domestic policy has been random, even trivial: he paid close attention to relatively minor appointments. Especially after October 1995, Chirac consciously stood aloof from the details of domestic policies, publicly affirming that while the President presides, governments should govern. This semi-detached attitude was best illustrated by the President's response to the mass strikes that followed premier Juppé's proposed social security reform in November–December 1995; Chirac intervened publicly only once during this period – and then on a matter relating to foreign policy!

This conscious division of labour (high politics for the President; the management of contentious policy dossiers by the Prime Minister or ministers) recalled more than any other the relationship maintained between de Gaulle and his Prime Ministers. The classic role of the French Prime Minister is to act as a *fusible*: a fallguy for the President. The nature of the Chirac–Juppé relationship was no exception. After one year in office, premier Juppé's political credit appeared virtually exhausted by unpopular, but essential reforms of the social security system, and by austerity measures taken to prepare France to meet the convergence criteria for participation in the single European currency.

As with individual government ministers (Chapter 7) and the Prime Minister (below), French Presidents are assisted by their own presidential office. Although it has no formal organisational existence, the presidential office is composed of three components: the Cabinet, the Secrétariat général and the Chef d'état major particulier. Under Mitterrand, the press office and the President's special adviser also became important. The Cabinet is involved in controlling the President's diary and managing his mail. Strategic policy reflection takes place in the General Secretariat of the Elysée. This consists of upwards of twenty advisers. Presidential policy advisers do not usually manage specific items of government policy, although their role has been more affirmative at certain stages than at others, and they assist in important committees chaired by the President. Their role is to engage in strategic reflection in areas of presidential interest. In total, French Presidents are assisted by 30–40 civilian and 5–10 military advisers (Stevens, in Hayward, 1993). By comparison with the genuinely tentacular American presidency, these figures appear derisory (Seurin, 1986). This modest presidential infrastructure, while more extensive than that at the disposal of a British Prime Minister, has to be set in the context of the extensive bureaucratic machine officially co-ordinated by the French Prime

Minister, as well as the administrative capacity at the disposal of the larger government departments. A specific role within the presidential office is performed by the Chef d'état major particulier. This military cell advises the President on aspects of foreign policy, defence and security (Howorth, in Hayward, 1993). The sensitive nature of the unit is testified by the fact that new presidential incumbents have invariably altered its composition, starting by replacing the Chef d'état major himself. Thus, Admiral Lagardère, who had been closely associated with President Mitterrand, was replaced shortly after Chirac had been elected.

The role of the staff varies with presidential incumbent. Staff members are usually young civil servants, seconded to work in the presidential staff from their ministries. Under Mitterrand, the evolution of presidential staff followed the general direction of the presidency: early *compagnons de route*s (political allies from various stages of Mitterrand's career) were later replaced by apolitical technocrats (Cole, 1994a). In a novel departure, President Chirac accepted several close confidants of premier Juppé into his presidential office: the new General Secretary of the Elysée staff, Dominique de Villepin, had headed Juppé's office in the Foreign Affairs ministry from 1993 to 1995. Once established as General Secretary, de Villepin insisted that his primary loyalty lay with President Chirac.

As Anne Stevens (1992) affirms, the Elysée is not the Whitehouse. It is a relatively light infrastructure. Its proximity to the centres of decision making, however, inevitably fuels accusations of the office exercising power without responsibility. There have been occasions when presidential advisers have appeared to exercise a powerful role. Under President Pompidou, for instance, the part performed by M.-F. Garaud and P. Juillet received much critical attention. Under President Mitterrand, the involvement of presidential advisers in various scandals (notably concerning illegal phone tapping, and insider dealing on the Paris stock exchange) relaunched accusations of power without responsibility. Under President Chirac, the rehabilitation of de Gaulle's former adviser Jacques Foccart as a special adviser on African affairs reawakened accusations of clientelism with respect to France's relations with several African states.

Presidents have controlled key political and bureaucratic nominations. They have exercised their constitutional duty (article 8) to nominate the Prime Minister; each President has also exceeded his constitutional brief and insisted upon his right to dismiss incumbent Prime Ministers. The model of presidential dismissal established by de Gaulle with Debré in April 1962 was repeated on numerous subsequent occasions, most notably with Pompidou in 1968, Chaban-Delmas in 1972, Rocard in 1991 and Cresson in 1992. Presidents have also intervened closely in the nomination of individual ministers; indeed, key ministers have often been encouraged to bypass the formal governmental hierarchy headed by the Prime Minister, and to deal directly with the President. Such a pattern occurred at various stages of Mitterrand's presidency, notably with respect to the Finance Minister, Bérégovoy.

Presidential patronage extends beyond the *de facto* selection and dismissal of the political élite, to include top civil servants, the heads of nationalised industries and banks, prominent positions within the media, rectors, prefects, judges, ambassadors and appointments to a myriad of governmental quangos. Incumbent Presidents have also generally been able to ensure that their nominees have controlled the top positions within the parliamentary party and the extra-parliamentary party leadership. As a rule, the model for political appointments has been one of bargaining and compromise between President and Prime Minister, with the former exerting a greater degree of influence than the latter (Chagnollaud, 1988). This pattern was reversed during the first period of cohabitation (1986–8). President Mitterrand reserved a right of oversight over certain defence appointments, but elsewhere had to incline to the wishes of the Chirac government. The president's oversight over nominations was even less effective during the second cohabitation of 1993–5.

Presidential styles

Each presidential incumbent has portrayed his office as being the supra-partisan embodiment of national unity. Upon election, the successful presidential candidate claims to be the President of all the French: this is intended to disguise the fact each President is initially a representative of a party, a coalition or a set of interests. This monarchical style of presidential political discourse is essential, in order to facilitate the transition from being a presidential candidate to being President.

The two prevailing images of the French President are thus as a supra-partisan republican monarch, and as an interventionist and partisan political leader. The ability to combine the monarchical and partisan functions of the French presidency has become a test of political strength for French Presidents. A partisan identity is an indispensable precondition for building an electoral coalition to fight a presidential election, and for establishing a presidential party, or pro-presidential coalition, to provide disciplined support for presidentially inspired policies. As any other political leader, a President needs a partisan base of support, notably a supportive parliamentary majority. The President is the key executive leader, involved in the overall conception of government policy and the selection of governmental personnel. The monarchical posture is essential for posing as a head of state embodying national unity, rather than as any run-of-the-mill Prime Minister. The diplomatic precedence accorded to French Presidents as head of state in international summit meetings should not be underestimated in its domestic political importance.

The role model of presidential political leadership was provided by de Gaulle, whose lofty presidential style was imitated to a greater or lesser extent by his four successors. A strong sense of national identity underpinned de Gaulle's presidential practice. The General's concern with restoring French diplomatic and political prestige coloured his practice as President: his priority areas of interest lay in foreign policy, European affairs and defence. De Gaulle's primary preoccupation with restoring France's greatness also had clear implications for the organisation of its domestic political system. The republic must be a form of government sufficiently strong to enhance France's international prestige, and to allow France to re-enter the group of 'first-rank' nations. This patriotic imperative underpinned de

Gaulle's Fourth Republic crusade for a stronger executive, and reappeared in the formative years of the Fifth Republic. By consolidating the presidency first as a form of heroic, then as a type of institutionalised strong leadership, de Gaulle inaugurated a new style of political leadership which had a profound impact on the subsequent evolution of the Fifth Republic. When performing certain key rituals (for instance, official televised addresses to the nation) associated with the presidential office, each subsequent President has consciously imitated de Gaulle. Paradoxically, President Chirac appeared to have departed from the Gaullist press conference, in favour of an American-style pulpit presentation.

The strong personal element of legitimacy underpinning de Gaulle's leadership allowed the first President to present himself as the embodiment of national unity more effectively than any of his successors. The Olympian style imparted to the presidency by de Gaulle was to some extent disingenuous: as Jack Hayward (1993) points out, 'de Gaulle made it abundantly clear from the start that the Fifth Republic President would be in command'. De Gaulle came closest to disguising the partisan function behind his public display of monarchical aloofness. And yet the anti-partisan discourse adopted by de Gaulle appeared increasingly superficial, notably after he had been directly elected as President after being forced to a second ballot in the 1965 presidential election (see Appendices 3 and 4).

None of de Gaulle's successors was able to boast a personal legitimacy in the least comparable to that of the General. Whatever his qualities, de Gaulle's successor, Georges Pompidou, lacked the former's historic stature and relied upon far tighter control of the governing Gaullist party to provide a personal source of legitimacy. Whereas de Gaulle (rather like Mitterrand) was representative of a patriotic idea of France steeped in the nineteenth century, Pompidou was more openly representative of a conservative and moneyed business élite, distrusted by the devout Catholic de Gaulle. The different backgrounds and political upbringings of the first two Presidents of the Fifth Republic were reflected in their political styles and preoccupations. As a strong patriot and former military commander, de Gaulle was primarily interested in foreign policy, although circumstances forced his decisive intervention in other spheres of policy. While unable to ignore foreign policy issues (and while actively engaged in French European policy), President Pompidou's real interests lay elsewhere (Roussel, 1984). The second President entered politics after a successful business career, and one of his principal preoccupations as President was in the sphere of industrial policy, over which he imposed a large measure of presidential control.

Pompidou's successor, Giscard d'Estaing, possessed neither a strong majoritarian party support nor a political personality of historic proportions. President Giscard d'Estaing compensated for his political weakness by an enhanced presidential interventionism, and an attempt to move towards a more overt presidential interpretation of the regime. This took several forms. In the early stages of his presidency, there was a considerable expansion in the number of interministerial policy arbitration committees directly chaired by the President, or by one of his representatives in the Elysée staff (*conseils restreints*), rather than the Prime Minister. Giscard d'Estaing's insecurity was revealed by the fact that his Prime Ministers were asked to sign undated letters of resignation upon their nomination, and that detailed policy programmes were publicly outlined by Giscard d'Estaing to premier Chirac, in the form of six-monthly 'directive letters' drafted by the President. This move towards enhanced presidential supremacy was based on fragile foundations. Giscard d'Estaing could not count upon the support of a disciplined presidential party or coalition; indeed, he revealed an aristocratic disdain for all forms of party organisation.

With the resignation of premier Chirac in 1976, the political foundations for the third President's rule were weaker than under either of his predecessors (Chapter 2). The increasingly regal image displayed by Giscard d'Estaing contrasted with his relative political isolation after 1976. Herein lay another facet of the French presidency. The republican monarch aspect of the presidency had negative as well as positive features. In the case of Giscard d'Estaing, the dissemination of the image of the unresponsive, secretive and arrogant monarch contributed to the image of decadence, scandal and impetuosity which surrounded the end of his presidency. An analogous conclusion was drawn by certain commentators in relation to the final years of Mitterrand's presidency (Montaldo, 1994).

President Mitterrand's style varied according to events, opportunities, personal evolution and political strength. His presidential practice demonstrated the apparent paradoxes and contradictions imposed on any French President. Arriving in office as the most openly partisan President of the Fifth Republic, for instance, Mitterrand was re-elected in 1988 as the embodiment of supra-partisan consensus. By 1993 the Socialist president had been deserted by his formerly stalwart lieutenants in the Socialist Party (Cole, 1994a). By 1995 Mitterrand was an isolated, lonely figure: it was difficult to recall the highly interventionist President of the early Mauroy premiership (1981–2). Both Mitterrands were accurate reflections of the presidential function and style at a given point in time. The longevity of Mitterrand's rule as President gave occasion for several legitimate portrayals of his presidential style and practice, probably more so than for any other President.

Early indications of the presidential style of Jacques Chirac suggested a far more direct approach than that adopted by his predecessor. While opinion polls in May 1996 portrayed a majority of French people as dissatisfied with the content of government policy, President Chirac was personally appreciated as being 'sympathetic' and 'close to the people'. His repeated visits to the French provinces surprised certain observers, as did his practice of public walkabouts. At the same time, while early pronouncements revealed inexperience (especially in foreign policy) , Chirac progressively demonstrated an ability to internalise the gravitas of the presidential function, notably with his funeral oration for former President Mitterrand in January 1996. Observation of Chirac's first year in office implied that the exercise of the French presidency is a learning process, with individual competence gradually increasing over time, and with a particular political style emerging as much as a result of trial and error, as of conscious design.

Each presidential incumbent has left his distinctive mark upon the presidency. The most effective synthesis of the monarchical and partisan functions of the

French presidency, for the reasons outlined above, was that provided by de Gaulle. His successor, Pompidou, appeared as a more obviously partisan political leader, who relied more openly upon the Gaullist presidential majority as his source of legitimacy, but who was incapable of imposing his authority upon the historical chiefs of classical Gaullism. The third President, Giscard d'Estaing, entertained ambitions for a more overt presidentialism, but without a solid presidential party to underpin his political activity, he appeared isolated and out of touch. During his most effective periods as President (1984–91), Mitterrand combined a solid political base with the cultivation of an Olympian manner in imitation of de Gaulle. By the end of his presidential tenure, however, Mitterrand appeared rather more like Giscard d'Estaing: an isolated, solitary individual whose power was on the wane. It is as yet too early to judge President Chirac. In fact, all French Presidents have been subjected to a tendency for diminishing political returns as their presidencies have progressed; this suggests a natural threshold (variable for each incumbent, but not surpassing ten years) beyond which the effectiveness of presidential political leadership is seriously impaired.

Presidents and Prime Ministers during periods of cohabitation

Challenges to presidential supremacy have been most obvious during the periods of cohabitation. The model of presidential pre-eminence outlined above depends upon a coincidence of presidential and parliamentary majorities. After a long period (1958–86) which commentators generally viewed as one of encroaching presidentialism, the election of a narrow centre-right RPR–UDF majority in 1986 inaugurated the first period of cohabitation, between the Socialist President Mitterrand and the Gaullist premier Chirac (Cohendet, 1993; Duverger, 1987).

From being the potentially omnipotent and omnipresent chief executive, the French President was reduced to a rather more modest role as an arbitral observer. For once, the constitution was applied as written in 1958. The Prime Minister led a government responsible to the RPR–UDF parliamentary majority, rather than to the President. By nominating Chirac as Prime Minister in March 1986, Mitterrand recognised that power had to be vested in the victors of the most recent decisive election. During the period 1986–8, President Mitterrand withdrew from detailed policy making in the arena of domestic politics, although he did make use of those weapons reserved for the President in the 1958 constitution, notably by delaying certain pieces of legislation. Mitterrand insisted on preserving his constitutional prerogatives in matters of foreign policy and defence, and was by and large successful, in spite of a powerful push on behalf of premier Chirac. One expert concluded that presidential pre-eminence was retained in high diplomacy and defence policy, whereas the government held the upper hand in relation to African affairs, with European policy resulting from carefully prepared compromises between the two (Cohen, 1989).

A similar pattern reproduced itself in 1993, when the RPR–UDF coalition won a crushing victory at the expense of the incumbent Socialists. During the second cohabitation, Mitterrand no longer had either the energy or the political prestige to intervene in domestic politics, but retained a measure of influence in European affairs, defence and foreign policy. From 1993 to 1995, President Mitterrand and Premier Balladur spoke of foreign policy being 'a shared sector'. In an interview in September 1994, President Mitterrand protested that: 'There is no fundamental disagreement between us on foreign policy. We are both anxious to preserve the French national interest.' In fact there were divisions between Mitterrand and the Balladur government, notably over the French moratorium on nuclear testing, NATO and Algeria. In his memoirs, Balladur admitted that he had been unable to resume French nuclear testing while Prime Minister because of the President's opposition.

The major difference between the 1986–8 cohabitation and the experience commenced in March 1993 related to the deterioration in President Mitterrand's political standing in between these periods. In 1986 Mitterrand could count upon the support of a powerful Socialist parliamentary group in the National Assembly. He enjoyed the prestige of presidential incumbency without the responsibility for executive decisions. Finally, he profited from the monarchical, supra-partisan qualities of the French presidency to refine his sage, father-figure image for a renewed presidential bid in 1988. By 1993 Mitterrand had become a lame-duck President. There was no prospect of his standing for re-election in 1995. His Socialist Party had been reduced to a fractious rump of 63 deputies; worse, his arch-rival Rocard captured control over the Socialist Party only weeks after the election. Several of Mitterrand's closest political associates had been involved in corruption scandals. The tragic suicide of former premier Pierre Bérégovoy added a note of finality to the Mitterrand era. Quite apart from the President's limited powers on a strict reading of the 1958 constitution, President Mitterrand's position was far weaker during the second cohabitation than the first, on account of the wearing-down effects of over a decade in power.

5.4 Prime ministerial political leadership

Whether under cohabitation or not, the hybrid nature of the French executive is very much in evidence. The obvious alternative model of national political leadership to the presidency is that offered by the Prime Minister (Massot, 1993; Elgie, 1993). Before considering the evolving role of the French Prime Minister, it must be stressed that the relationship between President and Prime Minister does not encompass the totality of relationships within the French executive. Following from the insights of UK core executive theory and French organisational theory, we can identify various types of overt and covert policy actor within the French executive: apart from Presidents, Prime Ministers and their advisers, these would include ministers (notably the Finance Minister), differing grades and types of civil servant (spread across multiple *directions* and *corps*), members of ministerial cabinets and unofficial advisers. In a comprehensive study of the community of central government policy-makers, attention would be drawn not only to various types of actor, but also to their differing sources of legitimacy and expertise (for instance, political, bureaucratic or professional). Governance processes do not limit themselves to an isolated space (central government), but are increasingly multilayered and interdependent in character, requiring consideration of other actors: namely, foreign governments, EU officials and certain non-governmental interests. A full overview of patterns of governance lies beyond the scope of this chapter, but this diversity should be kept in mind when considering French political leadership.

Relations between Presidents and Prime Ministers have been the subject of many rather simplistic assessments, which betray a complex reality. No single model can account for the complexity of the President–Prime Minister relationship, which is simultaneously conflictual and co-operative, routine and non-static. There is effectively a perennial and institutionalised tension between the Elysée (the President's official residence) and Matignon (that of the Prime Minister). As the chief presidential representative, the Prime Minister is expected to defend presidential policy priorities and translate them into legislation. As a transmission belt for the President, the premier has been expected to assume responsibility for unpopular policies. But he or she is also anxious to assert his or her political identity, not least because the premiership has occasionally been a pedestal for a later bid for the presidency itself. The attempt to reconcile the conflicting roles of faithful presidential lieutenant and policy initiator has proved too difficult for several ambitious premiers (see Table 5.1 for a list of Prime Ministers in the Fifth Republic).

The chief roles performed by a French Prime Minister are those of political leader, government manager and presidential lieutenant. As a political leader, the Prime Minister is responsible for guiding the government's policy programme through parliament, and smoothing relations with the parliamentary majority. This task is often arduous; Barre or Rocard had to rely on restrictive constitutional

Table 5.1 Prime Ministers in the Fifth Republic

Prime Minister	Office	Party
Debré	1959–62	Gaullist
Pompidou	1962–8	Gaullist
Couve de Murville	1968–9	Gaullist
Chaban-Delmas	1969–72	Gaullist
Messmer	1972–4	Gaullist
Chirac	1974–6	Gaullist
Barre	1976–81	UDF
Mauroy	1981–4	PS
Fabius	1984–6	PS
Chirac	1986–8	RPR
Rocard	1988–91	PS
Cresson	1991–2	PS
Bérégovoy	1992–3	PS
Balladur	1993–5	RPR
Juppé	1995–	RPR

mechanisms to ensure their survival. Each Prime Minister suffers the indignation of quasi-permanent media speculation on his personal relationship with the President, and on the identity of his likely successor. As a governmental manager, the Prime Minister possesses powerful resources, but is aware that presidential support is required for maximum impact. Unlike in most parliamentary systems, it is rare for the premier to head the main political party, and thus to enjoy the legitimacy of popular election. As a presidential lieutenant, the Prime Minister is conscious that his or her legitimacy stems primarily from being the President's appointee.

In short, as a political leader, the Prime Minister appears often doomed to navigate the horns of an intolerable dilemma. A successful Prime Minister is likely to arouse presidential jealously, inviting dismissal or at least an effort to claim presidential credit for successful prime ministerial policies. This was the case notably for Pompidou under de Gaulle (1962–8) and Rocard under Mitterrand (1988–91). A Prime Minister who fails to protect the President from unpopularity – or who contributes to executive unpopularity through inept management – is likely to suffer even greater indignity: the fate which befell Edith Cresson, Prime Minister for barely eleven months. The election of Chirac as President in 1995 confirmed that the Fifth Republic remains governed by a principle of presidential initiative. The key measures announced by Prime Minister Juppé's 'Declaration of government policy' in May 1995 had figured in Chirac's campaign platform. Premier Juppé's rapid descent in popularity from May to November 1995 demonstrated the existential problems faced by French Prime Ministers. As Prime Minister, Juppé was expected to manage the contradictions of Chirac's own presidential campaign, to implement policies with which he was in partial disagreement (notably over Europe) and to take the blame if things went wrong.

The constraints weighing upon the French Prime Minister were revealed with the formation of premier Juppé's government in May 1995. As is habitual practice in the Fifth Republic, Alain Juppé only partially controlled the nomination of his own government: the precise contours stemmed from a bargaining process between President Chirac and his first Prime Minister. Juppé had to respect a delicate dosage between RPR and pro-Chirac UDF ministers, as well as fulfilling Chirac's campaign promises in relation to female representation (12 ministers out of 42), and the rejuvenation of political personnel. As a result, Juppé led an overmanned and inexperienced government team, whose indiscipline and amateurism contributed towards record unpopularity ratings for both President and Prime Minister after only five months in office.

During the periods of presidential ascendancy (especially from 1958 to 1986) French Prime Ministers suffer from several accumulated disadvantages which limit their capacity to exercise the *political* role that their status as head of government requires. These include their insecurity of tenure; presidential control over the composition of the government; the special relationship maintained by individual ministers with the President; the sporadic nature of presidential interventions; presidentially inspired policy agendas; the inputs of the presidential party; and rivalry with the President in relation to public opinion. The constraints on the freedom of manoeuvre of French Presidents (such as public opinion, the economic and social environment, and the foreign policy climate) apply all the more forcefully to Prime Ministers on account of their insecure position and their dependency on the President. As illustrated above, the success of the Prime Minister as a policy-maker does not ensure his or her political longevity; arguably the three most successful policy-makers (Pompidou, 1962–8; Chaban-Delmas, 1969–72; Rocard, 1988–91) were negatively rewarded for their services with dismissal by a resentful President. Their political dependency does not, however, deprive French Prime Ministers of all substantive leadership functions. From the inception of the Fifth Republic, various key functions have (with greater or lesser efficiency) been performed by the Prime Minister.

The Prime Minister is usually more involved than the President with the co-ordination and formulation of detailed government policy and the arbitration of intergovernmental disputes. In particular, the premier is in control of making difficult arbitrations between spending departments in the annual budget negotiations. In broad areas of domestic policy, most French Presidents have refrained from consistent intervention, except during periods of crisis, or immediately after coming to office. Economic and social policy typically falls into this category. Even in this mainly 'non-presidential' sector, however, each President periodically defines broad directions that governments are invited to follow, and occasionally intervenes directly.

As head of government in the 1958 constitution, the Prime Minister is conferred a co-ordinating role. For this reason, most government agencies with a clearly interministerial function are placed under the official tutelage of the Prime Minister's office. It does not automatically follow that these agencies form part of the Prime Minister's powerbase. The constitutional role of the French Prime Minister in co-ordinating government policy is undermined by several cross-cutting pressures. The appeal against the Prime Minister to the President by disgruntled ministers provides one example; the powerful position occupied by the Finance Minister is another. Policy initiatives undertaken by ambitious premiers have frequently run up against the opposition of the Finance Ministry. The example of Mme Cresson is indicative in this respect. France's first female premier was deprived of the means of effectively co-ordinating government policy when President Mitterrand and Finance Minister Bérégovoy formed an insuperable coalition to prevent her interventionist industrial ideas from being put into practice.

The Prime Minister possesses greater administrative resources than the President to assist in the task of policy co-ordination and formulation. The President's Elysée staff, appraised above, is relatively modest by comparison with the expertise available to the Prime Minister. The Prime Minister is in a stronger day-to-day position in relation to the permanent bureaucracy than the President. As the official head of government, he or she controls the services responsible for evaluating and monitoring government policy (notably the General Secretariat of the government, not to be confused with the President's Elysée staff), and maintains close relations with key politicians and bureaucrats within the ministries. The General Secretariat is composed of 15–20 civil servants, whose function is to attempt to minimise bu-reaucratic rivalries and to co-ordinate government policy, before and after deci-sions are ratified by the Council of Ministers (Py, 1985; Long, 1981). As its name implies, the General Secretariat assists the Prime Minister in the preparation of the government's work. It prepares meetings of the Council of Ministers, and of inter-ministerial committees, and – crucially – writes up the minutes of these meetings. This function is not always politically neutral: under the first Juppé government, for instance, unofficial members of ministerial *cabinets* were allowed to speak in interministerial committee meetings, but – by order of the premier – their remarks were not recorded.

The General Secretariat is formally attached to the Prime Minister, as are most other interministerial structures, whose role is to co-ordinate between various gov-ernment departments. In theory, it is above political conflicts, being headed by a senior civil servant. In practice, as with its British homologue the Cabinet Office, the General Secretariat is responsible to the incumbent government, to the extent that incoming governments have replaced the head of the General Secretariat with one of their own. Thus, Marceau Long was replaced in 1982 by Jacques Fournier, who in turn gave way in 1986 to M. Reneau de la Portière. There is little doubt that the General Secretary is a key politico-administrative actor, who derives his or her influence from formal control over the government machine and the information that this provides. The close contacts maintained between the General Secretary and the key political decision-makers (the Prime Minister, but also the President) enhance the influence of the General Secretariat. This influence, of a secretive nature, is difficult to 'measure' in an objective sense.

The Prime Minister is assisted by a powerful private office (Cabinet), responsible for intervening on his behalf in the work of other government departments and for assisting the head of government in the process of interministerial arbitration and policy formulation. As with ministerial *cabinets*, each Cabinet performs rather different functions according to the personality of the Prime Minister, and the individuals involved. Certain prime ministerial offices have enjoyed a reputation as fearsome defenders of a Prime Minister's political and policy interests (Huchon, 1993). The staff available to the Prime Minister (upwards of 100 advisers in his or her office) facilitates a detailed oversight of prime ministerial initiatives. The infor-mation provided by these advisers is one of the premier's most valuable resources. Even outside of periods of cohabitation, the Prime Minister disposes of significant sources of patronage, to some extent in competition with those of the President: nominations falling within the prime ministerial sphere have included appoint-ments to the Legion of Honour, to the Court of Accounts and to the Council of State, and the Prime Minister will usually be consulted on all senior bureaucratic appointments.

As with the President's Elysée staff, the Prime Minister's office has no official legal existence, leaving the premier free to determine its missions. As a rule, his or her advisers mirror the principal spheres of government activity, with a particular interest in matters of current and forthcoming legislation. Most members of the prime ministerial office are young civil servants on secondment from their own departments; some are always close political allies of the individual Prime Minister concerned, which can also complicate relations between President and Prime Minister. This system also produces tensions between permanent civil servants working in the government departments and those serving the President or Prime Minister.

The Prime Minister performs an important role in arbitrating interministerial conflicts. Such conflicts are a routine feature of government activity, few policies lying exclusively within the sphere of one ministry. When conflict arises, arbitration between conflicting demands is necessary, in the interests of co-ordination of government policy. Arbitration occurs in both a formal and an informal sense. The bulk of formal arbitration takes place in meetings chaired by the Prime Minister or one of his representatives. Although the President defines the general parameters of policy and can intervene at random, the Prime Minister usually performs a more important role than the President in co-ordinating specific governmental policies.

Alongside these formal mechanisms, many intergovernmental conflicts are solved in an informal manner: by the interministerial telephone; by *ad hoc* meetings of all sorts, by corridor discussions and around the dining table, a privileged instance for the resolution of conflicts in the French case. These mechanisms were particularly in evidence during the Mitterrand presidency: President Mitterrand's governing style in some senses encouraged such a deinstitutionalisation of the resolution of conflicts. Only occasionally are disputes resolved in the full Council of Ministers, which meets weekly under the chairmanship of the President of the Republic.

5.5 Conclusion and summary

From the evidence presented above, it is clear that political leadership has been rather more subtle in France than elsewhere. Formally, a pattern of presidential pre-eminence, and indeed encroachment, from 1958 to 1986 was replaced in 1986 by a reversion to a parliamentary model of executive power. Even during periods of presidential pre-eminence, however, the Prime Minister has performed certain leadership functions: notably, policy co-ordination, arbitration and (to some extent) initiation. It is also clear that Presidents retained a measure of influence during periods of cohabitation. The variable performance of French Prime Ministers was related in part to their personal qualities and style, in part to their strategic mastery of the resources available to them. The source of political legitimacy is the crucial variable in assessing prime ministerial power. The major disadvantage suffered by most premiers was that they owed their position to presidential favour. The occupancy of Matignon at times became an intolerable burden for Prime Ministers who were condemned to ultimate presidential disavowal, whether or not they succeeded in their policy objectives. By contrast, the strength of the Prime Minister's position during periods of cohabitation related to their retention of a clear electoral mandate to govern the country. The experiences of cohabitation revealed that the balance between presidential and prime ministerial powers depended to a large extent upon the state of political forces, as measured by the democratic verdict of the electorate at the most recent election, rather than upon any unambiguous constitutional provisions.

In the case of French Presidents, it would appear that Pompidou, Giscard d'Estaing and Mitterrand derived their authority from their occupancy of the French presidency, one of the key political institutions in western liberal democracies. Their room for manoeuvre was shaped in large measure by the possibilities opened up by this office. A convincing case might be made that de Gaulle possessed a stature which transcended the limitations of the presidency, on account of the precise historical circumstances surrounding his extraordinary political career. No subsequent President could follow de Gaulle, but each has contributed to building the French presidency as a bipartisan institution imposing a measure of cohesion upon a potentially unworkable system.

Indicative bibliography

Bigaut, C. (ed.) (1993) *Le Président de la 5e République*, Documentation Française, Paris.

Cole, A. (1994) *François Mitterrand: A study in political leadership*, Routledge, London.

Duverger, M. (1986) *Les Régimes semi-présidentiels*, PUF, Paris.

Elgie, R. (1993) *The French Prime Minister*, Macmillan, London.

Fournier, J. (1987) *Le Travail gouvernemental*, Presses de la FNSP, Paris.

Gaffney, J. (1989) 'Presidentialism and the Fifth Republic', in J. Gaffney, *The French Presidential Elections of 1988*, Dartmouth, Aldershot.

Guettier, C. (1995) *Le Président sous la 5e République*, PUF, Paris.

Hayward, J. (ed.) (1993) *De Gaulle to Mitterrand: Presidential power in France*, Hurst, London.

Lacroix, B. (1992) *Le Président de la République: usages et genèses d'une institution*, Presses de la FNSP, Paris.

Massot, J. (1987) *L'Arbitre et le capitaine*, Flammarion, Paris.

Chapter 6

A parliamentary democracy?

6.1 Introduction and objectives

As with the other chapters in Part II, Chapter 6 is concerned with the distribution of power between the main institutions and political actors of the French polity. The chapter considers the role performed by the French parliament in the Fifth Republic, notably by assessing the constitutional provisions regulating parliament's operation, and comparing the resources available to the executive with the remaining powers at the disposal of parliament. The specific objective of this chapter is to focus on the rationalised role of the French parliament in the Fifth Republic, and the relative weakness of checks and balances against the abuse of executive power. Parliament has performed a restricted role since 1958. While it continues to accomplish some significant political and policy functions, other institutions and actors – such as the judiciary and the mass media – have arguably proved more adept at controlling the executive.

6.2 Parliament in the Third and Fourth Republics: an elusive sovereignty?

A primary feature of the French republican tradition evoked in Chapter 1 was that the general will was to be entrusted in a sovereign assembly. A belief in parliamentary supremacy against arbitrary executive government guided republicans from the eighteenth century onwards. During the Third and Fourth Republics, deputies referred constantly to this parliamentary republican tradition to resist any attempts to encroach upon their power. There probably was a brief golden era, when the realities of parliamentary control approached the declarations of the parliamentarians: the period opened by the Macmahon crisis of 1877 was one of parliamentary dominance, with governments reduced, in the words of one observer, to 'the role of a mere committee' (Wright, 1989).

However, the rhetoric of parliamentary supremacy co-existed uneasily alongside a progressive yielding of decision-making authority to the executive throughout the twentieth century. This process had its origins in the inter-war period, when governments were first given discretionary powers to issue decrees. It gathered pace during the post-war Fourth Republic. Because of their unwillingness or their inability to take responsibility for unpopular decisions, deputies delegated responsibility for policy making to the executive, notably by allowing governments to issue 'decree-laws' to settle contentious and unpopular decisions. The appearance of parliamentary sovereignty was preserved, but the reality was one of progressive disengagement from detailed policy making. To this extent, the severe checks on parliament's authority in the 1958 constitution consolidated a tendency which was already well engaged.

The restraints upon parliamentary sovereignty in France were similar to those observed in other liberal democracies. These involved the growing role of the state in economic management, the post-war creation of the welfare state, the increasing technical complexity of policy making and the expansion of the government machine. In France, the enhanced role of the state in economic policy and post-war reconstruction should be signalled for particular attention. The economic planning mechanisms inaugurated in the 1940s bore witness to a new spirit of state *dirigisme*, rather than parliamentary incrementalism, as the motor for French post-war reconstruction (Chapter 13).

Weakened in relation to policy making, the French parliament retained its capacity to make and unmake governments. Unlike in Britain or Germany, prior to 1958 French governments only rarely changed as a consequence of electoral defeat. Instead, shifting parliamentary alliances brought down coalition governments with alarming regularity, but they were usually unable to propose any coherent alternative. The particular devices used by parliament to shackle the executive retained the fascination of Anglo-Saxon observers such as Philip Williams (1964). According to the rule of 'interpellation', for instance, deputies could demand an explanation of any aspect of government policy at any time; this would be followed by a vote which, if it went against the government, could bring it down. This was a particularly blunt weapon of parliamentary control. Private members' bills were a favoured means of securing favours for constituents and pressure groups, so that individual deputies became hostages to entrenched interests, such as the notorious wine growers. Powerful parliamentary committees performed a major role in determining the fate of government bills. The presidents of these committees were leading political players in their own right. It was not unknown for ministers to resign their portfolios in order to take charge of the ranking parliamentary committee, since committee chairmen were regarded as being more powerful than ministers. Parliament also retained control over its own timetable, which, put simply, meant that the government had to barter with the party leaders to ensure that its own proposals were placed on the agenda.

The negative features of parliament's oversight during the Fourth Republic drew critical attention from domestic and foreign observers. They were foremost in the mind of the Gaullist constitution-makers of 1958, who attempted to introduce a rationalised parliamentarianism to replace the despised *régime d'Assemblée*.

6.3 The organisation of the French parliament in the Fifth Republic

The National Assembly

The French parliament is composed of two chambers, the National Assembly and the Senate. Parliament meets for a minimum of 130 days per annum, in one continual session of nine months. The National Assembly presently consists of 577 deputies. This figure has varied throughout the Fifth Republic. Deputies are currently elected to represent single-member constituencies under the second-ballot system. All elections except one (1986) have been fought under this electoral system (see Appendix 1). To secure election on the first round, candidates require over 50 per cent of valid votes cast, and over 12.5 per cent of registered electors. Most constituencies require a second ballot: candidates having polled the support of over 10 per cent of the registered electorate on the first ballot are eligible to contest the run-off. The candidate with the most votes wins the second-ballot election. Unlike the presidential election, the parliamentary contest does not require that a candidate obtains an absolute majority of second-round voters to secure election. With the rise of parties such as the Front national and the Greens (Chapter 11), three- or four-cornered second-ballot contests have become more frequent.

The National Assembly is the popularly elected first chamber. Elections to the National Assembly take place at least once every five years, more frequently if the President exercises his right of dissolution as Chirac did in April 1997. During the Third and Fourth Republics, the results of general elections bore little relationship to the process of government formation: governments rose and fell as a result of bargains struck between party leaders in between elections. During the Fifth Republic, in contrast, elections for the National Assembly have tended to provided electors with a clear choice: either to return a majority loyal to the President, or to elect the alternative governing coalition. The emergence of a disciplined party system within parliament has restored parliamentary stability, while at the same time reducing the supervision exercised by parliament over the executive.

The National Assembly disposes of clear advantages over the Senate, in that it can claim to be vested with popular sovereignty. In disputes between the two chambers, the National Assembly has the last word. It is more important than the Senate in the process of passing legislation. Both government bills (*projets de loi*) and private members' bills (*propositions de loi*) can begin life in either the National Assembly or the Senate. After a first reading, bills are then sent to one of the six parliamentary legislative committees existing within both houses. Committees prepare reports on each bill, attempting to ameliorate proposed legislation by way of proposing amendments. These reports are eventually presented to the full house. Committee reports are either accepted by the chamber concerned, or sent back to committee, after which they are presented again at a later date. After completing their passage through the first house, bills are then sent to the second, where this procedure is repeated. In the event of the two houses failing to agree upon an identical text, the government has several available options at its disposal. It will usually establish a Mixed Parliamentary Committee (Commission mixte paritaire, CMP) comprising representatives of the National Assembly and the Senate, with a view to arriving at an acceptable compromise. Should this body fail to agree on a text admissible by the government, the latter will invite the National Assembly to decide.

The Senate

The second chamber is known as the Senate. It is currently composed of 321 senators, each serving for a nine-year term. Senatorial elections are held once every three years, to replace one-third of the Senate. The role of the second chamber has been somewhat controversial throughout its existence. Due to its mode of indirect election, the Senate has traditionally been overrepresentative of small town and rural France, at the expense of more dynamic urban areas. This imbalance was more marked under the Third and Fourth Republics than it is today, but the Senate retains somewhat of a conservative bias. Senators are indirectly elected by electoral colleges based on the 96 departments (metropolitan France only). Each department returns, according to its size, a minimum of two senators. The electoral college for each department is formed of: the deputies, members of the departmental council and delegates from each commune, depending upon its size. The key principle is that each of France's 36,518 communes is entitled to contribute towards electing senators: for this reason, the Senate has been labelled as the 'Council of the communes of France'. The changing balance of power within France's local councils is a useful guide to understanding the changeable composition of the Senate. Shifts in local election results are usually reflected shortly afterwards in the composition of the Senate.

The 1958 constitution clearly designates the Senate as the subordinate parliamentary institution, but the second chamber retains certain delaying and ratifying powers. Its inputs into government bills are not always devoid of effect, notably in relation to amendments of a technical nature. On occasion, the Senate can have an important political impact by becoming a focus of opposition to government policy: it performed this role *par excellence* during the resistance to the Socialists' 1984 Education Bill, for instance. The Senate has proved its political existence on several occasions. Its obstinate resistance to General de Gaulle's attempts to reform it in 1969 was approved by public opinion, which dared to say no to the General. The second chamber illustrated a similar tenacity during the period 1981–6, when it became transformed into a bastion of opposition to the Socialist government.

The most powerful resource possessed by the Senate is that its consent is necessary before constitutional reform can be engaged (see Chapter 4). This gives the second chamber an effective right of veto over constitutional reform. The prerogatives of both the National Assembly and the Senate have been severely reduced during the Fifth Republic. In the ensuing section, an attempt will be made to outline the imbalance between parliament and the executive established by the 1958 constitution, and consolidated by the subsequent political evolution of the Fifth Republic.

6.4 Resources controlled by the executive

John Frears (1991) put it admirably: 'The 1958 constitution is unusual in that it lays down in minute detail innumerable acts of parliamentary procedure – all designed to ensure that the government can govern free from parliamentary harassment.' The constitution of 1958 explicitly set out to ensure that executive government could govern. Parliament was to be limited to a bare oversight role, and to the passing of (executive-inspired) legislation. There were numerous restraining features in the 1958 constitution. We shall consider five: executive control over parliamentary business; restrictions on parliamentary sovereignty; limited means for parliamentary oversight; motions of censure; and budgetary constraints. To complete this section, we shall consider the political resources at the disposal of the executive.

Executive control over parliamentary business

The first type of constraint relates to those provisions giving the executive control over the organisation of parliamentary business. During the Third and Fourth Republics, control over the parliamentary timetable was confided in a parliamentary committee representative of the political formations present in parliament. Governments had to make continual concessions to secure parliamentary consideration for their proposals. Executive control over the parliamentary timetable since 1958 has been of major importance in regulating the operation of parliament. It enables a government to pursue its business with minimal regard to parliamentary harassment. Government bills (*projets de loi*) account for some 80–90 per cent of the legislative timetable, with private members' bills (*propositions de loi*) completing the shortfall. Government bills have priority over private member's bills; to stand any chance of success, a private members' bill must have the support of the government. Private members' bills can no longer propose to increase or reduce government expenditure, which limits their scope. This was in response to the inflationary impact of private members' bills during the Fourth Republic, and the manner in which they made deputies hostage to interest group demands.

The length of the parliamentary session is another aspect of executive control over the legislature. Whereas parliament used to sit for at least nine months during the Fourth Republic, from 1958 to 1995 there were two statutory sittings of the National Assembly lasting for no more than a total of five and a half months. Parliament convened as of right in April and October. Special sessions could be convoked, but only on the initiative of the executive. The short duration of parliamentary sittings proved inconvenient for the executive itself, since it left scant time for the passage of necessary legislation, and forced greater reliance on the unpopular restrictive clauses of the constitution, such as articles 44 and 49 (see below). In order to speed up their legislative programme, governments have invoked article 45 of the 1958 constitution, which allows them to declare a bill to be 'urgent': in this case, the bill requires only one reading in each chamber before a Mixed

Parliamentary Committee is convoked. This speeding-up clause is rather similar to the guillotine in the United Kingdom.

A restoration of the rights of parliament was a feature of Jacques Chirac's successful presidential campaign of 1995. The main proposal enacted in the July 1995 constitutional reform was the creation of a single parliamentary sitting of nine months, from October to June. This was justified in terms of improving parliamentary oversight. The extended parliamentary session would allow the government to process more legislation without having to resort to unpopular accelerating measures of the type detailed below. The extended parliamentary session also illustrated the distorting effects of multiple office holding (*cumul des mandats*) in the French system. After one year in operation, numerous deputies complained that the longer parliamentary sitting had left them with inadequate time to manage the cities of which they were simultaneously mayors. Absenteeism continued to be rife among French deputies.

Limitations on parliamentary sovereignty

A chief feature of the French republican tradition was that popular sovereignty should be vested in an elected assembly. The Fifth Republic constitution of 1958 directly challenged this principle. In article 34, the constitution draws a fine distinction between 'matters of law', requiring parliamentary endorsement, and 'matters of regulation', for which the government alone has responsibility. Furthermore, those matters deemed to fall within the 'sphere of the law' were subdivided into two categories: those where detailed parliamentary legislation and scrutiny were needed, and those where parliament was only required to approve general principles, allowing government departments to fill in the details of implementation. Those areas of policy in which parliament decides upon only general principles include such key matters as defence, local government, education and social security.

The pro-executive battery of weapons is reinforced by articles 37, 38 and 41 of the 1958 constitution. Article 37 sets out that: 'Matters other than those which fall within the domain of legislation shall have the character of regulations': no parliamentary approval is needed for these executive orders. Article 38 allows the government to request parliament for authority to rule by decree even in those policy sectors falling within the normal legislative domain. This provision has allowed governments to speed up the process of policy making when faced with an abnormally charged timetable. It was used, for instance, by Juppé in 1995 to push through sweeping reforms of the social security system. Article 41 forbids parliamentarians from proposing any bill on an issue falling within the 'executive sphere', as determined by article 34. The Constitutional Council has assumed the function of referee between the executive and parliament in determining the boundary between law and regulation.

The 1958 constitution envisages other situations where parliament is excluded from the policy-making process. The provisions for referendums are a case in point

(Chapter 4). The provisions of article 16 are more draconian, in that they assign emergency powers to the President to rule by decree throughout the duration of an emergency that the President himself is instrumental in defining. The only safeguard is that parliament sits 'as of right' throughout the emergency. On the one occasion that such an emergency has been declared, the parliamentary sitting met as usual, but its competence to take any policy decisions was ruled as being out of order by de Gaulle.

Motions of censure

The constitutional provisions relating to motions of censure are particularly severe. Along with article 16 (the emergency powers clause), article 49 must be a strong contender for being the most draconian in the 1958 constitution. The fundamental defining feature of any parliamentary democracy is the right of the elected assembly to overturn the incumbent government. This right is formally assured by article 49, which provides in its second paragraph that a motion of censure may be tabled against the government on the signature of one-tenth of deputies. An absolute majority of the National Assembly is required to carry the motion of censure. Only votes in favour of a motion of censure are counted for the motion; whatever their cause, abstentions and absentees are counted as being votes for the government. Only one successful motion of censure has been carried in the Fifth Republic: in 1962, against the government of Georges Pompidou.

The most sweeping aspect of article 49 relates to its third paragraph, which stipulates: 'The Prime Minister may, after deliberation by the Council of Ministers, pledge the government's responsibility on the vote of a text. The text shall be considered as adopted unless a motion of censure is voted under the conditions laid by the preceding paragraph [i.e. abstentions being counted as votes for the government].' This allows governments to stake their survival of the passage on a particular bill. Article 49, clause 3 (49.3) has been used for several distinctive reasons:

- To speed up parliamentary debate of contentious government bills, when the government has a charged parliamentary timetable. This occurred notably during the Socialist government of 1981–6, despite the Socialists' past criticism of the undemocratic character of the article. The use of article 49.3 has also on occasion stifled dissent from among the ranks of the government's own supporters.
- To preserve a minority government in office. An explicit consideration of the 1958 constitution-makers, this use was endemic to the experience of the 1988–93 Socialist governments. With only a relative small overall majority, the governments led by Rocard, Cresson and Bérégovoy were constrained to apply article 49.3 fairly systematically in order to ensure passage of vital government legislation.
- To force an unwilling coalition partner into line. This occurred most notably during the premiership of Raymond Barre. With Chirac's RPR in a situation of

semi-opposition, Barre repeatedly invoked article 49.3 to force the Gaullists either to support the government, or to take the responsibility for precipitating a general election. On each occasion, the RPR fell into line.

A reduced capacity for parliamentary oversight

The fourth manner in which parliament's control has been circumscribed relates to its reduced capacity for oversight of the executive's actions. The current means at the disposal of the French parliament to oversee the executive are weak by comparison with past republics. In part, this reflects a more general evolution away from legislatures in developed liberal democracies: even the most powerful American congressional committees cannot realistically expect to be kept informed on every aspect of executive policy. There is a specifically French angle too. The 1958 constitution reduced the number of permanent standing committees of the National Assembly and the Senate from nineteen to six. Standing committees consider all *propositions de loi* and *projets de loi* once they have received their first reading in either the National Assembly or the Senate. Their size is such that they are unwieldy instruments of public policy: the two largest committees contain up to 121 members, with four smaller committees composed of a maximum of 61 deputies. Actual attendance on parliamentary committees is far more restrained than these figures suggest. Whether governments accept amendments proposed by parliamentary committees depends in part upon political circumstances, and in part upon their parliamentary position.

It is clear that even governments with no overall working majority (such as the Socialist administrations of 1988–93) are under no constitutional obligation to accept amendments proposed by committees. Article 44 provides another example of a constitutional clause expressly designed to minimise unwelcome parliamentary interference. It allows a government to insist that only its own amendments to bills be considered by the assembly concerned; furthermore, the government can demand a single vote on all amendments. In the last resort, government can insist that parliament debate its own text. This contrasts greatly with the situation of parliamentary committees in an active legislature such as the American Congress, or the French parliament under the Third and Fourth Republics: in both instances, executive-inspired texts could be changed out of all recognition in their passage through committee.

Budgetary constraints

Parliamentary input into the complex budgetary negotiations is usually slight, although not inconsequential. Article 47 allots both parliamentary assemblies a maximum of 70 days to agree upon the government's budget, after which the government's text can be enforced by decree. We should note that the tight control exercised over parliament is in line with traditions in most liberal democracies; the open horsetrading that pits the American President against Congress is rare in other countries. By comparison with past French regimes, budgets are no longer held up to ransom by the pork-barrel demands of key deputies. But parliamentary influence – direct and indirect – has not completely disappeared: premier Juppé felt obliged to accept an important amendment to the 1996 budget passed through the National Assembly's Finance Committee. In preparation for the annual budget round, secret negotiations will take place between the Finance Ministry and various interests, including representatives of the pro-government parliamentary parties (and occasionally the opposition parties as well).

Political resources controlled by the executive

The final series of resources controlled by the executive are political ones, ultimately underpinning the constitutional devices noted above. Any government is secure as long as a hostile majority can be prevented from forming against it. Even minority governments, such as those of 1976–81 and 1988–93, have generally been secure in their positions, on account of the mechanisms analysed above. Unlike in the Third and Fourth Republics, changes of government have occurred either as a result of general elections, or as a consequence of presidential manoeuvring; changes of government as a result of shifting parliamentary alliances between elections are unheard of. The emergence of the presidential party, analysed in Chapter 9, has provided a solid political underpinning for the constitutional subordination of parliament.

The French parliament is not devoid of all influence. For sound political reasons, governments are not insensitive to party or coalition pressures; nor, on occasion, to demands formulated by the opposition parties. Wherever possible, governments will attempt to appease their own backbench supporters, usually by adopting a carrot-and-stick approach, balancing the threat of sanctions with the promise of sympathetic concessions. Regular caucus meetings between the parliamentary groups of the governing parties and representatives of the executive ensure that backbench demands are filtered to key decision-makers in the executive.

6.5 The French parliament: *pour quoi faire*?

The decline of parliaments is a constant theme of comparative politics. The diminished significance of the French parliament stems in part from the pressures noted in relation to other European countries: the increasing technical sophistication of policy making, the expansion and expertise of the bureaucracy, the increase in the extent and scope of government, the rise of party government, the input of well-organised pressure groups and the emergence of external actors such as the European Union. These developments were under way before the creation of the Fifth Republic in 1958. To accept that the French parliament is a diminished institution should not lead us to overlook the functions it does perform, or attempts to perform. These are as a representative forum for political parties; as the chief formal institution of representative government; as an instrument for scrutinising the executive; and as a political training ground.

Parliament is a major representative forum for political parties

Parties fiercely contest elections for the National Assembly. On account of France's electoral system, there is not an exact match between the party line-up within the National Assembly and parties' relative significance within the nation as a whole. Indeed, powerful forces within public opinion are excluded from parliamentary representation, such as the FN and the Greens. Taking the period 1958–97 as a whole, there is little doubt that a rationalised party system within parliament has facilitated the emergence of strong government, just as much as the constitutional devices within the 1958 constitution (cf. Chapter 9). It might be argued, indeed, that the party system, providing disciplined parliamentary support for stable governments, has acted against traditional formulations of parliamentary sovereignty, which required weak governments and ill-disciplined parties.

The character of the parliamentary majority has an impact upon the type of legislative programme envisaged by the government. This was revealed in Chapter 2 with our appraisal of the governments presided over by Chirac (1974–6) and Barre (1976–81): the lack of a reform-minded parliamentary majority, as well as the weakness of the presidential party, definitely had a constraining effect on the type of policies that could be pursued during this period. President Giscard d'Estaing's early reformism was quietly shelved after one year, on account of the fundamental conservatism of his parliamentary majority. An earlier example had been provided by premier Chaban-Delmas (1969–72), whose radical intentions were frustrated as a result of a tacit alliance between a conservative President Pompidou and an even more conservative parliamentary majority.

Parliament is the chief formal institution of representative government

As we illustrated in Chapter 4, upon a strict reading, the 1958 constitution establishes a system based upon government responsibility to parliament. In theory, a determined parliamentary majority can rid itself of an undesirable government. As in other parliamentary systems, government formation must in practice reflect the balance of political forces within the National Assembly. To be more exact, a government cannot survive in the event of a hostile parliamentary majority forming against it. This explains why the Socialist President Mitterrand on two occasions, in 1986 and 1993, preferred to call upon the leader of the victorious centre-right coalition to become Prime Minister, rather than to attempt to name a Socialist or an 'apolitical' premier, who would have then been disavowed by the National Assembly.

The two instances of 'cohabitation' since 1986 have revealed the strengths, but also the weaknesses of the French parliament. That President Mitterrand felt constrained to call upon Chirac to form a government in March 1986 confirmed that

France was a parliamentary democracy. Experiences of cohabitation have also demonstrated that 'parliamentary' executives are no more inclined to involve parliament in policy making than 'presidential' ones. Backed by an extremely tight majority, and faced with an alert, politically astute President, Chirac's government of 1986–8 made full use of the restrictive clauses in the 1958 constitution to keep parliament in check. Article 49.3 in particular was repeatedly used to speed bills through parliament. The situation was somewhat different after the 1993 election inaugurated a second period of cohabitation: the return of a vast RPR–UDF majority led to problems of a different kind, notably those of disciplining enthusiastic young deputies determined to leave their mark. Due to the political pressures within the RPR, for instance, the Balladur government felt constrained to go further than it had intended in its 1994 reform of the Nationality Act.

Parliament is an instrument for scrutinising the executive

Since 1958 the French parliament has had a poor reputation as an agency for scrutinising executive activity. Absenteeism is rife within the National Assembly, in part because of the practice of electronic voting, in part because of the *cumul des mandats*, but also because parliament is felt to be a subordinate institution. Parliamentary standing committees have proved too large and cumbersome to appraise government bills; at any rate, the government is free to ignore their conclusions. Convinced of their own impotence, parliamentarians for long proved inept at exploiting the weapons available to them.

Apart from censure motions alluded to above, scrutiny of the executive has taken two rather crude forms: questions to ministers, and the setting up of special committees of inquiry and control. Written questions to ministers have proved to be a damp squib: overwhelmingly they concern local constituency issues of interest only to individual deputies and – possibly – their electors. Oral questions have had little more impact. There is no exact equivalent of Prime Minister's Question Time in the British House of Commons. The procedure of 'questions to the government' was established during the Giscard d'Estaing presidency. Government ministers respond to prepared questions delivered by deputies. These sessions have proved ineffectual, partly because no supplementary questions are permitted, partly because of a lack of public and media interest. The fate of parliamentary questions is symptomatic of a broader antipathy towards viewing parliament as a forum for great national debates. The political irresponsibility of the French presidency has something to do with this: French Presidents have repeated at will that they are responsible only to the people, not to the intermediaries gathered in parliament. The sense of drama aroused by Prime Minister's Question Time or by the great parliamentary debates in the UK is quite absent in France. French national political debate occurs in television studios more firmly than in other western European nations, where parliamentary debates can have an important political impact.

The other form of executive scrutiny is that provided by special parliamentary committees of inquiry or control. They are pale imitations of the powerful US congressional committees, with freedom to obtain information and question officials. They suffer from several flaws, which limit their effectiveness. They can be established only if a majority of deputies or senators supports their constitution. Only a small proportion of requests for the creation of committees are agreed to by the Legislative Committee (Commission des lois), which is usually dominated by the government's supporters. The framework of reference of duly constituted committees is invariably established by the incumbent government. Most pertinently, access to official information is limited, ministers can refuse to co-operate and civil servants are not required to attend meetings.

Despite the constraints placed upon it, the French parliament is a conscientious legislative body. Frears (1991) presents compelling evidence to suggest that there has been a steady increase throughout the Fifth Republic in the proportion of successful amendments to government bills. It is clear, however, that a proportion of 'parliamentary-inspired' amendments to government bills is in fact imposed upon the relevant deputy or senator by the government itself.

Parliament is a political training ground for ambitious politicians

As in other parliamentary systems, the National Assembly is a breeding ground for political talent. Many politicians make their political reputations in parliament, although other avenues, such as party and local government, are probably more important in France than in most comparable democracies. Effective political performance in the National Assembly remains a certain recipe for political attention: the efforts of several young RPR and UDF deputies in contesting the Socialist Nationalisation Bill in 1982 provided a springboard for their future political promotion. At the other end of the spectrum, the Senate has proved to be a coveted retirement post for experienced politicians: for instance, Pierre Mauroy, Socialist premier from 1981 to 1984, and Socialist Party leader from 1988 to 1992, preferred to end his career in the Senate rather than contest an Assembly seat.

Important strategic positions occupied within parliament are coveted by leading politicians, since they are clearly capable of influencing the conduct of government policy. The President of the National Assembly is one such position: the post has been occupied by former premiers such as Chaban-Delmas and Fabius, as well as by former President Giscard d'Estaing. The post is the fourth in the official state hierarchy, and offers its occupant a measure of influence over parliamentary procedure, the right to nominate one-third of the members of the Constitutional Council, the occupancy of a splendid official residence and permanent contact with ministers. From 1993 to 1997, Philippe Séguin, has transformed the presidency of the National Assembly into a public platform from which to criticise the Juppé government that he in theory supported. To a lesser extent, the presidency of the Senate is a comparable position of influence. The presidents of the parliamentary committees, while no longer the barons of old, are assiduously courted by government ministers. According to one former president of the social affairs committee, the leverage of such a position can be considerable (J.-M. Belorgey, interview with the author, 1993).

6.6 Beyond parliamentary scrutiny: the judiciary and the media

As in other liberal democracies, classic parliamentary functions either have been ceded to the executive (in terms of policy making) or are more convincingly performed by other bodies (in terms of scrutiny and political communication). Certain representative functions are in practice devolved to the party system (Chapters 9, 10 and 11); others are performed by interest groups and voluntary associations (Chapter 12). The principal function that remains with parliament is that of democratic legitimisation: no government can survive for long without the confidence of the democratically elected Assembly.

In relation to political communication and executive scrutiny, the role of the mass media should be signalled for attention. Long a subservient arm of the Gaullist and Giscardien regimes, the partial liberalisation of broadcasting during the Mitterrand presidency introduced an unpredictable new actor (Kuhn, 1995). Prior to 1981, tight executive control over television output was enforced both by means of direct state intervention and by autocensure on behalf of broadcasters. Mitterrand's creation of the High Authority for broadcasting in 1982 broke new ground, in that it ensured a degree of political pluralism and removed control of the media from the state's direct tutelage. Broadcasting standards are currently controlled by the High Audiovisual Council (Conseil supérieur de l'audiovisuel, CSA), a successor to the High Authority. The CSA is a relatively tame watchdog with a narrow remit, but one which at least has the merit of ensuring fair television coverage at election times.

Government secrecy and the absence of a Freedom of Information Act curtail genuinely investigative television journalism. As a means of executive scrutiny, for instance, critical television documentaries remain rare. As an instrument of political communication, television has become the theatre of political competition between political parties and politicians. This is especially visible during presidential election campaigns. The role of the face-to-face televised debate between the two leading candidates is a case in point (Hayward, in Cole, 1990). The belief that the presidential debate has affected the outcome of successive presidential elections is firmly established, but has never been convincingly demonstrated. Giscard'd'Estaing's tart reply to Mitterrand ('you do not have a monopoly of compassion') is believed to have delivered his victory on points in 1974. The challenger Mitterrand's jibe that Giscard was a 'man of the past' struck a chord in 1981. Neither Jospin nor Chirac managed to secure a decisive advantage in 1995. Unlike in the United States and the UK, little real evidence has been presented in the French case to test the effects of television in determining partisan outcomes. That television has assumed an increasing importance in the daily routine of politicians is unquestionable, however: an ability to cope effectively with television has become more important in most respects than parliamentary performance. The concentration of the mass media on the presidency as the cornerstone of the political system, and on the personal merits of rival candidates during presidential elections, has strengthened a parliamentary reading of the political system. In the absence of televised parliamentary debates, public interest in the institution is weak.

The role of investigative journalism should also be highlighted as a form of executive scrutiny. Apart from the crusading *Le Canard enchaîné*, investigative journalism of the American or British variety has little tradition in the French press. The press has assumed a growing importance, however, in focusing attention on executive malpractices and corruption under successive administrations. The example is the role of *Le Monde* and *Libération* in uncovering phone-tapping abuses among Mitterrand's Elysée staff. In terms of political orientation, the bulk of national and regional dailies are conservative leaning, without the overt partisanship of their British counterparts. The importance of the apolitical French regional press, the absence of a tabloid tradition and the highbrow character of French national dailies serve to highlight the contrast between France and certain other European countries, most notably the UK.

The role of the judiciary

Judicial and semi-judicial bodies have become increasingly important in French politics. French politics has been transformed in important respects by the affirmative presence of its judicial and quasi-judicial institutions. There is an argument that these bodies have become more effective in scrutinising executive abuses of power than parliament or the media. The Constitutional Council (Chapter 4) and the Council of State (Chapter 7) are appreciated elsewhere. In the course of the 1980s and 1990s, judicial actors (especially the investigating magistrates, *juges d'instruction*) have become important actors in their own right, far less inclined than previously to bow to executive pressures. In the French legal system, these magistrates are instructed to inquire into alleged breaches of the law and to present reports recommending (or not, as the case may be) further action to the French Chancellery. To carry out their functions, they are invested with certain powers, such as the right of search, the confiscation of documents and the interviewing of suspects.

Inspired by their Italian counterparts, French investigating magistrates have meticulously uncovered abuses of executive and municipal power, as well as widespread but illegal practices of financing political parties. Their fervour has made a handful of magistrates into household names, such as Van de Rumbeyke, Thierry Pierre and Halphen. These figures have used their powers to the full, including making spectacular visits to headquarters of the main political parties (the PS, the RPR and the PR), and even conducting investigations inside the Prime Ministers' office. In at least one case – the 1990 law on the financing of political parties – the activities of the investigating magistrates led to important legislation being enacted, as well as legal sanctions being taken against several party treasurers and a handful of former government ministers.

Alongside these well-publicised cases, however, insiders complain of executive pressures being brought to bear against magistrates who are too meticulous in their inquiries, especially when these touch political parties, the inner workings of the state or the murkier sides of state activity, such as the secret services and government slush funds. Moreover, many important judicial appointments (notably the public prosecutors) are made by the executive branch (either by the President of the Republic or by the Justice Minister) after consultation with the Higher Council of the Magistrature, a body representing both the political executive and the legal profession. Accusations of political considerations influencing judicial appointments were levelled against the Juppé government in 1996, as they had been against its predecessors. Thus, M. Benmakhlouf, the former Directeur du cabinet of the Justice Minister J. Toubon, became public prosecutor for the Paris area in July 1996, despite being very closely associated with the ruling Gaullist party.

6.7 Conclusion and summary

Traditions of executive scrutiny and parliamentary control are comparatively weak in the modern French polity. Foreign policy decisions in particular have usually escaped serious parliamentary scrutiny, on account of the President's constitutional pre-eminence in foreign policy and defence. President Chirac's unilateral decision to resume French nuclear testing in July 1995, without any reference to parliament, party or public opinion, suggested that the French exception remains alive in this sphere. The contrast with President Clinton's travails with the US Congress over resisting arming the Bosnian Muslims illustrates the difference between the two systems. The real issues raised by the emasculation of parliament for most of the Fifth Republic relate to the blurred lines of political accountability created by presidentialism, to excessive government secrecy and to hidden politico-administrative circuits of decision making that escape parliamentary oversight.

The high level of centralisation in France has traditionally insulated political and administrative authorities from scrutiny. By comparative European standards, there are few checks and balances on executive power. The spheres of government secrecy, misappropriation of public finances and attempts to limit judicial independence give some cause for concern. The experienced American observer Ezra Suleiman (1991) argues strongly that checks and balances against executive misuses of power are inadequate: 'All mechanisms of control – the National Assembly, the *Cour des comptes,* the judicial system, the *Inspection des finances* – are ineffective, or, in sensitive matters, find their independence to be inexistent.'

In a context of globalisation, European integration and international financial capitalism, even national governments can only pretend to exercise limited sovereignty. The functions of national parliaments everywhere are either in decline or being reinvented. The French parliament has suffered more than most since 1958, on account of the constitutional straitjacket within which it functions, and the tendency of the French party and electoral systems to produce clear electoral verdicts. The *raison d'être* of the French parliament is not as an institution capable of controlling the policy process, or as an instrument of detailed executive scrutiny. It is too weak to perform either function alone. Insofar as these functions are performed at all, they are shared with other institutions or actors, such as the judiciary, the mass media, and social or political movements. The real justification of the French parliament is as a foundation of democratic legitimacy, upon which French governments must rest their claim to govern, in at least equal measure as they are dependent on presidential support for their appointment and continuing existence.

Indicative bibliography

Ameller, M. (1994) *L'Assemblée nationale*, PUF, Paris.

Baguenard, J. (1990) *Le Sénat*, PUF, Paris.

Belorgey, J.-M. (1991) *Le Parlement à refaire*, Gallimard, Paris.

Bodiguel, J.-L. (1991) *Les Magistrats: un corps sans âme*, PUF, Paris.

Frears, J. (1991) 'The French parliament: loyal workhorse, poor watchdog', *West European Politics*, vol. 14, no. 1.

Kimmel, A. (1991) *L'Assemblée nationale sous la cinquième république*, Presses de la FNSP, Paris.

Kuhn, R. (1995) *The Media in France*, Routledge, London.

Robert, J. (1988) 'De l'indépendence des juges', *Revue du droit publique*, no. 1.

Chapter 7

An administrative state?

7.1 Introduction and objectives

It is common usage to regard France as the bureaucratic state *par excellence*. Metaphors of bureaucratic power in France abound, typified by references to an *énarchie*, to the ubiquitous influence of 'technocracy' and to the administrative state. These are predicated upon the perception of a powerful, usually coherent and homogeneous bureaucracy.

In important respects, the state has performed a pre-eminent role throughout French history. In Chapter 1, we perceived how the state acted as a source of imposed cohesion, a tool for overwhelming centrifugal pressures of all varieties. The ideology of the state was in some sense a defining feature of the republic. The state was held to represent the 'general will', superior to the particularistic interests of regions, political castes or interests. This underpinning ideology strengthened the organisation of a powerful bureaucracy, which germinated in the *ancien régime*, and rapidly matured in the Napoleonic order. Far from representing a unified entity, however, France's bureaucratic leviathan contains countless conflicting interests within its midst. In the course of Chapter 7, we shall investigate whether the French state has been as strong and coherent as some (both detractors and supporters) would like to believe, and what challenges the French state has had to face in the 1990s.

If only for the subsequent criticism it raised, Michel Crozier's *The Bureaucratic Phenomenon* (1963) was the most significant early contribution to the study of the French 'bureaucratic mentality'. It remains a landmark more than 30 years after its initial publication. The key theme of Crozier's portrayal was that of compartmentalisation (*cloisonnement*): this referred to the compact, impenetrable character of different bureaucratic agencies, and the lack of communication between them. Taking issue with Max Weber's belief in the 'absolute superiority of a regimented, hierarchical form of organisation', Crozier affirmed that each level of a bureaucratic hierarchy operates in accordance with its own norms, usually in complete ignorance of the overall objectives of the organisation. The term *cloisonnement* became used as a code to depict the inward-looking, defensive character of French bureaucratic agencies. It could be applied to bureaucratic mentalities at all levels. It was used by J.-P. Worms, for instance, in his study of the French prefectures in the 1960s (Worms, 1966). Public perceptions of French bureaucracy have gradually changed, not least as a result of the powerful movement of political and administrative decentralisation which occurred in the 1980s. But the image of the bureaucratic society remains a powerful one.

7.2 Features of the French civil service

The metaphor of the administrative state, or of the bureaucratic society, implies a strong unitary state. However, the evidence presented below suggests that, despite the undeniable weight of administrative procedures and interests in France, the French civil service is fragmented at all levels of operation. Several features characterise the French administration, certain ones shared with bureaucracies in comparable nations; others specifically Gallic.

The first observation relates to the classification of who comprises a 'civil servant'. Entry to the civil service at all levels is based on competitive public examination and carries with it security of tenure. Several public sector professions depending directly upon the central state are also classified as belonging to the national civil service. This greatly inflates the official number of civil servants in comparison with other European countries. The fact that policy implementation has traditionally been the responsibility of civil servants working in the ministerial field services, rather than local government (as in the UK), has also inflated their number.

Primary school teachers are a case in point: the most humble school teacher carries the status of a civil servant (*fonctionnaire*) with security of employment and specific rights and duties. The vast majority of 'civil servants' have no visible impact upon policy making, except in their indirect capacity of operating in professional interest groups. The élite civil servants with which this chapter is concerned number approximately 5,000, highly concentrated in the Parisian headquarters of the various ministries, or in certain key posts in the provincial prefectures and ministerial field services.

The second obvious point relates to the educational base from which the French administrative élite is recruited. Nominations to top administrative positions are determined on the basis of competitive examinations, internal promotion procedures and political appointments. Key civil service appointments are largely dependent upon having transited through one of France's *grandes écoles*, followed by success in the highly competitive examinations for the National Administration School (*Ecole nationale d'administration*, ENA). The School was created in 1945 as a means of conferring upon the state the responsibility for the training and recruitment of its top civil servants. Prior to this date, civil servants had been recruited according to the norms in operation in different *corps* and ministries, which each operated its own entry examinations. Since 1945 ENA has served as the privileged channel for recruitment to top civil service positions. The annual intake of ENA students is of the order of 120, with the most frequent entry route being the School's competitive examination, taken on completion of a university degree. Each individual is classified in relation to his or her performance, and compared with co-students. The individual performance of each ENA student determines the civil service posts to which he or she can aspire:

- High flyers strive for the Council of State, the Court of Accounts or the Financial Inspectorate: these three bodies are collectively known as the *grands corps*.
- Other postings open to ENA graduates are the administrative inspectorates of the various government departments, the prefectoral corps, the Foreign Affairs Ministry, overseas commercial attachés, administrative postings in a range of government departments, the Regional Courts of Accounts and the Paris town hall (Ecole nationale d'administration, 1992).

The essential point is that mere entry to ENA secures a prestigious civil service post, with the possibility of a lucrative transfer to the private sector at a later date. The end product of this system is sometimes contemptuously referred to as an *énarque*, with the same mixture of enmity and admiration reserved for Oxbridge graduates in the UK. Whatever the efficacy of this system, it is resented in the provinces, for producing out-of-touch Parisians from narrow educational backgrounds. It was in recognition of this resentment that the Socialist government of Edith Cresson partially delocalised the school to Strasbourg in 1991, causing furore among ENA students for whom study in Paris was the height of social achievement. ENA is not the only route for access to the higher echelons of the civil service: to some extent individuals can work up from lower gradings, or else join one of the *corps* via a different route (notably the Ecole polytechnique). Technical specialists working in government departments, for instance, have usually studied at the Ecole polytechnique, which has an identity just as strong as ENA.

A third feature of the French civil service relates to its 'politicisation'. Two rather different interpretations might be given in relation to the notion of a 'politicised' civil service. It can refer either to the nomination of top civil servants according to political criteria, or to the proportion of civil servants entering into politics. If it is true, as Wright (1974) argues, that the first political nominations occurred in the Fourth Republic, the movement has accelerated in the Fifth Republic, notably with the repeated changes of government of the 1980s and 1990s. A series of top administrative posts are now effectively determined according to political criteria: prefects, rectors and ambassadors are regularly shifted when governments change. Other posts are not open to political interference, being determined uniquely by internal administrative promotion procedures (Le Pourhiet, 1987). The fact that key posts are subject to political interference has led to accusations of a 'spoils system' being in operation. This is rather misleading in the French context, especially since political appointments within the French bureaucracy are limited to the top élite (rather than reaching the middle ranks as in the United States), but the principle of political appointment might be held to contravene the neutrality of the state.

The other definition of politicisation refers to the involvement of civil servants in posts of political authority. These can be subdivided into two different types: civil servants substituting for party politicians in positions of political authority; and ministers having at one stage or another exercised a civil service function. The first category was much in evidence under de Gaulle, but has declined subsequently. In his reaction to the *Régime des partis* of the Fourth Republic, de Gaulle ostentatiously favoured the appointment of apolitical 'technocrats' as government ministers, preserving the myth of the neutral state. By the end of his presidency, however, 'technocrats' had given way to the near-total penetration of the Gaullist UDR within the Council of Ministers (Charlot, 1970). This reliance upon the presidential party to provide the bulk of government ministers has continued under each of de Gaulle's successors, including Giscard d'Estaing. The second type of indirect bureaucratic input relates to the high proportion of government ministers having served at one time or another as civil servants, considered immediately below.

Closely related to the above, a fourth feature of the French civil service relates to the interpenetration of political and administrative personnel (de Baecque and Quermonne, 1981). This is a peculiar feature of the French system. Individuals initially trained as civil servants frequently opt for a political career. This is less surprising than it appears at first sight. The fact that teachers and university professors are considered as civil servants partly explains this penetration; a high proportion of 'civil servant' Socialist deputies elected in 1981 were in fact secondary school teachers. A second line of explanation lies in the role performed by ENA. Far from being 'merely' a training ground for France's civil service élite, ENA has become a nursery for France's political élite as well, in a broad sense that surpasses political cleavages. This is in part because of the existence of a powerful network of relationships between former ENA students. It is also attributable to the fact that ENA attracts the best students, who, naturally ambitious, are often driven towards pursuit of political office. The creation of ENA has arguably accentuated this process, since it is legitimate for members of a self-conscious élite, recruited ostensibly for state service, to harbour aspirations of political or economic success. This explains the importance of ENA graduates among cabinet ministers, as well as on the boards of private industries. Moreover, because civil servants enjoy security of tenure, they are able to take time out of their administrative careers in order to engage in political activity; should they suffer an electoral setback, they can always re-enter their *corps* at a later date.

For critics, this interpenetration of personnel lends support to a bureaucratic power thesis: the permanent administration in France has proved remarkably effective at diffusing an administrative ethos among politicians. The boundary between politics and administration has become blurred: a common career trajectory for members of the political élite involves a passage through ENA, attachment to a *grands corps*, service in a government department or a ministerial *cabinet*, and an overt political engagement. The fact that a majority of ministers in the Fifth

Republic (55 per cent) before 1981 started out their careers as civil servants testifies to this (de Baecque, 1991). These figures were less overwhelming under the Socialist administrations of 1981–6 and 1988–93, but they remained significant.

The interpenetration of political and administrative élites is one key feature of the French system; another is *pantouflage*. By *pantouflage*, we mean the transfer of personnel between top civil service positions and lucrative posts in private industry. As in other European democracies (such as the UK), strong evidence points to a regular transfer of former government ministers to lucrative posts within state or private industry. Nominations to leading positions in state industry are often barely concealed 'golden handshakes' for former ministers: in 1995, for instance, Balladur's former Finance Minister, Alphandéry, was named as Director-General of Gaz de France, to replace Gilles Ménage (himself a former adviser of President Mitterrand). The French government's privatisation programme has added a new dimension to this traditional practice. A furore was created in 1986–7, when the Chirac government was accused (rightly) of ensuring that industrialists close to the Gaullist RPR were placed in key positions on the boards of the industries to be privatised. This traditional practice has recently come in for fierce criticism. The involvement of key French companies in repeated corruption scandals has made it a hazardous exercise for former politicians to embrace a practice that was for long accepted as one of the perks of state service.

The role of the *corps* is a sixth distinguishing feature of the French civil service, one often underestimated by Anglo-Saxon observers. The *corps* are bodies without obvious parallels in the British or American contexts. Rather than designating an institution or a government department as such, the term is used to describe the different state grades to which all civil servants must belong. Entry to each *corps* is based on competitive examination, and carries with it rights, responsibilities and prospects for career development.

A small number of administrative *grands corps* stand out as objects of particular prestige; in this way a definite sense of internal hierarchy exists within the French civil service. These administrative *grands corps* are the Council of State, the Financial Inspectorate and the Court of Accounts. Competition to enter these *corps* is fierce, and they attract the best ENA graduates. As Anne Stevens (1992) points out: 'the three leading administrative *grands corps* are all concerned with controlling and checking the work of other civil servants'. The prefectoral corps and the diplomatic corps fall slightly lower in the administrative hierarchy, but retain considerable prestige. Alongside these administrative corps, two technical corps – Mining, and Highways and Bridges – recruit engineers to serve in several technical government departments (Equipment, Agriculture, Industry) and their field services.

Both the technical and the administrative *grands corps* represent the centralising traditions of the French state; as such, both have attempted to put a brake on the decentralisation process appraised in Chapter 8, which they have experienced as involving a weakening of their power. The technical *grands corps* have proved to be particularly obstructionist in relation to the process of decentralisation, since the new responsibilities of local and regional authorities have deprived these engineers and central planners of a traditional and coveted role.

Each of these bodies is different, but each shares the distinction of attracting the educational élite, and of retaining the loyalty of its members throughout their careers. Civil servants are loyal to these corps more than to individual government departments. The *esprit de corps* is often cited to illustrate an homogeneity of outlook of these politico-administrators, deeply imbued with the ideology of serving the state. As with most other generalisations, this is only partly true; educational background does not ensure a similar distribution of partisan loyalties, or attitudes. But it might help explain the extent to which the *grands corps* are rarely subject to political controversies. The attention paid to Council of State judgments is an illustration of this. Governments of all political persuasions listen attentively to the Council of State, even when (as in most instances) its advice is only indicative.

The Council of State

The Council of State is the most prestigious of the *grands corps*, with one of the prize placements for ENA students being as an *auditeur*. On average, the top six students each year are recruited to the Council of State. The Council is composed of some 300 members, divided into six grades according to length of service. The collegial identity of members of the Council of State is one of its significant features; each member is conscious not only of belonging to a venerable institution, but also of forming part of the inner circle of the French élite.

The functions of the Council of State are diverse. Its activity lies at the interface between the political, judicial and administrative spheres. Three principal roles emerge:

■ As a privileged government adviser, the Council of State performs a key role in the preparation of government laws. Before French government bills (and decrees) are considered in the Council of Ministers, or the National Assembly, they must be submitted to the Council of State for an appreciation of their legality and administrative feasibility. Although Council of State judgments are not binding, governments of all persuasions listen attentively to its deliberations. The Council of State also intervenes when called upon to give general advice to governments on a broad range of issues (e.g. electoral reform). Finally, the Council of State passes most of the decrees implementing laws voted by parliament. In the opinion of a former vice-president (Long, 1992), the Council of State lies at the heart of the French administrative system. It is 'an obligatory reference point before any important decision is taken'. Because of the prestige of its function and membership, 'its recommendations, though non-imperative, are at the intersection between advice and decisions'.
■ The Council of State has major judicial and juridical-administrative functions. The French Republic has a separate system of administrative courts, apart from

the ordinary legal system. These courts, which judge on the legality of acts of French civil servants and government agencies, hear grievances from members of the public. The Council of State is the ultimate appeal court in relation to matters of alleged maladministration.

■ As the pinnacle of the French system of administrative courts, the Council of State operates at various different levels: as an administrative court of first instance, as an appeals court and as a court of cassation. As an administrative court of first instance, the Council of State acts as a referee in relation to major disputes involving the legality of ministerial regulations (decrees and ordonnances) and government decrees, and potential major abuses of public authority. As an appeals court, the Council of State adjudicates in relation to certain specific types of dispute, notably those involving election results. As a court of cassation, the Council of State exercises judicial and administrative control over other key administrative bodies such as the Court of Accounts, the Higher Council of the Magistrature and the Higher National Education Council, and can be called upon to arbitrate in disputes between public authorities (Stirn, 1991).

As the guarantor of the integrity of French administrative traditions, the Council of State has been critical of many aspects of moves towards closer European integration, especially insofar as this process threatens the pre-eminent role it performs within the French administrative system. As much as any other organisation, the Council of State can pretend to represent the unity and indivisibility of the French state.

7.3 A unified and indivisible state?

In 1973 Jack Hayward could legitimately entitle his classic work *The One and Indivisible French Republic*; over twenty years later, such a title would be a hazardous one. Although the unity of the state is repeated incessantly in official governmental discourse, and the theme of *l'administration au pouvoir* is a popular one, on closer inspection this appears exaggerated. The omnipresence of the French state is real; its omnipotence and unity are far less certain. Several types of differentiation exist within the French administration. Certain of these are present in all liberal democratic-political systems, whereas others are more specifically French. In a rather schematic manner, we might identify at least seven sources of potential and real conflict within France's one and indivisible state. We will examine these in the following sections.

Competition between ministries

As in other western European nations, there is an inbuilt tension between the Finance Ministry and the spending ministries. The annual budget round bears testament to this. In his study of the French Prime Minister, Elgie (1993) illustrates how the budget division (*direction du budget*) of the Finance Ministry exercised a tight control over the budgetary process, marshalling all means at its disposal to resist spending increases by ministries such as Education, Defence and Health. The budget of 1989 studied by Elgie (1993) provided limited evidence for a bureaucratic model of the policy-making process. The key resources at the disposal of the budgetary division were essentially financial and technical. But they were also political, in the sense that they were charged with implementing tough government guidelines ultimately determined by the President (guidelines that the Finance Ministry itself was instrumental in pressing upon the incumbent government).

Competition between ministers and civil servants

Tensions between high-ranking civil servants and ministers are obvious, although they should not be overstressed. In spite of their common outlook in many respects, political and administrative actors pursue rather different logics. The bureaucratic logic is justified by reference to the general interest and the service of the state, an appeal with a particular resonance in France. From a bureaucratic perspective, politicians look to their particularistic interests, notably to the need to get re-elected. The need for continuity in public policy is used as a powerful argument by bureaucrats to justify attempting to orientate decisions in particular directions. From a politician's perspective, bureaucrats often reason in terms of longer-term departmental agendas, which take inadequate account of political realities and the democratic legitimacy of politicians. These diverging outlooks should not be overstressed, however: the defence of specific sectoral interests (such as Health, Education and Defence) usually unites the ministers and civil servants within a particular government department, since their mutual interests are tied up in maximising their resources and influence.

One specific mechanism adopted in the French case is that of the ministerial office (*cabinet*). Each minister is assisted by a team of advisers, whose function it is to follow particular briefs, write speeches and provide advice, although, as Carcassonne (1986) explains, 'no two *cabinets* are the same'. The size of ministerial cabinets varies from four or five advisers to over 100 in the case of the Prime Minister. The status of the *cabinets* is rather ambiguous; with no statutory existence, they tend to mirror the qualities and priorities of the minister involved. They are often composed of young ENA graduates. Their interventions can cause resentment both in other branches of the civil service and among permanent officials (especially the *directeurs*) of the department concerned. Because individuals generally serve in *cabinets* at the beginning of their careers, and because they are identified with particular ministers, they rarely remain in any one *cabinet* for more than two years. From the perspective of the permanent career civil servants, the capacity for disruption represented by the *cabinets* can be great.

Paradoxically, the *cabinet* system testifies to the influence of the administrative recruitment process: ministers usually nominate junior civil servants to serve in their *cabinets*, despite the fact that one of the functions of the *cabinet* is to attempt to control the civil service. This is because only those trained in administrative techniques really understand how the system works, a testament to the insidious power of the French civil service. As a counterpart, it might be contended that there is no settled pattern of relations within the *cabinets*: certain *cabinets* are dominated by representatives of the chief divisions (*directions*) within the ministry; others are openly political, determined to impose the will of the minister; still others lie somewhere in between these two cases.

The attempt undertaken in 1995 by the Juppé government to reform the operation of the *cabinets* revealed a sense of unease at their political irresponsibility, as well as the financial improprieties involved in certain cases. In theory, no minister is henceforth able to employ more than five advisers in his or her office. In practice, a detailed investigation proved that most ministers continued to employ far more than this number, relying on the indulgence of government departments to second their officials to serve on *cabinets* (Favereau, 1995).

Departmental interests and governmental co-ordination

As in all unitary liberal democracies, there are tensions between the interests of particular ministries and the overall cohesion of the government machine, requiring efforts at government co-ordination. This co-ordinating function is performed at different levels and rhythms by the presidential Elysée staff, the Prime Minister's Cabinet, the General Secretariat of the government and various interministerial committees (see Chapter 5).

The role of interministerial structures

Tension between individual ministries and interministerial structures can be extremely significant. Each government department has its own traditions, policy concerns and budgetary priorities, often cultivated by career civil servants whose longevity of service surpasses that of any individual government. However much it might be resisted, co-ordination by the Finance Ministry, the Prime Minister or the President is accepted as inevitable. Less welcome is co-ordination by specifically created interministerial structures, designed to demonstrate the government's commitment to a particular policy area. The creation of an Interministerial Delegation (Délégation interministérielle) is a means of ensuring permanent co-ordination in a policy sphere which falls between several ministries, but which has a high governmental priority. They have existed in areas such as training policy, drug prevention campaigns and regional policy. It is a classic problem of public administration that horizontal interministerial delegations suffer from bureaucratic resistance from vertically organised government departments. From the point of view of government departments, the interministerial organ will always make unacceptable demands which deflect the ministry from its mission. Departments wish to determine where and when their expenditure takes place, rather than being forced to finance programmes they do not completely control. A long-standing example of such an interministerial structure is the DATAR, the tool of Gaullist regional policy since the 1960s (Biarez, 1989).

In theory, the DATAR exists as an interministerial organ for co-ordinating all policies which have an effect upon planning (*aménagement du territoire*); in practice, its power tends to vary according to the political support it receives at any one moment. The DATAR is resented not only by individual ministries, but often by local authorities as well, since its existence symbolises the state's interest in local affairs. After a long period of disorientation following the decentralisation reforms of the 1980s, the DATAR is increasingly in evidence in French regional policy. A more recent – and probably less enduring – example is that of the Interministerial Delegation for the City (Délégation interministérielle à la ville, DIV). This was created in 1989 in order to stress the Rocard government's commitment to an audacious urban policy: the invention of an interministerial structure was intended to give urban policy greater prominence within the administrative apparatus. The efficiency of such structures depends upon a strong political will in order to facilitate their co-ordinating task: the DIV had to deal with over 40 divisions spread across several ministries (Le Galès and Mawson, 1994).

Tensions between different interests within a single sector

Government departments are highly complex entities. Competition between rival divisions (*directions*) can be acute, as each attempts to maximise influence and budgets against the claims of rivals within the same ministry (as well as against similar *directions* in other departments). Within the French education sector, for instance, competition for resources between the secondary and higher education divisions is endemic. These divisions are sometimes called upon to cohabit in the same department; on other occasions they form separate ministries. In his study of the Industry Ministry, Friedberg (1974) pointed to the minimal contact between the heads of rival divisions, and to their preference for cultivating outside contacts rather than seeking compromise with each other.

Paris and the provinces

Tensions within a single ministry can also arise from conflicts of interest and appreciation between the Parisian headquarters of a ministry and the regional and departmental field services of the same ministry. This has always existed, but the situation has become immensely more complicated since the *déconcentration* reforms of the 1980s and 1990s. By *déconcentration*, we mean the granting of greater autonomy to the regional and departmental offices of the main ministries; to some extent, these agencies can decide how they implement laws and decrees issued from Paris. The field services have been known to make common cause with other local and regional actors – local authorities, the prefectures, other services – against their own ministries. Their autonomy is – in theory – counterbalanced by the requirement that they submit to the co-ordinating role of the prefect, rather than the hierarchical command of their Parisian headquarters. In practice, however, the field services still have closer contacts with their own ministries than with the prefectures, whose co-ordinating appetites are resented by the field services in a similar manner to the oversight role exercised by the Prime Minister on a national level.

Cross-cutting pressures

Finally, several sources of tension criss-cross those explored above. They include rivalries between members of the administrative *grands corps* and others; between *énarques* and others; between different territorial levels of administration (the centre, the regions, the departments), between the prefectures and the ministerial field services. The omnipresence of the state gives these rivalries an intensity in France that is absent in such an obvious form in most other European nations. Far from representing an administrative monolith, this situation has been likened to a bureaucratic jungle with few fixed ground rules. This is to overstate the case: there are several key elements of cohesion in the system. The sense of duty possessed by a caste of high-ranking civil servants is no less marked in France than it is in the UK, and in both instances certainly more so than in the United States. The existence of a unitary system of government and the concentration of most bureaucratic resources in the central government are another source of cohesion. The financial and technical resources possessed by the central ministries – and their field services – continue to give the state a real presence at all territorial levels of administration. But it is probable that the unitary character of the French state has been overemphasised.

7.4 Conclusion and summary

The variety of situations lends further support to an appraisal recognising the heterogeneity of the French state, based on numerous agencies pursuing their own interests with varying degrees of autonomy. Rather than a centralised, uniform entity, the French state can often be disaggregated into its component units; this is important, since it enables us to understand how different components of the state are able to engage in relationships with different types of policy actor in local government and elsewhere.

The rigidly centralised and static state emphasised by Crozier in the 1960s has had to adapt to changes in its internal and external environment. On an internal level, administrative reforms introduced by the Rocard government (1988–91) have modernised the operation of internal civil service management rules. More scope is allowed for internal promotion procedures based on merit, although in the middle ranks the system remains one based on seniority. The continuing hold of the *grands corps* on key civil service positions reveals the limits of this movement. But the French state is not a unified entity. A multitude of different actors exist, often with different sectoral and territorial logics. These logics have been strengthened by the changes in the 1980s and 1990s, notably by decentralisation (see Chapter 8). This dual movement has appreciably modified the operation of the ministerial field services in the departments and regions. Externally, the context within which the French civil service operates has been challenged by changes in the international economy, and by the combined processes of decentralisation and closer European integration (Muller, 1992). Faced with new types of responsibility, the state has been called upon to reinvent the roles it performs and to legitimise its existing functions.

Indicative bibliography

Crozier, M. (1974) *Où va l'administration française?*, Editions de l'organisation, Paris.

De Baecque, F. (1973) *L'Administration centrale de la France*, Armand Colin, Paris.

De Baecque, F. and J.-L. Quermonne (1981) *Administration et politique sous la Ve République*, Presses de la FNSP, Paris.

Gaffney, J. (1991) 'Political think tanks in the UK and ministerial cabinets in France', *West European Politics*, vol. 14, no. 1.

Grémion, C. (1979) *Profession décideurs: pouvoirs des hauts fonctionnaires et réformes de l'état*, Gauthier-Villars, Paris.

Long, M. (1995) 'Le Conseil d'état: rouage au coeur de l'administration et le juge administratif suprème', *Revue administrative*, vol. 48, no. 283.

Muller, P. (1992) 'Entre le local et l'Europe: la crise du modèle français des politiques publics', *Revue française de science politique*, vol. 42, no. 2.

Stirn, B. (1991) *Le Conseil d'état: son rôle, sa jurisprudence*, Hachette, Paris.

Thullier, G. (1985) *Les Cabinets ministeriels*, PUF, Paris.

Wright, V. (1974) 'Politics and administration under the French Fifth Republic', *Political Studies*, vol. 22, no. 1.

Local and regional governance

8.1 Introduction and objectives

One of the most apparent paradoxes of the French polity lies in the co-existence of rigid centralised judicial norms and rules, and a rich diversity of local and regional situations and practices. This diversity exists in spite of (or because of) the uniform presence upon the territory of metropolitan France of three levels of subnational government and administration: the commune (36,518), the departmental council (96) and the regional council (22). Following on from the discussion of the French state in Chapter 7, Chapter 8 analyses the formal units of French local and regional government, with particular reference to the Socialist decentralisation reforms of the early 1980s. An attempt is made to formulate some conclusions in relation to the impact and consequences of these reforms more than one decade after their implementation.

8.2 Patterns of French local governance

The commune

As the oldest and most revered territorial unit in France, the commune demands attention. With the commune, France has probably the smallest local politico-administrative structure of any country. France's 36,518 communes elect 550,000 local councillors, almost 500,000 of whom represent 34,000 rural or small town communes with fewer than 1,500 inhabitants. The modern commune is based on the parishes drawn up by the church between the tenth and twelfth centuries. Communal boundaries were redrawn during the French Revolution, but they usually respected the older parish boundaries. The basic structure of French municipal government is laid down by the 1884 Municipal Government Act. Although the size and character of communes vary enormously, each disposes of the same legal rights and obligations. This poses major difficulties, given that the policy problems faced by municipal authorities in large French cities have little in common with those of rural hamlets. Apart from the special exception of Paris, the same municipal laws have traditionally regulated local government in large cities as well in small rural communes.

This system was established to cope with a rural society. The judicial status of the commune is thus disconnected from specific urban problems. Around ten metropolitan cities have developed rapidly, and can now boast over 500,000 inhabitants, but except for Paris, Lyons and Marseilles no new political or administrative structures have emerged to cope with this expansion. Until 1977, Paris did not have a mayor, but a prefect and a prefect of police named by the central government. In 1977 the first direct election of the Mayor of Paris transformed the office into a major national political prize. No government can henceforth ignore the Paris town hall, the power base from 1977 to 1995 of President Chirac. Special regimes were also introduced for Lyons and Marseilles in 1982.

However inefficient the communes appear on paper, most French citizens identify with their commune, and express confidence in their mayor. Attempts to reform local government by regrouping communes into larger units have usually been met by hostility. The commune is a symbol of civic identification. The next echelon, the canton, is a far more artificial institution, which often regroups communes with diverging interests and different socioeconomic compositions.

Their diverse situations mean that it is difficult to make too many generalisations concerning France's 36,518 communes. The size and geographical location of a particular commune are more indicative of its nature than the mere fact of its being a commune. An accurate portrayal of the French commune has to distinguish between small and medium-sized communes (up to 20,000 inhabitants), which generally exist in a dependent relationship with, and look for protection from, higher-placed local, regional and state authorities (especially the 96 departments); and larger urban communes, which adopt characteristics of city governments. The preoccupations facing the two types of authority are completely different: small rural communes usually have to combine forces to provide even such basic services as water provision and waste disposal. Large urban communes are genuine city governments, often employing thousands of local authority employees, disposing of large budgets and providing a wide range of social, economic and cultural services.

Communes are distinguished from other layers of French subnational government by their proximity to local citizens. The demands placed on municipal governments far outweigh their material possibilities, as well as their legal responsibilities. Their core service delivery responsibilities involve housing, primary education, water, fire prevention, land use, streetlighting, sewerage and waste disposal. Ambitious communes provide a range of additional services such as cultural animation and economic development. Aside from their role as service providers, municipal governments are the focal point of France's thousands of local communities. They are also the site for the playing out of local political rivalries and personal ambitions.

The sheer number of French communes requires intercommunal co-operation in order to provide basic service provision in domains such as transport, road maintenance and waste disposal. This is especially the case in rural communes, but urban problems also are rarely confined to the boundaries of a single commune, especially in large cities. City-centre authorities are usually associated with outlying communes in order to provide services such as housing, fire prevention and urban planning. Such associations can take several forms: these range from intercommunal syndicates performing basic service functions, to highly complex districts and urban communities that take over many of the traditional communal functions.

The key resource that all communes share (and jealously guard for themselves) is that they control the development of the land over which their jurisdiction is based. This comprises a total of 90 per cent of national territory. Within the confines of the Urban Code, communes can grant or withhold planning permission for public or private sector developments. Such a resource is becoming increasingly important as the demand for development land intensifies. Environmental critics complain that weak planning controls – and the general lack of a Green Belt policy – have led to uncontrolled expansion initiated by irresponsible local authorities. Urban expansion has occurred in part because communes compete with each other in order to attract business and consumer investment into their areas. The system of local government taxation increases such competition between communes.[1]

The central figure in French small town and rural society is the mayor, who performs the combined roles of locally elected politician and servant of the state. The contrast between the mayor of a small town of up to 10,000 inhabitants and the mayor of a large metropolitan city is striking. Whereas the former personally or indirectly knows most of the town's citizens, the relationship between the big city mayor and his or her electors is based on more indirect channels of communication. The big city mayor is usually a national political figure as well, with severe constraints on his or her time. In small communes, the mayor is usually the only person who can co-ordinate the activities of the different administrative agencies. In the large cities, mayors will use their national influence to ensure – as far as possible – that the decisions taken by local administrative agencies do not discriminate against their interests. In both types of commune, mayors attempt to consolidate their local influence by sponsoring a range of local associations. Another means of influence lies in the manner of delivery of local services, which can create faithful clients anxious for the survival of the municipal team. A successful mayor attempts to maintain good relations with the principal interests of his or her commune, including the main local associations and charities, local businesses, representatives of the state (prefectorial, ministerial and departmental civil servants) and political interests (especially the local party and local electors).

In the main cities, French mayors have performed a prominent role in promoting local economic networks to attract funds and investment into their localities in an era of increasing municipal competition (Le Galès, 1993). The mayor-entrepreneur metaphor should not be overstressed, however. Mayors must interest themselves in everything that goes on in their cities, including in the insalubrious poorer quarters:

efforts to improve living standards in visibly deprived areas are probably more important for their survival than high-level prestige projects, especially in a climate of municipal corruption. If French mayors have forged closer links with business interests since the early 1980s, these are not exclusive; close links with networks of non-economic associations have proved essential for their survival. The decentralisation process has also strengthened the role of the mayor's fellow executive officers (*adjoints*), sometimes capable of building their own powerful networks independently of their mayor.

A long-standing theme of the French literature has been that the political prestige of the local *notable* with national connections facilitates access to other local actors: the prefect, the ministerial field services, the departmental and regional executives, and the local and national civil servants (Crozier and Thoenig, 1975; Dupuy and Thoenig, 1983). The practice of multiple office holding (*cumul des mandats*) is a central feature of the French political system. The logic of this system preceded the decentralisation reforms of the early 1980s. Given the dispersal of decision-making authority across a range of separate institutions, individual politicians felt compelled to accumulate political offices in order to consolidate their own political positions and to strengthen their bargaining position in relation to others, especially the departmental prefect. A classic example is that of a mayor who was also elected deputy. As a simple mayor, he or she occupied a relatively weak bargaining position *vis-à-vis* the departmental prefect or other local authorities. A deputy-mayor, on the other hand, could defend local interests more effectively, since national connections could be called upon to overcome the resistance of a departmental prefect. Any genuine *notable* could usually ensure the defence of his or her essential interests against the prefect, the state's departmental representative.

The shortcomings of this system were obvious. Individuals sometimes accumulated five or six political offices, in addition to unofficial duties. They were unable to fulfil all the obligations involved with these offices, but they were determined to prevent a political opponent from gaining ground within any one of their fiefs. In its defence, this system was functional, since it ensured a degree of linkage between otherwise disconnected local and national spheres of government. In 1990 individuals were limited to holding two 'significant' political offices. 'Significant' offices included deputy, senator, member of the European Parliament, mayor of a town with over 20,000 inhabitants, regional councillor and departmental councillor. However, political *notables* continue to combine two 'significant' offices with the less important elective positions, such as mayor of a small town or rural commune.

The practice of multiple office holding remains deeply embedded in the mentalities of French politicians. Thus, the campaign for the 1995 municipal elections was enriched by the spectacle of former President Giscard d'Estaing attempting (and failing) to be elected as Mayor of Clermont-Ferrand. In the same elections, eleven members of Alain Juppé's government sought election or re-election as mayors, including the Prime Minister himself, who succeeded another former premier (Chaban-Delmas) as Mayor of Bordeaux. Despite certain abuses, the practice of *cumul des mandats* is an essential mechanism for enabling the smooth functioning of France's politico-administrative system. There is a problem of link-age between the different layers of government; the practice of *cumul des mandats* facilitates such communication.

8.3 Decentralisation

In the past decade, studies of the Socialists' decentralisation programme have pro-liferated, both in France, and amongst external observers (Dion, 1986; Keating and Hainsworth, 1986; Rondin, 1986; Mény, 1987; Biarez, 1989; Ashford, 1990; Schmidt, 1990a). The principles underpinning the decentralisation reforms were rather contradictory, reflecting the pressures of the competing interests at stake. Greater democracy and citizen participation were declared objectives of the 1982–3 reforms. In opposition in the 1970s, the Socialists had called for an increase in citizen participation and self-management, notably by creating neighbourhood councils, and promoting associations and consumer groups to encourage new forms of access to local decision making. The Socialists argued that the proximity of municipal, departmental and regional authorities made them the appropriate suppliers of an extensive range of services. Proximity was more democratic. It was also more efficient, since it avoided unnecessary bureaucratic delays and allowed local authorities greater choice in prioritising their activities. For critics, the real issue at stake involved not democratisation, but the removal of constraints on the power of entrenched municipal *notables*, especially prominent within the ranks of the Socialist Party.

The decentralisation reforms of 1982–3 were of such complexity that their im-pact is only becoming clear over a decade after their implementation (Lorrain, 1993). The reforms created 22 elected regional assemblies, replacing previously co-opted institutions, and greatly enhanced the decision-making powers of the 96 departmental councils and of the larger communes. The decision-making respon-sibilities of a range of local actors were increased, with the extension of their influence into policy sectors within which they previously exercised a marginal influence, or from which they were excluded altogether (such as social affairs, economic development and education). The three layers of French subnational government – the region, the department and the commune – were all strengthened, with increases in budgets, staff and powers.

Observers agree that the subnational system in France has become more frag-mented since 1982. There is a larger number of local actors than ever before. There is also a great deal of confusion in relation to who should do what. The de-centralisation reforms attributed spheres of competence (*blocs de compétence*) to each type of local authority. These spheres of competence consisted of specific services that were best executed at a particular level. The 22 regions were invested with important powers of economic planning, infrastructure development, trans-port and secondary education. The 96 departments were to take over from the state the responsibility for social affairs and post-primary education (excluding pedagogy). The communes were strengthened in matters of urbanism, planning permission, land use and primary education. In practice, this neat division has proved impossible to implement. The situation bequeathed by the Socialist decentralisation reform has proved an extremely complicated one. The responsibility for delivering services is divided between several layers of local and regional authority, as outlined in Table 8.1.

The various subnational authorities have overlapping territorial jurisdictions and loosely defined spheres of competence. Above all, there is no formal hierarchy between them. In theory, no single authority can impose its will on any other, or prevent a rival authority from adopting policies in competition with its own. The prefecture has lost its role as traditional arbiter of local conflicts. Local and

Table 8.1 Subnational authorities in France

Type	Number	Functions
Communes	36,518	Varying services, including local plans (POS), building permits, housing, building and maintenance of primary schools, waste disposal and some welfare services
Intercommunal syndicates*	Not available	Groups of communes with a single function (SIVU) or delivering multiple services (SIVOM)
Districts*	62	Permanent voluntary organisations in charge of intercommunal services such as firefighting, waste disposal, transport, economic development and housing
Urban communities*	9	Statutory intercommunal organisations; similar services to districts, with a more constraining character
Departmental councils	96	Social affairs, some secondary education (*collèges*), road building and maintenance
Regional councils	22	Economic development, transport, infrastructure, state–region plans and some secondary education (*lycées*)

* These organisations are legally considered as local public establishments, rather than fully fledged local authorities.

regional authorities have overlapping areas of responsibility. Even when the spheres of competence are clear, they are not always respected: communes, departments and regions often appear in a position of open competition with each other, with each adopting policies designed to appeal to its particular electorate.

8.4 Who gained the most from the decentralisation reforms?

The communes

On paper, the communes gained least. Municipal governments already had an elected executive. The mayor has always had responsibility for drawing up the commune's budget and executing the decisions of the municipal council, although traditionally this power depended upon creating a *modus vivendi* with the prefect (or subprefect for mayors of smaller communes). Active municipal councils in the major French cities were already pursuing ambitious progammes of urban renovation in the 1960s and 1970s (Le Galès, 1993). Since the 1982–3 legislation, the prefect can no longer veto the mayor's decisions, which must be implemented if they respect the law. The prefect retains the right to challenge their legality or financial probity in the administrative courts or regional Courts of Accounts, but this control is exercised *a posteriori* (contesting decisions already taken by local authorities, rather than vetoing them in advance). It is used sparingly. The mayor's powers have undoubtedly been reinforced in numerous spheres: for example, over town planning, municipal housing, employment and local economic policy.

As measured in terms of budgets and staff, the communes remain by far the most important local authorities in France, but their situation varies dramatically. The ability to exercise an influence beyond their traditional duties depends upon the financial and logistical resources that communes have at their disposal. Small communes continue to depend upon outside advice and assistance in order to carry out their legal functions. The mayors of small communes used to depend upon the prefect or subprefect for advice; they now seek protection from elected representatives of the departmental councils. The smallest communes are often incapable of deciding upon the merits of planning applications, for example. Preceding decentralisation, small communes called upon the field services of the Equipment Ministry (DDE) to examine applications for building permits. Since 1983, they have as often called upon the technical services of the departmental council, but they continue to call for outside assistance. The mayors of large towns fared better from decentralisation. Only large cities are in a position to create extensive bureaucracies. Urban planning agencies have expanded in the main French cities, which testifies to the determination of local authorities to plan their local environment. Dynamic entrepreneurial mayors have succeeded in launching major local renovation projects in large metropolitan centres, such as Grenoble, Toulouse and Lille.

The departmental councils

The most obvious victors of the decentralisation reforms were the 96 departmental councils (*conseils généraux*). The battle between 'regionalists' and 'departmentalists' was lively during the decentralisation debates of 1982–3. The departments emerged as the clear victors, invested with larger budgets, more staff and more service delivery responsibilities than the regions. Powerful entrenched interests already operated through the departments, while the regions were untried and untested. Central government preferred to deal with the relatively subservient departments, rather than strong regions which might contest its authority.

Decentralisation conferred new functions on the departments, but these were not new institutions. Departments are composed of cantons, of which there are some 2,000, generally concentrated in rural and small town areas. Along with the commune, the canton has subsisted since the French Revolution. The original justification for the department was to enable any inhabitant to travel to and from the prefecture on horseback in one day; this makes no sense in the age of the high-speed train, the TGV. Due to population movements and demographic changes, the boundaries of France's 2,000 cantons are heavily overrepresentative of rural areas. Inequalities in representation are enormous: in 1992 the smallest canton had 261 inhabitants; the largest over 60,000 (Bréhier, 1994).

The departmental councils have benefited from a new democratic legitimacy, in addition to increased staffs and budgets. The presidency of the departmental council has become one of the coveted positions in French local government. Since 1982 the president of the departmental council has been legally recognised as the fount of executive power within the department, replacing the centrally nominated prefect. In the opinion of one interviewee: 'the change at the level of the departments was enormous, far more significant than for the communes'. The president of the departmental council has inherited certain functions of the prefect, notably that of advising and co-ordinating the activities of small communes. For this reason, the presidency of the departmental council has been a favoured resting place for ex-ministers (and even ex-Presidents of the Republic).

The key resources at the disposal of the departmental councils are financial, bureaucratic and legal. The financial resources of the departments are important: benefiting from the transfer of state funds (in the form of specific grants-in-aid and a general block grant), the departments also have the right to raise local taxation and to charge for services. The departmental president is responsible for preparing the council's budget, previously drawn up by the prefect's services. Departmental budgets can be considerable: that of the Nord department in 1995 was Ff 8,000 million ($1,600 million), twice the amount of the Nord/Pas-de-Calais regional budget, although the region catered for 4 million inhabitants, as against 2.5 million for the department. The key advantage held by the departments over other territorial authorities stems from their powerful bureaucratic resources: with decentralisation, the departments took charge of most of the civil servants previously attached to the prefectures. In certain rare cases, the departmental councils have

also taken direct control of the personnel of the field services of government ministries, notably the DDE. The departments were able to rely upon a tested bureaucratic personnel, while the regions had to experiment and innovate.

These inequalities reflect the differing services that are delivered by the two types
of authority. The services that the departmental councils are legally obliged to
deliver include social services, health care, post-primary education and departmental road-building programmes. Defenders of the departments point out that these
basic services rarely occupy the limelight, but involve an extremely sophisticated
financial and organisational infrastructure. The cost of social service provision has
escalated dramatically, plunging several departmental councils into a severe financial crisis. Departments have also taken over responsibility for services they did not
ask for: this is notably the case for the minimum income, created by the Rocard
government in 1988.

Apart from their statutory obligations, departmental councils can engage in
policies in other areas, except where they are specifically forbidden to do so. The
departmental councils compete with the regions and the communes in the economic development sphere, adopting their own policies usually concerned with
safeguarding non-urban interests. As for big city mayors, the launching of major
infrastructure projects is often a matter of prestige; each departmental president
wants to associate his or her name with a major project.

The constraints weighing upon France's 96 departmental councils are multiple.
In common with other territorial authorities, many departmental councils have
fallen seriously into debt in carrying out their new responsibilities. In spite of their
powerful organisation and financial resources, the departments are felt to lack
political legitimacy. Departmental councillors are renewed by halves every three
years. They represent individual cantons, rather than places on a party list. Unlike
the mayor, the departmental president is not directly elected as head of a party list,
but represents an individual constituency (or canton). His or her status is that of
primus inter pares (first among equals), rather than that of executive mayor. Presidents must strike bargains to rally support from other councillors, who are often
notables in their own right. This electoralism militates against the promotion of
coherent long-term policies. Departmental presidents might be *notables*, but they
have to deal equally with other *notables*, especially the mayors of large cities. They
must also co-operate with powerful deputies or senators, and party chiefs.

Departmental councils must also cope with the competition of other layers of
subnational government: namely, the regions and the cities. Relations between the
departmental council and the department's leading city are often acrimonious, on
account of the overrepresentation of rural and small town areas in most departmental councils. The political affinities of the large cities and the countryside are
frequently opposed, with the left strongly represented in urban areas and the right
in the departments (three-quarters of which are under UDF or RPR control). Large
cities and the departmental councils are often the focus of conflicting local interests.
The departmental council feels more at ease with the small and medium-sized
communes, for which it performs the role of adviser and benefactor. Insofar as they

are capable of performing such a role, the departments attempt to act as arbiters between the traditional ethos of the French countryside and the dynamic, growth-oriented towns.

The regions

The regions were created in 1972, but in most areas they had a nominal existence prior to 1986. The innovation of the decentralisation legislation of 1982–3 lay in the provision that the regions should be directly elected. To the extent that the regions owe their existence as full authorities to the decentralisation legislation, they can also claim to be victors of the decentralisation process. They benefited indirectly from the removal of prefectoral control, and from the creation of a directly elected executive. This gave them an authority they had never possessed before. Most experts today consider that France's system of subnational government has 'one layer too many'. While the department has its defenders, for many the region would appear as a more logical structure, especially in the context of European Union regional policy, which only recognises states and regions as possible recipients of EU aid.

As argued above, the 'regionalists' lost out in the debates surrounding the decentralisation legislation. Relations between the departments and the regions are often acerbic. At their inception, the regions had neither the organisational past nor the bureaucratic resources of the departmental councils. Unlike the departments, they were unable to rely on the transfer of state personnel, although many state civil servants opted for the challenge of serving the new regions. In contrast to the sizeable bureaucracies serving the large cities and the departments, the organisational resources available to the regions are minimal: there are fewer than 100 salaried staff in most regions.

Moreover, as the regions were untested institutions, existing *notables* preferred not to invest their time in adding regional posts to their existing offices. This had the initial effect of making most regional presidents second-rank politicians, placed in position by departmental élites who were anxious to ensure that the regions did not discover a real existence. A few powerful regional presidents emerged, but their power had been established prior to acceding to the regional presidency. Examples were Olivier Guichard in Pays de la Loire, Michel d'Ornano in Basse-Normandie, and Jacques Chaban-Delmas in Acquitaine. Except in these isolated cases, regional political leadership was no real match for that of the large cities or departments. This situation has changed gradually, but there remains a penchant for other elective offices before those of the region.

The president of the regional council is elected by his or her peers at the first council meeting; this usually involves horsetrading between several parties, and subtle coalition arrangements which vary from one region to another. The regions have suffered from the electoral system used for the six-yearly elections to the regional assemblies. The use of a highly proportional version of proportional representation for elections to the regional assemblies has produced numerous hung councils since 1986, which have proved incapable of imposing a clear political direction. In contrast, at the level of the departmental councils, the use of the majority two-ballot system in cantonal elections has encouraged single-party majorities, or at least coherent coalitions. For this reason, regionalists have urged a reform of the electoral system, whereas departmentalists have declared themselves satisfied with it.

The regional councils are invested with the executive powers over regional policy in a specified number of areas: certain aspects of secondary education (buildings and investment), regional transport and certain types of infrastructure. As they have become established, they have added new policy responsibilities, notably that of adult training policy. But rather than being a major service delivery institution, the role of the region is above all one of consultation, co-ordination and planning. There is considerable debate among French specialists as to the real extent of the regions' influence. For certain observers (Le Galès, 1995) the essential distinction rests between cities and departments, with the regions left almost as bystanders. There is a new mode of urban governance concentrated around dynamic municipal teams, counterbalanced by the role of the departments in safeguarding rural and small town interests. This view might be tempered by observing that the regions have exercised a growing influence in certain specific policy sectors, notably education, training and economic planning. However, the situation has been variable: where there are genuinely strong regional identities (such as in Brittany), the regional assemblies have had a real political existence; where there is no tradition of regionalisation (such as in Limousin, Auvergne and the centre), this has been less the case.

The regions possess two powerful resources: they are the natural negotiating partners of the state, through the mechanism of the state–region contracts; and the regional level is that favoured by European Union regional development policies. This brings them into permanent contact with the regional field services of the French state, especially those involved with European policy. As their authority has become established, there is some evidence that the regions have acted as the intermediaries between the state and other local authorities, and that they are acquiring new policy responsibilities. On occasion, they have been invested with authority to negotiate in the name of the other local authorities. These factors promise a brighter role for the regions in the future, but for the moment they remain the newcomers in the French system of local governance.

8.5 The French prefect and the decentralised state

Local policy implementation, co-ordination and arbitration were classically the domain of the French prefect, the official representative of the centralised post-Napoleonic state in the French departments. Directly appointed by the Interior Minister, until 1982 the prefect was able to exercise a considerable degree of supervisory control – *la tutelle* – over local authorities. As representative of the central state, the prefect retained formal hierarchical control over local authority budgets and policy implementation, leaving locally elected authorities in a clearly subordinate position.

However, the reality was more complex than this formal hierarchical model suggests. The exercise of the prefect's influence depended not only upon support from Paris, but also on striking compromises with mayors, departmental presidents and other local *notables*. The successful prefect was both a central agent in relation to the local political community, and a firm advocate of the department's cause in Paris. The extent of any prefect's influence depended traditionally as much upon the position he or she occupied within a local political community, as upon the formal powers invested on the prefect by the state. Even before the decentralisation reforms of 1982–3, the mayors of large French cities were able to override departmental prefects on account of their national standing and their access to government departments (Crozier and Thoenig, 1975). The prefect's influence was more obvious in small communes (where he or she acted as adviser and occasional provider of funds for investment projects) than in large cities.

The prefect undoubtedly lost prestige during the early stages of the decentralisation process, symbolised by the material fact of losing many staff. But there is a case for arguing that the prefect has gained more influence as the recognised co-ordinator of the state at the level of the department than he or she lost as the *tutelle* authority. The traditional prefectoral control role has weakened. True, the prefect retains two principal formal powers in relation to local authorities. The prefect can refer all local decrees to regional administrative tribunals to ensure their legality. This power is used sparingly, but its tempo does vary according to political circumstances. The threat of decrees being referred to administrative tribunals is usually sufficient to ensure that municipal acts are rigorously in accordance with the law. The prefect also has the right to refer local authority budgets to the new regional Courts of Accounts. *A posteriori* control over local decisions has been used extremely sparingly, and usually on minor issues. Prefects continue to act as advisers to mayors of smaller communes, but the latter turn increasingly to departmental councillors and officials instead. Prefects have recognised their diminished status; a considerable number have gone 'on sabbatical' in order to take up the position of chief of staff under the presidents of regional or departmental councils. Prefects retain their traditional control over law and order.

To some extent the post-decentralisation French state of the late-1990s is witnessing a return of the prefect as arbiter and co-ordinator of the local state. As the chief representative of the state, the prefect formally exercises authority over the ministerial field services. In the 1992 Deconcentration Charter, the prefect was recognised as the sole co-ordinator of the government's activities. The impact of the 'deconcentration' measures of the 1980s was rather paradoxical and uneven across the different ministries concerned. As a general rule, deconcentration combined more autonomous decision-making powers (or at least discretion) for the ministerial field services with a reinforced co-ordinating role for the prefect. These two principles were not obviously compatible. Tensions within the regional state might be illustrated by considering relations between prefects and officials working for government departments.

The prefect and the ministerial field services

The extent of the prefect's control over the field services of the Parisian ministries varies considerably according to locality, as well as the nature of the government department involved. In a recent study (Im, 1993), three distinct types of relationship were diagnosed: those where the field services were placed under the direct control of the prefect (Employment, Youth, Sports); those deconcentrated ministries which enjoyed independence, but where the prefect could prevail if necessary (Equipment, Agriculture); and those ministries which fiercely resisted any prefectoral oversight (Finance, Justice, Education).

The greatest threat to prefectoral oversight resides in the fact that Paris-based ministries insist on transmitting orders directly to their field services, seeking thereby to bypass the prefect's co-ordinating role. In spite of the prefect's claim to co-ordinate government activity within the departments and regions, ministers (and leading civil servants) often insist upon transmitting orders directly to their representatives on the ground, and marshal their own political resources to ensure that unfavourable prefectoral arbitrations do not occur. The resources at the disposal of the prefect to prevent this are limited.

The official means by which the prefect ensures co-ordination is via the inter-ministerial mail service (*service du courrier*): all correspondence and government circulars must first be addressed to the departmental prefecture, before being distributed to the relevant agencies. But, as one General Secretary admitted, there was nothing to stop Parisian civil servants from sending faxes to their field services. More official co-ordination occurs via the Regional Administrative Conference: this monthly meeting unites the departmental prefects of a region, along with key representatives of the ministerial field services, in an attempt to co-ordinate government policy. A participant of these meetings was of the opinion that they tended to ratify agreements reached informally elsewhere. The various field services receive their budgets directly from their department's expenditure total. They do not depend upon the prefecture for their resources; the role of financial probity is ensured by the Trésorier-Payeur général (TPG). This departmental representative of the Finance Ministry remains vigorously independent of the prefecture, although in practice the two are often called upon to work together.

In conjunction with the observations made in Chapter 7, the above appraisal points to a process of redefining the role of the French state, challenged from below by the pressures of local governance, and from above by the consequences of globalisation and European integration. This movement has had an impact upon the internal organisation of the state, notably with respect to internal management practices and patterns of recruitment. Notwithstanding the uniformity of administrative rules governing relations within the French state, detailed case studies from the departments and regions have demonstrated that the situation of the field services of Parisian ministries on the ground varies greatly: some enjoy almost total local autonomy, others depend tightly upon hierarchical commands from their ministries, others are effectively co-ordinated by the prefecture (Jeannot and Peraldi, 1991; Im, 1993). This depends partly on the culture of a particular region, and partly on the type of government agency involved.

8.6 Whither decentralisation?

There is little dispute that decentralisation reforms have had a major impact upon French centre–periphery relations. There remains much confusion about the division of policy making and administrative tasks between central and subnational units, and among the local authorities themselves. To some extent, new patterns of policy making have emerged, based on networks of decision-makers and the influence of new actors, including those from the private sector (Lorrain, 1993). It appears certain that the proliferation of policy actors has blurred responsibilities and diminished political accountability.

The consequences of the decentralisation reforms were not those initially predicted. The most obvious impact has been in relation to new financial arrangements, partnerships, municipal corruption and the complexity of subnational decision making. These consequences were not tied only to the decentralisation reforms, which either amplified movements already under way (such as urban renovation) or shed new light on practices that had probably already existed (such as municipal corruption).

New financial arrangements

State financial transfers form an important part of the budgets of communal, departmental and regional councils. In addition to a general central government block grant (*dotation globale de fonctionnement*), regional and local authorities receive financial support from the *dotation générale de la décentralisation* (DGD), a fund specifically designed to compensate for new policy responsibilities under decentralisation, and the *dotation générale d'équipement* (DGE), a general fund to cover investment items.

The proportion of state transfers in local government revenues has diminished progressively since 1982, with an increasing proportion of local government revenue spent on servicing debt. The problem of municipal debt emerges as one of the principal legacies of decentralisation. With diminishing real central government income for local authorities, ambitious economic development or cultural projects in the 1980s had to be financed through borrowing, raising local taxes or soliciting support from the private sector. The room for manoeuvre at the disposal of mayors is limited: revenue raising by increasing local taxes hits companies which are relied upon to provide local employment. As in other European countries, central

Table 8.2 Local government finance (Ff billions)

Year	1980	1985	1991	1993
Communes				
Total expenditure	132.3	249.4	377.4	409.9
Income	137.1	252.6	374.7	410.9
of which:				
Taxes	49.2	103.3	158.7	180.8
Central transfers	49.4	87.8	125.2	132.0
Borrowing	18.2	29.5	37.3	45.0
Other sources	20.3	32.0	53.5	53.1
Departments				
Total expenditure	70.1	119.7	186.7	205.8
Income	71.4	122.5	182.8	208.4
of which:				
Taxes	21.8	59.0	98.6	106.8
Transfers	41.8	49.2	61.9	65.7
Borrowing	5.3	10.2	14.4	27.4
Other sources	2.5	4.1	7.9	8.5
Regions				
Total expenditure	5.0	18.3	55.4	62.7
Total income	4.8	18.2	53.7	63.0
of which:				
Taxes	2.5	9.8	27.5	31.4
Transfers	0.5	2.8	15.1	18.5
Borrowing	0.8	2.6	8.8	10.3
Other sources	1.0	3.0	2.3	2.8

Source: INSEE, *Tableaux de l'économie française*, 1995–6, p. 119.

controls over local government expenditure form part of a more general effort to rein in public expenditure, but the evidence points to limited success in this sphere.

Partnerships

One unintended impact of the decentralisation process has been to increase the number and variety of partnerships with which local and regional authorities are involved. Certain public sector partnerships are virtually imposed by the central state: the quinquennial state–region contracts, for instance, determine the rights, responsibilities and financial contributions of the various public sector partners called upon to participate in mainly centrally defined programmes. In a context where responsibilities are blurred, major infrastructure projects require co-operation between several actors. Other forms of partnership encouraged by de-centralisation have included joint venture projects between local authorities and private sector capital (the Mixed Economy Societies), and the more systematic tendering out of municipal services (such as waste disposal and heating) to the private sector (Lorrain and Stoker, 1995).

Corruption

The granting of control over new resources to local politicians coincided with a spate of local corruption scandals. These practices were not necessarily new, but became more visible with decentralisation. In several cities (for instance, Grenoble), the role of mayors in determining public works contracts, or in granting land use permission for development, was exposed as a powerful incentive for corruption. One side effect of decentralisation has been to lessen the esteem with which municipal élites have traditionally been held, although the high rate of re-election of incumbent mayors in the 1995 municipal elections suggested that one's own mayor was generally exempt from excessive criticism. While there is much evidence of local corruption, those involved in municipal politics often suspected the anti-corruption campaign of being co-ordinated by the Parisian *grands corps*, determined to recover their lost influence.

The weakening of the state?

The losers of the decentralisation process were the *grands corps* and the central ministries considered in Chapter 7. The technical corps – notably Mining, and Highways and Bridges – experienced the whole decentralisation process as an affront to their own legitimacy and prestige. These *corps* sought to recover power, especially since the bureaucratic services of the regions and cities escaped from their influence. The enhanced role of cities in urban development has occurred at the expense of central planners and engineers, whose role has undoubtedly diminished. A continuing reaction is to be expected.

8.7 Conclusion and summary

On a positive reading, decentralisation has improved local democracy, reduced the tutelage of the central state and strengthened the checks and balances within the French political system. A less positive interpretation might point to a confusion of service delivery responsibilities and an absence of genuine political accountability. Whichever interpretation is favoured, decentralisation was a reform with unintended consequences. While the debates surrounding the reform of 1982–3 centred on democracy, participation and proximity, the legacy of decentralisation has been in part one of corruption, municipal debt and the greater input of private sector actors into local policy making. The term 'governance' is useful in this context, since it allows a fuller understanding of the broad range of actors involved in the new governing processes. Alongside the various local government and state actors analysed in this chapter, other players with an influence in local and regional politics include the chambers of commerce, voluntary associations, professional interest groups and party organisations.

At the level of the departments, decentralisation has been portrayed as 'a three-way contest for influence among the prefects, the state field services and the council presidents' (Garraud, 1989). To this should be added the mayors of large cities and a host of other actors who are more or less important depending upon the policy sector concerned, the attitude of central government and the nature of the local political community. The outcome of this contest depends in any one department upon the local political and economic circumstances, the talents and determination of the actors involved, and the role that the state actors choose to play. There is no uniform model of local political influence stemming from the decentralisation legislation.

If certain segments of the state have suffered from the effects of decentralisation, it would be unwise to conclude that there has been a general weakening of the state. The French state retains enormous regulatory and fiscal powers, and remains deeply involved in local affairs. It acts as an arbiter between the conflicting claims of different local authorities. It defines the conditions under which decentralised units function. It retains control over most local government finance. It continues to determine apportionment criteria for grants to subnational units. The taxation instruments available to local councils are crude; and they are not at liberty to avail themselves of new instruments. Finally, unlike Germany or Belgium, France re-mains a unitary system of government, at liberty to increase or reduce the preroga-tives of local government in accordance with the perceived interest of the centre.

Note

1 Communal revenue is based on four separate taxes: the professional tax, levied on companies present within the commune; the habitation tax, levied on all residents, and two minor land taxes. The most important of these is the professional tax, the level of which is determined in part by each commune. The professional tax sets communes against each other, and leads them to attempt to 'poach' each other's firms and commerce.

Indicative bibliography

Bernard, P. (1982) 'La Fonction préfectorale au coeur de la mutation de notre société', *Revue administrative*, vol. 45, no. 2.

Biarez, S. (1989) *Le Pouvoir local*, Economica, Paris.

Bréhier, T. (1994) 'Le Conseil général, pierre angulaire de la politique française', *Le Monde*, 19 March.

de Forges, J.-M. (1989) *Les Institutions administratives françaises*, PUF, Paris.

Dupuy, F. and J.-C. Theonig (1983) *Sociologie de l'administration française*, Armand Colin, Paris.

Garraud, P. (1989) *Profession homme politique. La carrière politique des maires urbains*, Harmattan, Paris.

Le Galès, P.(1993) *Politique urbaine et developpement local*, Harmattan, Paris.

Loughlin, J. and S. Mazey (1994) 'The end of the French unitary state? Ten years of regionalization in France', *Regional Politics and Policy*, vol. 4, no. 3.

Mabileau, A. (1991) *Le Système local en France*, Montchrestien, Paris.

Schmidt, V. (1990) *Democratising France*, Cambridge University Press, Cambridge.

Part III

Political forces and representation

Chapter 9

The development of the French party system

9.1 Introduction and objectives

Chapter 9 is the first of three chapters on the French party sytem. The themes addressed in this chapter include a brief history of French parties, an overview of the evolution of party and electoral competition since 1958, and the impact of presidentialism on the organisation and objectives of French parties. In the final section, an attempt will be made to situate French parties in the broader context of theories and typologies of European party systems.

A system of competing political parties is generally held to be a key defining feature of a liberal-democratic political system. Although the 1958 constitution recognises the legitimacy of political parties as 'representative institutions', a powerful strand of Gaullism has denigrated political parties as divisive, fractious organisations, whose existence is barely tolerated, and this on condition that they do not threaten the superior interests of the republic. In the Gaullist tradition, parties have never been wholeheartedly accepted as instruments of democracy, reflecting a distrust of representative democracy in favour of a direct relationship between the providential leader and the nation. But a distrust of intermediary bodies between the citizens and the state (such as parties and pressure groups) is not limited to Gaullism. It is deeply embedded in the ideology of the unitary state itself. In the Rousseauite tradition, the state represents the general will, superior to the particularistic interests represented by parties, groups and regions. There is no natural sympathy for doctrines such as pluralism which emphasise the importance of the *corps intermédiaires* between the citizen and the state. In part, this is a natural consequence of France's historical development.

9.2 The origins of the French party system

What we might label as modern-day parliamentary factions first emerged in the course of the nineteenth century in Europe, in those liberal European regimes with representative assemblies or parliaments. Such factions existed initially at a parliamentary level. Only later did parliamentary factions organise throughout the nation as a whole. Within France, the moderate republicans of the early Third Republic fitted this description well. Prior to the twentieth century, what passed for political parties were often little more than constellations of supporters based around political *notables*, whose power lay in their social, economic or political control over a local community. Centralised, coherent and disciplined parties were non-existent on the centre and right, and deficient or fractious on the left. In the Third Republic (1870–1940), the French party system reflected the profound divisions within French society. It was highly unstable and fragmented. During this period, there were multiple lines of social cleavage which meant that no one party, or even combination of parties, had a natural majority of support within the country. France of the Third Republic was above all a localised society, divided into a multitude of different regions, each suspicious of the other, and of the centralising authority of Paris.

The localised bases of society had consequences for the organisation of political parties. In Paris, the deputy was a fervent constituency ambassador before being a party representative. Indeed, many independent-minded deputies were not elected on any party label, or would be elected for one party, but sit with another in the Chamber of Deputies. The significance of party labels varied in different parts of the country. For this reason in the Third Republic, it was somewhat misleading to talk of national parties. The obvious comparison was with the pork-barrel politics that still characterise elections to the US Congress. Finally, policy divisions between parties were aggravated by the nature of the parliamentary-dominated system: small parties frequently changed coalitions in order to obtain temporary advantage. This exacerbated a situation of inherent governmental instability.

By the end of the nineteenth century, parties had spread throughout most European nations, in response to the gradual extension of the suffrage. In the course of the twentieth century, freely competing political parties were repressed for authoritarian alternatives in a number of European countries: this occurred notably in Italy, Germany, Spain and Portugal. Except for the Vichy interlude of 1940–4, this did not occur in France. The French party system is marked by a measure of underlying continuity which belies the baffling array of party labels, the rise and fall of minor parties, and the emergence of new political movements such as Gaullism. These political families will be considered in the next chapter.

In M. Duverger's terminology, the earliest French parties were formed as cadre parties of the bourgeois variety (Duverger, 1964). They first developed within the Chamber of Deputies as parliamentary factions, and only gradually extended their coverage downwards and outwards towards the grass roots. These parties were forced to establish wider party organisations in order to cope with the need to organise elections, but they remained essentially parliamentary-dominated and centred. The moderate conservative factions (*modérés*) of the late nineteenth and early twentieth centuries best corresponded to this model. In certain key respects, this heritage was carried over into the first half of the twentieth century by the Radical Party.

In the early twentieth century, these elitist cadre parties were complemented by a series of 'outsider' or mass parties, which first developed as extra-parliamentary organisations in order to represent groups excluded from the political system, and only later became parliamentary groups as well. Within these 'outsider' parties, the extra-parliamentary organisation has traditionally been more important *vis-à-vis* the parliamentary representatives than in the insider parties. The examples of the Communist Party (PCF) and, to a lesser extent, of the Socialist Party (the SFIO, later the PS) best fit the outsider model: party statutes in both parties subordinated parliamentary representatives to control by the party executive. In this respect, French parties continue to be differentiated according to their origins. Thus, the National Bureau of the French Communist Party exercises a tight supervision over the activities of its deputies, whereas centre-right UDF deputies are not even certain of forming part of the same parliamentary group.

The origins of the French party system were laid in the Third Republic. The Radical Party was created at the turn of the century in order to defend the anti-clerical Republic against the Catholic Church. From 1900 to 1940, the Radicals acted as the pivotal party of the Third Republic. Radical participation was often essential to enable government coalitions to survive, and consequently the Radical Party became highly opportunistic, prompt to change alliance partners when it served its interest. This was revealed with alacrity during the inter-war period: on three occasions (1924, 1932 and 1936), the Radicals allied with the Socialists during general elections only to desert their Socialist allies for the centre-right after two years. Politically republican, the Radicals were usually conservative in socioeconomic matters, determined to support the cause of small anti-clerical peasant farmers and artisans. The survival of Radicalism is limited to certain pockets of south-west and central France, where the movement articulates a republican, anti-clerical and rural tradition.

The Socialist and Communist Parties were the first powerfully organised mass parties. The SFIO (Section française de l'internationale ouvrière) was created in 1905 as France's first unified Socialist Party, after the Second International had ordered France's six existing Socialist movements to fuse into a single organisation. Under the impact of the Russian Revolution, the SFIO in turn split in 1920 into two parties: the French Communist Party (PCF), supporters of Lenin's '21 conditions' for joining the Third International, and the Socialist Party, which retained the party's existing title (SFIO), claimed to represent continuity with the old party, and resisted the Leninist model of socialism. The division of the left into two rival parties was a fundamental structuring feature of the French party system from 1920 onwards. Relations between these two parties oscillated between long periods of fratricidal strife and brief spells of unity (such as during the 1936 Popular Front election campaign). The Communist and Socialist Parties have survived intact since 1920, despite a period of illegality for the PCF, and a change of name for the Socialists in 1969. These parties are considered in some detail in Chapter 10.

On the centre and right of the French party spectrum, it would be fruitless to try and differentiate the myriad of factions that existed during the Third Republic. A distinction might, nonetheless, be drawn between the *modérés*, conservative, parliamentary republicans, and the *ultras*, opposed to all forms of parliamentary regime. The former category prevailed for most of the period 1870–1940, especially after the Third Republic had overcome the early challenges to its legitimacy. The *ultras* adopted different guises, but never completely disappeared. The proliferation of reactionary, anti-parliamentary leagues during the 1930s represented a real challenge to the legitimacy of the Third Republic, and contributed to its collapse under the impact of German invasion in 1940.

Parties in the Fourth Republic

A pattern of party fragmentation was carried through into the Fourth Republic. This occurred in spite of the efforts of the founding-fathers of the Fourth Republic at the liberation to stimulate the emergence of a few large disciplined parties. Legitimised by their role in the French Resistance, three large parties initially dominated the political landscape: the PCF, the SFIO and the new Christian-democratic party, the Popular Republican Movement (MRP). The creation of the MRP represented the final rallying of Catholics to the republican form of government. The three resistance parties served under de Gaulle in the post-war provisional government of 1944–6. After de Gaulle's departure in January 1946, the PCF, the SFIO and the MRP formed the tripartite government of 1946–7, a government which enacted many landmark social reforms (Johnson, 1981).

The disciplined tripartite coalition broke down in May 1947, with the expulsion of the PCF from government, and the party system reverted to type: the early discipline of the Fourth Republic revealed itself to be illusory faced with the onset of severe domestic and international pressures. The rivalry between Socialists and Communists in particular postponed any prospect of renewed left-wing co-operation for a generation. The departure of de Gaulle from office in 1946 was a prelude to the formation of the Rassemblement du peuple français (RPF), a tough Gaullist organisation campaigning for a presidential-style regime which prefigured the Fifth Republic.

By the mid-1950s, a pattern of party proliferation had reappeared. Many of these parties were tiny, with only a few deputies. But in the parliamentary-dominated regime of the Fourth Republic, small parties were often able to exercise a political influence far greater than their numbers merited. This was especially the case for parties in the centre of the political spectrum. For much of the Fourth Republic, the Radicals continued to perform this function, although they were greatly weakened by comparison with the Third Republic, and they split into left- and right-wing components in the early 1950s.

It was undeniable that the major parties were more disciplined in the Fourth Republic. This was especially the case on the left (Communists and Socialists), but held true also for de Gaulle's RPF and the early MRP. But even strong parties fell victim to the decaying effects of the political system: notably, the tensions caused by participation in coalition governments; the ability of issues (such as the

European Defence Community and decolonisation) to divide parties; and the short duration of governments, preventing parties from being judged on the basis of their performance in office. Ultimately, political parties were scarcely more cohesive during the Fourth Republic than under its predecessor. In the Third Republic, the large number of parties reflected the profound divisions irrigating that society, and in particular the localised nature of French politics. In the Fourth Republic, parties continued to represent a broad variety of divisions within French society. But most observers agreed that the manner in which the political system operated – in particular, the destructive quality of the National Assembly — exaggerated the extent and nature of political cleavages within the nation as a whole. Parties were accused of keeping alive old divisions for their own partisan purposes.

However disingenuously, General de Gaulle was able to attract overwhelming support in May 1958 by condemning the instability induced by the *régime des partis* of the Fourth Republic, a regime he had actively sabotaged. At the beginning of the Fifth Republic, the term 'party' was hurled as one of abuse. It was instructive in this respect that the *Union pour la nouvelle république* (UNR), the movement formed to support de Gaulle in 1958, refused to call itself a party, but preferred to think of itself as a rally behind a charismatic leader.

9.3 Parties in the Fifth Republic

Presidentialism and the party system

The French Fifth Republic was created in 1958 on the basis of an official antipathy towards political parties. The ancillary position of political parties was officially recognised in the constitution of 1958. In spite of this constitutional ambiguity, the Fifth Republic has witnessed the emergence of a new style of renovated, presidential party, of which the Gaullists and later the Socialists provided the best examples. Such parties developed in part as a consequence of the new institutions of the Fifth Republic (especially the strengthened presidency) largely created and bequeathed by de Gaulle, although other variables also underpinned the evolution of the party system. The origins and evolution of the major French political parties are summarised in Table 9.1

The most obvious impact of presidentialism upon the development of the party system lay in the emergence of the presidential party as a key feature of the Fifth Republic. The existence of disciplined, pro-presidential coalitions controlling the National Assembly for most of the period since 1958 has been in stark contrast to the chaos of the Fourth Republic, where governments were short lived and multifarious, usually based on unstable coalitions and shifting party alliances. To all intents and purposes, the presidential party, either comprising a majority on its own (1968–73, 1981–6, 1995–), or else as the dominant partner in a governing coalition, has been an important feature of the Fifth Republic (Cole, 1993a).

This pattern of presidential domination has, however, been challenged on several occasions. In a subtle manner, this occurred in the course of Giscard d'Estaing's

Table 9.1 Major French political parties: origins and evolution

Party	Initial creation	Current initial	Past initials
Communist	1920	PCF	PCF
Socialist	1905	PS	SFIO, FGDS
Radical	1900	Radical/Radical Party	MRG, Radical
Christian-democratic	1945	FD	MRP, CD, CDP, CDS
Gaullist	1947	RPR	RPF, UNR, UDR
Conservative	1946	CNI	CNIP
Republican	1962	PR	RI
National Front	1972	FN	FN

presidency (1974–81), when the presidential party never comprised more than the 'minority of the majority': the incumbent President had to face the growing hostility of RPR deputies from 1976 to 1981. The breakdown of the president–party relationship arose more openly during the two periods of 'cohabitation' (1986–8, 1993–5), when the Socialist President Mitterrand was constrained to 'cohabit' with the Gaullist Prime Ministers Chirac and Balladur. On these occasions, the 'presidential party' (the PS) was returned to opposition with little, if any, impact on government policy.

The early aversion to political parties in the Fifth Republic could be explained by the peculiar circumstances surrounding the creation of the regime, and by the forceful personality of Charles de Gaulle, whose immense political authority subsequently shaped the presidential institutions of the Fifth Republic. Until 1986, the presidential party depended upon the authority of the directly elected President for its privileged position, as well as upon the electorate's unfailing tendency to re-elect the party or coalition supporting the President. Once the providential leader had acceded to the supreme office, his political party was destined to perform a subordinate role, provoking accusations levelled at all governing parties of 'bootlicking'. The fact that presidential majorities have rarely, if ever, been as submissive as the image of the 'bootlicker' suggests should not detract from the evidence that their room for manoeuvre is limited, especially if the parliamentary majority has been explicitly elected to support the President.

An original situation was produced after the 1995 presidential election. The fact that the new President, Jacques Chirac, already commanded a huge parliamentary majority when elected, the fruit of the RPR–UDF's landslide right-wing victory of March 1993, proved a mixed blessing, since it removed any pretext for a dissolution of the National Assembly. As his predecessors Pompidou (1969) and Giscard d'Estaing (1974) discovered by default, an incumbent President's authority is only really established when a parliamentary majority has been elected in his name (as in 1962, 1981 and 1988). President Chirac's premature dissolution of the National Assembly in April 1997 represented, in part, just such an attempt to associate more explicitly a centre-right governing majority with his election as President in 1995. The 1997 election campaign was also called in an effort to obviate the ambiguities of Jacques Chirac's 1995 presidential campaign. The presidential candidate of 1995 had emphasised the need to heal the 'social fracture' dividing French society, and advocated caution in relation to further European integration. In 1997, the centre-right (RPR-UDF) campaign, led by premier Juppé, was far more explicitly pro-European, notably imploring for a final effort to ensure that France would participate in the launch of the single European currency in 1999.

The strength of the presidency as shaped by de Gaulle (and imitated by his successors) transformed the direct presidential election into the decisive election of the Fifth Republic from 1965 onwards. This has had an important effect upon the performance of parties in parliamentary elections: it gives a strategic advantage to those parties which can hope to elect presidential candidates. The most successful parties in the Fifth Republic have been presidential parties, able legitimately to envisage the conquest of the regime's greatest institutional prize, the presidency. At different stages during the Fifth Republic, the PS, the UDF and the RPR have been able to pretend to the status of presidential parties.

In association with the emergence of the presidential party, there has been a presidentialisation of party structures. The most fortunate parties have become rallies for their leaders; the least fortunate have been torn asunder by the competition between rival candidates for the presidency. The negative effects of presidential competition have been most obvious on the right of the political spectrum. This might be illustrated by the 1995 presidential election campaign. The division of the French right into two or three families is not new: shades of René Rémond's three families of the French right (bonapartism, orleanist conservatism and the counter-revolutionary right) could be discerned in the three rival right-wing candidates of 1995: Chirac, Balladur and Le Pen (Rémond, 1982). Previous presidential contests have invariably experienced competition between rival candidates from the conservative camp: in 1981 and 1988, right-wing divisions facilitated François Mitterrand's victory. The original feature of the 1995 election stemmed from the fact that both Chirac and Balladur came from the ranks of the RPR. In the aftermath of Chirac's election as President, the RPR assumed an original posture: a presidential party containing a minority of deputies having campaigned against the President! Faced with a similar prospect of presidential-inspired factionalism, the Socialist Party leadership agreed in 1995 on the procedure of internal party primaries. The Socialist Party primary pitted First Secretary Henri Emmanuelli against Lionel Jospin, a former party leader (1981–8) and Education Minister (1988–92). Rejecting the advice of key figures in the Socialist hierarchy, party activists overwhelmingly backed Jospin (65/35 per cent). The democratic legitimacy of having been invested as candidate after a secret ballot was in marked contrast to the right's inability to organise a right-wing primary to separate Chirac and Balladur.

9.4 The evolving party system: from confusion to bipolarity, 1958–83

In section 9.3, we addressed the divided and fragmented nature of political parties during the Third and Fourth Republics. No single party, or coalition of parties, could muster a lasting majority of support either within the country or within parliament. This pattern changed abruptly with the creation of the Fifth Republic. After an initial period of confusion from 1958 to 1962, the party system became enormously simplified throughout the 1960s, 1970s and early 1980s on account of the process known as bipolarisation. By bipolarisation, we mean the streamlining of parties into rival coalitions of the left and of the right. This process of electoral bipolarisation reached its height in the 1978 National Assembly election, when RPR–UDF and PS–PCF coalitions divided the vote almost evenly between them. Since the mid-1980s, the structure of the French party system has become less neatly balanced, as a result of both the emergence of new parties and a shift in the balance of gravity between left and right to the detriment of the former.

In order to understand the bipolar French party system, such as it existed in 1978, it is necessary briefly to enumerate the reasons most frequently cited for the development of left–right bipolarisation during the 1960s and 1970s. Varying explanations have been forwarded. The most common relate to the political, constitutional and institutional structure of the Fifth Republic; the historical role performed by Gaullism; sociological explanations, in particular the return of class politics; and the role of the second-ballot electoral system.

The political, constitutional and institutional structure of the Fifth Republic

Those commentators who stress the importance of politico-institutional factors in explaining left–right bipolarisation point in particular to the enhanced prestige of the presidency as modelled by de Gaulle between 1958 and 1969; to the bipolarising pressures of the direct election of the president after 1962 (only two candidates go through to the decisive second ballot); and to the strengthening of executive government in the constitution of the Fifth Republic. With the emergence of strong, stable governments encouraged by the 1958 constitution, parties were deprived of their former capacity for byzantine political manoeuvre in an Assembly-dominated regime. The key contenders for office gradually refocused their attentions upon the presidential election. These various pressures combined to stimulate the emergence of stable government coalitions, and in turn more purposeful oppositions. One of the paradoxes of direct election was that the actual development of the Fifth Republic (partisan and bipolar until the mid-1980s) was in contradiction to de Gaulle's conception of the presidency and the Republic as being above parties.

The historical role performed by Gaullism

The second explanation commonly forwarded to explain left–right bipolarisation relates to the historical role performed by Gaullism, and the development of party strategies on the non-Gaullist right, the left and the centre to respond to this. The progressive emergence after 1958 of Gaullism as a federating force of the right, and eventually of most of the centre, forced the disunited left to react in order to secure its own survival. Greater electoral co-operation between Socialists and Communists occurred from 1962 onwards against the common threat represented by Gaullism. In turn, the so-called independent centre (in fact composed mainly of conservative and centrist politicians left over from the old Fourth Republic), which maintained the pretence of autonomy from both Gaullism and the left throughout the 1960s, ultimately rallied in stages to the Gaullist-led majority from 1969 onwards. By 1978 the independent centre had completely disappeared and had been subsumed into Giscard d'Estaing's UDF. The continuing survival of the centre-right UDF confederation for some twenty years testifies to the structural need to organise the various small parties of the centre and non-Gaullist right to prevent complete domination by the RPR.

Sociological explanations to account for left–right bipolarisation

Sociological explanations were favoured especially by left-wing analysts. They pointed to the emergence of social class as the central political cleavage during the 1970s, which gave a structural basis to left–right bipolarisation artificially created by the institutions and electoral system of the Fifth Republic. The capacity of Gaullism to attract a core working-class electorate during the 1960s had blurred natural class divisions. During the 1970s, the increasingly stark division between the left and right reflected a genuine class division. It was contended that unemployment and the onset of sustained economic crisis (especially after the 1973 oil crisis) had revived latent class divisions.

This explanation appeared superficially attractive during the 1970s: the proportion of industrial workers voting for left-wing parties, for instance, increased dramatically from 1968 to 1978. Within the left, the PCF claimed to be *the* party of the industrial working classes: as late as 1978, the Communists (36 per cent) still obtained more support from industrial workers than the revitalised Socialists (33 per cent) (Capdeveille, 1981). Mitterrand's PS attracted support from many of the new social groups produced by post-war socio-economic change: clerical workers, middle management and the new expanded professions (such as teaching and social work). It also proved remarkably successful at poaching the support of a traditional left-wing electoral clientele (industrial and clerical workers), at the expense of the Communist Party. With the decline of Gaullism after 1973, the right-wing parties represented a more classic conservative electoral base: traditional élites, a fraction of the managers, the traditional professions, farmers, the lower middle classes in the private sector and a diminished proportion of industrial workers.

However, this neo-Marxist class thesis hardly stood up to developments in the 1980s – a decade marked by extreme electoral volatility, by a marked decline in working-class support for the PCF and the PS, by a collapse of the Socialist electoral coalition, and by the emergence of new political parties such as the Front national and the Greens. In fact, in a decade of electoral instability, the political cleavage based around religious identity remained by far the most predictive indicator of voting choice, as it had since surveys were first carried out in the 1965 presidential election (Michelat and Simon, 1977). In the 1995 presidential election run-off, Chirac obtained the votes of 74 per cent of regularly practising Catholics, as against only 31 per cent of those declaring themselves to have 'no religion' (Le Monde, 1995b).

The electoral system

For certain French political scientists, it is a self-evident truth that the structure of the party system in the Fifth Republic can be attributed primarily to the electoral system. For Jean-Luc Parodi, for instance, the single-member constituency, second-ballot electoral system was destined to produce a *quadrille bipolaire*, a system with four main parties and two electoral coalitions (Parodi, 1978). Certain commentators were guilty of constructing general models by observing the contours of the party system at that particular time: there is no political reason why this (or any other) electoral system should produce four major parties. But, in practice, it was undoubtedly the case that the use of the second-ballot system in legislative elections since 1958 had a salutary effect in stimulating electoral co-operation on left and right. The bipolarising effects were enhanced by the fact that a similar electoral system was used for the presidential election.

Eschewing for the moment the debate between electoral systems and party systems, the practical effect of the system was to provide an additional stimulus for coalition building on the left and right. Under the second-ballot system in use in parliamentary elections, a candidate must obtain an absolute majority of votes (and at least 25 per cent of registered electors) on the first round to be elected, failing which a second round is held, at which the candidate with the most votes wins. A 5 per cent voting threshold was introduced in 1958 to bar small minorities from contesting the second round. This was raised to 12.5 per cent of registered electors in 1976 (Bartolini, 1984). The effect of the 12.5 per cent threshold has been to exclude candidates from significant minority parties contesting the second round, especially where they lack great regional concentrations of strength. The performance of the Greens in the 1993 legislative elections was an adequate testament to this: with 7.6 per cent of the first round vote, only two Green candidates managed to obtain more than the 12.5 per cent threshold and contest the second ballot. Neither was elected. The electoral system has helped to preserve, rather artificially, a bipolar, left–right outcome to elections, notwithstanding the clear existence of a multiparty reality since the mid-1980s.

The parties' reactions to the new electoral rules of the game were variable. Initially inspired by the discipline and unity of the Gaullist movement, the main formations of the French right have generally agreed since 1962 to support only one candidate from the first ballot, although this has never prevented dissident conservative candidates from fighting disputed seats. A small number of officially approved 'primaries' has allowed difficult local cases to be arbitrated by the electors. Only in 1978 was there a general practice of competing RPR and UDF candidates on the first round. The presentation of a single candidate minimises the problem of vote transfers on the second round that has classically afflicted the left-wing parties.

The pattern of electoral co-operation was somewhat different on the left. In 1958 Socialists and Communists fought each other throughout France, effectively cancelling out the left-wing vote, and allowing the election of numerous Gaullists on a minority of the vote. In 1962 the two parties formed the first of many second-ballot withdrawal agreements. Under the rules of such agreements, the left-wing parties each agree to stand down if their rival obtains more first-round votes in a particular constituency. Thus, if a Communist candidate arrives ahead on the first round, the Socialist withdraws and calls on his or her supporters to back the Communist. If a Socialist comes in first, the Communist withdraws and calls upon his or her supporters to back the Socialist. From 1967 to 1997, with the exception of the 1986 election (fought under proportional representation), the Communists and Socialists have agreed national withdrawal pacts in legislative elections fought under the second ballot. PS–PCF electoral pacts have historically been necessary for each party to maximise the number of its deputies, but they have also greatly increased tensions within the left, as each party competes for first-round supremacy. In 1997 the PS also concluded a wide-ranging agreement with the main ecologist groups, the left-Radicals, and the small Citizens Movement party (MdC), whereby joint candidates would be presented from the first ballot in selected constituencies.

During the 1970s and 1980s, this arrangement appeared to discriminate against the number of Communist deputies, since a significant fraction of Socialist first-round voters would always refuse to back the Communist candidate in the second round, whereas Communist voters were far more disciplined. In 1962, Communists arrived ahead of Socialists in three-fifths of constituencies, reflecting the parties' respective electoral strengths. By 1988, however, Socialists came in front in 19/20ths of constituencies. By 1988 the once great Communist Party had become reduced to a reservoir of left-wing votes for electing Socialist candidates. The poor performance of both left-wing parties in 1993 had the paradoxical effect of reducing the gap separating Communists and Socialists.

It has become increasingly apparent that traditional bipolar electoral alliances, such as between Socialists and Communists, no longer accurately reflect the real divisions between France's political parties, but are a legacy of what are perceived to be the dictates of the electoral system. Socialists and Communists continue to ally with each other in elections for the National Assembly, but disagree at all other times. In terms of economic policy, for instance, the Socialist record from

1981 to 1993 had more in common with monetarist norms espoused elsewhere in Europe than with the expansionary policies advocated by the French Communist Party. This disassociation between electoral alliances and political coalitions has increased the electorate's distrust of the party system as a whole.

The influence of the electoral system must not be discounted. At a given period, the electoral system encouraged the parties of the left and right to form coalitions to fight the common enemy. By its discriminatory effects against smaller parties, the second-ballot system forced the centre parties to choose between the Gaullist-led majority or the left in order to survive. The electoral system has also hindered political movements such as the Greens at an early stage in their development. However, the structure of the bipolar French party system of the late 1970s must not be reduced to the electoral system alone, but must incorporate all other elements mentioned above.

9.5 The evolving party system: from bipolarity to confusion, 1983–96

The height of left–right bipolarisation occurred in 1978. In that year's National Assembly election, the four leading parties (PCF, PS, RPR and UDF) obtained over 90 per cent of the vote, with each party polling 20–5 per cent. In 1978, the structure of the party system was that of a *quadrille bipolaire*: four parties of roughly equal political strength divided voter preferences evenly between left and right coalitions. These parties were the PCF and the PS on the left, and the neo-Gaullist RPR and the liberal conservative UDF on the right. The French party system was transformed beyond recognition during the twenty years separating the 1978 and 1997 National Assembly elections (see Appendix 2). It was appropriate to portray the French party system in 1997 in terms of six significant political families, in addition to a number of more marginal groupings. These families were the Communist left (PCF), the Socialist/centre-left (PS), the Greens, the centre-right (UDF), the central right (RPR) and the extreme right (FN). These formations are analysed in more detail in Chapters 10 and 11.

No single explanation ought to be forwarded to interpret the breakdown of the *quadrille bipolaire*. In part, the weakening of left–right bipolarisation stems from features peculiar to each party. The decline of the PCF is clearly a central theme. Any attempt to chart this decline must combine appraisal of the mistakes committed by the Communist Party leadership with longer-term sociological and ideological trends, and the impact of the new post-communist world order. A comprehensive overview would require a similar approach to be applied to each single party, a task that lies outside of the scope of this chapter (cf. Cole, 1990). Apart from party-specific explanations, several more general hypotheses are plausible, which we will now consider.

Party performance

After the economic miracle of *les trente glorieuses* (1945–74), political parties in government have proved incapable of dealing with the perception of prolonged economic crisis since 1974. In comparative European perspective, the reality of the French crisis is highly debatable, but the perception of economic malaise (combined with a marked French cultural pessimism) has had a destabilising effect on all incumbent governments since 1974. Mitterrand's election as President in 1981 was regarded by many as fortuitous, an unforeseen consequence of premier Barre's inability to master the economy. For this school, Mitterrand was carried to power on a wave of negative dissatisfaction with Giscard d'Estaing, rather than by positive endorsement. By January 1982, a series of by-elections had revealed the Socialists to be in a clear minority. In elections from 1982 to 1986, the PS was consistently defeated, culminating in the right-wing victory in the 1986 election. The swing to the right registered in 1986 ought to have ensured the presidential victory of a conservative candidate, and yet Mitterrand was comfortably re-elected in 1988. Mitterrand's re-election was facilitated by a catalogue of errors made by Chirac's conservative government, but it was also greatly aided by right-wing divisions, especially the emergence of Le Pen's far-right National Front. Mitterrand was re-elected in 1988 due to crucial centre-right support, but betrayed this trust almost immediately. The Socialists' resounding electoral defeat in 1993 was inescapably linked to perceived poor economic performance and the misuse of political authority. In turn, the image of a government in permanent retreat augured ill for premier Balladur's prospects of being elected President. To the surprise of many commentators, the anti-incumbent reaction was repeated in the 1995 presidential election, with the election of Chirac. Since 1981, key elections have tended to go against incumbent governments, in a manner which suggests the electorate's dissatisfaction with the performance of successive governments.

The end of ideological solutions?

By the end of the 1980s, there was clear evidence from opinion polls that many French voters had grown tired of older ideological divisions and programmes, which had structured French party competition until the early 1980s and Mitterrand's election. This disillusionment was heightened especially after the high expectations and subsequent disappointments created by the 'dual alternation' of 1981–2, when the left took power, and 1986–7, when a Thatcher-style government led by Chirac attempted to roll back the frontiers of the state. The limitations of party performance in office were exacerbated by exaggerated claims made by parties while in opposition. This had a particularly damaging effect upon the Socialist Party. The Socialists in power (1981–6, 1988–93) were unable to satisfy the party's rhetorical demands made while in opposition. The reaction against the left was all the more keenly felt because these illusions had been maintained for so long. The myth of *l'autre politique* was exploded by the

Socialist experience of 1981–2, which revealed socialism in one country to be an illusion. The conservative government of 1986–8 suffered from a similar inability to match theoretical claims with practical results: what it defined as liberalism did not have the positive effects its supporters had claimed, such as a rapid reduction in unemployment, or an immediate economic recovery. In both cases, opposition parties had created false expectations which were disappointed once these parties obtained power. The crisis of classical French political parties, especially those on the left, relates in part to the fact that nothing has replaced these lost solutions.

Beneath the clash of rival political programmes between left and right lay a *de facto* convergence on many areas of public policy. This was particularly acute in relation to economic policy. With the left's abandonment of Keynesian reflationary policies in 1982, and its modification of its traditional statism, the dividing line between left and right became blurred, if not extinct as some commentators argued. The monetarist policies engaged by the French Socialists after 1983 were at least as rigorous as those undertaken in other European countries. Developments in the European Union further blurred the economic distinction between left and right: the key élites in the three leading parties (the PS, the UDF and the RPR) firmly supported moves towards closer European economic and political integration initiated at the Maastricht summit in 1991. The constraint represented by the European Union on the autonomy of party policy weighed increasingly heavily throughout the 1980s and 1990s.

There is some evidence of a return to a certain tradition of mobilising, voluntaristic political action. The key to Chirac's presidential campaign in 1995 lay in protesting against *la pensée unique*, the notion that there was only one economic path (the strong franc policy) if France was to meet the convergence criteria for a single European currency. Chirac's campaign combined a rather paradoxical alchemy of themes more normally associated with the political left, with the desire for an end to 'fourteen years of socialism'. Influenced by the theses of French sociologist Olivier Todd, Chirac diagnosed a 'social fracture' within French society, based on the exclusion of minorities, bad housing, low salaries and – crucially – unemployment. Given the lyricism of Chirac's campaign promises, and the near-monopoly of power held by the right, high expectations were raised in the 1995 campaign. Disappointment rapidly set in; one year after his election, President Chirac and his premier Juppé were deeply unpopular.

The Italian syndrome

In the 1993 election, the ruling Socialists were particularly afflicted by the wearing-out effects of power: the party appeared literally worn out by over a decade in charge of the state. The scale of the party's electoral defeat exceeded that normally reserved for incumbent governments by an electorate dissatisfied with relative economic privation. It was an historic disavowal. The poor Socialist performance occurred against a background of evidence of political corruption. Although no party escaped unscathed, the Socialists, after nearly ten years in power, fared worst.

The reality of political corruption in France ought to be placed in perspective; it would pale into insignificance beside the Italian case. Most 'corrupt' practices have been desperate manoeuvres to raise finance to fight prohibitively expensive election campaigns. Moreover, the 1990 law on the financing of political parties went some way to alleviating the root problem. However, well-documented evidence of corrupt practices aggravated the widespread sense of distrust of the political parties, more characteristic of the Fourth Republic than the Fifth. The controversy over *l'Etat-PS* further fuelled such sentiments. Such attitudes appear to renew a long-established strain of French political culture which considers the activity of politics to be the preserve of charlatans seeking to enrich themselves. The malaise currently affecting French political parties might thus be interpreted as a part of a more deeply rooted dissatisfaction with the Fifth Republic.

New cleavages and political movements

The bipolar contours of the French party system have also been challenged by the emergence of new political cleavages which existing parties are unable to articulate, leading in turn to the growth of new political movements. The issues of immigration, security and the environment fall into this category. The breakthrough and persistence of the Front national has been both cause and effect of a changed political agenda which the mainstream parties have been unable to control. Likewise, the rise and fall of the Green parties proved a test case of the disruptive force of new political issues and the difficulties experienced by the mainstream parties in articulating new political demands, notably those concerning the environment and post-materialist values. The Front national and the Greens are considered in more detail in Chapter 11.

9.6 The French party system in comparative context

The byzantine French party system has long been a source of fascination for French and foreign observers alike. However, models of European party systems popular in the comparative European literature appear rather unsatisfactory when appraising the historical evolution of the French party system. One of the most influential hypotheses pertaining to the evolution of the European party system was that formulated by Lipset and Rokkan in the 1960s (Lipset and Rokkan, 1967). For Lipset and Rokkan, the 'parties of the 1960s reflect, with few but significant exceptions, the structures of the 1920s'. Political loyalties had been 'frozen' since the 1920s: the principal parties in western Europe were those which expressed divisions which had first surfaced in the nineteenth and early twentieth centuries.

Even in the 1960s, there was little evidence to support this model in the French case. It presupposed a coherent and stable party system of the type that had never really existed in France. On account of the country's late industrialisation, there was no highly disciplined and structured industrial working class supporting a unified social-democratic party, as in Britain or Germany; nor its antidote, in the form of a unified bourgeois party to resist socialism. The rationalisation of the French party system occurred as a result of social, political and institutional change after 1958, rather than half a century earlier. Lipset and Rokkan also observed that loyalty to party in Europe was strong; parties persisted even after the divisions around which they had been formed had disappeared. This has a greater resonance in the French case. The survival of the Radical Party for most of the twentieth century, long after the resolution of the church–state dispute, and of the French Communist Party after the collapse of the Soviet Union, provided some (very limited) evidence to support this. For the most part, however, the cohesion of French political parties was inadequate to support the Lipset/Rokkan model. The rise of polarised left–right competition was a product of developments in the 1960s and 1970s; since the 1980s, new parties have emerged to disrupt this relatively stable pattern of party competition between left and right.

Other party systems experts emphasised that social changes in the post-war period led not only to changing sources of political division, but also to changing types of party resulting from divisions within society. Otto Kirchheimer (1966) diagnosed the emergence of the 'catch-all' party as a new type of European party. In order to rally support from an electoral majority (in a post-war Europe characterised by a weakening of old ideologies and social divisions), parties had to appeal for support to all groups within the population, rather than limiting their appeal to one class or interest. Such an appeal required a toning down of past political programmes, in an attempt to occupy the centre ground. The model catch-all party was the German Christian-Democratic Union (CDU), whose non-ideological political appeal cut across the boundaries of social class and religion. As we shall see when appraising the French left, this model underplayed the persistence of ideological traditions on the French left, notably the influence of Marxism, and the consequences of political competition between Socialists and Communists.

Other models more specifically tailored to explain Mediterranean political systems appeared unsatisfactory or outdated. Thus, Sartori's 'polarised pluralism' (with the mainstay of political competition being between an unelectable Communist Party and an amorphous centre-right governing coalition) enjoyed a brief popularity among certain observers of the French Communist Party, but it was difficult to transpose from its Italian setting (Sartori, 1976).

None of these explanations easily fitted the French case, shaped by particular historical and social conditions. But neither should the uniqueness of the French case be overplayed. The distinctive character of the French party system has been modified in important respects during the past two decades. The decline of the Communist Party has fundamentally reshaped the nature of French party competition (Chapter 11), liberating the Socialist Party from an overbearing ideological presence to its left. If rather belatedly, the 'catch-all' model allows some insights into the evolution of French party competition in the post-1981 period. The Socialists' experience in government during 1981–6 and 1988–93 forced a re-evaluation of its party programme and modernisation of its political discourse. As if to recall the exceptional stature of the French polity, however, the breakthrough and consolidation of the far-right FN in the 1980s introduced a new unpredictable player, performing certain protest functions classically associated with the Communist Party, and introducing a new political agenda to complicate the existing pattern of left–right polarisation.

9.7 Conclusion and summary

Viewed as a whole, the party system of the Fifth Republic has underpinned a political regime which, in French terms, provides a model of political stability. The emergence of cohesive majorities to support governments (albeit with assistance from the 1958 constitution and a majoritarian electoral system) represented a novel departure in French politics. Initial Gaullist hegemony incited opposition parties to increase cooperation in order to survive. Right-wing domination of the party system from 1958 to 1981 gradually produced its antibody in the form of a resurgent left which finally achieved power in 1981. A decade of Socialist-led government (1981–93) proved that the regime could withstand an alternation in power. With the return of Gaullism in 1995, in the form of the election of Jacques Chirac as President, the Fifth Republic seemingly reverted to its initial inspiration.

The *bipolar quadrille* no longer accurately describes the structure of the French party system. The challenge of new parties, the decline of certain older parties (notably the PCF) and the limited capacity of existing parties to master new political issues have called the effective functioning of the party system into question. The decline in public confidence in French political parties and politicians is a worrying sign; the 1995 presidential election once again went against the incumbent government. The rapid fall from public favour of President Chirac during the first year of his presidential term revealed a new depth of public dissatisfaction so shortly after a decisive election. These themes are addressed in more detail in Chapters 10 and 11.

Indicative bibliography

Appleton, A. (1995) 'Parties under pressure: challenges to established French parties', *West European Politics*, vol. 18, no. 1.

Avril, P. (1984) 'Les Chefs de l'état et la notion de majorité présidentielle', *Revue française de science politique*, vol. 34, no. 4–5.

Bartolini, S. (1984) 'Institutional constraints and party competition in the French party system', *West European Politics*, vol. 7, no. 4.

Bréchon, P. (1993) *La France aux urnes*, Documentation française, Paris.

Cole, A. (ed.) (1990) *French Political Parties in Transition*, Dartmouth, Aldershot

Frears, J. (1990) *Parties and Voters in France*, Hurst, London.

Machin, H. (1989) 'Stages and dynamics in the evolution of the French party system', *West European Politics*, vol. 12, no. 4.

Ysmal, C. (1989) *Les Partis politiques sous la Ve République*, Montchrestien, Paris.

Chapter 10

The presidential parties

10.1 Introduction and objectives

The evolution of the French party system having been traced in Chapter 9, Chapters 10 and 11 consider in further detail the fortunes of France's major and minor parties. The aim of these chapters is to provide a brief summary of the most important features of each of the main parties. In Chapter 10, we discuss the presidential parties (the RPR, the UDF and the PS), defined as those who have in the past elected their candidate to the presidency. In Chapter 11, we turn our attention to the anti-establishment parties (the PCF, the FN and the minor parties). Because these are different types of party, with varying historical, organisational and ideological traditions, the traits highlighted for each party are not necessarily the same. As a general guide, a brief history of each party will be followed by an overview of its beliefs, political appeal, organisation and leadership.

The study of French political parties has a long tradition. The academic literature in English alone on French political parties is vast. The main areas of analysis include the evolution of the party system (Bartolini, 1984; Machin, 1989; Cole, 1990); the cultural and discursive context within which parties have developed (Gaffney, 1989b); intra-party relations (Hanley, 1985; Cole 1989); and case studies of individual parties (Bell and Criddle (1988, 1994) on the Socialists and Communists; Knapp (1994) on the Gaullists; Shields (1990) on the Front national). The French literature is so abundant as to excuse any attempt at repetition here; several leading references are provided in the bibliography, but this is the tip of the iceberg.

In the systemic and political context of the French Fifth Republic in the 1990s, it is useful to divide parties across the dimension of presidential and anti-establishment parties. It might be objected that this division is imperfect and too schematic. The performance of the parties in local government, for instance, does not easily fit into this classificatory schema. Moreover, an anti-establishment party such as the Front national undoubtedly aspires to become a presidential party, and its leader has adapted skilfully to the political conditions of the presidential election. But the fact remains that only three of France's six political families can realistically aspire to elect their candidate to the presidency, which has proved to be the key office of political competition throughout most of the Fifth Republic. This has had a major structuring impact upon the contours of the French party system. It has also helped to shape the identity of French parties, whatever their origins. For these reasons, the division between presidential and anti-establishment parties is as pertinent as any other.

10.2 The Gaullists

History

The Gaullist movement derived its initial legitimacy from General de Gaulle's proclamation in favour of a Free France in 1940. The first organised Gaullist movement – the Rassemblement du peuple français (RPF) – was created by de Gaulle in 1947. It became a powerful mass movement, deriving its identity from a combination of vigorous anti-communism, nationalism, hostility to the parliamentary regime of the Fourth Republic and personal attachment to de Gaulle (Charlot, 1983). Although it was one of the principal movements of the late 1940s, by 1953 de Gaulle had dissociated himself from the RPF as a movement hijacked by conservative *notables* in quest of a bandwagon.

Gaullism as a political movement was resurrected by the events of May–June 1958, which carried de Gaulle to power and inaugurated the Fifth Republic. When de Gaulle returned in 1958, his followers formed themselves into the Union pour la nouvelle république (UNR) with the primary objective of supporting the General. Emerging as a major political force almost overnight in 1958, the UNR became the pivot of de Gaulle's Fifth Republic (Charlot, 1970). A distrust of organised political parties and interests comprised one of the essential features of classical Gaullism. In keeping with his suspicions of political parties, de Gaulle did not openly acknowledge any link with the UNR. Given his suspicion of parties, he could not admit his presidential authority being based upon a disciplined, partisan coalition, as opposed to the direct confidence of the French people expressed through referendums and the direct election of the President. Indeed, de Gaulle even refused to allow the UNR, created only weeks before the 1958 election, to label itself as the Gaullist party: 'not even in adjectival form' would he allow his name to be attached to a party. This policy was tempered in practice by the fact that from 1962 onwards the General called upon electors to support UNR candidates in elections for the National Assembly; and, as Duverger (1977) points out, de Gaulle 'never denied that the UNR provided his most solid basis of support'.

As the *de facto* presidential party, the UNR was a subordinate institution, with no formal influence over presidential decision making. Party organs were dominated by members of the government, limiting further any temptation towards autonomy: in this way, the subordination of the party executive to government decisions was ensured (Charlot, 1970). From the creation of the UNR in 1958, the first Gaullist Prime Minister, Michel Debré, insisted that the movement could only perform a subordinate role. In April 1960, Debré justified the decision to exclude a number of opponents of de Gaulle's Algerian policy from the movement with the proclamation that: 'the UNR's legitimacy and values are intricately bound up with the political priorities of General de Gaulle' (cited in Charlot, 1993b). The Gaullists were called upon by Debré and later Georges Pompidou (de Gaulle's second Prime Minister) to imitate what was perceived to be the practice of the British Conservatives and the German Christian Democrats: to provide unflinching public loyalty, and to keep criticisms away from the public eye.

To the extent that the UNR was the prototype presidential party, appraisal of its evolution is inseparable from that of the Gaullist regime itself (see Chapter 2). The party benefited from de Gaulle's unprecedented popularity and from public approval of the new regime to strengthen its position. In June 1968, taking advantage of the fears raised by the events of May, the Gaullists won an absolute majority of seats, the first occasion this had been achieved in French history. Moreover, the election of Pompidou as President in 1969 appeared to suggest that the Gaullist party could survive its founding-father. In time, however, the virtual disintegration of the UDR, culminating in the 1974 presidential election, revealed the limits of the institutionalisation of Gaullism as a political movement in its existing form. After de Gaulle had left the political scene, the Gaullists lacked a definite sense of purpose and ideological cohesion; the once-omnipotent UDR became riven by policy and personality-based factional disputes. There is a strong case for arguing that historic Gaullism died with de Gaulle: the UDR's difficulty in existing after 1969 testified to the personal rally facet of the Gaullist movement, a basis which eventually delegitimised the party in its existing form after de Gaulle's departure.

In the 1974 presidential election, former premier Chaban-Delmas, the official Gaullist candidate, obtained only 15.1 per cent, as against 32.6 per cent for Valéry Giscard d'Estaing, an independent conservative candidate. Giscard d'Estaing won the presidency in 1974 in part because the Gaullist Interior Minister, Chirac, led a powerful revolt of 43 Gaullist deputies in his favour. This act of treachery would never be forgiven by certain Gaullists. Shortly after his appointment as premier in 1974, Chirac took over control of what remained of the Gaullist party. President Giscard d'Estaing's acquiescence was bought in the belief that the Gaullist movement would be delivered to the new President, a preliminary to the creation of a new presidential party. Chirac intended otherwise: control over the UDR was a means of lifting Gaullism out of its electoral abyss, if necessary at the expense of President Giscard d'Estaing's own supporters. Conflict between Giscard d'Estaing and Chirac was thenceforth probable, and Chirac's resignation as Prime Minister in August 1976 accelerated this movement. In December 1976, Chirac transformed the old party into a dynamic new organisation, renamed the Rally for the Republic (Rassemblement pour la république, RPR), bearing a close resemblance to de Gaulle's RPF of the Fourth Republic. The RPR was originally intended to be a mass campaigning party to regenerate the French right. Although membership figures are notoriously unreliable, the RPR can claim to have an effective campaigning party organisation, along with the PCF and the FN.

From the vantage point of the late 1990s, the RPR appeared to be a successful political movement, though its fortunes have fluctuated greatly during its twenty-year history. As a general rule, the strengths of the RPR have lain in those areas of weakness for the early Gaullist movements: especially municipal government and party organisation. The failure of past Gaullist movements (especially the UNR) to secure a solid implantation in local government was a key source of weakness (Williams and Harrison, 1969; Goguel, 1983). The power base of the RPR has been its control over Paris, presided over by Chirac from 1977 to 1995. Chirac's decision to contest the Paris election in 1977 proved a political masterstroke. The patronage and political prestige of the Paris town hall made up for the fact that the RPR continued to trail the centre-right UDF in terms of overall presence in local government (the 96 departmental councils, 36,518 communes and 22 regions).

Most importantly, Chirac's election as President in 1995 heralded the return of a Gaullist to the Elysée after a period of 21 years crossing the desert. In addition to there being a Gaullist President in the Elysée palace, there was a large RPR–UDF overall majority in the National Assembly, RPR–UDF control over a majority of France's regional and departmental councils, as well as control of many leading French cities. However, this position was less impregnable than at first sight. Chirac's first-round total in 1995 (20.8 per cent) was by far the weakest of any successful presidential candidate in the Fifth Republic. This confirmed that the electoral totals available to RPR candidates bore little relation to the previous electoral feats of historic Gaullism. Moreover, Chirac's election came after a bruising battle with former premier Balladur, himself also a member of the RPR, supported by a minority of RPR deputies. Above all, Chirac's election could not conceal the fact that the French electorate was more fragmented than ever, notably in the light of Le Pen's strong showing (15 per cent).

Beliefs and political appeal

The RPR differed in key respects from historic Gaullism of the 1960s. The UNR was both a personalist rally behind a charismatic leader and a vehicle for mobilising support for the Fifth Republic. It was a movement with a broader sociological base than that typical of French right-wing parties: it obtained support from across the social spectrum, with a strong undercurrent of working-class Gaullism essential for its success (Knapp in Cole, 1990; Knapp, 1994). The beliefs propounded by de Gaulle's UNR also set the movement apart from traditional conservative movements. Strongly influenced by de Gaulle's brand of nationalism, the UNR advocated national independence, social and economic interventionism and popular participation. In the appreciation of Knapp (in Cole, 1990, p. 140), the Gaullist UNR was

> not a conventional European right-wing party. [It was] less European, less Atlanticist, more ready to accept state economic intervention, less trusting of private enterprise . . . To French voters, the Gaullist party offered a charismatic leader; the heroic aura of the resistance, loyalty to institutions that offered stable government for the first time in the twentieth century; *gloire*, a sure barrier against communism and economic prosperity.

This alchemy of nationalism and populism set the Gaullists apart from mainstream European conservative or Christian-democratic traditions, which were more integrationist and Atlanticist. Under President Pompidou (1969–74), the UNR became a more recognisably conservative movement, both in terms of the sociological composition of its electorate, and in its beliefs and policies. As surveyed in Chapter 2, the policies pursued during the Pompidou presidency brought the Gaullist movement broadly into line with other European conservative movements, most notably in relation to Atlanticism and European integration.

The RPR has oscillated between portraying itself as a French Labour Party (1976), a tough anti-communist movement in the style of de Gaulle's RPF (1979), a 'catch-all' party and a classic right-wing Conservative Party, a description which most accurately portrays the RPR. Its message has varied, according to climate and clientele. At some times it has stressed national populism (Chirac's 1979 Cochin appeal), at others European integration (the 1992 referendum). In the economic sphere, it has at some times laid stress on neo-liberalism (1986–8), at others on interventionist policies aimed at combating unemployment (Chirac's 1995 campaign). On the specifics of policy, the Gaullist movement has frequently been divided. The cleavage over Europe is probably the most significant in this respect. During the Maastricht referendum campaign of 1992, the RPR was openly divided between opponents of the treaty (Séguin and Pasqua) and supporters (notably Juppé). This division was to some extent repeated within the Gaullist government of 1995–7, with premier Juppé and Séguin, President of the National Assembly, representing opposing poles on this issue. Divisions among Gaullist deputies might be traced in relation to other policy sectors as well, such as constitutional reform, economic policy and popular participation.

This flexibility is an important part of the Gaullist party, a movement that has placed greater emphasis on leadership, patriotism and the tradition of *volontarisme* in domestic and foreign policy than on the specific content of policies. It should also be recalled that there are multiple strands of Gaullism, corresponding in part to specific generations, in part to the demands of different historical situations. To this extent, Chirac's 1995 campaign against the 'technostructure' and in favour of direct contact between the President and the people responded to a powerful strand of popular Gaullism – one rather distrustful of representative democracy and in favour of a direct contact between the leader and the people.

In spite of itself, the RPR is a recognisably conservative party, the key party of the French right. This was revealed by the nature of Chirac's first-round electorate in 1995, after a presidential election campaign based on the theme of radical change. Strong support for Chirac came from the youngest age cohorts and from students, but he also enjoyed a firm showing among more traditionally conservative categories such as business, the liberal professions and the farmers (Le Monde, 1995b). In contrast, Chirac's working-class support (15 per cent) trailed that of Jospin (21 per cent) and Le Pen (27 per cent). Although outperformed by Balladur in traditionally conservative categories such as practising Catholics, Chirac attracted a cross-class electorate unavailable to any other candidate.

Organisation and leadership

More than in any other presidential party, leadership has always played a consciously important role in the Gaullist movement. The style and dimensions of such political leadership have varied over time. De Gaulle's authority over the Gaullist party was immense; to label the UNR as a personalist movement accurately captures at least part of its essence (Cole, 1993a). However, his authority did vary somewhat according to different generations. The wartime *compagnons* were entirely devoted to de Gaulle, and accepted his decisions even when they disagreed with them (as leading Gaullists such as Michel Debré did over Algeria). But the younger Gaullist generation, first elected as UNR deputies in 1958 or 1962, were less inherently deferential towards de Gaulle, more concerned with their own career advancement. A strong sense of self-interest explained why the Gaullist UDR temporarily outlived the General: the new Fifth Republican élite, propelled to positions of influence under de Gaulle, was unwilling to allow Gaullism to disappear with its founder. It was in this sense that Gaullism aspired to represent more than just a personal rally.

President Pompidou (1969–74) possessed neither the personal charisma nor the historical dimension of de Gaulle; the second President was compelled to exercise a closer supervision over the Gaullist party in order to maintain his own authority, and to quell the fronde of the 'historical chiefs' (such as Debré) who contested his Gaullist credentials. Pompidou's presidential interference in the affairs of party was far more marked than de Gaulle's. The quality of the UDR as a presidential rally diminished greatly during Pompidou's presidency: from being in part a personalist movement dedicated to serving de Gaulle, the Gaullist party became less unconditionally devoted to its presidential leader, more a network for the dissemination of patronage.

The historical filiation of Chirac's RPR with Gaullism is undeniable, but Chirac's political leadership has been of a different nature than that of either de Gaulle or Pompidou. It was based on a different criterion: that of a party leader in all but name. The Gaullist party has changed in order to survive. Chirac's stewardship of the RPR from 1976 to 1995 was often criticised, including from within the ranks of the RPR itself. Internal dissent developed in several directions after the 1988 presidential election defeat. That Chirac managed to survive the outbreak of factionalism within the RPR after the presidential defeat of 1988, and retain his control over the leadership in spite of a strong challenge in 1990 from Seguin and Pasqua, confirmed the strength of his leadership. That he managed to retain the support of most RPR deputies and the bulk of party members when premier Balladur appeared best placed to carry the 1995 presidential election provided additional proof of the loyalty that Chirac had built up over a twenty-year period. The support of the RPR in the run-up to the 1995 presidential election was itself of great importance. In 1995 the support of a powerful political party appeared to be an important ingredient of presidential success, one commonly overlooked in an age of modern political communication.

10.3 The UDF: a failed presidential party

History

Of the three movements considered, the UDF has by far the weakest claim to comprise a presidential party. Its inclusion in this section is debatable, but justified by the observation that the movement was itself the creation of former President Giscard d'Estaing. The Union for French Democracy (Union pour la démocratie française, UDF) was formed in 1978 as a confederation of parties supporting the President. It continues to exist some twenty years later, in the form of an uneasy but functional co-existence between several political families with distinct political traditions. The chief political forces represented within the UDF are the Republican Party, the inheritors of Giscard d'Estaing's Independent Republicans (1962–77); and Force démocrate (FD), the successors of the French Christian-democratic tradition. The other three component elements of the UDF are the Radical Party, which can trace its origins back to 1901; Perspectives et réalités (a small party dedicated to former President Giscard d'Estaing) and the UDF's 'direct' members. Rather than being a party in the conventional sense, the UDF is a confederation of separate political parties, each anxious to preserve its identity and positions of political strength (Cole, 1990). Only the few direct members give the UDF any genuine existence as a federation.

The UDF might be considered as a successful electoral cartel, but as a failed presidential party. His election as President in 1974, against the powerful Gaullist party, confirmed Giscard d'Estaing's patrician disdain of political parties, in accordance with the traditions of French conservatism he represented. Because he had not had to rely on a political party for his election, the third President initially made little concerted effort to organise a disciplined presidential party. His belief that Chirac would 'deliver' the Gaullist movement appeared increasingly fanciful; Chirac's resignation as premier and launch of the RPR in 1976 dispelled any doubts he might have entertained. The creation of the Republican Party in May 1977 was a response to the threat represented by a reinvigorated Gaullist party, as was the creation in February 1978 of the UDF, in preparation for the National Assembly elections of March 1978.

The President's various parliamentary supporters (the PR, the CDS and the Radicals) were constrained to conclude an electoral agreement among themselves before the 1978 election, in order to stand a chance against rival RPR candidates. Each party agreed in advance which constituencies would be contested. The politico-institutional system of the Fifth Republic (in particular, the manner in which the electoral system had come to operate by 1978) and the prevailing atmosphere of conflict between President Giscard d'Estaing and his former premier Chirac combined to promote the creation of the UDF as a matter of electoral necessity. In 1978 UDF candidates faced first-round competition from RPR candidates, but in subsequent elections the UDF and RPR have agreed single candidates in most constituencies before the first ballot.

As an electoral cartel, the UDF has repeatedly proved its worth; it provides a loose structure allowing the non-Gaullist parties of the centre-right to co-operate in their mutual interest, and to bargain with the RPR. In 1988 for the first time, the UDF became the larger of the two right-wing formations in terms of deputies, a position it held until the 1993 election. The UDF and its allies have consistently outpolled the RPR in cantonal elections; UDF *notables* control a larger number of departmental councils (*conseils généraux*) than any other party, as well as several leading French cities (notably Lyons, Marseilles and Toulouse).

President Giscard d'Estaing had originally envisaged the UDF as the basis for the emergence of a great centre-right party, a dominant presidential party to replace the Gaullists. But even while Giscard d'Estaing remained at the Elysée, the UDF was too indeterminate an arrangement to serve as an effective presidential party. It lacked an effective organisational basis upon which to mobilise support. This was confirmed in the 1981 presidential election when, to all intents and purposes, the UDF was excluded from Giscard d'Estaing's re-election campaign. Once Giscard d'Estaing had lost the presidency, the UDF became little more than an electoral cartel.

As a parliamentary party, the UDF has been less than convincing: there has been no assurance that its member parties even form part of the same parliamentary group. From 1988 to 1993, the CDS formed its own autonomous group, before returning to the UDF fold in 1993. In the European Parliament, UDF deputies have also formed part of various separate parliamentary groups. As a presidential party, it is doubtful whether the UDF as such exists. In the 1981 election, Giscard d'Estaing completely ignored the UDF, as did Barre in 1988. In 1995 the UDF was hopelessly split between those advocating support for Balladur, those demanding a UDF candidate, and those backing Chirac. The fact that the UDF refrained from running a candidate in 1995 seriously called into question its status as a presidential party. The systemic and political constraints explained above probably mean that the UDF will survive as a loose electoral cartel, but little more.

Beliefs and political appeal

The history of the UDF is also the history of its component parties and the trajectories of a number of key individuals (such as former President Giscard d'Estaing and former premier Barre). The genealogy of the various member parties of the UDF reveals diverse origins, but common pressures inciting co-operation. Each party was forced to adapt to the political conditions of the Fifth Republic, notably the emergence of conquering Gaullism in the 1960s.

The largest party in the UDF is the Republican Party (1977–). Its forebear, the Independent Republicans (1962–77), was created by Giscard d'Estaing in 1962 in order to rally those old-style conservatives who wanted to support de Gaulle over Algerian independence and over the direct election of the President. Most Fourth Republic conservatives opposed de Gaulle on these issues, but they were progressively supplanted by Giscard d'Estaing's pro-Fifth Republic movement. From 1962 onwards, Giscard d'Estaing's Independent Republicans represented the bulk of the non-Gaullist fraction of the presidential majority, providing critical support for the Fifth Republic, for de Gaulle and later for Pompidou. The alliance between Giscard d'Estaing's Independent Republicans and the Gaullist party provided the core of the presidential majority during the de Gaulle and Pompidou presidencies. The Independent Republicans were replaced in 1977 by the Republican Party, as an ostensibly disciplined party capable of standing up to the RPR, and federating Giscard d'Estaing's other parliamentary supporters. In practice, the Republican Party has retained key features of the older formation: a weak central organisation, a distrust of party activists and a preponderance of conservative *notables*, with their independent bases of political power, usually in local government. The Republicans might be portrayed as the inheritors of the independent conservative traditions of the Third and Fourth Republics. Their loose style of organisation faithfully reflects their origins as provincial *notables* with a strong sense of independence, of innate superiority and of hostility to the organisational constraints of belonging to a political party.

The other principal party within the UDF is Force démocrate, a 'new' party born in 1996 out of the CDS and the tiny Social-Democratic Party. Its creation is too recent to enable any serious analysis to be undertaken. The creation of Force démocrate was intended to move the former CDS away from too close an association with Christian democracy, and to broaden its geographical appeal (with the party seeking to appeal beyond its Catholic strongholds in western, eastern and northern France). The CDS itself had been formed in 1976 as a fusion of two earlier centre parties, the CD (Centre démocrate)and the CDP (Dreyfus, 1990). In terms of its organisational filiation, broad philosophical outlook and geographical implantation, the CDS was the inheritor party of the MRP, the important Christian-democratic party of the Fourth Republic.

The CDS could probably lay the strongest claim to representing a 'centre' party in French politics. Until 1974, the forebears of the CDS (Lecanuet's Reformist movement of 1967 and Democratic Centre of 1973) attempted to preserve the centre as an autonomous political space between left and right. This proved virtually impossible. Overt centrist parties or presidential candidates have not performed particularly well in the Fifth Republic. Due to the constraints of the second-ballot electoral system, self-identified centre deputies in the Fifth Republic have generally owed their election to conservative electorates and to alliances with parties of the mainstream right. This was notably the case for most 'opposition' centrists from 1962 to 1973. In presidential elections, self-proclaimed centre candidates (such as Barre in 1988 and to some extent Balladur in 1995) have lacked credibility in the absence of enthusiastic support from one of the major parties. The bipolarising pressures of the Fifth Republic have thus made life difficult, if not impossible, for a centre party which is genuinely independent from the parties of the left and right. This reason more than any other explains why Force démocrate remains tied to the UDF cartel; it depends upon conservative solidarity for the election of its deputies, mayors and senators.

Force démocrate differs in important respects from the other principal party of the UDF, the Republicans. It is the inheritor of the social Catholicism of the old MRP. Its political identity has consistently been Catholic, social and European. It has been less inclined to accept an unregulated free market than the 'neo-liberals' of the Republican Party. There is, however, some degree of geographical complementarity between the CDS and the Republican Party: the latter is weak in the former's strongholds and vice versa. The Republicans tend to be strongest, for instance, along the Mediterranean coast, and in the Rhône-Alpes area, where there is no strong Catholic tradition. The CDS electorate is a (rural) conservative electorate, which limits the reformist aspirations of CDS leaders. As with the Republicans, the real strength of the CDS lies in its fortresses in local and regional government, and its strong parliamentary representation. Its influence is also manifested through a range of associations promoting semi-Catholic causes.

Leadership and organisation

Throughout its existence, the UDF has remained a loose confederation without a mass membership or a structured party organisation. The real rationale for the continuing existence of the UDF lies in the need to provide a loose structure to regroup the non-Gaullist elements of the right-wing coalition, and to allow for the survival of distinct political and geographical traditions resistant to Chirac's brand of Gaullism. These specific traditions include those of social Catholicism, independent-minded conservatism and the vestiges of peasant anti-clericalism. In the terms of Duverger's (1964) classic formulation, the UDF is composed of a loose collection of cadre parties forced to cohabit by the exigencies of the Fifth Republican political system. It is neither a presidential rally of the Gaullist type nor a well-structured party such as the Socialists. Its two largest parties (the Republicans and Force démocrate) mutually suspect each other of wanting to dominate the UDF. Neither party wants the UDF to be a genuine federation, or party, which would weaken their own identity.

More than in any other party, the role performed by the elected representatives (élus) should be signalled for attention. With its solid implantation in local government, and in the context of the French practice of multiple office holding (cumul des mandats), power within the UDF lies less with a designated leadership than with powerful regional barons, who combine strong positions in subnational government with leading roles at the national level. François Léotard (Republican Party) and Pierre Méhaignerie (CDS) provide two good examples to underline a general phenomenon. Both men combined leadership of their respective movements with important positions in local government and major national ministerial responsibilities. Neither exercised an inspirational, mobilising style of leadership. In the Christian-democratic tradition, leadership is generally understated and exercised in a restrained manner. In the Republican Party, leadership styles are more expansive, but the leader must respect the internal balance represented by the existence of rivals who also hold strong political positions. In both the PR and Force démocrate, the wisdom of the *élu* is held in greater esteem than the inspirational leadership qualities of a particular individual leader, or a mass membership. A distrust of individual leadership and continuing resentment towards his personality also explained why former President Giscard d'Estaing was unable to impose his will upon the constituent parties of the UDF, even after he had captured control of the Federation in 1988. There was no mass groundswell in favour of a Giscard d'Estaing candidacy in 1995. The history of the UDF came full circle when, in 1996, Giscard was replaced as President of the UDF by his former protégé turned rival, Léotard.

10.4 The Socialist Party

History

The first unified Socialist Party in France, created in 1905, carried the curious title of the French Section of the Workers' International (Section française de l'internationale ouvrière, SFIO) in deference to its formation on the orders of the Second International. It brought together a total of six small socialist parties, an early pointer to the divided nature of the French left. Each of these pre-parties represented different traditions, ranging from anarchism to French Marxism to reformist socialism. Throughout its existence (1905–20), the first (and only) unified Socialist Party was racked by conflict between orthodox Marxism and evolutionary, gradual socialism. To some extent, this conflict has remained present within the French left ever since. At the congress of Tours in 1920, the SFIO split into two parties in response to the challenge posed by the Bolshevik Revolution of October 1917. A majority (around two-thirds) of delegates voted to accept Lenin's 21 conditions and created the PCF (Chapter 11). A minority of delegates retained the title SFIO. This fundamental division of the French left into Communists and Socialists has never been overcome. The history of the French left since this date has been one of long periods of fratricidal strife interrupted by short-lived spells of alliance, themselves a prelude to renewed inter-party conflict.

The Socialist minority at Tours retained the party's initial title SFIO, in order to demonstrate its organisational continuity with native French Marxism. The SFIO vehemently rejected the Bolshevik model and declared itself committed to working within existing parliamentary and republican institutions. Although the Communists were the larger element in 1920, by 1932 the Socialists had come to dominate the French left, with the PCF reduced to being an isolated minority. In the 1936 election, a left-wing alliance of Communists, Socialists and Radicals won the first ever real left-wing majority in France's history. Following the Popular Front election victory, the Socialist leader Léon Blum formed a Socialist–Radical coalition government; the PCF, arguing that it was a revolutionary party, refused to join. Despite a series of important symbolic social reforms being enacted (paid holidays, the 40-hour week), the left-wing government rapidly ran into serious economic and political problems. It survived barely one year, collapsing when Radicals withdrew from Blum's government. What was the legacy of the Popular Front experience? The 1936 election revealed the left at its most effective when united; the brief duration of the Popular Front government suggested that it could be united only for short periods of time, around specific objectives, before natural rivalries gained the upper hand. The only periods of united left-wing government in French history occurred between 1944 to 1947 when Communists, Socialists and the Christian-democratic MRP joined together in the post-war resistance coalition; and from 1981 to 1984, when four PCF ministers participated in Mauroy's government.

During the period 1945–69, the history of the French Socialist Party was one of almost uninterrupted decline, whether this was measured in terms of electoral performance, party membership or political offices occupied. From a post-war high of 21 per cent in 1945, the SFIO had declined to 12.5 per cent in 1962, before sinking to 5.1 per cent in the 1969 presidential election. The Socialist Party experienced the first decade of the Fifth Republic as a stagnating party with few new ideas, an ageing political personnel, and an outdated political strategy that refused to acknowledge the direct presidential election or the need for a lasting alliance with the PCF. The role performed by the Socialist leader (and former premier) Guy Mollet in the Algerian crisis from 1956 to 1958 had led to further splits within the Socialist movement, notably on behalf of the anti-colonialist left. From the early 1960s onwards, key initiatives came from outside of the SFIO, in the form of several left-wing political clubs and the small Unified Socialist Party (PSU). Most future Socialist personalities had formed a part either of the clubs or the PSU; few had their origins in the SFIO, itself a damning testament to the stagnation of the old party. François Mitterrand took control of the party in 1971 at the congress of Epinay, heading a heterogeneous alliance principally directed against the former SFIO leader, Mollet. It was indicative that Mitterrand came from outside the SFIO, with the power base of the future President being a movement of left-wing political clubs known as the Convention of Republican Institutions (CIR).

The rise of the Socialists was the major political occurrence of the 1970s. No single explanation can account for their success. This stemmed from a combination of reasons, of which political strategy, sociological change, ideological evolution and Mitterrand's political leadership were all important (Cole, 1994a). During the

1970s Mitterrand's PS was a party well attuned to the institutional, social and political imperatives of the Fifth Republic and the social structures of French society. Unlike the PCF, the PS (created in 1969) was a party which, on an institutional level, could credibly contend to win the presidency, the supreme political prize of the Fifth Republic. Mitterrand understood that there was no future for a party, such as the old SFIO, which refused to respect the new political rules of the Fifth Republic, centred upon victory in the presidential election. Mitterrand finally achieved such a victory on his third attempt in 1981.

After the decade of revival (1971–81), the French Socialists experienced a decade of being the presidential party (1981–93), before being brutally rejected by the French electorate in 1993. The extent of the electorate's disavowal of the French Socialists in 1993 indicated the relatively fragile bases of their electoral renaissance in the 1970s.

Beliefs and political appeal

Mitterrand's Socialist Party came to articulate the demands of many new social movements arising in the 1960s and 1970s. New social movement activists figured prominently among the influx of new party members which by 1975 had transformed the old SFIO into a recognisably new party. On a sociological level, the new French Socialist Party of the 1970s appeared to be a genuinely interclass party, repeating a feat achieved previously only by the Gaullists in the 1960s. This was in marked contrast with the old SFIO in the Fourth and early Fifth Republics: the SFIO had become reduced to being an institutional expression of lower civil servants and public sector workers, penetrating neither the ranks of the industrial working class nor the new emerging social groups.

Mitterrand's PS attracted support from many of the new social groups produced by post-war socioeconomic and demographic change: new tertiary sector workers (especially in the public sector), the new and expanded professions (teaching, social work), as well as a high proportion of the *cadres*, the managerial strata whose ranks had increased dramatically in the post-war period. The party also proved remarkably successful at attracting the support of older, more traditionally left-wing constituencies, such as industrial workers and low-status office and shop-workers, over which the Communist Party had traditionally exercised a strong influence (Capdeveille, 1981; Bell and Criddle, 1988). The development of the PS during the 1970s and early 1980s under Mitterrand's leadership thus witnessed the party transformed into being a virtual microcosm of French society as a whole. At its height, the Socialist Party managed simultaneously (and paradoxically) to attract support beyond the left as a catch-all party; to appeal to the traditional left-wing electorate attracted by orthodox Marxism (the culture represented by the French Communist Party); and to articulate the concerns of new social movements and themes given expression in May 1968.

The progression of the Socialist Party was replete with contradictions, not least that the party proved capable of appealing for the support of the crucial swing groups in the electorate, while at the same time radicalising its political discourse and programme. The French PS maintained a far more radical language and programme than that of any other European socialist party. This was a product of three factors: the constraint represented by the need to take into account the PCF; the fact that it had been absent from power for almost 25 years; and the enduring radicalising influence of May 1968, which inspired a whole new generation of PS activists. It is interesting to compare the evolution of the French PS with that of other European socialist and social-democratic parties. In order to stand a realistic chance of forming a government, or else as a result of their experience in government, European social-democratic parties had generally moderated their political programmes, originally based on Marxism, in the post-war period. This had usually occurred *before* obtaining power, with the evolution of the German SPD providing a role model for other parties to imitate. The French Socialists apparently underwent a reverse process: in order to facilitate alliance with the Communists, the party made radical policy commitments on a scale no other European socialist party would envisage. The incompatibility between the rhetoric of a party in opposition and the limited possibilities of government action explained in part the difficulties of the early reformist period of the Mitterrand presidency (Chapter 2). The gap between theory and practice disorientated Socialist Party leaders, activists and voters, especially after the turn to economic austerity in 1982–3.

Leadership and organisation

The post-1971 Socialist Party (PS) represented, among other things, an uneasy compromise between a Gaullien-style presidential rally (inspired by Mitterrand's leadership after 1971) and a strong tradition of party organisation and self-sufficiency (as embodied in the old SFIO). The tension between traditions of party patriotism and the exigencies of presidentialism (notably Mitterrand's self-elevation above the party) was a constant feature of internal PS dynamics during its decade of renewal (1971–81). The post-1971 party laid great stress on its quality as a democratic party, as an aspiring mass party, even as a *parti autogestionnaire* inspired by the ideals of May 1968. Of equal importance was its character as a factionalised party: the resurrection of the PS during the 1970s was intricately linked to the fusion of a variety of pre-existing political groups into a single party (Cole, 1989). The PS is the most openly factionalised of French political parties, to the extent of career advancement depending upon belonging to one of the party's key factions. Factions are officially represented on the party's governing organs. As a general rule, in the 1970s factionalism could be portrayed as being synonymous with internal party democracy (hence positive). By the early 1990s, after over a decade of Socialist government, factionalism carried highly negative connotations, synonymous with patronage, policy division and power politics.

The problem of the role of the presidential party was complicated by the fact that the PS considered itself to be a mass party, rather than merely a personal appendage of a providential leader. As the earlier presidential parties had discovered, however, the PS was constrained broadly to provide ideological justifications for policies it had neither initiated nor approved. During the first Mitterrand presidency, potential tensions between the key pillars of the Socialist power structure (the presidency, the executive and the party) were smoothed over because there existed a virtual osmosis between party and government, to the extent that it was difficult to distinguish between them as separate analytical entities. The Socialist Party leadership was determined from the Elysée palace, and there was direct presidential involvement in the selection of PS candidates for parliamentary elections. The party was effectively co-opted into the governmental machinery and reduced to silence. Critics argued that the PS had ceased to exist as early as 1983.

In electoral terms, such a judgement was premature, as revealed in the party's honourable performance in the 1986 National Assembly elections (31.61 per cent). The PS victory in the 1988 National Assembly elections revealed the continuing solidity of Mitterrand's electoral coalition of the 1970s. But the party's identity problems were aggravated during Mitterrand's second presidential term (1988–95). Relations between party and president deteriorated to such an extent that the President's name was hissed at during a special PS conference in 1994. Differences between president and party surfaced at the level of policy, organisational interests and personalities. Party leaders deplored both their lack of influence and the general direction of government policy (especially during the Rocard government, 1988–91, when older factional rivalries were revived). PS leaders also feared that President Mitterrand's attempts to broaden the presidential majority from 1988 onwards were detrimental to the party's long-term interest. The Rocard government of 1988–91 contained several ministers from outside the Socialist Party, mainly those representing 'civil society', such as former Olympic champion R. Bambuck as Minister for Sports. But Rocard's government also contained men who not only were not socialists, but had previously participated in centre-right governments: J.-P. Soisson and J.-M. Rausch were the most prominent. Moreover, throughout the second term, President Mitterrand appeared to make strong overtures to political groups in competition with the PS; this was notably the case with respect to B. Lalonde's Génération écologie in the 1994 European election.

The real electoral disavowal of the Socialist Party came in 1993, when it was reduced to under 20 per cent of the vote, not far above the level when Mitterrand had taken over the party in 1971. While PS support held up honourably among its new middle-class voters in 1993, the party's popular vote collapsed. The divorce between the Socialist Party and the traditional left-wing constituency suggested a breakdown in the successful electoral coalition (new middle classes + popular electorate) that had brought Mitterrand and the Socialists to power in 1981. The Socialist Party finally paid the electoral price in 1993 for a decade of economic austerity and rising unemployment, which hit the party's traditional electorate with particular intensity. Apart from narrow economic issues, the Socialists suffered from their perceived inability to provide responses for 'new' issues such as immigration and the environment, and from the highly damaging impression that, with so many of its politicians involved in corruption scandals, the PS had lost its claim to occupy the moral high ground in French politics. The honourable performance of the Socialist candidate Jospin in 1995 only partially re-established confidence with the popular electorate; the PS candidate notably trailed Le Pen among industrial workers (21/27).

10.5 Conclusion and summary

Lionel Jospin's presidential campaign performance of 1995, and his overwhelming endorsement as the new party leader in October 1995, gave the French Socialist Party new hope. The secret of the success (in the circumstances) of Jospin's campaign lay in his recognition that the PS had to distance itself from the Mitterrand legacy, and from the personality of François Mitterrand, in order to survive. This illustrates a more general point in relation to the presidential parties appraised above.

An element of paradox surrounds the presidential parties. Each is at least potentially tied to a particular political leader. This has proved necessary for each of these political families to function in a political system that places a high value on personality and the direct presidential election. But each has also suffered from its status as a presidential party – to varying degrees and at different moments. The Gaullist UNR emerged almost overnight as a presidential rally to elect deputies sympathetic to de Gaulle and the new republic. It experienced some difficulty in defining a role beyond this. It did not long survive de Gaulle's departure in its existing form. The UDF, created four years after President Giscard d'Estaing's election, surfed on the presidential bandwagon for a limited period, but soon discovered the former President to be an encumbering figure. The PS was moulded in the image of François Mitterrand during the 1970s, faithfully served President Mitterrand for most of the 1980s, and was disavowed by the electorate in 1993. In the 1995 presidential election campaign, the Socialist candidate, Lionel Jospin, distanced himself as far as decently possible from Mitterrand's heritage. This was, however, problematic for Jospin, as he had been deeply implicated in the public policy choices of the time.

Notwithstanding the identities of individual parties, the weight of the systemic constraints imposed by the Fifth Republic has tended to reduce the capacity of parties to act in a manner autonomous from their *de facto* presidential leaders. These systemic constraints include: the principle of presidential initiative in policy formulation, personnel selection and elections; the generally subordinate elective relationship binding party to President, or *présidentiable*; and not least the strait-jacket imposed by the 1958 constitution, which tends to require a large measure of parliamentary subordination to the executive, whether presidentially inspired or prime ministerial.

All serious presidential candidates in the Fifth Republic have attempted to appear as being above party. Parties are forced to campaign for presidential candidates over whose behaviour or political programme they have little control. If their candidate is successful, parties have been constrained to respect the engagements of the President of the Republic, rather than develop their own programmes. This deprives parties of the critical policy-making capacity essential for a genuinely independent existence. This proved to be especially the case for the PS, a party with a strong tradition of self-sufficiency.

The presidential perspective has greatly increased tensions *within* parties and coalitions as well as between them. This was apparent in the 1995 presidential campaign: for the first time, the two leading conservative candidates (Chirac and Balladur) represented different coalitions within the same party, the RPR. Personal rivalries between these *présidentiables* were manifest, to the extent that Chirac defined the content of his presidential campaign in order to demarcate himself as far as possible from his rival. In common with the US model, the personalised basis of presidential competition depletes campaign platforms of much meaningful content; by ricochet, it reduces political parties to observer status during presidential campaigns, which is bound to limit their future influence.

Indicative bibliography

Bell, D.S. and B. Criddle (1988) *The French Socialist Party: The emergence of a party of government*, Clarendon Press, Oxford.

Bergounioux, A. and G. Grunberg (1992) *Le Long Remords du pouvoir*, Fayard, Paris.

Charlot, J. (1970) *The Gaullist Phenomenon*, Allen and Unwin, London.

Cole, A. (ed.) (1990) *French Political Parties in Transition*, Dartmouth, Aldershot.

Colliard, J.-C . (1971) *Les Républicans indépendants*, PUF, Paris.

Dreyfus, F.-G. (1990) 'Place et poids de la démocratie chrétienne: le CDS, un parti démocrate chrétien dans l'arène publique', *Revue française de science politique*, vol. 40, no. 6.

Dupin, E. (1991) *L'Après-Mitterrand: le Parti socialiste à la dérive*, Calmann-Levy, Paris.

Gaffney, J. (1989) *The French Left and the Fifth Republic*, Macmillan, London.

Knapp, A. (1994) *Gaullism since de Gaulle*, Dartmouth, Aldershot.

Portelli, H. (1992) *Le Parti socialiste*, Montchrestien, Paris.

Chapter 11

The anti-establishment parties

11.1 Introduction and objectives

The parties considered in Chapter 10 were labelled as presidential parties, in that each could aspire to elect its candidate to the presidency. The three parties considered in this chapter – the Communist Party, the National Front and the Greens – are all anti-establishment parties in terms of their political identity, in spite of their quest for greater recognition on behalf of existing parties. One of the key features of French 'exceptionalism' was the persistence for most of the post-war period of a strong Communist Party. The strength of the PCF – for long France's leading party – was a structuring feature of the political system, helping to shape the strategies of other French parties, and partially determining the direction of party competition. The existence of a powerful, if long dormant, far-right tradition also set France apart from Anglo-Saxon experiences of liberal democracy, if not from those of several continental European partners (most notably Italy). The breakthrough and persistence of the far-right Front national has durably shaped the structure of the French party system and the issues processed by the policy agenda since the early 1980s. In line with developments in other European nations, the breakthrough of the Greens testified to the presence of political ecology as a new social and political movement, albeit one of uncertain longevity and identity. A plethora of minor parties, political clubs and extra-parliamentary forces give a colourful dimension to the French party system; a brief typology of these parties will complete this chapter.

11.2 Whatever happened to the French Communist Party?

History

The creation of the French Communist party (PCF) at the congress of Tours in 1920 was one of the key developments in the history of the French party system. The decision of a majority of delegates to the SFIO's 1920 congress to accept

Lenin's 21 conditions and to affiliate to the Third International led to the creation of a new left-wing movement, which took the title of the French Communist Party. The consequences of the Tours split were long lasting. It gave the PCF a revolutionary identity, a belief in its destiny as the future harbinger of socialist revolution. It also ensured that the PCF accepted the leading role of the Soviet Union in world affairs, and subordinated itself to the CPSU. During the inter-war period, the PCF was gradually transformed from an ill-organised collection of romantic revolutionaries into a tough bolshevik organisation, dedicated to furthering the aims of the USSR, and tightly organised along democratic centralist lines (Tiersky, 1974).

Bolshevisation in the 1920s gave way to Stalinisation in the 1930s. The emergence of Maurice Thorez as uncontested PCF leader in 1934 symbolised the party's dependence upon the Soviet Union; Thorez was handpicked by Stalin. Domestic strategic orientations closely followed political evolutions in Moscow. The shift from a 'class against class' isolationist strategy between 1928 and 1932, to a Popular Front option in 1936 depended far more upon Stalin's evaluation of the dangers of fascism than upon any indigenous political reasoning on behalf of the Communist Party leadership. By lessening its isolation, however, the 1936 election proved that left-wing unity benefited the PCF even more than the SFIO. The PCF leapt overnight from 8 to 15.7 per cent of the voters, including for the first time majorities in many of the working-class suburbs surrounding Paris, suburbs which remain loyal to the party today.

The wartime Resistance movement transformed the PCF into the major political force of the left, a status it occupied until the mid-1970s. Its resistance legitimacy enabled the PCF to expand its bases of support beyond its core working-class base – conquered in 1936 – to include many rural areas, with French peasant communism particularly strong in south-west and central France. In 1944 the Communists joined with Socialists and the Christian-democratic MRP in a post-war resistance coalition, which collapsed under the impact of the cold war in May 1947, with the Socialists and the MRP combining to expel the Communists from government. Once again, mutual enmity between the left-wing parties replaced their brief period of co-operation.

The PCF during the Fourth Republic: a counter-community?

The decline of the Communist Party during the Fifth Republic becomes apparent when appraising its strength during the Fourth Republic. The party's weakest performance in the Fourth Republic (25.8 per cent in 1956) comfortably surpassed its best showing in the Fifth Republic (22.5 per cent in 1967). In the five general elections of the Fourth Republic, the party's vote varied between 25.8 per cent (1956) and 28.6 per cent (November 1946). Throughout the Fourth Republic, the PCF acted as a counter-community, in opposition to the rest of French society, in some senses a mirror image of the Catholic Church (Kriegel, 1985). The party was a highly organised community, which offered its members the emotional satisfaction of belonging to a cohesive, well-organised counter-society, with its own norms, duties and satisfactions. Party members would come into contact only with other party members, would go on party-sponsored vacations and attend party summer schools. The PCF was by far the best organised French party, the only one with an activist mass membership. At its height, the PCF conceived of itself as a tribune of the working class, articulating the demands of alienated industrial workers.

The PCF's obsession with workerism (*ouvrièrisme*) reflected its own position within the political system. The bulk of the party's electoral support came from industrial workers. In 1947 the PCF captured control of the CGT, the largest trade union, which gave the party unprecedented access to organised labour; it exploited its control of the union to further the party's political aims. After its conquest of the CGT, the PCF was the only party which could lay a genuine claim to be able to organise the working class politically. Communist party cells proliferated in factories throughout France, especially in the larger industrial concerns.

Inspired organisationally by Marxism-Leninism, the PCF also inherited older French anarcho-syndicalist traditions, which stressed the autonomy and self-sufficiency of the working class (Ridley, 1970; Lorwin, 1972). The marginal, alienated status of the working class reflected France's late industrialisation, and the high concentration of workers in geographically distinct proletarian areas, such as the Paris Red Belt, the Nord/Pas-de-Calais mining sectors, and pockets of heavy industry elsewhere, notably in eastern France (Lorraine) and along the Mediterranean coast (Marseilles).

The other key aspect of the PCF's identity as a counter-community lay in the almost mystical faith placed by French Communist leaders in the USSR. During this period, the PCF was the most Stalinised party in western Europe, although national revolutionary symbols also played their part in the construction of PCF identity. This might be explained by several factors, the most pertinent being that the PCF had been moulded into an effective pro-Soviet party during the inter-war period, whereas the other important western European Communist Parties – notably, in Italy and Germany – had been crushed under fascism and had effectively been reconstructed as new parties during the wartime resistance to fascism. PCF leaders felt they owed a great debt of loyalty to the USSR, and to Stalin in particular. In contrast particularly with the Italian party, the PCF had retained its organisational continuity throughout and had never lost its faith in the revolutionary leadership of the USSR.

The PCF's consistently high level of political support during the Fourth Republic had an important impact on the overall direction of party competition. Communist strength facilitated centre-right domination in three principal senses. First, the systemic opposition of the PCF after 1947 condemned the socialist SFIO to join a series of centre-right coalitions aimed at defending the republic against its enemies. Second, the cold war climate prevented any prospect of the formation of a united left (SFIO and PCF) alliance. Third, the strength of the PCF, and its stance as a determined anti-system party, enabled the non-communist centre and conservative parties to scare moderates against voting for the left. This mechanism continued to operate in favour of the centre-right and Gaullist parties until the left's electoral victories of 1981.

The PCF in the Fifth Republic: decline and resistance

The creation of the Fifth Republic marked a fundamental watershed for the PCF. The party strongly opposed the return of de Gaulle and paid a heavy price for it: in 1958 the PCF lost one-quarter of its electoral support for opposing de Gaulle, most of the lost voters being working-class people attracted by de Gaulle's blend of nationalism, charismatic leadership and promise of strong government (Ranger, 1981). From being France's largest party in 1946, with over 28 per cent of the vote, the PCF polled 8.6 per cent in the 1995 presidential election, itself a better performance than other recent showings.

No single explanation should be isolated to account for this decline, it being a combination of several related phenomena. On a purely institutional level, the PCF has suffered from the effects of the second-ballot electoral system, as well as from the direct election of the presidency. The rules of political competition in the Fifth Republic dictate that, to be a successful party of government, a party must be a presidential party, able to elect its candidate to the presidency. The PCF clearly is not such a party. Alongside this secondary explanation, the PCF's decline can be related to the process of social and ideological change, the collapse of communism and repeated mistakes made by the Communist Party leadership.

Social change

The PCF always relied disproportionately on the industrial working class for its electoral support. Unlike other western European communist parties, the PCF made little concerted effort to expand its electoral clientele beyond its working-class strongholds; in part, this was because the party conceived of itself as the 'party of the working class'. The party's traditional strongholds have been in the strong industrial conurbations of the Paris region, the north and the Mediterranean around Marseilles. In the Fifth Republic, it has rarely been able to attract much support outside these areas, except in certain rural strongholds where the party led the French Resistance movement, notably in south-west and central France. The PCF has fallen victim to the modernisation of French society and the economy. Not only has the industrial working class been declining rapidly in France, but the party's hold over its working-class constituency has dissipated to the point of extinction. From the mid-1970s onwards, the PCF faced fierce competition for working-class votes, first from Mitterrand's PS in the 1970s, latterly from Le Pen and the Front national. Since 1981 the PS has attracted substantially more electoral support among workers than the PCF, as a more credible party of the left. And since 1988, the Front national has also consistently outpolled the PCF among industrial workers, capitalising on the breakdown of the communist subculture to extend its influence in underprivileged working-class suburbs.

Strategic inconsistencies

The French Communist Party has been damaged by repeated changes of strategy, oscillating between unity with the Socialists and hardline anti-socialism. After the débâcle of the 1958 election (18.9 per cent, 10 seats), the PCF adopted a renewed Popular Front strategy of alliance with the Socialists. The PCF argued strongly in favour of a common programme of government with the Socialists from 1962 onwards, believing that it was their only means of obtaining a share in power, and ensuring that the Socialists were committed to radical change once in government. Such a programme – the Common Programme of the Left – was eventually signed with the Socialists in 1972. It committed the left to a range of radical reforms foreshadowing those eventually enacted in a milder form in 1981–2. Previous experiences of left-wing unity – in 1936 and in 1944–7 – had clearly benefited the PCF electorally, as the stronger, more organised party of the left. This did not occur from 1972 to 1977: the experience of the Common Programme greatly strengthened the Socialists, led by Mitterrand since 1971, while the Communists stagnated. For this reason, the PCF renounced the Common Programme in 1977, only months before the National Assembly elections of 1978, which the left had been expected to win. Although the left-wing parties agreed a second-ballot withdrawal pact in 1978, they lost the election (Johnson, 1981).

Once elected President in 1981, Mitterrand invited the Communists to join his government. From 1981 to 1984, the PCF had its second experience in government. This was largely an unhappy affair. There were only four Communist ministers out of a total of 44, and they had little impact on government policy. But merely by participating in the Socialist government, which adopted increasingly austere economic policies after 1982, the PCF lost face in the eyes of its more radical voters. The PCF finally quit the government in 1984 after its humiliating reversal in the 1984 European elections (11.2 per cent). The ensuing decade witnessed a return to harsh anti-Socialist rhetoric, suspended only to enable the PCF to conclude electoral pacts with the Socialists in 1988 and 1993. The party has progressively become marginalised on the extreme left of French politics, and the Socialists have come to dominate the mainstream left. Conscious of the limits of isolation, the new party leader, Robert Hue, has attempted to build bridges with the Socialist Party. Co-operation between PS and PCE was closer in the 1997 campaign than on any occasion since 1973.

The collapse of communism

For as long as it survived, the PCF was never really able to distance itself sufficiently from the USSR and the Soviet model of communism. With the collapse of the Soviet Union, the PCF has lost its most consistent model of reference. The PCF was created as a party dedicated to the defence of the USSR. It was the most Stalinised party in western Europe, due in part to its organisational continuity, in part to the situation of the French proletariat and its sense of exclusion from the national community. The French party reacted to Khrushchev's denunciation of Stalin in 1956 with disbelief . In contrast to the Italian Communist Party – which immediately defined an Italian road to socialism – the French remained committed to the salient traits of the Soviet model and to the defence of the Soviet Union. It was only in the course of the 1970s that the PCF declared itself a Eurocommunist party and made some timid criticisms of Soviet labour camps. By the time it attempted to liberalise its doctrines in the mid-1970s, it was probably too late: Mitterrand's Socialist Party had already succeeded in attracting the support of those who might have been tempted by a reformed Communist Party along the lines of the Italian example. After the break with the Socialists in 1977, the PCF reverted to its former deference to the USSR.

Marchais' leadership from 1970 to 1994, became synonymous with an orthodox defence of traditional communism, including against the reformist Gorbachev era in the USSR. Those within the party who argued that the PCF should be more forthcoming in its support for Gorbachev were either expelled or silenced (Raymond, in Cole, 1990). The real sentiments of the Marchais leadership were revealed when the PCF leadership failed to condemn the Soviet coup which briefly ousted Gorbachev in August 1991, leading to a fresh wave of resignations from the party. With the collapse of communism in eastern Europe and the former USSR, the PCF has become rudderless, having lost a deeply ingrained framework of reference provided by the 'real socialism' of the Eastern Bloc, and unable, or incapable, of replacing it with anything else.

Organisation and leadership

Its 'democratic centralism' (officially abandoned in 1994) was for long a fundamental feature of the French Communist Party's organisation. In principle, the doctrine of democratic centralism – invented by Lenin in 1902 to deal with the problems of a revolutionary party in Tsarist Russia – stipulated that democratic discussion was full and free until decisions had been taken, when organisational discipline and unity had to be respected. In practice, the organisational basis of the PCF was 'all centralism and no democracy'. At the height of its strength, this organisational principle ensured that orders reached at the summit were implemented in a disciplined manner throughout the lower echelons of the party. However, internal dissent was a reality of the French Communist Party even during its heyday. Open factionalism broke out in the 1980s, in the form of a succession of waves of opposition to Marchais' leadership. Marchais finally retired as General Secretary in January 1994, after 24 years at the helm, but only after handpicking the new General Secretary, Hue. In unreformed communist tradition, no discussion was allowed within the party in relation to who should succeed Marchais as leader. In certain respects, at its 28th Congress in 1994, the PCF appeared one of the last unreconstructed communist parties. Efforts undertaken by Hue to broaden the party's political appeal have met with real, but limited success, as revealed in the 1995 presidential election. Whether Hue will be able to impose reform on the Communist Party bureaucracy will be a key future test of the ability of the PCF to reform itself.

Despite its decline, the PCF retains certain important resources. It still controls the CGT, one of the two largest labour federations. After the 1993 National Assembly elections, the PCF managed to hold on to its parliamentary group, with 23 deputies and a number of senators. Moreover, despite serious losses in the 1995 municipal elections, it continues to hold powerful positions in local government, essential for the party's organisational survival. Finally, it continues to express a diffused radical sentiment which, arguably, lies deeply embedded in the French political tradition.

11.3 The National Front: the reluctant anti-establishment party

History and electoral evolution

If the National Front (FN) was born in 1972 as the 'latest attempt at regrouping the forces of the extreme-Right' (Shields, in Cole, 1990), it differed from previous manifestations of this tradition in several respects. From its inception the FN leader, Jean-Marie Le Pen, strove to demarcate the Front from earlier, especially violent, manifestations of the extreme-right tradition. The FN openly looked to the Italian far-right party, the Movimento Sociale Italiano (MSI), as a model to imitate, a movement which resurrected the Italian far right from the early 1970s on the basis of an electoralist strategy and a pursuit of democratic respectability. In order to preserve its 'governmental' vocation, the FN has attempted (with little success) to build bridges with mainstream conservative movements and their electorates. The imperative of respectability was not lost on Le Pen himself: in the early days, he wore a black eye patch over his left eye, which he claimed hid his injuries received in the Indochinese war; after 1981, Le Pen dressed in the smartest republican blue, and removed the pirate-style eye patch.

Somewhat like the example of the French Communist Party above, the FN has attempted to perform variable roles: as a federator of the French far-right tradition; as a vehicle for disseminating the influence of nationalist ideas; eventually as a partner in power. To this extent, it has been a reluctant anti-establishment party. In its early guise, the FN acted as a federator of various marginal groups of the extreme right, such as Occident and Ordre Nouveau, called upon to unify their forces in a 'non-sectarian' spirit. In its capacity as a rally of the far right, the FN attracted (and continues to attract) a rag-tag of marginal groups committed to various lost causes: monarchists, Vichyites, former Poujadists, *pieds noirs* (former Algerian settlers), *intégrist* Catholics, anti-communists, anti-abortion activists and self-proclaimed fascists. The ecumenicism of the FN is an essential part of the movement's appeal, since it limits competition from other far-right groups.

The FN's electoral audience was initially minimal. In 1978 the FN obtained 0.4 per cent. In the 1981 presidential election, Le Pen failed to obtain the 500 signatures necessary to stand as a candidate. The FN's electoral breakthrough first became apparent in 1983: scattered successes in the municipal elections were followed by good performances in by-elections towards the end of the year (at Dreux and Aulnay-sous-Bois). The first national breakthrough occurred in the European elections of 1984: 10.95%. This performance was better than any previous far-right showing since the beginning of the Fifth Republic. The no vote in the 1962 referendum on Algerian independence totalled only 9.3 per cent. In the 1965 presidential election, Tixier-Vignancourt obtained 5.3 per cent. In subsequent elections, the Front has polled an average of 10–12 per cent, with 15 per cent in the 1995 presidential election as its highpoint.

Interpretations vary as to why the FN was able to achieve a major breakthrough. At least five important explanations relating to the Front's initial successes appear credible, though none is satisfactory on its own.

1. The breakthrough of the FN was an ultra-conservative reaction to the radicalisation of politics in the aftermath of Mitterrand's victory in May 1981. For the most hardline faction of the right-wing electorate, the parties of the mainstream right appeared lacklustre in their opposition to the Socialists' radical reform programme of 1981–3; the Front offered uncompromising opposition to the Socialist–Communist government. The 1984 FN electorate was bourgeois in its socioprofessional profile; this suggested that early support for Le Pen came from the most hardline faction of the traditional right-wing electorate; the popular classes only joined the Le Pen bandwagon later on.

2. The breakthrough of the FN was facilitated by the existing political parties, insofar as these parties attempted to exploit concern over 'immigration' (or, more accurately, the coming-of-age of second-generation immigrants, and their entry on to the labour market) to score political points off their rivals. The PCF was the first party openly to exploit the theme of rising immigration for its own political purposes (Schain, 1987). Communist local authorities in the Paris region, well in tune with the sentiments of their own voters, adopted an increasingly antagonistic attitude towards Arab immigrant workers. In 1980 one PCF-run municipal council bulldozed a hostel housing immigrants. The mainstream parties also contributed in an indirect manner to legitimising the political message carried by the FN. The RPR–UDF opposition used immigration as a stick with which to beat the Socialists, notably during the 1983 municipal elections. The Socialists themselves retained an ambiguous attitude towards the FN, whose survival would weaken the parties of the mainstream right. Mitterrand's introduction of proportional representation for the 1986 National Assembly elections was inspired in part by the calculation that an FN parliamentary presence might prevent the RPR–UDF coalition from obtaining an overall majority.

3. The breakthrough of the FN was tied to economic crisis: neither left nor right had been able to come to terms with the post-1973 economic crisis. The

assimilation of unemployment with immigration was a central feature of Le Pen's initial political message. Simplistic solutions to the problem of unemployment were attractive to a proportion of the electorate alienated by the broken promises of left and right. As it became an established political force, the FN picked up substantial support in the deprived outskirts of leading French cities, where high levels of unemployment and crime co-existed with large numbers of 'immigrants'. Although detailed psephological studies repeatedly demonstrated that there was no easy correlation between FN support and the concentration of immigrants (Fysh and Wolfreys, 1992), post-electoral surveys also consistently portrayed FN voters as those for whom immigration and security were the principal political issues.

4.   The breakthrough of the FN was a manifestation of discontent with the political system. Popular distaste for mainstream politicians was increased by the spate of corruption scandals that occurred throughout the 1980s. This allowed the FN to attract support on the theme of 'clean hands', one of its 1993 election campaign slogans. Le Pen skilfully exploited an anti-political strand within French political culture. As a new party, the FN was not tainted with the failings of the existing parties, partly because it did not hold many positions of elected responsibility. It could be understood as a virgin party that stood outside of the existing 'corrupt' political system. Le Pen's attacks against the 'gang of four' should be understood in this sense.

5.   As a practitioner of demagogic political leadership, Le Pen has not been surpassed. He has astutely manipulated the personalisation inherent in the Fifth Republic's presidential system, and has exploited the mass media in order to spread his message. The simplistic solutions advocated by Le Pen make it difficult for mainstream politicians to compete on grounds that the FN leader himself has defined. Le Pen's leadership has not been exercised without criticism, however, including from within the FN. Within the context of the French far right, Le Pen occupies a median position between those urging an Italian evolution (moving into a governmental coalition with the parties of the mainstream right, as the MSI achieved in Italy in 1994) and those advocating a hardline far-right response.

Each of these explanations for the National Front's breakthrough contains partial truths, but also its own internal weaknesses. Explanations based on the resurgence of a national populist strand of political culture do not account for the fact that the FN emerged at a particular point in time. The personal leadership explanation underplays the social forces underpinning the FN's emergence. The initial political explanation (the idea that the FN was a radical reaction to the left in power) cannot account for the fact that the FN performed better under the right in 1986–8 and 1993–5 than it had done under left-wing governments. The economic crisis interpretation cannot account for the fact that the crisis had persisted since 1973–4 without political extremism. It is clear that all of these ingredients are necessary to explain Le Pen's breakthrough.

Despite predictions of its imminent demise, the Front has proved its capacity to resist in each type of election the regime has to offer, whatever the electoral system used. This sets it apart from past far-right movements, such as Poujadism of the Fourth Republic. It has performed well in elections fought under proportional representation (European and regional elections), but it has stood up well in other contests as well (cantonal, municipal and legislative elections). Its most spectacular performances have been in presidential elections. The 'earthquake' represented by Le Pen's performance in the first ballot of the 1988 presidential election (14.4 per cent) was surpassed only by his 1995 score (15 per cent). On both occasions, the first-round push of the FN leader had a major impact upon second-round campaigning by the remaining candidates.

The Front has occupied few positions of direct influence within the French political system. Until 1995 it ran no large councils. Its unique municipal experience in a town of over 10,000 inhabitants (St Gilles in the Gard department) ended in farce. It has no deputies (despite polling 12.41 per cent in 1993), although it had a group of 35 after the proportional representation election of 1986. In 1995 it had 10 members of the European Parliament, which formed an interventionist European group vilified by almost everybody else in Strasbourg. Its largest influence is within the 22 regional councils, where it elected hundreds of councillors in the 1992 regional elections. Even in the regions, however, it rarely has the power directly to block initiatives taken by mainstream parties. Evidence suggests that the patient electoralism of the FN has garnered certain rewards. The capture of three major councils in the 1995 municipal election (Marignane, Orange and Toulon) was an important breakthrough: for the first time, the FN had access to the various resources provided by control over municipal government (such as land use, housing, culture and municipal employment). The FN captured a fourth council – Vitroller – in early 1997.

The FN's principal weakness lies in its isolation. This is essentially political, stemming from the fact that nobody will ally with the movement. Sporadic local alliances between the RPR or the UDF and the FN, especially in the south of France, were terminated in 1990, on the orders of the national party leaderships. The second-ballot electoral system used for National Assembly, cantonal and municipal elections usually penalises marginal parties unable to enter into alliances with other parties. With 12.41 per cent in the 1993 National Assembly elections, the FN fielded 99 second-round candidates, but it elected no deputies. In contrast, the PCF obtained 9.12 per cent but returned 23 deputies; this was because it could count upon electoral alliances with the Socialists, and because of the geographically specific nature of Communist support.

The political appeal of the Front national

Interpretations of the character and appeal of the FN vary. Indeed, the movement itself has evolved during its existence.

A protest movement?

The appeal of the FN might be interpreted on different levels. At one level, it is certainly a vehicle through which the various undercurrents of the French extreme right are expressed; its subtle anti-Semitism, for instance, is designed to appeal to its hard core, extreme-right electorate. But these themes only appeal to a minority, even of Le Pen's electorate. At a more general level, the FN is a party which is used as a protest vehicle for a variety of different discontents with the existing political parties and political system, and with French society in general. In the words of John Frears (1990), 'The FN skilfully weaves together many of the themes of the post-war extreme-Right: Poujadist, anti-Parlementarism and rejection of politicians, nostalgia for the days of empire and of French Algeria in particular, anti-Communism, the cult of the leader, anti-semitism, above all the nationalist theme of France for the French.'

In terms of continuity with past traditions, it is clear that the Le Pen phenomenon represents the resurgence of a deeply rooted national populist strand of French political culture. The political message of the FN is best understood as a form of national populism, which is flexible enough to respond to changing public anxieties. Le Pen defends himself against the charge of being anti-republican. It is unlikely that the FN would enjoy the level of support it currently does if its political message was limited to expounding the themes of the French extreme right. The search for historical predecessors is probably necessary, but certainly insufficient in order to understand Le Pen. The FN bears certain similarities to the short-lived Poujadist movement of the 1950s. The latter – which polled some 12.5 per cent in the 1956 election – often evokes comparisons, but they are somewhat misleading. The Poujadist movement was an anti-tax, anti-modernism movement of shopkeepers, traders and small businessmen (Williams, 1964), whereas Le Pen recruits from a far broader social spectrum. While Le Pen obtains his highest support in large cities, the 1956 Poujadist movement fared best in the rural areas and small towns of west and south-west France.

A fascist party?

Fysh and Wolfreys (1992) conclude their study of the FN as follows:

> The FN has made its appearance in a country with mass unemployment, a social crisis, bankrupt politics; it has built a mass base on a personality cult and exploitation of a ready-made scapegoat; many of its leaders are psychotically anti-semitic; others have records for terrorism or other forms of violence. It is a new party, largely excluded from positions of power. This combination of phenomena is not new. It has occurred in the past. It has a name. Its name is fascism.

Two principal objections might be levelled against such a conclusion. First, it might be objected that fascism refers to a specific movement associated with unprecedented problems of dislocation and defeat in inter-war Europe. Second, it is debatable whether 'mass unemployment, a social crisis and bankrupt politics' accurately describes the state of contemporary French politics and society. Such appraisals can be historically misleading. They can also overdramatise the support received by a far-right movement such as the FN. On the other hand, a threatened sense of national identity, a feeling of anomie and menacing representations of the adversary all recall certain features of fascism, as well as the more obvious reference to the cult of the leader.

A single-issue movement?

The FN has been portrayed as a single-issue movement, rallying support around the theme of immigration-invasion (Mitra, 1988). While the FN is not exactly a single-issue party, Le Pen had made his political reputation by stressing one issue above all others. This might be summarised as 'France for the French'. Immigration and security are consistently cited as the essential policy issues by FN voters (Mayer, 1996). France has always been a country of immigration. But whereas past immigrants were Catholic Europeans (in the twentieth century, Italians, Portuguese and Spanish), post-war immigrants were mainly of North African origin, with their own well-developed culture and religion, which many feel to be antagonistic to mainstream French culture. The arrival of second-generation immigrants on to the French labour market, and manifestations of cultural difference, have reinforced the problem of the integration of ethnic communities into mainstream French culture.

The impact of Le Pen's FN should be measured in terms of influencing the policy agenda, rather than in a narrow electoral sense. Le Pen will never be elected President, but his political agenda on immigration is now widely accepted (in a modified form) by key elements of French society. Ever since the Front's breakthrough, sections of the main right-wing parties – the RPR and the UDF – have attempted to win back lost voters by imitating the Le Pen agenda on immigration. The indirect influence exercised by Le Pen on the French policy agenda was illustrated by the Nationality Act of 1993, which imposed tough new conditions for the acquisition of French citizenship; and by the practice of J.-L. Debré, President Chirac's Interior Minister, of forcibly expatriating illegal immigrants in chartered aircraft.

The politics of fear

Le Pen's politics are the politics of fear. The FN has proved capable of mobilising popular fears across a range of apparently unconnected themes, such as immigration, anti-Semitism, AIDS and European integration. Each appeared to threaten an idealised national identity. The politics of fear paid dividends, because France of the 1980s and 1990s was a society in the throes of an ideological vacuum, after the perceived failure of the right- and left-wing alternatives. Above all, the threat to national identity is the linchpin of Le Pen's mobilising appeal.

A populist movement?

The social bases of the FN are different from those of the classic right-wing parties. The FN's electorate is more masculine, young and popular than those of the traditional right-wing parties. In the 1995 presidential election, according to the BVA–Le Monde survey (Le Monde, 1995b), Le Pen outpolled any other candidate among industrial workers (27 per cent). As revealed in surveys since 1986, those groups supporting the FN most strongly are those on the wrong side of history: industrial workers, low-status clerical workers, artisans, small businesspeople, shopkeepers, farmers. Alongside this popular constituency the FN has always attracted the support of a more bourgeois constituency: from a fraction of the independent professions, in particular. As time has progressed, the FN's electorate has become more popular and less bourgeois. The centre of gravity of Le Pen's electorate has shifted. In 1984 the FN was supported primarily by traditional right-wing voters radicalised by the presence of the left in power, and their dissatisfaction with the divisions of the main right-wing parties. By 1986 these electors had returned to their traditional conservative base and they have been replaced by a more popular electorate. This sociological composition lends weight to the economic crisis thesis.

The Front obtains its best scores in the eastern half of France, especially in the large cities, where there are large concentrations of immigrants, combined with situations of urban deprivation. The large cities (especially the suburbs) provide fertile ground for the FN: this is the case in the north (Lille-Roubaix-Tourcoing); in Paris and its suburbs; in the east (Nancy, Strasbourg, Mulhouse); and in the centre (St-Etienne, Lyons, Grenoble). But the strongest concentration of support is along the Mediterranean coast: in Marseilles, Nice and Toulon. In these cities, urban tensions are complicated by the presence of large numbers of *pieds noirs*, white Algerian settlers forced to return to the mainland after Algerian independence.

The breakthrough of the FN is symptomatic of urban anomie, and of a measure of social and political disintegration. Polls show that FN voters are unlikely to trust anyone outside of family and a small circle of friends; outsiders are distrusted or despised (Perrineau and Mayer, 1992). The notion of crisis also explains why the FN performs well in localities where local political élites are in crisis: the FN performs so well in Marseilles, for instance, because of the disintegration of local political élites and the absence of anything to put in their place. By contrast, where local political élites are well implanted and respected, the FN has failed to make much impact.

11.4 The Greens: a flash in the pan?

Before 1989 the new wave of Green party politics which had influenced most of western Europe appeared to have bypassed France. Since the creation of Les Verts in 1974, the French Greens had experienced only intermittent minor successes, such as the 3.8 per cent vote for Antoine Waechter in the 1988 presidential election.

Environmental concerns had been placed on the political agenda by the May 1968 movement and resurged periodically throughout the 1970s, usually in the form of anti-nuclear protest. But aspirations of social change (including ecological change) rested firmly upon the mainstream left-wing parties, especially the Socialist Party, which partly resurrected itself in the 1970s by articulating the demands of a variety of new social movements. The ecological constituency was also represented by well-organised pressure groups, such as Friends of the Earth (Les Amis de la terre).

Between 1989 and 1992, Les Verts maintained a far more significant level of public support in the polls and electoral contests than hitherto (around 14 per cent). While the breakthrough of the FN had indirectly benefited the PS (by causing divisions among the RPR and UDF), the emergence of the Greens after 1989 had a detrimental effect on the Socialist Party, in part because the Greens provided a rallying point for disillusioned ex-Socialists. The breakthrough of the French Green parties represented part of a European-wide movement, based on the new saliency of the environment as a political issue. Within the context of the French party system, the success of the Greens was commonly interpreted as one further sign of the inability of the mainstream parties to articulate new political demands – in particular, those associated with the environment. The halcyon years of the French Greens were between 1989 and 1992. In the former year, the Greens first broke through into the European Parliament with 10.53 per cent of a resolutely volatile electorate. The unity of the French Greens – always imperfect – was damaged in 1990 when Brice Lalonde (a former Ecologist presidential candidate in 1981, later a minister in Rocard's Socialist government) announced the creation of Génération écologie, as a more pragmatic Green party.

Despite their divisions, in the 1992 regional election the two rival Green lists polled almost 14 per cent between them (7.1 per cent for Génération écologie; 6.8 per cent for Les Verts). 1992 was the year which saw the entry *en masse* of Greens into France's regional assemblies, where they participated in several regional executives. The jewel in the Green crown was reserved for the Nord/Pas-de-Calais region, where a Red–Green alliance was concluded between the Socialists and the Greens, presided over by Marie-Christine Blandin, a member of the Green party. Elsewhere regional diversity prevailed, and in both Green parties different strategies were adopted in different parts of the country. The failure to achieve heady expectations in the 1993 National Assembly elections (a combined total of 7.6 per cent) sparked off a devastating spiral of internal recriminations and divisions, which grew in intensity as the Greens' opinion poll fortunes diminished. By the 1994 European elections, the French Greens (2.84 per cent) had squandered the electoral capital carefully acquired in the course of the past ten years. Voynet's 3.3 per cent in the 1995 presidential election revealed the disoriented state of French political ecology.

Organisation and leadership

Under the informal leadership of Antoine Waechter from 1986 to 1993, the Greens stuck rigorously to a strict autonomy line, known as 'neither left, nor right', whereby the party refused to consider alliances with any other political parties. At the 1993 general assembly, Waechter was ousted by a heterogeneous coalition of factions spanning the extreme left to centre of Les Verts. Dominique Voynet articulated this new orientation. Whereas Waechter had prided himself upon retaining the Greens as an autonomous political movement independent of right and left, Voynet sees the Greens as lying in the tradition of the alternative left.

Unlike for most French parties, analysis of the official organisation of the Green parties is highly indicative of their character. The central organisation of Les Verts is extremely weak, with only minimal control over local and regional organisations. The internal decision-making processes are based mainly on direct democracy, with the party's sovereign annual assembly remaining open to all members: around 600–700 members usually attend out of a total membership of some 5,000. Rather than nominating an official leader, Les Verts designate four national spokespersons: the 'leader' (Antoine Waechter, 1986–93, D. Voynet, 1993–   ) has a far more precarious existence than in any other party. Alone among French parties, the party's activists exercise considerable control over the strategic choices made by the party leadership. As in other Green parties, there is no unified leadership in Les Verts; rather, fluid factions representing different sides in internal conflicts have risen and fallen. This informal type of party organisation has bred organisational chaos.

The decline of French political ecology, symbolised by Voynet's 3.3 per cent in the 1995 presidential election, is at least in part of its own making. The psychology of decline after the 1993 National Assembly elections was reflected in the outbreak of party factionalism of a particularly virulent nature: eleven separate tendencies were represented at the party's 1993 general assembly. There has, moreover, been a marked tendency for former leading personalities to quit the party once their influence has diminished: after Lalonde's desertion in 1990, former leader Waechter left Les Verts in 1994 in order to create his own minuscule movement (Mouvement de l'écologie indépendant). Taking these factors together, the French Greens appear increasingly to be a modern version of the old Unified Socialist Party (PSU), a movement bursting with ideas, but hopelessly divided, leading ultimately to paralysis and insignificance.

It would be misleading to judge the Greens merely by weighing their electoral performance. As harbingers of political ecology, the French Greens have contributed to placing new issues on the political agenda which mainstream parties have been forced to address. The influence exercised by environmental issues remains strong within French public opinion. As the German example reveals, the electoral fortunes of Green parties ebb and flow rather more than those of older established European parties. This is partly incumbent upon their representing a particular type of party. Rather than a party, in the classic sense of the term, the French Greens appeared to many as a single-issue movement, notwithstanding their efforts to produce coherent policies across the whole range of issues. There has never been a consensus that a political party is the most appropriate means of promoting Green issues: social movements such as Greenpeace and Amis de la terre have in the past been critical of any attempts to organise ecologists into a political party. Like their counterparts elsewhere, the French Greens appear as a radical new middle-class social movement. The social characteristics of party activists in Les Verts are consistent with the young, highly educated and new middle-class profile of activists in other Green parties.

11.5 The minor parties

Ever since its origins, the French party system has spawned a rich progeny of minor parties and personalities. To retrace the history of France's minor parties, political clubs and extra-parliamentary groups lies outside the scope of this chapter, but a brief attempt will be made to classify different types of minor party. Four main types might be identified:

- The first relates to former party factions transforming themselves into independent political parties. A recent example is that of the Mouvement des citoyens (MdC), a party created in 1990 out of the former CERES faction within the Socialist Party. The MdC retains certain pockets of support where the CERES faction was formerly strong, notably in Paris and in the Territoire de Belfort department, which leader J.-P. Chevènement represents as deputy.
- Since the inception of the Fifth Republic, political clubs have performed a major role, both in transforming parties from within, and in challenging them from outside. During the 1960s, left-wing clubs were instrumental in renovating the structures of the non-communist left outside of the SFIO. Since the 1980s, most club activity has occurred on the right, with certain clubs – such as Groupements des recherches et d'études pour la civilisation européenne (GRECE) – acting as bridges between the far-right and mainstream conservative politicians. Some of these clubs are genuine think-tanks; others are mini-political parties, or else operate as factions within or across parties.
- Certain parties form around particular individuals in dispute with their original party formations. The best recent example is that of Philippe de Villiers and the Mouvement pour la France (MPF). In opposition with the UDF over the Maastricht Treaty, and representative of an ultra-conservative strand of public opinion, de Villiers ran an independent list in the 1994 European elections, which polled over 10 per cent, a freak performance that de Villiers was unable to repeat in the 1995 presidential election (4.80 per cent).
- Since May 1968, various small but significant anti-system left-wing parties have provided real competition for the Communist Party in its control over the far-left electorate. These have included Trotskyites, Maoists and *gauchistes* of various guises. The most enduring (and endearing) is Lutte ouvrière (LO), a Trotskyite party which can trace its genealogy to the inter-war period. One of the principal surprises of the 1995 presidential campaign was the 5.37 per cent polled by LO candidate Arlette Laguiller in her fourth presidential campaign.

11.6 Conclusion and summary

The existence of such a broad range of anti-establishment and minor parties acts as a counterweight to the centripetal tendencies of the French party system analysed in Chapters 9 and 10. It helps to explain the continuing fragmentation of the party system, especially in non-decisive elections (such as European elections) and the first round of the presidential election. In the 1994 European elections, the two leading lists were reduced to a combined total of 40 per cent. On the first round of the 1995 presidential election, the two leading candidates polled just over 40 per cent of the vote, a far weaker proportion than in any other presidential election. The 1995 presidential election also witnessed an unusually strong showing of anti-system candidates, with the combined totals of far-left (14 per cent) and far-right candidates (20 per cent) surpassing one-third of the electorate, in addition to a higher than average abstention rate and number of spoilt votes (Cole, 1995).

The sudden emergence of the Greens in 1989, their peak in 1992–3 and their subsequent virtual collapse illustrates that the party system has to be analysed in terms of an active evolving structure, rather than a static range of pre-established political positions. In spite of the rich variety of anti-system parties (especially the FN) , the French party system has become rather more like those of its European neighbours. The mainstay of political competition is provided by a social-reformist PS, and the conservative RPR–UDF coalition. The major developments outlined in this chapter – the decline of the Communist Party, the breakthrough of the extreme right and the varying fortunes of political ecology – reflect broader European trends observable in countries such as Italy, Austria and Belgium. The major political blocs in France – conservative and social democratic – are broadly comparable to those present in comparable European countries. As in certain other European countries, however, the real dangers lie in the extent to which these blocs are challenged by political forces ambivalent towards liberal democracy.

In terms of the operation of the French party system, the image of French exceptionalism no longer comes from a strong Communist Party (which retains a significant political presence), but from an assertive and visible far-right movement which insists on its demands being taken into account, and which has exercised an indirect influence over the policy agenda. The ability to manage this movement poses a new test both for the integrative capacity of the French Fifth Republic and for the welfare of liberal-democratic values in French society.

Indicative bibliography

Bell, D. and B. Criddle (1994), *The French Communist Party*, Clarendon Press, Oxford.
Birenbaum, G. (1992) *Le Front national en politique*, Balland, Paris.
Frears, J. (1990) *Parties and Voters in France*, Hurst, London.
Hainsworth, P. (1990) 'Breaking the mould: the Greens in the French party system', in A. Cole (ed.), *French Political Parties in Transition*, Dartmouth, Aldershot.

Ignazi, P. and C. Ysmal (1992) 'New and old extreme right parties: the French National Front and the Italian Movimento Sociale', *European Journal of Political Research*, vol. 22, no. 1.

Marcus, J. (1995) *The National Front and French Politics: The resistible rise of Jean-Marie Le Pen*, Macmillan, London.

Mayer, N. and P. Perrineau (eds.) (1989) *Le Front national à découvert*, Presses de la FNSP, Paris.

Mayer, N. and P. Perrineau (1992) 'Why do they vote for Le Pen?', *European Journal of Political Research*, vol. 22, no. 1.

Newman, M. (1987) 'Conflict and cohesion in the British Labour Party and the PCF', *West European Politics*, vol. 10, no. 3.

Shields, J. (1990) 'A new chapter in the history of the French extreme right: the National Front', in A. Cole (ed.), *French Political Parties in Transition*, Dartmouth, Aldershot.

Chapter 12

The representation of interests

12.1 Introduction and objectives

In Chapter 12, the character of French group representation and mediation is discussed at some length. After a brief exploration of the various types of interest and pressure group activity, the weakness of economic interest groups is contrasted with the profusion of pressure group activity in the non-economic sphere, which belies traditional accounts of French *incivisme*. The actual mechanisms by which groups exert pressure are explored in some detail, as are the relations between groups and the state. It is contended that the French case cannot be fitted easily into the traditional pluralist or corporatist models of state–group relations. In the course of Chapter 12 it is hoped to investigate French pressure group politics in their full complexity, and to demonstrate that French history continues to weigh heavily upon the operation of groups in France. Despite certain modifications due to the changing role of the state, this is one sphere where the French 'exception' remains strong.

12.2 The context of French interest group activity

Pressure group activity appears at first sight weaker in France than in the north European democracies. This stems in part from the ideology of the indivisibility of the French state, a key legacy of the French Revolution. The process of state building arguably required the subordination of intermediary interests such as the church, the nobility and the monarchy, whose resources lay in a pre-revolutionary social and political order. The role of the state in forging national unity led to a distrust of intermediary interests as being detrimental to the general will, which was defined as being broadly synonymous with the welfare of the French state. Organised group activity was forbidden during the French Revolution; only in 1884, with the repeal of the *Loi le Chapelier*, were professional groups allowed to organise, but they remained weak (Guilani, 1991). The existence of a powerful central bureaucracy, imbued with the ideology of the higher interests of the state, contributed to the comparatively weak role of organised interest groups in policy making.

At the same time, powerful vested interests did manifest themselves within what remained until 1939 an overwhelmingly rural, agriculture-based society. The influence exercised by interests such as wine growers and North African settlers during the Third and Fourth Republics was well documented by Philip Williams in *Crisis and Compromise* (1964). During the parliamentary-centred Third Republic, interests focused their attention on key parliamentary committees with power to distribute resources. The capture of deputies, even parliamentary committees, by specific interests counterbalanced the official discourse valorising the higher role of the neutral state. In the course of the Fourth Republic, it became obvious not only that interests continued to capture parliamentary committees and certain ministries, but that agencies of the state themselves acted as powerful interests, weakening the myth of the unity and indivisibility of the French state. This was notably the case for the French military, which progressively detached itself from the tutelage of the republican state. Indeed, de Gaulle justified his return to power in May 1958 by castigating the influence of particularistic interests; it became obvious that de Gaulle included the military within this description. The official 'ideology' of the Fifth Republic reverted to the indivisibility of the French state and its superiority over organised interests. The 1958 constitution recognised, however, that political parties and interest groups had a legitimate right to exist.

Various attempts have been to explain the apparent weakness of French associational life, notably by referring to traits embedded in French political culture. Michel Crozier's 'stalled society' embodied this tendency; the French have a fear of face-to-face contact and are incapable of operating a normal model of political bargaining (Crozier, 1970). As a nation of individualists, the French are reluctant to join groups. Those who do belong to groups distrust the state, as well as each other, and are disinclined to enter into a political bargaining process. For its part, the French state continually contests the representative character of groups. The state occupies a powerful position because it is able to decide which groups are 'representative' of a particular sector. These arrangements benefit the group concerned in relation to its rivals. More than in most nations, the state thus arbitrates between which groups are 'good' and which are narrow and self-serving.

Political scientists have expended much energy attempting to define what pressure groups are and how they might be distinguished from political parties. In liberal-democratic polities, we might make several basic distinctions between groups and parties. The first distinction is that pressure groups articulate specific policy interests; parties aggregate a range of interests and attempt to formulate them into a coherent whole. As a consequence of this, political parties contest elections and seek to participate in power; pressure groups, on the other hand, seek to influence power, but do not normally contest elections or provide ministers in government. This rule is not watertight. Some groups, such as environmental groups, have on occasion transformed themselves into parties and fought elections:

the French Greens fall partially into this category. On occasion, prominent representatives of an interest group have served in government as ministers; this occurred in March 1986 when François Guillaume – leader of the powerful farmers' union, the FNSEA – became Minister of Agriculture in Chirac's conservative government.

It is useful to draw a distinction between pressure groups and interest groups. The term 'pressure group' might be used as a generic term to cover all types of group which engage in political activity of any sort. The term 'interest group' usually refers to professional groups, such as trade unions and employers' associations. In the terms of this definition, pressure groups in France have proliferated in the course of the Fifth Republic; the legendary French reluctance to join groups has been countered by an explosion of voluntary associations at all levels of society (especially locally). Occupational interest groups remain weak, however, with the notable exception of certain professions and the farmers.

12.3 French economic interest groups

The prevailing impression when studying French interest groups is one of fragility, although this masks an uneven pattern of influence. In certain policy sectors such as agriculture, well-organised professional interest groups enjoy a neo-corporatist style of relationship with the ranking state ministry, involving groups not only in the formulation of policy, but also in its implementation. The role performed by the FNSEA has been extensively researched in this sphere (Keeler, 1987). The weight of certain professional orders – notably among doctors, lawyers and architects – also lends itself to a corporatist-style analysis. In other sectors, contact between the state and organised interests ranges from the sporadic to the non-existent. This is partly because of the reluctance of the state to share policy-making responsibility with private interests, partly because groups are too weak and partly because the state itself is divided. In an attempt to link French experience with those of comparable liberal democracies, certain French public policy specialists have diagnosed a 'French' model of corporatism, based on the role of public sector professionals and the *grands corps*. This model will be considered below.

Business interests

Business represents the key cluster of interests in capitalist liberal democracies, both in the form of employers' associations and in the activity of individual firms (see Table 12.1). Employers' associations vary in their structure from one country to another. Employers in France are represented in different organisations according to their size: large firms are represented in the *Conseil national du patronat français* (CNPF); small and medium-sized enterprises in the *Confédération générale des petites et moyennes entreprises* (CGPME) or the *Union patronale des artisans* (UPA). The most important of these organisations is the CNPF. It is composed of representatives of the professional branches (e.g. the metallurgy industry, the

Table 12.1 French economic interest groups: a typology

Type	Organisation	Influence	Weaknesses
Business groups			
CNPF (Conseil national du patronat français)	Confederal. National Council unites representatives of sectoral branches (e.g. textiles, metallurgy, construction).	Lead employers' organisation. Representative of big business. Chief negotiator with government in most sectors. Helps run social security system with unions and state.	Large firms often act alone. Serious internal divisions in 1995.
CGPME (Conseil général des petites et moyennes entreprises)	Confederal.	Strength among small and medium-sized businesses.	Not an insider. Distrusted by governments.
Labour Unions			
CGT (Confédération générale du travail)	Confederal. Executive traditionally close to PCF. CGT was for long the largest French trade union, both in terms of votes cast in works council elections and in terms of membership.	Traditionally strong in ports, mines, shipbuilding, iron and steel and other heavy industry. Steep decline in works council elections (45% in 1967; 23% in 1995).	Long dominant in its industrial working-class bastions, the CGT has undergone a dramatic loss of influence. Haemorrhage of members (from over 3,000,000 in 1978 to under 1,000,000 in 1996). Unemployment, industrial rationalisation and ideological climate (decline of the PCF) all to blame.
CFDT (Confédération française démocratique du travail)	Confederal. The CFDT was created in 1964 out of the older CFTC. Traditionally Socialist inclining but suspicious of the PS, the CFDT was influenced by the strong ideological currents of May 1968. In maturity it has become the 'responsible' voice of French trade unionism. Nicole Notat only union leader to support Juppé's social security reform of 1995.	Traditionally poor sister to the CGT, the CFDT overtook the former in workplace elections in 1995 (24%). 5–600,000 members. Its zones of strength are less tied to heavy industrial plant than the CGT. CFDT took over from FO in 1996 as chair of Sickness branch (CNAM) of the social security sytem.	Certain branches traditionally opposed to leadership. Leadership contested for its co-operation with the Juppé government.

Table 12.1 (*continued*)

Type	Organisation	Influence	Weaknesses
FO (Force ouvrière)	Born out of a split with the CGT in 1947, FO is France's third most significant union. Marked by a tradition of anti-communism.	FO has traditionally been strong in certain white-collar professions and in the civil service. Until 1996, FO was the most important trade union representative in co-managing France's social security system. It was replaced in 1996 by the CFDT.	Serious internal divisions from Trotskyite factions. Marc Blondell's leadership contested. Loss of CNAM presidency a severe blow for the union. At most, 300,000 members.
Other economic interests			
Fédération syndicale unifiée (FSU) Fédération de l'éducation nationale (FEN)	Born in 1994 after a split with the FEN, the FSU has 11 member unions, the most important being the secondary school teachers' union (SNES). FEN retains majority support only among certain primary school teachers.	FSU less prone to co-operation or co-decision making than the FEN. Favours street demonstrations over negotiations.	The formal split within the FEN has weakened one of the strongest sectoral unions that France has ever known.
FNSEA (Fédération nationale des syndicats des exploitants agricoles)	Represents all interests in the agricultural sector. Shares features in common with labour and employers' unions.	Close contacts maintained between FNSEA officials and government ministers.	FNSEA increasingly contested by rural 'co-ordinations'.
'Co-ordinations'	'Spontaneous' groups arising in wildcat strikes with increasing frequency. Testament to the weakness of traditional unions.	Co-ordinations have appeared among nurses, health workers, railwaymen and farmers.	They are single-issue groups, which often disappear once a strike is over.

building federation and the textile employers' federation), as well as members of the 'interprofessional' local, departmental and regional unions. The CNPF and its member unions perform a range of functions: these include social and legal functions, and more classic lobbying activities. Much of the energy of the CNPF and of its local and regional federations is spent in providing representatives to sit on the tripartite committees that govern the social security regime, as well as the labour disputes courts. This activity is benevolent.

As a confederation, the CNPF has relatively weak control over the economic interests it represents. Moreover, it is frequently divided. In 1995, for example, a leadership struggle pitted the CNPF's largest professional union – the metallurgy industry union – against other employers' unions in a battle which the latter won. Its divisions can impair its bargaining position in negotiations with government ministries, which are apt to challenge the representative nature of the CNPF. Critics contend that the basis for joining the CNPF is completely anachronistic: most professional federations represent trades or professions that have evolved beyond recognition since the late 1940s when CNPF statutes were drawn up. Leading companies represented within the CNPF will more often than not operate as economic actors in their own right. This can also weaken the effectiveness of collective employers' action. The CNPF commands respect, however, on account of the vital importance of the interests it represents; its discrete pressure has been efficient under governments of different political persuasions. Its lobbying activities are concentrated upon Paris and Brussels. The CNPF has faced an increasingly vociferous challenge from the CGPME, representing small and medium-sized employers, whose interests often diverge from those of big business. Unlike the CNPF, the CGPME and the UPA will rarely, if ever, be drawn into the government's policy orbit.

Alongside employer's federations, the Chambers of Commerce, of Agriculture and of Trade perform an important role in representing industrial and commercial interests in the localities and regions, as well as performing a number of quasi-administrative functions. The Chambers of Commerce are the most important. They are semi-public organisations: in the words of one General Secretary interviewed, the Chambers have 'one foot in the public, one in the private'. They perform three essential functions. First, they represent the interests of local firms (industrial and commercial), in terms both of lobbying and of providing firms with business advice. Second, they are themselves important local economic interests (the Chambers run most of France's ports and airports, as well as many commercial and industrial zones). Third, they carry out important administrative and regulatory functions as local agencies of the Ministry of Industry and Commerce. Relations between the Chambers of Commerce and the local employers' federations are often tense, although there is a crossover of personnel between the two. This is due in part to the fact that the Chambers enjoy compulsory membership from all firms registered in their localities. This gives them substantial financial resources, since each firm has to pay 1 per cent of its turnover to the Chamber. Local employers' federations complain that this deprives them of financial resources, and point out that elections to the Chambers attract only 15–20 per cent of eligible voters.

Although French employers seek to present a united front, there are many sources of internal pressure: between small and big businesses, between industrial and commercial interests, between competitive and closed sectors, between export-driven and neo-protectionist sectors, and between conservative and liberal employers. The vital economic role performed by the larger companies places them in a strong bargaining position with the government, especially as the government will identify its aims with its industrial 'national champions'. Companies such as Peugeot-Citroën, Elf-Acquitaine and Rhône-Poulenc occupy a powerful bargaining position. In the industrial sphere, French traditions of powerful state interventionism have limited somewhat the freedom of manoeuvre of large indigenous firms, although this pattern is changing under the impact of privatisation and moves to closer European integration (see Chapter 13). The French state has less freedom in relation to multinational companies. The delocalisation of Hoover from Reims to Scotland in 1993 revealed the impotence of the French government to control the flow of industry in the open European market.

Labour unions

Trade unions constitute the second most powerful cluster of interests in the capitalist democracies. But they are generally far more divided even than employers' associations, and have suffered since the early 1980s from a steadily less favourable policy climate. European social-democratic governments have generally maintained closer relationships with trade unions than conservative governments, but this neo-corporatist model has been in decline across Europe. It has always been less relevant in France than in Germany, for instance, where the state routinely negotiates economic strategy with the 'social partners', in the form of the single employers' association and trade union federation. Although the term 'social partners' is used to designate labour and employers' representatives, economic interests are less integrated into decision-making machinery in France than in Germany or the Scandinavian countries. As with the CNPF and its member unions, the main trade union federations serve on the tripartite boards administering the social security system, and the labour disputes boards. Elections to these boards enable the strength of the various trade union federations to be gauged on an annual basis.

French trade unions are among the weakest in the EU (Mouriaux and Bibès, 1990). A combination of France's late industrialisation, the difficulties of legal existence and political divisions have meant that labour unions were never as firmly rooted in France as they were in Britain, Germany or the Scandinavian countries. The early history of the trade union movement was one of a struggle between the anarcho-syndicalist traditions of the craft unions and the collective proletarian ethos of later industrial unions (Lorwin, 1972). From the anarcho-syndicalist heritage emerged a deeply imbued sense of workerism (*ouvrièrisme*) and working-class self-sufficiency; this was later articulated by the *Confédération générale du travail* (CGT) and the PCF. The capture of the CGT by the Communist Party in 1947 aggravated political divisions between French trade unions, to the detriment of collective unified action. The division into five national trade union 'peak' federations, split along lines primarily of political affiliation rather than occupational status, proved a fatal weakness for French trade unions, which found it as difficult to speak to each other as to engage a dialogue with employers or the state.

At their height, French trade unions occupied powerful positions of strategic importance within French industry: in traditional heavy industries (mining, shipbuilding, automobile construction) the rate of unionisation was upwards of 50 per cent, with certain sectors (dockers, printers) operating an effective closed shop. Certain of these heavily unionised industries (mining) suffered an irreversible decline in the course of the 1980s, whereas others (automobiles) adopted new working practices less conducive to traditional union influence. Industrial rationalisation in the 1980s had a detrimental effect on union strength, as did the rise in unemployment. As well as there being a decline in traditional heavy manufacturing industries, unionisation is virtually absent in newer industries and in small-scale firms with fewer than 50 employees. Where unions are present in these small firms, they tend to be represented by the CFDT or the FO (which value collective bargaining), rather than by the CGT (which usually retains an oppositional stance).

Trade union representatives perform an important role in the administration of the social security system; in the works councils that have a statutory existence in all companies employing over 50 employees; on labour disputes boards, and in various local, regional and national consultative committees. But, even in elections for these boards, the largest union is that of non-union members. The overall proportion of non-union representatives elected to serve on professional bodies increased from 15 per cent in 1966 to 28 per cent in 1989; the CGT declined from 48 per cent to 24 per cent; while the CFDT's representation rose from 18 per cent to 22 per cent (Labbé and Croisat, 1992).

The crisis of French trade unionism forms part of a wider post-industrial movement. All trade union federations, whatever their ideological leanings, have suffered from the impact of the economic crisis, the effect of new technologies, declining working-class consciousness and the rise of individualism (Lasserre, 1985). In France, trade union decline has been superimposed upon a weak initial base of union membership: never more than 15–20 per cent of the overall workforce were unionised, a proportion well under 10 per cent today. Employers' associations and public policy-makers are often inclined to the view that French trade unions are too weak; there are scarcely enough activists to serve as union representatives on the social security committees, or to engage in collective bargaining negotiations with employers. Most industrial disputes that broke out during the 1980s and 1990s occurred by wildcat 'co-ordinations' or strike committees, completely outside the control of the official unions (Mouriaux, 1993; Hassenteufal, 1990). Such strikes were more difficult to control because of the absence of recognisable bargaining partners.

Farmers' and teachers' organisations

Two groups of workers have traditionally been powerfully organised in their own separate unions: the teachers and the farmers. The Fédération de l'éducation nationale (FEN) derived its strength from the fact that it represented teachers at all levels of the profession (from the maternity school to the university sector), as well as technical staff working in the schools. It was by far the most representative French trade union, which gave it considerable bargaining power in negotiations with the state. The FEN enjoyed traditionally close political relations with the Socialist Party, but these were embittered by a series of educational disputes throughout the course of the Mitterrand presidency. A major setback occurred when the left abandoned its project to reform private schools in 1984, a reform that had been strongly supported by the FEN leadership.

Throughout the 1980s, the FEN was weakened both by internal dissension between different political tendencies in its midst, and by competition from the teaching branches of the other unions (CGT, CFDT, FO). Itself a confederation of professional unions representing different levels of the teaching profession, the FEN was strongest among primary school teachers. The Syndicat national des instituteurs (SNI) had grown out of the conflict between church and state, and the defence of *laicité*. The FEN split apart in 1992, when the main secondary school teachers' union – the Syndicat national de l'enseignement secondaire (SNES) – was expelled from a movement controlled by the SNI. In response, a new trade union federation – the Fédération syndicale unitaire (FSU) – came into being, a federation which rapidly replaced the FEN in all branches except that of primary school teachers. As a federation, the FSU has eleven member unions, the most important being the SNES. The formal split within the FEN has weakened one of the strongest sectoral unions that France has known.

Farmers' unions display characteristics which are reminiscent of both trade unions and employers' associations. Despite the demographic decline of agriculture, these organisations continue to wield considerable influence in France, as well as in a number of other European countries. The political pressure brought to bear by farmers stems in part from the unity of the agricultural sector: employers and employees tend to make common cause in defence of agriculture, in a manner rare in the secondary and tertiary sectors. The near-monopoly of representation by the leading French farmers' organisation – the Fédération nationale des syndicats des exploitants agricoles (FNSEA) – has traditionally acted as a resource unavailable to labour unions, as have the close contacts maintained between FNSEA officials and government ministers. For these reasons, the FNSEA has a better claim to exist in a neo-corporatist relationship with the French state than any other trade union.

The modest economic weight of agriculture (Chapter 13) is counterbalanced by the fact that French farmers generally have political support, and employ pressure tactics to marshall this support to maximum effect. In particular, French farmers are defended by conservative-inclining parties, since they are perceived to symbolise essential features of national identity in a period of rapid social and economic change. The efficacy of the agricultural lobby was revealed during the Uruguay round of the GATT negotiations (1986–93), during which the negotiating stances of the French government were seriously curtailed by public support for a solution which safeguarded French farmers against the full effects of international competition.

There is undoubtedly a deep cultural sympathy for the plight of small farmers in France, a nation with a profound rural heritage (Boussard, 1990). To this should be added the fact that many constituencies are predominantly rural, and farmers' unions have proved successful in targeting unpopular deputies. The example of the farmers shows that the influence a group can exercise is considerably enhanced if it is backed by public opinion. The effectiveness of the farmers also reflects their willingness to resort to methods of direct action. The French farmers' unions have learnt lessons from early syndicalist movements; their violence is in proportion to their desperate plight and the uneconomic foundation of their livelihoods, especially after reforms to the EU's Common Agricultural Policy (Tacet, 1992). As with the trade unions, the position of the main farmers' union (FNSEA) has been threatened by the activities of unofficial rural 'co-ordinations', wildcat strike committees dedicated to the pursuit of narrow sectional interests, and less likely to compromise than the permanent partners of the state.

12.4 Non-economic associations and new social movements

Economic interests form only one type of group activity. Most groups are concerned with non-economic, voluntary or promotional activities. Pressure groups might include associations dedicated to the defence of the environment, feminist movements, regionalist movements, anti-nuclear movements, groups espousing specific moral causes, cultural movements, neighbourhood defence groups and so on. Certain associations might pursue overtly political objectives; others might be essentially non-political, becoming involved in politics only when government proposes to enact policy that affects its interests. Evidence presented below suggests that there has been an increase of participation in group activity in the French case, throwing into relief the traditional stereotype of the French as a nation of uncivic individualists.

There has been a growth of groups as the state has increased the scope of its intervention. In any area of policy, groups tend to crystallise on either side of the argument: for instance, pro- and anti-abortion associations; pro- and anti-hunting lobbies. This can be seen in relation to the environment, a relatively new area of political interest. Environmental groups sprang up in France in the 1970s, initially in an attempt to halt the construction of nuclear power plants. In response to environmental pressures, the French nuclear industry organised itself as a highly effective lobby against Green movements. As with the environmental groups, the pro-hunting lobby provides another example of the difficulties of maintaining a strict distinction between political parties and pressure groups: in the 1994 European election, the pro-hunting lobby ran its own list, Chasse, nature, pêche et tradition, which received 4 per cent, comfortably surpassing the vote of Les Verts.

In the course of the 1970s, the development of new social movements, such as environmental, feminist and regionalist movements, appeared less in evidence in France than in the UK or Germany. The French party system long remained impermeable to the disruptions of the new social movement politics of the 1970s and early 1980s, whereas these single-issue movements wreaked havoc in the UK and Germany. As argued in Chapter 2, the legacy of May 1968 expressed itself within existing political parties. Until 1981, aspirations of social change rested firmly upon the mainstream left-wing parties, especially the Socialist Party, which partly resurrected itself in the 1970s by articulating the demands of a variety of new social movements. The disappointment felt by these new social movements with the Mitterrand presidency (1981–95) was such as to stimulate more independent forms of political and group activity. As the example of the Greens illustrated, however, these movements were too heterogeneous to articulate a coherent political message. The demands voiced by new social movements in the 1970s have either been incorporated by mainstream political parties, or else (as with the nuclear issue) represented only a small minority of public opinion.

The '1901 associations'

According to French law, voluntary associations or clubs must be registered under a law dating from 1901 as 'non-profit-making' associations if they are to be assured of legal protection. '1901 associations' are required to adopt certain organisational characteristics (such as having written statutes and a management board) and are obliged to register their existence with the prefecture. In return, these 1901 associations can expect to receive public subsidies. This enables a fairly precise representation of the extent of civic participation in voluntary associations. According to one source, there existed 700,000 associations in 1995, employing a total of 800,000 salaried staff, making an important contribution to the non-profit-making sector of the French economy. These associations reputedly had a turnover of $50 billion, of which $20 billion came in the form of grants from public authorities (Kaltenbach, 1995). In 1992, 70,000 new associations were registered, compared with 20,000 in 1975. In its declaration of general policy in May 1995, the Juppé government estimated that 20 million French people were active in associations of one form or another. While the precise figure is impossible to verify, group activity – defined in its large sense – is the primary form of social mobilisation in France today. By way of comparison, the RPR can boast 150,000 active party members; the PS 100,000.

Whether these groups can be described as pressure groups, in the sense defined above, is debatable. Pressure groups are groups which seek to exercise pressure in order to secure their objectives; they are not simply groups of citizens coming together in pursuit of common interests. As Anne Stevens (1992) points out, however: 'many clubs and societies exist for purely recreational reasons, but even they may occasionally be stirred to political action'. The format of the 1901 association covers an infinite range of activities. The types of voluntary group activity have changed. Traditionally the 1901 association represented benevolent activity on behalf of charitable groups, such as Catholic aid organisations. Critics contend today that the 1901 format has become a cover to enable public funds to be channelled to organisations serving private interests. The distinction between genuinely private groups and those depending on public, or parastatal, authorities has become blurred. The boundaries between 1901 associations and private companies are not always clear: certain organisations benefit from both statutes. Moreover, the main economic interest groups – such as the CNPF and the CGT – have created pseudo '1901 organisations', in order to receive public subsidies. Even government departments have on occasion created '1901 associations' in order to overcome particular legal restrictions on their activity as public sector authorities. The most widespread distortion of the 1901 format is that instigated by municipal governments (see below). Along with the Mixed Economy Societies (public/private mixed societies established by public authorities), the 1901 associations have become one of the most prosperous – and least understood – areas of French democracy.

12.5 Interest groups and the French political system

The resources at the disposal of groups

The strength of an interest group will depend upon a number of factors: its strategic location within society, the degree of access it enjoys to decision-makers, its financial and technical resources, and the sympathy it attracts from public opinion. Most groups can be measured by these classic criteria. Others are less easy to classify. Groups espousing political violence – such as Action directe, or the Front national pour la libération de la Corse (FNLC) – fall outside of the parameters of normal political bargaining. There are different possibilities open to such groups: they can try to convince the authorities of their legitimacy, or they can adopt unorthodox methods, including various forms of direct action and political violence. Leaving aside these anti-system forces, a number of elements are likely to determine the effectiveness or otherwise of a group.

- *The extent to which an interest is structured.* Vast heterogeneous groups (such as pensioners, the unemployed and consumers) are hardly structured at all, whereas business or professional groups are more likely to have a precise agenda and powerful resources at their disposal. The most tightly organised French interest groups are the corporate professional orders, membership of which is compulsory for the professions concerned: the Ordre des médecins is the most notorious. Several French professional groups receive substantial financial contributions from the state, in return for performing a series of para-public functions (Guilani, 1991).
- *The attitude a particular government, or individual minister, adopts as to the legitimacy of groups.* A government in power is more likely to be sympathetic to groups with which it feels ideologically akin. Wright (1989) points out how successive Education Ministers in the 1970s and 1980s attempted to push through university reforms by relying upon the sympathetic teaching unions, at the expense of their rivals. That consecutive reforms floundered suggested that policy implementation required a more sustained, bipartisan effort. The capacity of the French administration to differentiate between groups sets the French state apart from most of its European neighbours.
- *Strategic position.* Certain interests impose themselves as major players because of their powerful strategic position. This is usually the case for the main

economic interests, notably large multinational firms which occupy specific market positions. Governments will often rely on large firms for detailed information concerning exports, markets and technologies. To act as such a specialised source of information is beyond the capacity of the state itself.

■ *Access to political and financial resources.* The largest groups (especially employers' associations and to some extent labour unions) tend to be self-financing, but for smaller, promotional groups, a lack of finance is often prohibitive. The fact that so many French voluntary associations depend for their survival upon grants from local government limits their autonomy and weakens their bargaining stance. In the absence of financial muscle, the rallying of public opinion to a particular cause provides a political resource that can radically enhance a group's bargaining position: overwhelming public support for the cause of the nurses and health workers in 1989, for instance, constrained M. Rocard's government into making concessions it had not initially envisaged.

Where do groups exercise pressure?

Groups apply pressure wherever power is held by the state, or by public authorities. They attempt to concentrate their activity in the arena where the state is at its most powerful. In modern complex democracies, this arena is invariably the executive. The highly centralised political executive of the Fifth Republic acts as an incentive for interest groups to 'network' with central state decision-makers. Interest groups will often employ full-time lobbyists to present their organisations' case. These figures are increasingly deployed in Brussels as well. There are, however, several points of access open to groups, with much French activity concentrated at the micro level.

The legislature

Classically, parliament was the central focus for pressure in the French republican tradition. Power appeared to reside in parliament, and deputies were far more accessible than remote civil servants. In the Third and Fourth Republics, individual deputies were often totally beholden to the pressures of particular vested interests, who provided financial support in return for supporting their cause. The case of the alcohol distillers (*bouilleurs de cru*) in the Third Republic was a celebrated one. With the general weakening of parliament in the Fifth Republic, the emasculation of the committee system, and stringent conditions for the introduction of private members' bills, such pressure tactics have proved less effective. Those groups that are forced to lobby deputies to support their causes are usually those without direct access to government departments.

The executive

The political executive and the bureaucracy are nearly everywhere the primary targets of interest groups. The capacity of a group to maintain a network of national contacts within government departments is testament to its influence, or to its 'insider' status. Serious negotiations between government departments and large firms take place 'behind closed doors': for example, in a myriad of formal committees and informal meetings. Large French firms – such as Elf-Acquitaine – have teams of lobbyists specifically trained to target government departments; they are received as partners by the ministers or civil servants concerned. In contrast, in most policy sectors, trade unions remained outsiders even during the Mitterrand presidency.

The French executive provides conflicting evidence of the penetration of interest groups into the decision-making machinery. All other things being equal, government agencies seek alliances (or at least good relations) with their corresponding professional groups; it is far less clear that these alliances will be successful in achieving results. In certain policy sectors, powerful interest groups – such as the FNSEA – appear to colonise their corresponding ministry, although this impression is not really accurate. In other sectors, groups are largely disconnected from the executive agencies. In still others, there is a continual and ongoing bargaining process between groups and agencies, both aware of the benefits of co-operation, but both attempting to maximise their influence *vis-à-vis* the other. The image of the 'policy community' has been used by Hayward (1986) to characterise policy making in the sector of industrial policy. While the policy community is useful as a metaphor to describe which actors are involved in policy making in a given sector – and which actors are excluded – it leaves many questions unanswered, notably the extent to which a given policy community really determines the outcome of policy. In the French context of a powerful central state, policy communities are rarely able to act in isolation.

Direct action

In most European democracies, groups which resort to street demonstrations will generally tend to exercise the least pressure, except where demonstrations are massive and highly symbolic of widespread support. This explained why the mass of anti-nuclear demonstrations had such an impact in West Germany in the early 1980s, for instance. In France, such methods have a long history. Direct action tactics have become a regular feature of pressure group activity, superimposed upon a distant memory of a revolutionary tradition. French farmers, fishermen and lorry drivers have perfected strategies designed to cause maximum possible disruption to the normal functioning of French life. The apparent success of such procedures has encouraged their protagonists. It has been argued that dissatisfied groups engage in such activities because they are excluded from regular participation in decision making in a highly centralised and secretive politico-administrative system. This thesis has almost certainly been exaggerated. For groups such as farmers, direct action tactics go alongside private negotiations between interest group representatives and state officials. A more serious problem revealed during the 1990s has been the inability of interest group representatives to conclude deals which are acceptable to their members; this has afflicted such venerable institutions as the FNSEA, the FEN and the main students' unions.

Subnational government

As illustrated in Chapter 8, the strengthening of local and regional levels of subnational government by the decentralisation reforms of 1982–3 created new arenas for group influence and activity. Bargaining between local politicians, local administrators and representatives of local interest groups takes places regularly across the range of policy issues that are decided at these levels (Le Galès and Thatcher, 1995). Since the decentralisation reforms, associations have had much closer contact with the various local and regional authorities, whereas previously groups would target their attention on the prefectoral and ministerial field services (Rolin, 1990). Alongside the municipal authorities, the departmental councils have become privileged partners for associations. Voluntary associations which dispense services (for instance, in the health or social spheres) have become rather more equal partners, as opposed to mere clients of local or central government. The notion of the contract between public authorities and voluntary groups expresses this new relationship. We should note, however, that the principal economic interest groups – employers' federations, trade unions – aspire to influence national policy processes as a priority, in the belief that decisions taken nationally will filter down to regional and local levels. Lobbying in Paris or Brussels bears more weight than regional or local lobbying.

Most voluntary associations exist at a local or subnational level. The interpenetration between municipal governments and 1901 associations reveals the dependency that exists between the two types of organisation. Many 1901 associations are created on the initiative of local authorities themselves, such as municipally inspired sports clubs, social or cultural associations. These groups can in practice be difficult to distinguish from agencies of local government. The system of local authorities providing financial support for local voluntary associations means that even groups bitterly opposed to the local authority often depend upon grants for their continued existence. Most French associations are usually in a weak position with regard both to elected authorities and to governmental agencies. They depend upon the latter both for financial support and for information. Only local authorities or government agencies can confer legitimacy on associations by bringing them within their orbit. The relationship between local pressure groups and the town hall is a particularly complex one: the mayor claims to personify the general interest, whereas local associations can only claim to represent one fraction of the population. To implement policy effectively, however, the town hall needs a network of associations in all different spheres of local society. These reinforcing pressures usually create a *modus vivendi* between the municipal government and the principal local associations.

The European Union

Lobbying tactics are increasingly directed towards the institutions of the European Union. Sites of pressure vary: they include the Commission, the European Parliament, the European Court of Justice and the biennial summits of European leaders. Types of pressure also vary: they range from direct action tactics adopted by French farmers in Brussels; to transnational trade union co-operation; to lobbying on behalf of French cities (usually in European networks of similar cities); to lobbying by industrialists representing particular sectors (such as the steel industry). Such forms of lobbying have developed exponentially in recent years, as groups attempt to reverse unfavourable arbitrations at the national level (Mazey and Richardson, 1993).

12.6 Pluralism, corporatism and the 'French exception'

In the Anglo-Saxon tradition, most democratic theorists regard the freedom to organise interests into groups as a fundamental prerequisite for the operation of liberal democracy. For sound historical reasons, prevailing French theoretical frameworks – equating democracy with a Rousseauist general will – have been less inclined to accept groups as a legitimate expression of the democratic process. The French state has historically been less tolerant towards autonomous groups than in comparable countries. In the French republican tradition, the state is held to be superior to the total of competing interests; groups exist in a subordinate relationship with the state. This order of priorities was written into the 1958 constitution, and is constantly reiterated in the discourse of politicians and civil servants. In the USA, by contrast, a system of freely competing interest groups is held to be synonymous with democracy itself: the state prefers to see itself as a referee between the key interests in society. The French and American examples provide two differing views of liberal democracy: in the first, the people's representatives (and the state) express the general will; in the second, the popular will emerges as the result of the confrontation of conflicting private interests. These historical, cultural and political traditions affect the role of groups and patterns of group–state relations in both countries.

Two ideal-type models of state–group relations (and their adjectival extensions) have prevailed in the academic literature on interest groups. The pluralist model portrays democracy in terms of the free interplay of competing groups, with the state reduced to an arbitral role. The corporatist model describes a pattern of state–group relations within which groups are fully integrated into the machinery of the state, and where relations between groups are largely non-competitive. Neither is applicable in the French context. Pluralism is alien to the institutional and philosophical framework of the Fifth Republic. The pluralist portrayal of politics in terms of a system of groups competing on a relatively level playing field underestimates the role of the state in arbitrating between groups, and deciding which ones are legitimate. This is particularly important in France. Pluralism appears ill-adapted to explain the French traditions of a strong, directive state defining the parameters of group activity, and a relatively weak system of national bargaining.

Neither does the corporatist model, as defined by Schmitter, appear appropriate when considering French state–group relations. Schmitter defined neo-corporatism in terms of a number of principles: non-competition between groups, recognition of groups by the state, representational monopoly of the single group, and compulsory membership of professional groups (Schmitter and Lehmbruch, 1979). In the corporatist schema, groups do not compete with each other, as much as co-operate closely in their mutual interest. This is typified notably by national collective wage agreements negotiated between the state, employers and the unions; by the representation of capital and labour on key policy-making committees; by the existence of single powerful labour and employers' federations; and by the existence of closed shops and compulsory membership. As with pluralism, this model does not appear particularly well adapted to the French experience, although certain features inevitably occur. Groups are too divided, or else there is insufficient evidence that points to the involvement of labour and capital in economic policy making. Corporatist features have been partially diagnosed in relation to agricultural policy and in the operation of several professions. The Chambers of Commerce also share certain features of the corporatist model. The corporatist label appears less pertinent elsewhere.

A French version of the notion of corporatism has been applied by certain specialists (Jobert and Muller, 1987; Mény, 1989). While recognising that a full application of neo-corporatism is inappropriate in the French context, these observers maintain that the French case is characterised by certain corporatist features, notably the institutional incorporation of the main social partners (employers and trade unions) into the state, especially via the tripartite system. The specific character of the French model relates to its strong public sector corporatism and its pattern of representing interests within the state. The French system of the *grands corps* gives French corporatism a stato-centrist coloration absent in other European nations. The role of *grands corps* (especially the Mining, Highways and Bridges, and Rural Engineering corps) surfaces in numerous public policy studies. Separate studies have highlighted the importance of engineers from the Bridges and Highways corps in urban policy in the 1960s and 1970s (Thoenig, 1973); that of mining engineers in energy policy; and that of arms engineers in civil aviation (Muller, 1989). The advantage of such studies is that they highlight the role of powerful actors within the state, as much as the incorporation of outside interests into the decision-making machinery. Even so, not all French observers are convinced of the wisdom of adapting a foreign concept such as corporatism to fit the murky reality of the French situation. Fontaine (1996) points to the forces challenging the French model of public sector corporatism, notably the evolution of the state faced with pressures of European integration and decentralisation, and the changing role of the *grands corps*.

12.7 Conclusion and summary

It is difficult to fit the French case into either of these models – or their variants – which appear designed to depict different social and political realities. The above analysis would suggest that state–group relations are one sphere in which the French exception remains alive and strong. In part, this is the inescapable heritage of France's past historical development, which has ensured that trade unions perform a subaltern role, that direct action tactics can pay dividends, that technical state *corps* have great prestige, and that the state exercises an essential role in defining the parameters of legitimate group activity. This conclusion needs to be modified in certain respects, however. First, state interests (such as the technical *grands corps*) have been weakened, especially in the 1990s, and new public and private actors have emerged to contest their role. Second, French pressure and interest groups have discovered new arenas for their activity, notably at a European and a subnational level. Finally, though measurement tools are crude, the number of new associations created annually suggests that French citizens participate more actively than ever before in groups, at least some of which have an incidence on public policy.

Indicative bibliography

Basso, J. (1983) *Les Groupes de pression*, PUF, Paris.

Defrasne, J. (1995) *La Vie associative en France*, PUF, Paris.

Guilani, J.-D. (1991) *Marchands d'influence: les lobbies en France*, Seuil, Paris.

Jobert, B. and P. Muller (1987) *L'Etat en action: politiques publiques et corporatismes*, PUF, Paris.

Keeler, J. (1987) *The Politics of Neo-corporatism in France*, Oxford University Press, Oxford.

Le Galès, P. and M. Thatcher (eds.) (1995) *Les Réseaux de politique publique: le débats autour des 'policy networks'*, Harmattan, Paris.

Mouriaux, R. and G. Bibès (1990) *Les Syndicats européens à l'épreuve*, Presses de la FNSP, Paris.

Weber, H. (1986) *Le Parti des patrons*, Seuil, Paris.

Wilson, F. (1987) *Interest Group Politics in France*, Cambridge University Press, Cambridge.

Part IV

Reshaping modern France

Chapter 13

French society and economy

13.1 Introduction and objectives

Neither the political institutions appraised in Part II, nor the representative forces analysed in Part III of this book can be dissociated from their surrounding social and economic environments. While both institutions and political movements have changed, often dramatically in the period since 1981, these changes have resulted as much from external forces as from the internal traits of these organisations themselves. In the course of Chapter 13, we will appraise the forces modifying the social and economic context within which contemporary French politics operate, with a view to illuminating further the debate over whether we are witnessing the end of the French 'exception'. After considering various interpretations of the evolution of French society since 1945, Chapter 13 attempts to demonstrate how the French model of economic and industrial policy has been modified since the early 1980s.

13.2 The evolution of French society: social consensus or social fracture?

Table 13.1 portrays the changing French class structure during the post-war period. Even a cursory glance reveals that the old French class configuration has been greatly modified. The peasantry and the traditional bourgeoisie have virtually disappeared. The popular classes (industrial workers, low-status clerical workers and shop assistants) have declined. There has been a marked expansion of the new middle classes (clerical workers, managers and related workers in the public and private sectors). However, if French observers broadly agree on the contours of the evolution of French society, they disagree firmly upon the interpretation that should accompany this evolution.

The optimistic school argue that France, like many other advanced industrialised states, has moved towards a happy state of social harmony and prosperity, with the growth of an affluent middle class. They celebrate the emergence of a new national

Table 13.1 Social change and the evolution of the French workforce

	1954	1962	1975	1982	1988	1993
Farmers	21	15.5	7.5	6.5	6	4
Artisans, small businesspeople, shopkeepers	13	10.5	8	8	8	8
Higher management, intellectual and liberal professions	3	4.5	7	8	11	13
Intermediary professions (teachers, social workers, middle management, civil servants, etc.)	9	11.5	17	18	20	21
Non-managerial clerical workers (*employés*)	17	18.5	24	26.5	27	28
Industrial workers	37	39.5	36.5	33	28	26

Source: INSEE, *Tableaux de l'économie française*, 1995–6 (1993 figures); INSEE censuses and employment surveys, 1954–88 figures. Cited in Dirn (1990), p. 160.

consensus, based on an end of ideology, an enhanced material well-being and a virtual eradication of class conflict. Imitating Daniel Bell in the USA, they refer to the new middle classes as the purveyors of a new focal culture disseminated to the rest of French society. Not only have the middle classes expanded in number, but members of the older social classes, such as farmers and industrial workers, have come increasingly to imitate the middle class in their lifestyles, so much so that they have lost many of the specific traits associated with their class of origin. The boundaries between different social classes have become blurred. This extolling of the beneficial effects of social change was pushed furthest by Mendras (1989), who discerned a Second French Revolution. Mendras argued that the structure of French society had been overhauled during the post-war period in a manner just as radical as that following the 1789 French Revolution. There were seven principal characteristics of this Second French Revolution:

■ There was an unprecedented demographic and economic expansion during the first 30 years of the post-war period, labelled by Jean Fourastié as *les trente glorieuses*. After a century of demographic stagnation (1840–1940) France's population rose dramatically after the war, from 42 million to 55 million within one generation. Economic production multiplied fivefold within several decades; national wealth increased in an unprecedented manner; the structure of the French economy was radically altered.

■ Economic take-off caused the expansion of tertiary sector employment, which produced an overhaul in the nation's social class structure. The two dominant social classes produced by the French Revolution, the peasantry and the bourgeoisie, have disappeared, replaced by a new dominant middle class.

- Despite the post-war economic boom, industry and the industrial working class are in decline, leading to a weakening of subcultural resistance to national integration.
- The spread of urbanisation has weakened the traditional opposition between the town and the countryside; an urban lifestyle now prevails everywhere.
- The great national institutions, such as the army, the church and the republic, are no longer challenged in principle by particular sections of French society. They have lost their symbolic importance and ideological character.
- The uniformity promoted by the French education system and the post-war development of the mass media have contributed to the sense of a unified national community.
- Individualism has made such progress that it is no longer considered an ideology, but merely a manner of living shared by everybody.

Such optimism is challenged by other sociologists and social historians. Todd (1995), for instance, directly challenged the thesis of the end of ideology, and insurged against the conformity (*la pensée unique*) that this notion implies. Todd diagnosed a 'social fracture' based on the division of French society into two antagonistic camps of approximately the same numerical weight: the middle classes (*classes moyennes*) and the popular classes (*classes populaires*). The former had benefited from the process of European integration, industrial modernisation and tertiary sector expansion. The latter had been sacrificed, especially during the 1980s, to the exigencies of economic austerity and capitalist rationalisation. The popular classes were alienated from the more privileged section of French society. Although the middle classes had increased in numbers, the popular classes continued to represent a small majority of the population (Todd, 1995). Rather than a broad social consensus, a social fracture had come into existence, with whole swathes of French society being abandoned as victims of the process of social and economic modernisation. The divorce of the popular classes from the Socialist left was particularly marked, since their conditions of existence had worsened during the Socialist decade of the 1980s. The fears of the disadvantaged half of the French population were expressed in the emergence of a new cleavage: one based around national identity and a rejection of cosmopolitanism. This was articulated with particular clarity during the referendum on the Maastricht Treaty in 1992 (see Appendix 5). Traditional left-wing areas were in their majority opposed to ratification of the Maastricht Treaty, and among the popular electorate, opposition to the ratification of Maastricht reached two-thirds of those voting.

These two portrayals of the evolution of French society contain alternative visions of social reality, but both would concur that the post-war period has witnessed the development of new social groups of a composite range and nature (Vincent and Aubert, 1977). As in other European countries, the emergence of new social groups (especially managers and clerical workers) was related to the social and economic transformation of French society during the post-war boom, and to the expansion and democratisation of the education system. France's industrial take-off during the 1950s led to changing demands being placed upon the work-force: more technical and managerial staff were needed to run new industries and services, at the expense first of farmers, latterly of manual workers. The result of these developments was that France became far less of a rigidly class-bound society than it had been in the 1930s. Social mobility has increased and class has become less of a structuring element in most people's daily lives; but this does not signify that social class has disappeared altogether. The new middle classes are themselves fragmented, especially in relation to whether they work in the public or private sector, but also with regard to their political beliefs, their socioeconomic status and their cultural preferences. Among the new middle classes, there is considerable diversity in terms of occupation, lifestyle, income and education. Whether we prefer an optimistic or a more pessimistic reading, it is clear that the fate of the new middle classes is in marked contrast with the virtual disappearance of the peasantry and the fragmentation of the industrial working class.

The end of the peasantry?

At the height of the crisis in Franco-American relations occasioned by the GATT agreement in 1993, the French daily *Libération* rebaptised the French revolution-ary slogan to read *Liberté, égalité, fraternité, ruralité* (freedom, equality, brother-hood, rusticity). Images of France as a traditional rural society continue to permeate the perceptions of the country held by French people and foreign ob-servers alike. As illustrated in Chapter 12, the success of French farmers in impos-ing their corporatist demands represents one of the constant features of the French exception. It is a testament to the historical conscience of a nation whose identity was forged on the land. France of the nineteenth century was often portrayed as an inward-looking autarky, a rural, believing society, pervaded by an all-encompassing distrust of Paris and the outsider. Outside of the handful of cities, the lives of most French people were confined to their immediate locality and kinship networks. During the nineteenth century, the occupational background of most working Frenchmen was linked to the land: France was still overwhelmingly a rural society at the turn of the twentieth century (Tacet, 1992).

At the end of the Second World War, France was the most rural of all western nations: 45 per cent of the population lived in rural communes and one-quarter of the labour force worked in agriculture. As Williams put it: 'Agriculture was far more important than in Britain: in 1946, France still had one industrial worker for every agricultural worker, while Britain had nine' (Williams, 1964). Fifty years later France had become a heavily urbanised nation, in which agriculture directly employed under 5 per cent of the working population. There were as many as six million agricultural workers in 1946, but only just over one million in 1986, with five times fewer workers producing twice as much as 40 years previously. Throughout the course of the twentieth century, France became an industrialised nation comparable with other European industrialised nations. It is today a post-industrial nation comparable with the others. Notwithstanding this evolution, the nation's rural conscience has remained intact. The French peasantry might appear as a historic relic to outside observers, but the rural myth is one which continues to motivate political action and to have a major impact upon political choices. The farming lobby has attracted considerable support from *citadins* in part because of the sentiment that the splendid French countryside must be managed, rather than left to decay. The process of rural desertification is considered as part of a broader social problem. Protection of farming communities not only protects an endangered economic activity, but helps to preserve the nation's rural patrimony as well.

Whither the *classes populaires*?

The structure of protest politics in France is another feature setting the French apart from her north European neighbours. Traditions of direct action stem in part from the consequences of France's late industrialisation. By the end of the nineteenth century, France was barely industrialised, outside of a number of geographically specific areas. Throughout the nineteenth century, French industry remained essentially small scale and rural, concentrated in small companies employing fewer than 100 workers. By the end of the nineteenth century, only the metallurgical industries (such as iron and steel, and mining) were beginning to take the shape of modern heavy industries. The great working-class strikes at the beginning of the twentieth century were as much the product of pre-industrial workers, such as winegrowers, shoemakers and woodcutters, as they were of genuine industrial workers (Ridley, 1970).

By comparison with the United Kingdom or Germany, France industrialised in a late and imperfect manner. The early decades of the twentieth century witnessed the growth of a heavily concentrated urban working class, with a strong sense of its own identity. Industrial workers were geographically separated from the rest of French society. They lived in tightly knit communities, where proletarian consciousness was high. Such proletarian communities existed, for instance, in the mining areas of the Nord/Pas-de-Calais, in the Paris industrial suburbs and in the large Mediterranean cities such as Marseilles. Unlike the peasantry, whose ancestry was ancient, the lineage of the French industrial working class was far more recent. Indeed, the survival of a large peasantry retarded the development of an industrial working class in France.

France's industrial take-off began in earnest from 1900 onwards and continued uninterrupted, despite the war, until 1930. The birth of heavy industry in urban conurbations brought about the creation of the modern working class and the beginnings of a new feeling of class consciousness. The older artisanal pre-industrial working class, which had prevailed until the turn of the century, had prided itself upon its trade consciousness, based on the exercise of skilled occupations which gave it professional autonomy and self-confidence. The new industrial working class of the early twentieth century adopted a more genuine proletarian consciousness based upon poverty, deprivation and the performance of menial, unskilled tasks. Both these rival forms of class consciousness became part of the modern working-class mentality in France. The French Communist Party (PCF) was traditionally the only party capable of expressing these two different forms of working-class consciousness. The working class could in some senses be considered as a subculture, with a high sense of class consciousness and a belief in its destiny as the harbinger of socialism. Its grandiose demands were in part an extension of its minority status and its besieged mentality. More than most of their European counterparts, French workers believed in the Marxist-inspired myth that the working class was the class of the future, and that it was destined to play a central role in the creation of a socialist society.

Divisions produced by France's late industrial revolution of the twentieth century continue to manifest themselves in a variety of forms. The bitter class-against-class confrontation of the 1930s to the 1950s has given way to a less structured urban anomie, where a new type of urban poverty sets immigrants and paupers against the traditional proletariat. The ranks of the traditional industrial working class have been decimated by unemployment and the shift to a post-industrial society. The structure of the industrial working class has altered as well. It is no longer a male bastion, since 40 per cent of workers are women, often part-time workers. France's large immigrant community is also concentrated within the working class, and performs most of those menial tasks that native French workers now refuse to do. In political terms, the weakening solidity of the industrial proletariat has accentuated the decline of the French Communist Party. The breakdown of traditional working class subcultures has also facilitated the emergence of the FN as a new urban protest movement of a rather different type (Chapter 11).

13.3 The French economy and economic management

As French Presidents love to recall, the French economy is the fourth largest in the world. Thirty years of spectacular economic growth from 1945 to 1974 – *les trente glorieuses* – placed France second in the ranking of European nations, trailing only the Federal Republic of Germany. Although France has maintained its ranking as Europe's second economic power, the 'thirty glorious years' were followed by over two decades of painful adjustment to depressed conditions in the world economy. The effects of the oil crises of 1973 and 1979, of the processes known as globalisation and internationalisation, and of the march of European integration during the 1980s and 1990s were to highlight the importance of the external constraints weighing upon the French economy, and the limited room for manoeuvre of its governments in inventing new economic policies. The pressures facing French economic policy-makers in the 1990s are rather similar to those facing policy-makers in other developed European countries: namely, how to combine effective anti-unemployment strategies and economic growth with a tight control over inflation, limited budget deficits and a balance of trade surplus. These pressures have become more urgent as France prepares itself to take part in moves towards European monetary union (see Chapter 15). Comparative data on the European economies are given in Table 13.2.

Table 13.2 France in the European Union: some comparative data

Country	Date of entry into EU	Population (1993) (millions)	GDP (ecus per inhabitant)	Inflation (1993–4)	Unemployment (1994)
Austria	1995	7.9	19,684	2.6	6.9
Belgium	1958	10.1	17,822	1.9	10.2
Denmark	1973	5.2	22,212	2.3	10.2
Finland	1995	5.1	14,020	1.6	18.4
France	1958	57.7	18,250	1.6	12.5
Germany	1958 (1990 ex-GDR)	81.1	20,177	2.7	8.4
Greece	1981	10.5	7,305	10.8	9.4
Ireland	1973	3.6	11,222	2.4	15.1
Italy	1958	57.8	14,659	4.2	11.5
Luxembourg	1958	0.4	26,750	2.0	3.5
Netherlands	1958	15.2	17,368	2.6	7.7
Portugal	1986	9.8	7,378	4.0	6.9
Spain	1986	39.1	10,445	4.3	24.1
Sweden	1995	8.7	18,299	2.5	9.8
United Kingdom	1973	58.0	13,876	2.9	9.5
USA		258.3	20,780	2.7	6.1
Japan		124.8	28,851	0.5	2.8

Source: INSEE, *Tableaux de l'économie française*, 1995–6, p. 6.

The French economy has been transformed during the post-war period from 'a partly agricultural to a service economy, with the relative weight of industry (broadly defined) remaining constant' (Flockton and Kofman, 1989). The decline in agricultural employment appraised above has been outstripped by increases in farming productivity, which have made France into the world's second largest food exporter behind the United States. The inbuilt French surplus in agricultural products is of great benefit to the French balance of trade account, counterbalancing the nation's energy deficit.

French performance in manufacturing industry has proved variable. France is the world's fourth largest exporter of manufacturing goods. A consistently high performance has been achieved by capital goods industries reliant on heavy state investments: this is notably the case in aerospace, telecommunications, the railways, the armaments industry and civilian nuclear power. Each of these industrial sectors benefited from specific state investment plans launched in the 1960s and 1970s. French public policy experts refer to 'high-tech Colbertism' to describe the interventionist model of French industrial policy during the period 1945–74 (see below). Certain Anglo-Saxon observers doubted whether these industries would be in a position to compete in a fully open European and global market, when deprived of past levels of state subsidy (Flockton and Kofman, 1989; Flockton, 1990). For others, the success of French 'high-tech Colbertism' rested not only upon state investment, but also on a synergy with dynamic private sector industrial actors, and the production of goods which were competitive on the world market.

Alongside its mixed record in the high-technology activities such as information technology, computers and consumer electronics, the French economy has performed credibly in intermediate branches such as car manufacturing, glass, rubber and chemicals. These were also sectors where long-term state investments facilitated economies of scale. On the debit side, a decline in the traditional manufacturing sector (textiles, steel, mining, shipbuilding) has occurred in France, as in other European nations such as the UK, in spite of the considerable financial efforts of the French government in favour of these 'lame ducks'. One informed analyst puts state investment in industry into context by pointing out that the bulk of the Industry Ministry's intervention budget was directed towards supporting the declining coal industry, rather than high-technology firms (Cohen, in Hayward, 1995).

French performance in the service sector of the economy has more than compensated for its mixed industrial performance. In line with other European nations, the service sector in France has assumed new importance as a source of wealth creation and economic development. France can claim to be the world's second largest exporter of services, with particular strengths in tourism, retailing, transport, banking and insurance. With agricultural and industrial employment in permanent decline, tertiary sector employment is the source of most new job creation. Service sector growth has proved sluggish since the early 1980s, however, reflecting lower growth rates throughout the French economy.

Analysts disagree upon the precise causes of France's economic 'miracle' of the period 1945–73. Recurrent explanations include the role of state economic interventionism and Keynesian economic management, the strength of public and private investment in industry, the sustained level of foreign demand for French industrial and agricultural goods, the foundation of the EEC, which created new markets for French industrial and agricultural products, and the political stability induced by the Fifth Republic (1958–). It lies beyond the limited scope of this chapter to develop these arguments in more detail.

From inflation to integration

French government economic policies are shaped in part by the environmental conditions within which governments function. The high economic growth rates of *les trente glorieuses* facilitated the type of interventionist policies adopted by French governments. With the onset of world economic crisis in 1973, the room for manoeuvre open to governments has been limited, as have their policy responses. The high growth rates of 1946–73 were accompanied by consistently high levels of inflation, a phenomenon aggravated by the oil crises of 1973 and 1979. From 1976 onwards – with the exception of the Socialist relaunch of 1981–2 – the anti-inflation strategy has officially been the centrepiece of French macroeconomic policies. The credibility of such a strategy increased steadily once it became apparent that it was supported by the main principal élites on left and right.

The attempt by the conservative premier Barre to rein in public expenditure and to master inflation in 1976–81 floundered in part because of the belief that there was an alternative economic strategy, a belief not confined to the ranks of the left-wing opposition. The failure of the Socialist government's attempt at reinvigorated Keynesianism in 1981–2 revealed that this was not the case (see Chapter 2). If the Socialist experiment of 1981–2 taught anything, it was that economic policy could not be confined to the barriers of a single nation-state, and that there were major dangers for a nation pursuing markedly different economic policies from those of its main trading partners.

Mitterrand's decision in 1983 that France should remain within the European monetary system was a defining moment in recent French history (Cole, 1994a). It promoted a measure of consensus among French governments that Keynesian policies were no longer adapted to the economic environment of the 1980s, at least not within the context of a single nation-state. It also impressed upon France's rulers the interdependent nature of relations between countries, especially those within the European Union. The recognition of limited economic sovereignty was the practical lesson of the 1983 economic U-turn. It was a powerful calling into question of the French model (based on high growth, high inflation, state interventionism and competitive devaluations) in favour of the German model (one of low inflation, high productivity, balanced budgets and stable currencies).

With the left's abandonment of Keynesian reflationary policies in 1982–3, and its modification of its traditional statism, the dividing line between left and right in economic terms became blurred. The monetarist policies engaged by the French Socialists after 1983 were at least as rigorous as those undertaken by conservative administrations in other European countries. The strong franc economic policy reduced the room for manoeuvre in other policy sectors throughout the period of Socialist administration, 1983–93. The need to compete in international markets, and above all to fulfil the economic convergence criteria imposed by membership of the European Union, has led to a significant weakening of the hidden protectionism characteristic of much of the post-war French economy.

The discipline of French governments since 1983 has brought definite economic rewards. The policy of the strong franc pursued by governments of the left and the right since 1983 has led France to overcome its traditional economic weaknesses: namely inflation and the balance of trade deficit. In the course of the 1980s and 1990s, the French disease of high inflation and regular trade deficits gave way to low inflation and trade surpluses. This occurred at the expense of sluggish growth rates (by French standards) and an exponential rise in unemployment, a major political issue in the 1995 presidential campaign. A powerful theme of Chirac's presidential campaign in 1995 was his refusal of *la pensée unique*, the notion that there was only one economic path (the strong franc policy) if France was to meet the convergence criteria for participating in a single European currency. This suggested that the political problem posed by unacceptably high unemployment might force governments to relax their strict codes of economic management at some date in the future. This depended in part upon whether the EMU project would prove a viable proposition in 1999 or beyond, or whether economic policy would be 'renationalised' when faced with the costs of full European economic integration.

13.4 *Dirigisme* and its limits

State intervention in economic policy making formed the core of the French economic model, a critical aspect of the French 'exception'. During the post-1945 period, this involved both direct state management of important industrial sectors and indirect state involvement through the planning process. The nationalisation programme of 1946 created large state firms in key sectors such as energy (GdF, EdF, CEA, CDF), transport (Air France), industry (Renault), banking and insurance. This had a major impact upon economic development. Through its control over the banking system and the distribution of credit, the French state occupied a powerful position to influence the investment choices of French firms. The state was thus simultaneously a gatekeeper, a mobiliser and an agent of economic development.

The formal role of the state in economic management was expressed through the French planning procedure. From 1947 onwards, the French state introduced a series of five-year plans, drawn up by civil servants in association with employers' and labour union representatives. These plans fixed goals for particular industrial sectors, and singled out priorities for economic development. Heavy state investment in industrial plant helped French industry recover during the early years after the war. However, most contemporary observers argue that, except in the period of immediate post-war reconstruction in the late 1940s and early 1950s, the importance of state planning should not be exaggerated. Only the first plan (1947–52) was of a command nature. Unlike the Soviet plans, which set compulsory targets for industrial sectors, the French plans were indicative: they attempted to influence private investment decisions and to mobilise social actors in favour of economic growth. There was little relationship between the sectoral priorities outlined in French plans and public finance. The French state spent far more on housing, infrastructure and agriculture than it did on industry. The plans were unable to dictate investment decisions even in public sector industries. Of the greatest importance, the Finance Ministry was not required to take into account the objectives outlined in the five-year plans, which singularly limited their effectiveness (Flockton and Kofman, 1989). These quinquennial plans continue to exist, but their impact on economic management has become far less important.

As indicated above, a belief in industrial policy nonetheless formed an integral part of the French economic model. Various types of instrument were used to attempt to promote French industry. These involved first the promotion of state-led prestige projects (*grands projets*) in sectors considered vital for national independence, such as nuclear power, space exploration, the railways, the defence industry, aerospace and telecommunications. Industrial efforts were sometimes co-ordinated by nationalised industries, but public ownership was not a condition for state involvement. Private sector actors (e.g. the aerospace firm Dassault and the conglomerate Alcatel-Alsthom) could also benefit from state aid, notably by indirect protectionist forms of assistance such as state procurement policies, low-interest credits and export credits. Government–industry relations were complex. While state planners could orientate the activities of private sector firms in sensitive industrial spheres (notably by procurement policies), there was evidence that large private firms were able to 'exert subtle influence over the government machinery' in order to promote their objectives (Cohen, 1995). Once established in the international market place, the most successful French firms demanded greater autonomy from the state, including in their detailed investment decisions, whether they were in the public or the private sector. In the course of the late 1980s and 1990s, the French state acceded to these demands, in order to assist the transformation of French firms into global players. Apart from the *grands projets*, industrial policy also involved direct government grants to industrial sectors in difficulty, such as coal, textiles, machine tools and shipbuilding. Such state grants and sectoral plans have virtually ceased since the Single European Act.

Under governments of the Gaullist right, as well as of the Socialist left from 1981 to 1983, the official aim of industrial policy was to promote national champions in technically advanced sectors, especially in the spheres of transport and energy. The policy of creating national champions depended upon fulfilling certain criteria that assumed a strong (if flexible) state and a high degree of national economic sovereignty. According to Cohen (in Hayward, 1995), the preconditions were offensive protectionism, technical innovation, public procurement policies, direct state aid and long-term political support (but weak political interference). In truth, the original features of French post-war economic management (such as planning) had faded in importance long before French governments attempted to harmonise economic policy with European Union partners in the 1990s. The about-turn of Mitterrand's Socialist government in 1982–3 should be signalled for particular attention in this respect.

At its height, the French state justified its economic activism with the argument that it intervened directly in areas where private capital was absent, and where the national interest was at stake. Gaullist policy-makers in the 1960s interpreted the national interest in terms of giving France a lead in the most technologically advanced industrial sectors. Likewise, Socialist ministers justified nationalisation in 1982 as a means of giving the state a lead in major infrastructure projects unattractive to private capital. The success of state investment depended upon the sector involved: massive financial investment gave France a technological edge in sectors such as aerospace, nuclear energy and transport, but it had less impact elsewhere (as with the steel plans of the 1970s and the failed bio-technology, satellite and cable plans).

In addition to the extension of direct state ownership in 1946, the Socialist government's 1982 Nationalisation Act took into public ownership all large private banks, several of France's largest industrial groups and a number of smaller concerns. The result was that the public sector increased from around 8 per cent to around a quarter of French industrial capacity and 50 per cent of industrial investment, while the nationalisation of the main banks left the state in control of virtually all credit. The Socialist nationalisation programme represented the apogee of French economic interventionism. Direct state involvement in economic development has subsequently diminished. This is partly the result of budgetary constraints, but it is also due to European policy fashions, promoting greater marketisation and privatisation. Whatever its industrial logic, nationalisation proved expensive. Within two years of the 1982 Act, the French Socialist government began backtracking. In 1984 state firms were allowed to issue 'investment certificates' to private sector investors, in an attempt to raise capital. This preceded the large-scale privatisation programme of the Chirac government of 1986–8, which was resumed with a new vigour in 1993 by the Balladur government and continued in the Juppé administration of 1995 (Bauer, 1988; Dumez and Jeunemaitre, 1993; Maclean, 1995).

State-led national industrial strategies, aimed at promoting national champions across a range of industrial sectors, have given way since 1982–3 to French state support for these champions becoming international firms able to compete in the global market. In practice, this has involved French governments supporting their return to the private sector, where they are better placed to engage in global strategies. The old national interventionist model is no longer in fashion. It arguably runs against the spirit and the letter of the Single European Act (although the Maastricht Treaty refers to industrial policy) and is possibly irrelevant in a context of globalisation. It is rejected as much on grounds of cost as of efficiency. State economic intervention has become subject to tight budget constraints on account of economic austerity policies pursued by all governments since 1982, as well as because of the ground rules of the European Union's competition policy. The need to control government expenditure in order to be eligible to move to a single European currency, as specified in the Maastricht Treaty, has acted as a further brake on industrial policy expenditure.

Given this, it is also the case that a plurality of different industrial and economic models co-exist within the EU, from Anglo-Saxon liberalism, through the German social-market economy to the vestiges of French *dirigisme*. The notion of the national champion has in part been replaced by that of a European-wide industrial policy, with traditional French ideas extrapolated to a wider arena. French governments have often advocated pan-European industrial policies, which would enable development costs to be shared among several partners, and would facilitate the 'internationalisation' of national champions. This orientation can on occasion lead to highly *dirigiste* actions being undertaken, such as President Chirac's insistence in 1996 on the merger between the state-run Aerospatiale and the private Dassault, as a preliminary to closer co-operation with other European defence firms.

Several examples illustrate that, if France has moved closer to the European norm, it remains committed to a larger measure of state economic interventionism than Anglo-Saxon or Germanic economic liberals consider appropriate. The nature of the French privatisation programme in 1986–8 illustrated this: the French state preserved a powerful oversight role for itself, notably through the policy of creating a 'hard core' of institutional shareholders close to the state's economic interests (Bauer, 1988). The 1993 privatisation programme has been less stato-centrist, but links remain close between political and economic élites. The ability of the French state to bail out public sector firms or banks with huge deficits continues to attract attention, even if such programmes depend in each case on approval of the EU Commission. Recent examples would include the 1995 rescue of the state bank Crédit lyonnais, and the 1996 reconversion grant accorded to the national airline Air France.

13.5 Conclusion and summary

In recent years, many observers of French society have pointed towards greater social harmony, resulting from the development of a prosperous middle class. More recently, attention has been focused on the social 'fracture' dividing French society, and the large number of losers in the process of social and economic modernisation. Both visions correspond to a genuine perception of reality. There is a paradox here. French society undoubtedly appears as more homogeneous in cultural terms in the 1990s than in the 1950s. Without accepting all the tenets of the optimistic school, social change has tended to enhance the sense of national community – up to a point. As old cleavages based on class and sub-cultural identity have diminished, however, new ones have emerged, notably those tied up with the advent of a post-industrial society, European integration and immigration.

In relation to economic and industrial policy, on balance France has been forced to succumb to changing policy fashions, rather than initiating them. The combined impact of globalisation and European integration has been to lessen the possibilities open to the French state to engage in a 'heroic' policy style, a style traditionally more visible in industrial policy than anywhere else. The obvious losers of this process are the state's technical experts in the *grands corps*, whose mission is to engage in state prestige projects.

As in the other areas surveyed, the redefinition of the French model in economic policy has led to a redefinition of the role of the state. External constraints weighed increasingly heavily on the freedom of manoeuvre of governments of both sides throughout the 1980s and 1990s. In key sectors of domestic policy, difficult choices were imposed upon governments of all political hues. But if French governments were subjected to similar social and economic challenges as their European counterparts, these were interpreted in a manner suitable to French customs. Traditions of state economic intervention are deeply rooted in France. The public sector remains stronger in France than elsewhere, as does the weight of the state in French economic management. The French notion of public service remains distinct from that of other European nations. Competitors still complain of hidden barriers to free trade, and of the effectiveness of lobbying by representatives of the French government in Brussels to obtain derogations. The French model has undoubtedly been weakened during the period since 1983. But old habits die hard.

Indicative bibliography

Bauer, M. (1988) 'The politics of state-directed privatisation: the case of France', *West European Politics*, vol. 11, no. 4.

Bloch-Liané, J.-M. and B. Moschetto (1987) *La Politique économique de la France*, PUF, Paris.

Cohen, E. (1995) 'France: national champions in search of a mission', in J. Hayward (ed.), *Industrial Enterprise and European Integration*, Oxford University Press, Oxford.

Dirn, L. (1990) *La Société française en tendances*, PUF, Paris.

Flockton, C. and E. Kofman (1989) *France*, Paul Chapman, London.

Fourastié, J. (1980) *Les Trente glorieuses ou la révolution invisible de 1946–1975*, Fayard, Paris.

Le Bras, H. (1995) *Les Trois France*, Odile Jacob, Paris.

Mendras, H. (1989) *La Séconde Révolution française*, Gallimard, Paris.

Schmidt, V. A. (1996) *From State to Market?*, Cambridge University Press, Cambridge.

Vesperini, J.-P. (1993) *L'Economie de la France sous la cinquième république*, Economica, Paris.

Vincent, G. and V. Aubert (1977) *Les Français 1945–1975: chroniques et structures d'une société*, Masson, Paris.

Chapter 14

Immigration, integration and cultural diversity: the case of the Maghreb community in France

14.1 Introduction and objectives

Chapter 14 examines notions of ethnicity, of national identity and of cultural pluralism, with particular reference to the plight of Maghrebians in France. After a brief overview of the history and nature of immigration in France, Chapter 14 examines why the French Jacobin tradition has traditionally been reluctant to admit the existence of distinct cultural and ethnic identities, and has preferred notions of assimilation of ethnic communities into the dominant French culture, rather than their autonomous integration. After exploring new forms of participation by Maghrebin groups in the French polity, the chapter examines three case studies of cultural diversity and national identity: the 'headscarf' affair; the Gulf War; and the rise of Islamic fundamentalism in the Maghreb.

14.2 French immigration policy, 1945–95: an overview

France can lay a plausible claim to be the 'crossroads of Europe'. It shares a land border with six European countries (Belgium, Germany, Switzerland, Luxembourg, Italy and Spain), and is connected to England by underground tunnel. Its proximity to former colonies, especially in the Maghreb, makes it an attractive destination for would-be immigrants. Its population has consistently been the most cosmopolitan of any European nation.

According to the 1990 census, the total immigrant population presently stands at 4.1 million, or 6.4 per cent of the entire French population. However, over three-quarters of these belong to seven main nationalities. Portuguese are the largest single group (504,604 in 1990), closely followed by Algerians (473,384) and Moroccans (396,470). Initially immigrants into France came from neighbouring European countries such as Belgium, Italy, Poland and Spain. However, since 1945 there has been a marked shift away from countries bordering France to those on the extremes of the Mediterranean basin (the countries comprising the Maghreb in particular) and further afield in central Africa and more recently southeast Asia.

At the end of the Second World War, for a combination of demographic and economic reasons, France needed to supplement its existing workforce. Immigration was one of the easiest ways to achieve this, and thus a policy of recruiting migrant workers was commenced. The policy laid down that immigrants would work and reside in France for a fixed period of time, contributing to economic development, at the end of which they would return to their country of origin. In order to achieve this end, a strictly controlled policy of entries and departures was to be put in place. This included the establishing of an official body regulating migratory flows, the Office national d'immigration (ONI), and the prioritising of single male migrants who would be housed separately from French nationals in foyers. What happened in reality, though, was that the sheer volume of immigrants overwhelmed the ONI and in practice it proved impossible to halt the flow of illegal immigrants, much sought after by employers, since they did not have to pay the former the same wages. Instead of initiating policy on migratory movements, French governments were able to exert relatively little control over the number of foreign nationals entering France. From 1974 onwards, several types of policy response have been adopted to deal with the complex phenomena of immigration, cultural assimilation and ethnicity.

The Giscard presidency, 1974–81

Valéry Giscard d'Estaing was elected President at a time of major economic and social instability. The effects of the economic crisis, set off by the oil embargo in 1973, began to be felt, and in July 1974 France decided to suspend all further immigration. This step was in fact predated by the Algerian authorities' decision to halt their own emigration a few months previously as a result of a spate of racist-inspired attacks in France, notably against Algerians. Thereafter the Giscard d'Estaing presidency embarked upon a series of repressive reforms aimed at reducing the presence of foreigners in French society. The measures included forbidding the reuniting of immigrants' families (*le regroupement familial*). They were designed to reinforce the perception that immigration was a short-term phenomenon and to encourage migrant groups to return to their country of origin, despite their substantial economic contribution to French society.

A major step was taken in 1977 when the Minister for Social Affairs, Lionel Stoléru, introduced measures promoting voluntary repatriation (*aide au retour*). This was a sum of 10,000 francs to be paid to immigrants for their 'voluntary' repatriation to their home country. While it was targeted at Maghrebians, relatively few took up the offer, and it was instead Portuguese immigrants, who traditionally engage in rotational migration, who benefited most. A form of forced return was also practised in reality since the *carte de séjour* (a ten-year permit enabling immigrants to reside in France for a fixed period) was not renewed. This text was eventually withdrawn after opposition from the Council of State and the

RPR. In 1980 the Bonnet law enabled procedures to be put in place for the immediate expulsion of immigrants, reinforcing the existing control that the state exerted over foreign nationals.

The PS in power, 1981–6, 1988–93: liberalisation and defensive reaction

The Socialist candidate François Mitterrand had fought his 1981 campaign on a manifesto which explicitly opposed the measures initiated by Giscard d'Estaing. Upon entering office, Mitterrand immediately cancelled the previous laws of the right and introduced a series of new measures. Three in particular are noteworthy. First, those foreign nationals without official documentation could 'regularise' their status. Second, the policy of family reuniting was re-established. However, perhaps the most innovative new measure was repealing the 1939 law with regard to foreign associations. Henceforth foreign nationals would no longer require prior government authorisation in order to create their own associations. This provided a useful framework within which youths, particularly of Maghrebian origin, were able to gain associational experience, and it resulted in a considerable increase in new associations being created. Two of these, SOS-Racisme and France-Plus would gain national notoriety. In addition to these measures, the rights of immigrants could now be put forward officially via the creation of the Ministry for National Solidarity. Furthermore, an October 1981 law transferred any deliberation on the contentious stay of foreign nationals from an administrative authority to judicial tribunals. Arguably, the latter were better guarantors of public freedom.

However, while all the above measures worked in favour of a less hostile environment for minority groups, public opinion in France remained sensitive to the permanent settlement of immigrants in French society. This was displayed with regard to the question of foreign nationals being able to vote in local elections, a policy which Mitterrand publicly endorsed. Public opinion polls were repeatedly hostile to the idea and as a result the government relegated the subject to one of secondary importance. Nonetheless Mitterrand continued to reaffirm his support for the theme before each electoral campaign, partly in order to remobilise the left and divide the traditional right, even if this meant in reality strengthening the hand of the extreme right.

In 1983 the FN made its first inroads into the political arena at the municipal elections and this was reinforced a year later at the European elections. The traditional political parties were taken aback by the rise of the extreme right and were immediately forced on to the defensive. For the Socialists in power this meant rethinking and changing policy to take account of public dissatisfaction. As a result, some of the policies that the Socialists had criticised under the Giscard d'Estaing presidency were reintroduced under a different guise. These included the former measure of *aide au retour*, renamed *aide publique à la réinsertion*; new restrictions on family unification; an intensification of the battle against illegal immigration; and the suppression of the Secretary of State for Immigrants.

In the run-up to the 1986 legislative elections, the PS stood on a platform that was clearly cautious in its references to the question of immigration. Pursuing the battle against illegal immigration was again spelled out, as was encouraging 'reinsertion' into the country of emigration. This time, though, the right to vote of immigrants was at best to be examined, sparing the PS from having to commit itself to the policy if public opinion remained hostile.

The overt support lent by Mitterrand personally to minority groups, and in particular to youths of Maghrebian origin, was a non-negligible factor in his re-election to the presidency. Exit polls conducted in 1988 indicated that French youths of north African descent voted overwhelmingly for the Socialist candidate. In the following year, the PS was instrumental in facilitating the election of almost 100 French nationals of Maghrebian origin to office at municipal level. However, in general the final five years of Socialist government were characterised by the adoption of a more aggressive tone with regard to migrant groups. In January 1990, Michel Rocard, the then Prime Minister, argued at a conference attended by PS political representatives of Maghrebian origin that 'We cannot import everybody else's misery', precipitating the protestations of many present and the walk-out by some. In 1991 the new Prime Minister, Edith Cresson, talked openly of using chartered aeroplanes to send back illegal immigrants, and backed this up in practice by returning a number of Malians to their home country in this manner. Even Mitterrand himself stressed the limits of French willingness to accept the presence of foreign nationals, by evoking the notion of the 'threshold of tolerance' to justify limitations.

The right in power: 1986–8 and 1993–6

The right was to provide further impetus for political mobilisation on the part of French youths of Maghrebian origin via the actions of the Chirac government during the period 1986–8. Uppermost in the minds of Maghrebian youths, and indeed the entire Maghrebian and migrant populations, was the government's proposed reform of the French Nationality Code. Whereas previously any person born on French territory, but of foreign parents, automatically acquired French nationality at the age of eighteen, the Chirac government was now proposing to modify this provision so that the children of immigrants would have in effect to 'earn' the right to acquire citizenship. This potential change was especially alarming to youths of Maghrebian origin, since if it were to be adopted they might be refused French nationality, and thereby rendered liable to expulsion. From the viewpoint of political rights, however, the proposed actions of the Chirac government crystallised in the minds of these youths the belief that, if they did not participate fully in the political process, there would be others quite willing and able to take decisions which could change their very status. Hostility from migrant and civil rights groups eventually led to the proposed changes being dropped.

With the election of an RPR–UDF government in 1993, a change in policy was anticipated. The Balladur government adopted a two-pronged approach with respect to questions of immigration and integration. On the one hand, it projected an outwardly tough stance on immigration. This was exemplified both by the stricter controls on acquiring French nationality as a result of the Pasqua laws (so called after the then Minister of the Interior, Charles Pasqua) and by the intransigent attitude towards illegal immigrants resident in France. Like its Socialist predecessor, the RPR–UDF government was anxious not to appear lax in its actions and discourse, particularly with the FN ever ready to criticise. The Balladur government also attempted to facilitate the settlement and 'integration' of migrant groups into French society. Attempts were made to continue the dialogue started off under the Socialists, of discussing the provision of Islam in France with representatives of the Muslim population.

14.3 Immigration, integration, assimilation and ethnicity: conceptual problems and the Jacobin state

With settlement of migrant groups in western industrialised nations accepted as a long-term reality, emphasis has shifted from the reasons for their emigrating from the country of origin to the nature of their permanent installation in the country of immigration. It is therefore important to understand the gradual distinction between the term 'immigration' and those of 'integration' and 'assimilation'. Immigration can be defined in a straightforward manner as referring to migratory movements from one country to another. Integration, assimilation and ethnicity are more problematic.

Until recently assimilation, with a stronger meaning than integration, has been the preferred term in France, since historically it has been allied with the Jacobin concept of the 'one and indivisible' republic. According to this concept, immigrants became part of French society by adhering to its values, rules and institutions on an individual basis. In this sense, assimilation refers to a *rapprochement* between French nationals and immigrants, but with the latter eventually adopting the identity of the former. This ideology was particularly useful when dealing with regionalist/autonomist movements that wished to differentiate themselves from the rest of France. As shown in Chapter 1, any serious analysis of French history would reveal that the 'one and indivisible' republic was anything but that in reality. Up until 1789 France was broadly divided linguistically into two (though Alsatian, Basque, Breton, Catalan, Corsican and Flemish all existed), and it was not until the early part of the twentieth century that the French language became the first medium of communication in all major cities. Despite this, the Jacobin concept has remained and continues to influence debate. With the first wave of immigrants entering France predominantly from neighbouring countries and often with shared cultural characteristics (e.g. religion or ethnic origin), there was a conscious attempt by some to conceal any differences. Thus foreign-sounding names were frenchified (Ivo Livi becoming Yves Montand is but one example). One of the most often cited ways of assimilating into French society was by adhering to French social movements, notably trade unions. In so doing, immigrants from Belgium, Italy, Poland and Spain were able to become an integral feature of one France by combating another (Jazouli, 1986).

While questions of immigration and integration have become the focus of national debate in France over the last decade, the notion of ethnicity has been noticeably absent from discourse, giving rise to the opinion that it remains a taboo subject. Until recently, its usage in France was confined to studies of anthropology and ethnology, but was never included in any general political debate. We shall adhere to the following definition provided by Isajiw (1974) and argue that ethnicity refers to 'an involuntary group of people who share the same culture or to descendants of such people who identify themselves and/or are identified by others as belonging to the same involuntary group'.

In France not only have the media, politicians and social scientists been wary about discussing ethnicity, but there has been a reluctance in many cases even to acknowledge its existence, despite the fact that groups such as Maghrebians can be and in practice are distinguished from the white French population on ethnic grounds. The reluctance and even refusal to acknowledge the existence of the notion of ethnicity in France can be attributed not simply to historical reasons, but crucially to those of an ideological nature. Let us examine the former. Distinguishing citizens on the basis of ethnic criteria is not a phenomenon new to France. It was in fact an integral feature of government policy during the Vichy period, when French citizens of the Jewish faith were discriminated against. In the minds of many academics and politicians, reintroducing the concept would be tantamount to conjuring up the divisive nature of the Vichy period once again. Consequently, the study of ethnicity has, to a great extent, been discredited and the parallel with discrimination against Jews by a French administration has not been lost upon French academics.

Second, the Jacobinist ideology of the 'one and indivisible' republic has discriminated against the notion of ethnicity. This notion has continued to predominate despite clear differences between regions existing for centuries, and despite members of certain regions (i.e. Alsace, Brittany and Corsica) perceiving themselves to be distinct from the rest of the French population and even in some cases the victims of internal colonialism from the French state. In the Jacobin tradition, the concept of ethnicity evokes images of a segregated society, with parallels with the Unites States often being cited. Traditionally influenced by republican ideals, social scientists in France are almost unanimous in their rejection of and opposition to the emergence of potentially divisive 'community' mentalities in their own country.

For the above reasons, little attention has been paid to the status of minority groups within French society and their access to full social, economic and political rights. One consequence is that there has been a weaker commitment to equal opportunities policies. Thus there is no equivalent body in France to the British Commission for Racial Equality, with responsibility for ethnic monitoring of job applications. This throws up broader questions of citizenship and in particular of the participation of migrant groups in the political process.

14.4 The political participation of Muslim groups in France

The political participation of Muslim groups in French politics takes three principal forms: first, national pressure groups existing within political parties; second, ethnic minority associations defining themselves as external to established political parties; and third, national political leadership, or more to the point, its absence, and what factors may hinder the establishment of a common agenda.

Ethnic minority pressure groups within political parties

The existence of ethnic minority pressure groups within political parties is rooted in a political contradiction, insofar as there is an implicit recognition of the reluctance and/or failure of political parties in the dominant society to take on board the demands of minority groups. The two main pressure groups in existence both operate within the Socialist Party (PS).

The first of these, the Cercle des socialistes de culture musulmane, was created in reaction to French society perceptions of Muslims during the 'headscarf' affair. It aims to bring together French Muslims who sympathise with socialist beliefs, while working towards a greater knowledge of Islam and its civilisation in French society. The Cercle also combats prejudices faced by the Muslim populations in France. What is significant about the organisation's existence and logic is its insistence upon defining itself around Islam. Its members are predominantly, but not exclusively, of Maghrebian descent; black African Muslims are also members, for example. However, they are overwhelmingly of the Muslim faith, with sympathisers of the Jewish faith excluded from membership. The use of the term 'Muslim' in the group's title is a deliberate attempt to provoke French society as a whole into recognising the existence of Muslims as an integral feature of that society. This is deemed necessary since, according to the Cercle, Maghrebians in particular are underrepresented in the political sphere and their views are not allowed to be expressed freely in the media.

The second organisation, the Conférence nationale des élus socialistes originaires du Maghreb (CNESOM), was set up in an attempt to define what PS policy should be to ensure a 'better integration of populations originating from the Maghreb'. As the name suggests, this organisation claims among its supporters a diverse cross-section of people who have resided in the Maghreb. These include not only Muslims, but also *pieds noirs*, *harkis* (those Algerians who fought on the French side during the Algerian War and their descendants) and citizens of the Jewish faith. Like the Cercle, the CNESOM seeks to provide a mouthpiece for Maghrebians in France. However, it differs from the CNESOM in that one of its specific objectives is to provide a positive image of *maghrébinité* in France. This concept is one which both researchers and activists have taken issue with; such an aim is idealistic and even paternalistic, in the sense that it harks back to a colonial past. In both pressure groups there has been an attempt to influence the decision-making process of the PS from within the party. The

CNESOM was instrumental in securing the election of almost 100 municipal councillors of Maghrebian origin in 1989.

Ethnic minority pressure groups external to political parties

Two groups predominate at a national level: SOS-Racisme and France-Plus. Both claim to be apolitical and to represent the interests of ethnic minority groups in general, or Maghrebians more specifically in the case of France-Plus. However, in both cases and despite claims to the contrary, there have in reality been close links with political parties, notably the PS. SOS-Racisme was initially the brainchild of Julien Dray, now a PS deputy. France-Plus was conceived of by Georges Morin, a long-time PS activist in affairs concerning the Maghrebian population in France. Symbolic figureheads were placed in charge of both organisations: Harlem Désir for SOS-Racisme and Arezki Dahmani for France-Plus. In both cases, individuals from the PS leadership were involved behind the scenes in promoting the groups at their outset. For SOS-Racisme there was also financial support from sponsors sympathetic to the association's ideals of promoting racial harmony, as illustrated by the 'Ne touche pas à mon pote' campaign.

Subsequently, both groups have sought to distance themselves from the PS. Dahmani in particular has been at pains to proclaim his willingness to engage in dialogue with parties on the left and right of the political spectrum. A change in leadership of SOS-Racisme, with Fodé Sylla now president, has resulted in ever more distant links between itself and the PS. SOS-Racisme, while initially created to combat racism, subsequently concentrated its efforts on concrete action at local level. France-Plus has aimed at facilitating and promoting political activism on the part of Maghrebian youths. This has included civic rights campaigns to enrol youths on the electoral lists.

Neither organisation has succeeded in gaining widespread acceptance from the Maghrebian population in France, in part due to the lack of a popular mandate. SOS-Racisme, because of the existence of French nationals of the Jewish faith among its leadership, has alienated some youths. France-Plus, because of the concentration of a subsection of the Maghrebian population of Kabyle origin in its organisational structure, and the perception of the association as an élite divorced from the mass of Maghrebians, has been criticised by others.

The absence of a common national agenda

From this brief examination of political mobilisation, a number of factors become apparent. First, the fragmentation of political activity has prevented the adoption of a common approach. Organisations have sought diverse and often opposing strategies. Second, the close identification of both internal and external pressure groups with political parties has either restricted their freedom of action, or led to marginalisation. Third, there has been little attempt to work together on areas of common interest between organisations, as a result of personality and ideological differences that have surfaced.

Given the lack of contact between the political élite and the population at large, in addition to the absence of a charismatic figure able to unite all Maghrebians, political activism has been seriously undermined. Furthermore, since no one voice can justifiably claim to represent the views of this population as a whole, individual political élite opinions have been expressed which are not necessarily representative of this subsection of French society. This in turn has created confusion among the national media as to whose views should be sought, with a possibly detrimental effect on the perception that French society as a whole might have of Maghrebians.

14.5 The place of Muslims in French society

As we have discussed already, in the present debate on ethnic minorities in France what is at stake is not so much the large-scale entry of immigrants into the country, but rather the long-term settlement of minority groups. However, when the media focuses attention on the questions of assimilation and integration (however these terms might be defined or interpreted), they are not merely talking in abstract general terms, but are aiming primarily at Maghrebians. This is explained by the fact that Maghrebians are perceived by academics, politicians and the public at large as being the least 'integratable' group in French society, and are the most often cited targets of discrimination. In this section we will examine the manner in which this specific migrant group is perceived in French society by means of three national/international issues in which Maghrebians have been directly or indirectly concerned: the 'headscarf' affair; the Gulf War; and the rise of the Front islamique du salut (FIS) in Algeria. These events are important in that they are seen as testing points for the loyalty of French Muslims when faced with issues where French interests were at stake. They are important also in that they indicate whether or not there has been a gradual acceptance of the diverse nature of the French population as a whole.

The 'headscarf' affair

The headscarf affair in 1989 demonstrated these conflicting loyalties. On the surface it may have appeared to be a somewhat banal refusal by two French school-girls of the Muslim faith to remove the *foulard* or veil while at school. However, underlying the whole debate were two diametrically opposed views of French society.

On the one hand, there were those who championed the Jacobin notion of the one and indivisible republic and the concept of secularity. The principle of secularity is in fact one traditionally espoused by the left, and this dates back to the Third Republic when, as a result of the laws of 1881 and 1882, national unity in France was cemented by a system of secular schools. The separation of church and state became law in 1905.

According to the partisans of this vision of society, the Muslim girls wearing the veil at school were in fact negating republican values, since they were visibly differentiating themselves from other pupils and thereby drawing attention to their religion. The secular school should permit no distinctive sign indicating the religious denomination of the pupil. Instead the defenders of the republican vision argued that Islam and indeed any religion should be practised in private, and Muslims should be persuaded to endorse secular values. The supporters of the notion of secularity included Socialist MPs and intellectuals of the left such as Elisabeth Badinter.

In the opposing camp were those who had forged close links with minority groups in French society, or who believed that the Jacobin vision no longer corresponded to the realities of life in contemporary French society and most certainly did not reflect the diversity of its population. According to the proponents of this vision, Islam was not incompatible with the rules, institutions and values of French society. The then Minister for Education and present National Secretary of the Socialist Party, Lionel Jospin, appeared at first sight to be an ally of this second school of thought. He stressed the importance of dialogue with the Muslim girls, arguing that French society was pluralistic and that secularity no longer needed to be antagonistic in nature.

What is revealing about the debate that ensued is that French Muslims were, to a large extent, excluded from it. When the views of Muslims were sought, invariably they tended to be those of individuals or groups on the extremes, who were not necessarily representative of the views of French Muslims in general.

What does the whole issue tell us about how Muslims are perceived in French society? One conclusion that may be drawn is that the debate on secularity intruded upon the question of the presence of ethnic minority groups in French society. The two issues were confused. They resulted in the misleading impression that being Muslim implicitly inferred that one could not be French. This was clearly an erroneous impression, given that Muslims in France had in their overwhelming majority settled permanently in France and on the whole abided by the laws and rules of that society. Nonetheless the impression undoubtedly exists. It is a view cultivated by the Iranian revolution in 1979 and the fundamentalist image projected. It was further influenced by the increasing visibility of Maghrebians in French society. This is illustrated both by the emergence of the so-called second-generation of youths, largely born and bred in France of one or more north African parents, and by the strikes of car workers in 1982 when French Muslims were visible participants in the struggle. Consequently, a feeling of wariness and even hostility has greeted the recognition that Maghrebians would henceforth be an enduring feature of French society.

Second, in practice different standards were seen to apply depending on the religion which one was alluding to. This was particularly the case for children of the Jewish faith, who had not been prevented from wearing the kippa at school, and those of the Catholic faith, who were allowed to wear crucifixes whereas Muslim youths were not permitted to wear headscarfs. This was the source of a great deal of bitterness and frustration among Muslims.

Third, the headscarf affair was a litmus test of the acceptance or not of a diversity of cultures in French society. The vociferous defence of the Jacobin concept suggested, perhaps, that large sections of the French public were not yet prepared to accept the reality of a permanent Muslim presence, and that the latter continued to be regarded as illegitimate actors by French society. Others, particularly those in positions of authority, were prepared to give at best a begrudging acceptance, and even this was within certain limits.

The Gulf War

During hostilities in the Gulf, the Maghrebian populations in France were the subject of considerable media attention, the fear being that they might in some way constitute a 'fifth column' of support for Saddam Hussein. The implicit rationale behind this argument was that Maghrebians would automatically support Saddam because he was an Arab and they would be more likely to find sympathy with him than with the western forces of which France was an active member.

To what extent were such fears justified? Surveys conducted at the time of the war indicated that Maghrebians in France as a whole did not support Saddam. A SOFRES poll published in the weekly magazine *L'Express* (8 February 1991) revealed that 66 per cent of French Muslims questioned disapproved of Saddam's policy. This was backed up by a study of Maghrebian municipal councillors in the Paris region and Rhône-Alpes in the aftermath of hostilities. The interviewers found little evidence of support for the idea that there might be a pro-Saddam 'fifth column' in France (Hargreaves and Stenhouse, 1991).

Clearly there were nuances expressed by some Maghrebians concerning official French government policy. Where opinions were divided among Maghrebians, however, was on the question of the nature of French participation. There was a division of opinion on the policy adopted by François Mitterrand, with 43 per cent of Muslims in favour and 43 per cent against according to the aforementioned SOFRES poll. However, given that a climate of fear reigned, both among white French nationals, who were anxious about the potential for inter-ethnic conflict, and among Maghrebians, who were worried about white French anger towards Saddam being vented against them, French Muslims chose in their overwhelming majority to keep their opinions to themselves. This was hardly the behaviour of citizens posing a potential threat to the French state.

Government circles appeared genuinely to fear the potential for conflict between minority groups, especially between those of the Jewish and Muslim faiths, and with the dominant society at large. This explains in part why procedures for the entry and departure of students and personnel in higher education establishments were significantly tightened, and why the army was deployed at various strategic points in the capital, including the main railway stations.

Government fears of conflict erupting between French citizens of the Jewish and Muslim faiths may have been partly fuelled by the Palestinian issue, where there is clearly a deep divide. French youths of Maghrebian origin identify their own plight with that of Palestinian youths. Saddam Hussein repeatedly played on the theme of the Palestinian question during hostilities. Nevertheless, to counter media speculation in France about the potential for intercommunal fighting, pressure group leaders such as Dahmani for France-Plus went to the extent of meeting openly with representatives of Jewish organisations and made joint appeals for calm. The Circle was far less open to such initiatives. It argued that such meetings were diverting attention away from the real differences which had surfaced between those of French society as a whole and those of Arab origin in particular. Divisions were silenced after a confidential directive had been sent out by the PS national leadership instructing local party officials that discussion and, in particular, criticism of government policy on the Gulf should be confined within party structures. In so doing there was clearly an official recognition of the existence of diverse communities within French society, as well as divisions within the Maghrebian community.

The rise of the FIS in Algeria and its repercussions for French society

Since the banning of the Front islamique de salut (FIS) by the Algerian government in 1992, a *de facto* state of civil war has reigned between the security forces, loyal to the government, and the Islamic fundamentalists, also referred to as the 'Islamists'. In France the presence of a sizeable population of Algerian origin and the close links between the two nations in recent history have alerted the media to the potential repercussions for France. This is particularly the case since the French government has not remained neutral, but has openly supported the Algerian government in its actions, providing economic assistance and arguing that there are no moderate Islamists. Since the FIS has waged war on the government in Algeria, sympathisers have been engaged in clandestine activities in Europe, including France. The trafficking of funds and goods has taken place for the FIS cause. This is illustrated by students in the Paris region and Rhône-Alpes, who have been found to harbour and provide arms, ammunitions and radio equipment for the movement. Illegal immigration networks controlled by Tunisian Islamic fundamentalists have also been discovered in Germany, with payment for illegal entry being channelled into supporting activists in Algeria. As a result of internal strife in Algeria, there has been a 'brain drain' of intellectuals and artists, who have principally settled in France. This has been used by the extreme right to fuel fears of a large-scale 'invasion' of Muslims. Finally and perhaps most dramatically, sympathisers of the FIS engaged in terrorist activity in France, notably the hijacking of an Air France aeroplane in Marseilles in December 1994. The FIS was the prime suspect in a series of bomb attacks in the Paris underground system in the summer of 1995.

As a result of the above actions, the French government embarked upon a policy of wholesale spot checks on anyone suspected of being sympathetic to the aims of the FIS. This meant in reality anyone looking remotely north African being systematically requested to show their official identification. The entire population of

Maghrebian origin has consequently been stigmatised and singled out, reinforcing the view of some white French nationals that Muslims and Islamic fundamentalists are one and the same. While stepping up security measures has resulted in a limited number of arrests, success in preventing FIS actions and catching those engaged in terrorist actions has been due more to undercover operations. The spot checks have merely soured what are already sensitive relations between police and youths of Maghrebian origin, in addition to restricting the freedom of movement of all Maghrebians residing in France.

To what extent can the wholesale control of Maghrebians be justified? Surveys conducted on the opinions of youths, in particular, of Maghrebian origin (accounting for approximately half the total population of Maghrebians in France) towards religion suggest that fears of a spread of Islamic fundamentalism among them are largely unfounded. A survey conducted by SOFRES in November 1993 for the weekly magazine *Le Nouvel Observateur* indicated that only a small minority (14 per cent) of respondents were attracted by an extreme form of Islam. Only 5 per cent of youths questioned claimed to be actively involved and only a further 9 per cent approved of it. The overwhelming majority (63 per cent) were opposed, while another 20 per cent were indifferent to such matters. Studies on the degree of religious observance (Hargreaves and Stenhouse, 1991) have repeatedly concluded that French youths of Maghrebian origin do not as a whole practise Islam on a regular basis, but consider it rather to be an integral feature of their identity.

14.6 Conclusion and summary

France's immigrant population frequently adopts the characteristics of a poor sub-culture at one time associated with the industrial working class. The geographical concentration of first- and second-generation immigrant communities in the suburbs of France's major cities in the industrialised eastern half of the country recalls (and to some extent coincides with) that of the industrial proletariat. Problems of race relations are concentrated in the large cities. As France divested itself of its remaining colonies in the 1950s and 1960s, members of colonial communities (mainly north African immigrants, from Morocco, Tunisia and Algeria) were attracted to France in order to provide a cheap, unskilled labour force. Because these workers were unskilled, they were the first to be affected by the economic crisis of the 1970s. This explains why unemployment rates are far higher among immigrant communities (except the Portuguese) than they are within the rest of French society. The problems immigrants have to face (education, unemployment, poverty) are in part those which afflict other sections of French society as well, but they are usually experienced in a more acute form. Assimilationist patterns have proved stronger in France than in most other European countries. This is tied up with a particular conception of Frenchness, predicated upon a long experience of assimilating different regions and peoples into a single entity, and the persistence of a Jacobin tradition distrustful of distinct cultural identities. Assimilation proved successful in relation to the pre-1940 European immigrant communities, who shared common religious and political beliefs. Arab immigrants have been less easy to assimilate.

Our three case studies demonstrate that French Muslims have been forced to question their own place within French society. In the case of the 'headscarf' affair, the most fundamental question of all was being posed. Can one be both Muslim and French? With respect to the Gulf War, Maghrebians on the whole did not support the actions of Saddam Hussein, nor did they engage in inter-ethnic conflict as was feared by some. This suggests that Maghrebians acknowledge their permanent position within French society. What is at issue, rather, is the nature of that position.

In fact, there has been a renegotiation of the specific place of Muslims in French society. This has taken the form neither of outright assimilation, as was the case for previous waves of immigrants, nor of an acceptance of pluralism where diverse cultural systems are able to co-exist (Hargreaves, 1995). Instead there has been a policy of co-option where differences have been tolerated, but where government has sought to limit divergent behavioural patterns in order that they be compatible with the cultural norms of the dominant society. This is, perhaps, best exemplified by the manner in which French governments, and in particular the Minister of the Interior between 1993 and 1995, Pasqua, strove to provide an organisational framework for Islam in France, similar to that of the Judeo-Christian religions. By creating organisational structures, and by supporting mosque building programmes, governments have aspired to prevent external forces from exerting influence over the French Maghrebian community. They have also attempted to exert a greater degree of control over this community themselves.

The acceptance of distinct ethnic groups was officially legitimised by President Mitterrand in a speech made after the end of hostilities in the Gulf on 3 March 1991. He publicly expressed his gratitude to French citizens of the Jewish and Muslim faiths for the restraint they had displayed during the war. Did this represent the beginning of a long overdue acceptance of Maghrebians as legitimate actors in French society? Only time will tell.

Indicative bibliography

Brubaker, R. (1992) *Citizenship and Nationhood in France and Germany*, Harvard University Press, Cambridge, MA.

Etienne, B. (1989) *La France et l'Islam*, Hachette, Paris.

Hargreaves, A.G. (1995) *Immigration, 'Race' and Ethnicity in Contemporary France*, Routledge, London.

Hargreaves, A.G. and T.G. Stenhouse (1991) 'Islamic beliefs among youths of north African origin in France', *Modern and Contemporary France*, no. 45.

Jazouli, A. (1986) *L'Action collective des jeunes Maghrébins de France*, Harmattan, Paris.
Stenhouse, T.G. (1996) *La Participation politique des Maghrébins de France*, Harmattan, Paris.
Withol de Wenden, C. (1988) *Les Immigrés et la politique*, Presses de la FNSP, Paris.

Chapter 15

France in the European Union

15.1 Introduction and objectives

A recurrent theme running through many of the preceding chapters has been the manner in which the process of European integration has called into question prominent features of the French model. Some analysts have gone as far as to suggest that, in important areas of public policy, the French model has been replaced by a German model. The London *Economist* even suggested in 1995 that 'the secret to understanding French politics in the 1990s lies across the Rhine'. The French model – based on centralism, state intervention in economic management, high inflation and growth – has been replaced by a German model, with its insistence on low inflation, high productivity, central bank independence and a strong currency. French economic policy has been driven since 1983 by a determined effort to match Germany in terms of economic performance, a precondition for preserving the rank of France as a pre-eminent European power. France's role in Europe has been further redefined since the end of the cold war and German unification in 1990, and the Maastricht Treaty of 1992. French governments have not merely emulated Germany, however. They have played up those areas in which France preserves an advantage, notably in terms of diplomatic prestige, international peacekeeping missions and troop deployments.

In the 1990s, the impact of European integration has weighed increasingly heavily on the conduct of domestic French politics (Tiersky, 1994; Stevens, 1992). This process has increased in tempo as preparations to participate in a single European currency under the Maastricht Treaty are refined. In the course of this chapter, we shall address the paradoxical nature of France's relationship to the European Union, a body which appears simultaneously as a powerful constraint on domestic public policy and a source of unrivalled opportunity for contemporary French governments to exercise influence on a wider world stage.

236

15.2 France and the history of European integration

French statesmen were in the forefront of the process leading to the creation of the EEC by the Treaty of Rome in 1957. In the opinion of Hilary Winchester (1993):

> Much of the credit for the organisations of European unity must go to France; not only were individuals, such as Jean Monnet, influential in setting up the early European structures, but France as a whole adopted an expansive view of European unity, in which a strong Europe was viewed as an extension of French national interests.
>
> (p. 157)

This was vital. Underlying its supranational discourse, the European Union (EU) has always been regarded as a means of enhancing French national prestige. To this extent, Europe was a French invention, and served French interests as much as those of any other nation. As surveyed briefly in Chapter 1, the principal moves towards closer European co-operation in the 1950s were of French or Franco-German inspiration: the European Coal and Steel Community of 1951, the abortive European Army of 1954, the Treaty of Rome of 1957. The reasons under-pinning moves towards closer European integration were multiple. Foremost was the need to end the ruinous European civil war which had plagued the continent for the past century, and to make future wars impossible. The genuine federalist ideal-ism of the founding-fathers co-existed alongside harsh calculations of national self-interest. European integration rested upon a reconciliation of France and Germany; co-operation between these hereditary enemies underpins the history of the Euro-pean Union. In effect, as the Community progressed, what amounted to a bargain was struck between the two countries: France would offer political leadership, while recognising Germany's economic primacy.

The current organisation of the European Union stems from 1965, when the separate institutions of the European Coal and Steel Community (ECSC), Euro-pean Atomic Agency (EURATOM) and European Economic Community (EEC) were fused into a single European Community. The European Community (EC) (1965–92) was governed by a single Commission, a Parliament (directly elected since 1979), a Council of Ministers, composed of representatives of national gov-ernments, and a Court of Justice. The European Council was added in 1974 as a permanent six-monthly summit of the heads of European governments. The Euro-pean Community became transformed into the European Union after the Maastricht Treaty of 1992.

The European Union contains two types of decision-making structure: *supranational*, as embodied by the European Commission, the Parliament and the European Court of Justice; and *intergovernmental*, as embodied in the Coun-cil of Ministers and the European Council. These decision-making structures reflect differing approaches towards the objectives of European organisation. The supranational approach seeks global integration. Voluntary co-operation is in-adequate; sovereignty is pooled for the mutual benefit of each member. The intergovernmental approach insists that crucial decisions must be taken by key national leaders invested with democratic legitimacy. Nation-states must reserve the right to veto (or opt out of) unpalatable decisions. The balance between supranational and intergovernmental pressures has evolved according to the interests at stake, and the weight of the players involved. French Presidents have generally preferred an intergovernmental institutional approach, which preserves their own decision-making power in relation to European policy. But they have espoused common interventionist European policies when these have favoured French interests, and have to some extent accepted supranational extensions of EC authority in the broader interests of European union.

15.3 French Presidents and Europe in the Fifth Republic

Since the inception of the Fifth Republic, Europe has been a personalised part of the presidential sphere of interest. It is the President who represents France at international summits even during periods of 'cohabitation'. This does not imply that French Presidents alone have determined French policy towards Europe. The President of the Republic might be the most important actor, but others are also influential: the Prime Minister, individual ministers, high-ranking civil servants, local and regional authorities, and representatives of French companies. French European policy is officially co-ordinated in the *Secrétariat général du comité interministériel* (General Secretariat of the Interministerial Committee, SGCI), a bureaucratic agency composed of representatives of the main departments involved in European issues. The SGCI is formally attached to the Prime Minister's office. In practice, this policy-making infrastructure is primarily at the disposal of the President, as the foremost representative of French European policy. The importance of the SGCI has been emphasised in detailed discussions of French European policy making (Lequesne, 1993; Harmsen, 1996). This valuable finding should be qualified. The SGCI does not substitute itself for political decisions. The principal policy decisions of the Mitterrand presidency were taken by Mitterrand himself, rather than by advisers or officials. The process of EMU, for instance, was characterised by strong political leadership on behalf of President Mitterrand, with the SGCI not obviously involved at any stage of the decision (Dyson and Featherstone, 1996). French monetary policy is co-ordinated by the central bank, rather than by the interministerial SGCI. To a large extent, French European policy has resulted from the personal priorities of successive Presidents, and their evaluation of whether the European balance of power permitted specific policy initiatives.

President de Gaulle

The creation of the Fifth Republic in 1958 interrupted any evolution of the EEC into a supranational federation, as envisaged by certain of its founding-fathers.

Before becoming President, de Gaulle had a less than enthusiastic record towards European integration: he had opposed the European Coal and Steel Community of 1951 and the abortive European Army of 1951–4. More than any other French President, de Gaulle personified one of two recognisable tendencies in French European politics: that which stressed the value of co-operation between nation-states, rather than the vision of a federal United States of Europe, as espoused by the European visionaries Jean Monnet and Robert Schuman.

Co-operation between nation-states was intended to enhance French influence within Europe. As President of the Fifth Republic after 1958, de Gaulle first proposed a Franco-British-American 'directorate' over the affairs of the West. Faced with Anglo-Saxon indifference, de Gaulle then advanced a Franco-German partnership, aimed at weaning Germany away from NATO, and proposing a dual leadership of a Europe which was neither Atlanticist nor *communautaire*. The opening to Germany bore fruit in the signing of the Franco-German friendship treaty of 1963.

The prevailing judgement is that de Gaulle was the least pro-European of all French Presidents, with each of his successors becoming progressively more pro-European, at least until the election of President Chirac in 1995. In certain respects, this judgement is rather superficial. De Gaulle certainly regarded himself as pro-European; indeed he did not separate European and French national interests. Europe was to be led to independence from American hegemony under France's enlightened military and political leadership. Only France, the lone continental European nuclear power, was strong enough to provide an alternative to American leadership. Thus, de Gaulle's decision to withdraw from NATO was justified by the imperative of French military independence (although the General was careful not to discard the safety of the US military umbrella). Other European nations (especially Germany) were dubious of the French alternative, and remained committed to NATO. De Gaulle's repeated vetoes of British entry to the EC, in 1963 and 1967, stemmed from the belief that the UK was an American trojan horse within Europe, and that British influence would be to the detriment of French influence. In this way, a 'French' Europe was juxtaposed to an Anglo-Saxon non-Europe.

As illustrated above, de Gaulle's preference for a Europe of the nation-states contrasted with the federalism of Europe's early visionaries. In terms of the EC's institutional structures, this meant that de Gaulle preferred an intergovernmental organisation to a supranational one. It was the duty of national leaders to preside and decide. De Gaulle's empty chair policy of 1965 testified to his determination to preserve French national interests. In conflict with its European neighbours over extending the use of majority voting for EC decisions, France refused to attend meetings of Community institutions for a six-month period. France would not be bound by decisions with which it did not agree. This stalemate was ended by the 1966 Luxembourg compromise, which gave any member state a right of veto over EC policies which it considered harmful to its vital national interests. The Luxembourg compromise represented a victory for the French government against the federalist enthusiasm of the smaller European nations. De Gaulle's intergovernmental conception of the EC was not seriously challenged again until the mid-1980s.

General de Gaulle was determined to defend essential French interests. This was illustrated in his defence of the Common Agricultural Policy (CAP). The CAP introduced several measures aimed at protecting European (and especially French) farmers. These included minimum prices for agricultural products, EC preference for local producers, external tariff barriers and provisions for export subsidies on third markets. The CAP embodied the new French neo-protectionist approach to Europe. The CAP was also typical of the Franco-German bargaining which has underpinned decision making within the European Community since the 1960s. By guaranteeing minimum prices for agricultural produce, the CAP ensured that France would benefit from an enlarged market for its agricultural products. In turn, Germany would profit from the expansion of industrial markets implicit in the removal of tariff barriers promised in the Treaty of Rome.

De Gaulle was above all a French patriot, one for whom European identity was important as a means of enhancing the continent's independence from the superpowers. De Gaulle's Europe was predicated upon a dominant Franco-German axis, upon French leadership within that axis, and upon a distrust of Anglo-Saxon influence. These themes represented the core of the Gaullist heritage which his successors had to take on board.

President Pompidou, 1969–74

Pompidou accepted the main traits of the Gaullist heritage, while demonstrating more flexibility in relations with the United States and the United Kingdom. The second President of the Fifth Republic was less averse to the accession of the UK to the EC, with British entry finally accomplished in 1973. Acceptance of the CAP was one of the conditions that the UK had to fulfil before being allowed to enter into the Community. In the early 1970s, British entry favoured French interests, for it was felt to counterbalance a reviving Germany.

Apart from the question of British entry, there was much continuity in the transition from de Gaulle to Pompidou. Both were determined to preserve French political pre-eminence within the Community, to favour common policies which were in French interests, and to resist federalist developments. It was noteworthy that British entry into the EC was agreed only when the Common Agricultural Policy was firmly in place. With respect to relations with Germany, President Pompidou lessened, but did not fundamentally alter, the Franco-German basis of the European community. Decision making usually took the form of bargains between France and Germany, although President Pompidou and Chancellors Adenauer and Schmidt did not enjoy warm personal relationships.

President Pompidou's 1972 referendum on British, Irish, Danish and Norwegian entry to the Community revealed how the issue of Europe could serve domestic purposes. The April 1972 referendum, called at a low point in his domestic popularity, was intended to produce an easy electoral victory for the President one year away from the 1973 National Assembly elections. The fact that over 40 per cent of the electorate abstained from voting deprived the President of the expected electoral tonic. The precedent of using the European issue for domestic purposes was not lost on Pompidou's successors, notably President Mitterrand, who called a referendum to ratify the Maastricht Treaty in 1992.

President Giscard d'Estaing, 1974–81

Like his predecessors, President Valéry Giscard d'Estaing regarded the European option as the best means of strengthening French influence.

Tight Franco-German co-operation was again revealed as the driving force of European integration, a co-operation facilitated on account of the warm relations between French President Giscard d'Estaing and the German SPD Chancellor Schmidt. Two decisions in particular helped to relaunch the process of European integration. In 1974, President Giscard d'Estaing and Chancellor Schmidt agreed to create an institutional basis for the regular summit meetings that took place between the heads of EC member states. Henceforth, summits were to take place at least once every six months, with these meetings known as the European Council. The creation of the European Council relaunched the process of European integration on an intergovernmental basis. Major EC policies would be decided in these six-monthly meetings between the heads of government. The Gaullist lineage was evident; each head of government would have the right to veto EC policies. In practice, the European Council has acted as a *de facto* EC executive, in competition with the European Commission in proposing policy initiatives (a body composed of Commissioners nominated by member states). Summit agreements lay behind major EC initiatives, such as the launching of the European monetary system in 1978, the enlargement negotiations leading to the accession of Spain and Portugal in 1986, and the calling of an intergovernmental conference in 1985 to introduce revisions to the Rome Treaty, which resulted in the Single European Act.

The second principal policy based on a Franco-German initiative was the creation of the European monetary system (EMS) in 1978. As with his predecessors, President Giscard d'Estaing promoted closer European co-operation as an alternative to economic domination by the United States. The creation of the EMS (which tied leading European currencies to narrow exchange rate variations) was crucial in this respect, since it laid the bases for future moves towards a single European currency.

The European Council was a continuation of the Gaullist legacy. The Third President of the Fifth Republic was as suspicious as his predecessors of the European Commission, and sought to limit the influence of the Commission President, Roy Jenkins. In other respects, Giscard d'Estaing proved more amenable than his predecessors to the reform of Community institutions. To satisfy the Germans, for instance, President Giscard d'Estaing accepted the principle of direct elections to the European Parliament, on condition that there be no strengthening of the Parliament's authority. Against much domestic opposition, President Giscard d'Estaing supported the membership aspirations of the Mediterranean countries (Greece, later Spain and Portugal), but on condition that the Common Agricultural Policy would preserve the interests of French farmers. President Giscard d'Estaing also agreed in principle that the second enlargement of the EC (to include Greece in 1981) had made necessary more majority voting within the Council of Ministers (the regular intergovernmental meetings of ministers from EC governments, not to be confused with the European Council).

President Mitterrand, 1981–95

His European mission gave a sense of direction to President Mitterrand's long presidential term in office (1981–95). In European policy, in symbolic and substantive terms, Mitterrand's Europe was far more integrationist than that espoused by de Gaulle (Lemaire-Prosche, 1990). Initially preoccupied by domestic politics, Mitterrand left his personal mark on French European policy, arguably more so than any President since de Gaulle. President Mitterrand could claim a major input into the two principal European decisions of the period 1981–93: the launching of the process leading to the Single European Act of 1986, and the Maastricht Treaty of 1992 (Cole, 1994a; Dyson and Featherstone, 1996).

There was much continuity in European policy between Mitterrand and his predecessors. Mitterrand preferred a compact, cohesive Community, based on a Franco-German directorate, rather than a broader nebula of less cohesive nations. This explained his initial reluctance to envisage the enlargement of the Community to include Spain and Portugal, as well as his later resistance to closer ties with the new democracies of eastern Europe. Both stances were later reversed, in order to placate Mitterrand's chief European ally, Chancellor Kohl of Germany. As with previous French Presidents, Mitterrand's Europe was conceived of as an intergovernmental rather than a federal entity: the same suspicion of the European Parliament and of the Commission (even when led by Frenchman Delors after 1985) surfaced on many occasions. But, in the broader interests of European integration, Mitterrand proved more willing to sacrifice elements of national sovereignty than any of his precursors had been. In the Single European Act of 1986, the French President accepted that majority voting should become the norm for EC decisions, although the Luxembourg compromise (right of national veto) formally remained intact. Not even over GATT in 1993 did the French government feel confident enough to use its veto. In the Maastricht Treaty, further provisions for majority voting were enacted, along with some strengthening of the powers of the European Parliament and the European Commission, traditionally anathema to French Presidents.

From 1984 onwards, Mitterrand concentrated upon portraying himself as a great European statesman, with a coherent vision of Europe's future. Mitterrand's close co-operation with Chancellor Kohl and Commission President Delors after

1985 produced a powerful coalition in favour of a more cohesive European Community. Mitterrand's European commitment was allied with a patriotic sense of the need to enhance French influence as a primordial political force within the European family of nations. As with past French Presidents, Mitterrand juxtaposed French European culture to Anglo-Saxon non-European culture. Mitterrand's preferred European Community was one strong enough to survive in an increasingly interdependent age. This implied a commitment to common policies to enable Europe to exist as a political, social, economic and military entity. If necessary, the European community should consider protectionist measures, especially to protect European industries against unfair Japanese and Asian competition.

President Mitterrand's espousal of common European policies was more advanced than his predecessors', including in the sphere of defence policy. Mitterrand was in the forefront of those statespersons espousing a common European foreign and security policy, and a European defence corps, both of which could easily be construed as being in the French national interest. In the late 1980s and early 1990s, a common foreign and security policy appeared to offer France a means of participating in the west European security debate at a vital stage in European history. It was perceived to be in France's interests to promote a European foreign and security policy, which it could be confident of influencing, rather than relying on NATO, from which it had excluded itself voluntarily in 1965. The development of the (French-dominated) Eurocorps was another means of enhancing European defence capacity independently of NATO. The Maastricht Treaty of 1992 went some way to addressing French defence concerns. It established a European defence corps, based initially around the Franco-German brigade created in 1987, in accordance with a political initiative strongly promoted by Mitterrand. It also laid down a complicated procedure for a common security and foreign policy, based on unanimous decisions within the West European Union (WEU, a body which contained representatives of most European Community member states, including France). In fact, however, the Maastricht treaty was highly ambiguous in this sphere. It asserted that 'the WEU will be developed as a defence component of the European Union, and as the means of strengthening the European pillar of the Atlantic alliance'. This fudge was intended to satisfy both France and the UK.

Paradoxically, however, in spite of attempts to move towards closer European defence co-operation independently of NATO, the most successful French foreign policy initiatives since 1990 have occurred as a result of co-operation with allies either under the umbrella of the United Nations (as in the Gulf War of 1991) or within NATO (as in the latter stages of the Bosnian conflict, 1991–5). The conflict in former Yugoslavia witnessed the major European powers at loggerheads with each other, incapable of disciplined joint decision making. Only when NATO (and the Americans) took charge was order restored.

Mitterrand also became a firm supporter of economic and monetary union, a cause that the French President promoted with insistence at Maastricht. Mitterrand's conversion to EMU reflected French fiscal and monetary rectitude during the 1980s; moreover, a central European bank would give the French more control over monetary policy, at present dominated by the German Bundesbank. In exchange for German support for monetary union, Mitterrand supported the German demand for closer European political union. The model of Franco-German bargaining proved its utility on this occasion as on others.

President Chirac, 1995–

François Mitterrand left the stage as a respected European elder statesman. The style adopted by his successor, Jacques Chirac, was in stark contrast. This became clear at the Cannes summit of June 1995, which terminated France's presidency of the European Union: in language unusual for diplomatic gatherings, Chirac publicly accused the Italian premier, Dini, of engineering a competitive devaluation of the lira in order to harm French agriculture, and clashed with the Dutch premier over the Netherlands' policy on drugs. This was followed by criticism of the Greeks for indulgence towards the Bosnian Serbs. These early skirmishes faded in significance beside the uproar caused by Chirac's decision of July 1995 to resume French nuclear testing in the South Pacific. This decision, taken without any negotiation with France's European partners, was condemned virtually unanimously by other nations, including most of France's European allies. In turn, this led President Chirac to accuse its European partners of a lack of 'community solidarity', for failing to support the resumption of nuclear tests. The tensions in Community relations between France and most of her European neighbours recalled those existing during the 1960s, when General de Gaulle had adopted unilateral initiatives and then accused French allies of a lack of solidarity. The isolation of the French government over nuclear testing rendered more remote the prospects for a genuinely common European foreign and security policy, as laid down in the Maastricht Treaty. French involvement in the Bosnian conflict was effective because it occurred within the framework of a NATO resolution and combined military action with American and British troops, rather than being part of concerted European action.

In his 1995 presidential election campaign, Chirac delivered an ambiguous message in relation to European integration, notably criticising the widespread belief that the strong franc policy (and its deflationary economic consequences) were inevitable, the indispensable corollary of closer European integration. Although Chirac had supported the Maastricht referendum of 1992, two-thirds of RPR supporters had voted against the ratification of the Maastricht Treaty. Torn between a sceptical electorate and the need to reassure financial markets, and prevent a run on the franc, President Chirac maintained an ambiguous attitude towards European integration for the first six months of his presidential term. Any lingering doubts over France's commitment to the Maastricht Treaty (especially the single European currency) were forcibly dispelled in a press conference in October 1995. President Chirac affirmed that the primary economic goal of the French government was to cut public sector deficits, in order to meet the convergence criteria for

French participation in the single European currency. That this decision was announced only two days after an official visit to Germany reinforced the belief that France had fallen into line with German wishes, confirming that the new European balance of power lay to the east of the Rhine.

Each President has left his personal imprint on French European policy. Several underlying themes reveal a measure of consensus among the five Presidents:

- There has been a cultural attachment to European values and civilisation, notably as exemplified by France. This has often manifested itself by a declared anti-Americanism. During the GATT negotiations of 1993–4, for example, the French Gaullist government of Balladur (supported by the Socialist President Mitterrand) held out for protectionist measures in favour of defending French cinema, a move justified by the need to support European civilisation against Anglo-Saxon encroachment.
- French governments have been forced to modify traditional interventionist economic and industrial policies under the impact of the European Commission's competition policy. But French governments continue to lobby hard in order to channel state aid to sectors in difficulty. Thus, in 1995–6 the European Commission agreed the French government's rescue package of Crédit lyonnais, as well as an expensive conversion plan for the national carrier Air France.
- The French have traditionally advocated a Europe prepared to protect its industry and agriculture. All Presidents have criticised unbridled economic liberalism, in a manner which sets France at odds with partners such as the UK (and to some extent Germany). In advocating neo-protectionist industrial policies, French governments have extrapolated their *dirigiste* economic traditions to the European level. In practice, however, the European Union as established by the Single European Act and the Maastricht Treaty is a liberal-capitalist club bound by the rules of the market. French governments have had to adapt their economic policies to fit in with these rules; there has been a notable lessening of state economic interventionism since Mitterrand took the 'European' option in March 1983.
- The French have been adept at suggesting common European policies, especially when these benefit French interests. The CAP is the classic example. Other examples include the creation of the European monetary system in 1978, which aligned the franc against the German mark; EUREKA (the European Space programme); and other related industrial projects with beneficial spin-offs for French industry. France has been in the forefront of suggesting these policies, aimed at creating a European community capable of competing with other trading blocs, notably the USA and Japan.
- In spite of the federalist rhetoric of men such as Jacques Delors, French politicians have shown limited enthusiasm for extending the powers of the European Union's supranational institutions, the European Commission and the European Parliament. In a traditionally centralist political regime, federalism

remains a foreign concept for French governments, embraced, if at all, in order to humour the Germans. French political parties themselves have shared a range of opinions over Europe. No French party has been an unequivocal champion of federalism, save the Christian-democratic FD. National independence has remained a key reference point. As the Maastricht referendum campaign of 1992 illustrated, moreover, each of the major parties was divided over Europe, with the Gaullist RPR the most divided of all.

■ France has always been suspicious of EU enlargement; this has manifested itself at each new widening of the Community to include new members (1973, 1981, 1986 and 1995). For France, 'widening' the Community is usually felt to be incompatible with its 'deepening' and its construction as an entity capable of imposing common policies. France's main partner, Germany, has supported both widening and deepening. It is, however, indicative of the tide of history that France has been powerless to prevent successive widenings of the European Union, most notably that of 1995, which introduced Sweden, Austria and Finland to the European club. More than any other indicator, this reveals that the new European balance of power created by the collapse of communism and German unification has gradually strengthened German influence at the centre of a broader European Union.

15.4 The bare essentials: Franco-German relations

As illustrated in the introductory section of this chapter, Franco-German reconciliation underpins the history of the European Community. Ever since 1963, it has become commonplace to depict the Franco-German axis as the pivot upon which closer European integration turns. The Franco-German couple is another metaphor in common use, one which has the disadvantage of underplaying the external pressures which interact upon the internal operation of Franco-German relations. Whichever epithet is preferred, personal relations between French and German leaders have always been important. De Gaulle and Adenauer enjoyed warm personal relations, whereas those between the General and Erhard or Kiesinger were far more difficult. Pompidou and Brandt distrusted each other; Giscard d'Estaing and Schmidt enjoyed a relationship based on mutual confidence. From the moment of Kohl's inception as German Chancellor, Mitterrand and Kohl endeavoured to recreate a great personal relationship, in conscious imitation of the de Gaulle–Adenauer partnership. Chancellor Kohl's ill-advised intervention in favour of Jacques Delors ahead of the 1995 French presidential election embittered relations between the German Chancellor and President Chirac, relations made worse by French nuclear testing, against the grain of German public opinion. But business being business, by October 1995 Chirac and Kohl had publicly patched up their differences, and in December 1995 a joint Franco-German letter attempted to recapture the spirit of earlier co-operation between France and Germany.

Franco-German political and military co-operation thus underpins the history of the EC. It has its roots in the friendship treaty signed between de Gaulle and Adenauer in 1963, in which French and German motivations were somewhat different. For de Gaulle, the principal incentive was to reduce Anglo-American influence over European affairs, and to enlist the support of West Germany in pursuit of this goal; for Adenauer, lasting reconciliation with France was important for reasons of continued economic recovery, as well as for securing eventual French support for new German initiatives towards eastern Europe. Adenauer was a dedicated francophile; the Franco-German friendship treaty was considered to be a major accomplishment. The relationship continued under Erhard, who took over as German Chancellor in 1965. Although the new Chancellor was less sympathetic to French foreign policy aims, he recognised the importance of maintaining the arrangement: for the first time in its history as a nation, Germany had a friendly country to its west, fulfilling a major psychological need. The special relationship has continued under all successive French Presidents and German Chancellors, although with marked variations in tempo. The Franco-German relationship in time became a powerful axis, with which all other European powers had to compose; moves towards closer European political integration and co-operation revealed themselves to be dependent upon Franco-German agreement, without which the EC could not progress.

For different reasons, France and Germany have both adopted visionary approaches towards Europe; this separates both nations from the United Kingdom, which has consistently attempted to dampen integrationist ardour. In terms of substance, both France and Germany have envisaged a political presence for the EU that goes beyond the Union as an 'extended free trade zone'. The French version of a more closely integrated Europe was traditionally 'Jacobin and interventionist' (McCarthy, 1993); the German version was federalist and socially progressive. In fact, both French and German leaders have extrapolated their vision of Europe from the governing realities in their own countries. For President Mitterrand, for example, a politician raised in the centralising, statist traditions of French radical republicanism, federalism remained an awkward reference. By contrast, the federal allusion came naturally to Helmut Kohl, for whom federalism followed logically from a decentralised reading of the German Federal Republic. A federal Europe was desirable because it was Germany writ large. Whatever their differences in approach, both French and German leaders have believed in the existence of a European finality. This has separated them from most British premiers, for whom Europe is at best an unavoidable constraint.

Preceding German unification, post-war Franco-German collaboration had been based upon an overall equilibrium between the two countries, according to which German economic supremacy was counterbalanced by French political primacy within Europe. To the extent that it kept Germany divided, and deprived it of great power status, the 40 years of cold war and the post-war division of Europe had generally benefited French interests. From the early 1960s onwards, the historical circumstances of the Second World War, combined with the legacy of Gaullist foreign policy, promoted a subtle disequilibrium within the Franco-German axis: France exercised a political leadership out of proportion to its economic weight. Germany was an economic giant, but a political pygmy.

German unification has altered this delicate balance. The balance of power within Europe has shifted to the Germans, and a new competitive edge has made itself felt within Franco-German relations. Since the events of 1989, the Franco-German partnership has suffered severe strains. France and Germany start from opposing positions on many of the issues facing Europe. In a range of policy sectors, French and German interests have diverged. In the period since Maastricht, these have included the GATT negotiations, CAP reform, the Atlantic alliance, Yugoslavia, Bosnia and relations with the new democracies of eastern and central Europe. Tensions were obvious during the 1993 GATT negotiations, for instance, when the Germans were torn between French and American demands. But French and German leaders have repeatedly expressed their belief in continuing European unification, and in the decisive role that the German Chancellor and the French President must perform in this process. Disagreement over specific policies, and even over more fundamental aspects of the European integration process (such as the finer details of monetary and political union, or foreign policy), cannot detract from this belief that Franco-German co-operation is critical to the future of Europe. The continuing benefits of reconciliation between two hereditary enemies are sufficiently broadly accepted to prevent either nation from deviating too far from the path traced by de Gaulle and Adenauer in 1963. The future direction of the European Community is as likely as in the past to depend upon tight Franco-German co-operation.

15.5 The European Union and the French political system

As the *Economist* affirmed in 1991, 'The recent paradox of France is that France made Europe, but then Europe remade France.' This can be seen most obviously in the sphere of economic policy: in the French obsession with tough, anti-inflationary economic policies, breaking decades of a loose attitude towards inflation. Above all, France is determined to be in the first division of European nations, even if this means trying to beat the Germans at their own economic game.

The process of monetary union enshrined in the Maastricht Treaty of 1992 has had an impact upon the operation of the French state in several recognisable ways. First, the policy agenda has shifted. The criteria outlined in the Maastricht Treaty stipulate strict conditions that member states must fulfil in order to qualify for membership of the single European currency. These include: annual budget deficits limited to no more than 3 per cent of GDP; public sector borrowing below 60 per cent of GDP; and inflation targets within 1.5 percentage points of the best-performing member state. The treaty affirms that a political decision would be made by EC Finance Ministers in 1998, on the basis of 1997 statistics. In order to meet the tough Maastricht convergence criteria to participate in a single European currency, French governments – like their counterparts elsewhere – have pursued policies of budget retrenchment, privatisation and welfare state reform. In November 1995, premier Juppé announced severe cuts to France's generous social security system, which many attributed to the French government's preparations for the single European currency. The popular protest movement provoked by welfare reform pointed to the difficulties ahead in educating French public opinion as to the full implications of European monetary integration and a single currency. There would be winners and losers – though no one could predict precisely who these would be.

Second, the preparations for economic and monetary union introduced new policy actors into the fray, most notably the French central bank. The independence of the French central bank since 1 January 1995 – on the lines of the German Bundesbank model – has reduced executive control over instruments of monetary policy such as interest rates. Tensions between the President of the French central bank, Jean-Claude Trichet, and Jacques Chirac resurfaced on several occasions, both during and after the 1995 presidential election campaign. On the basis of preliminary judgements, central bank independence appeared to have strengthened the role of monetary policy technocrats at the expense both of the Finance Ministry and of the traditional political leadership.

The European debate has polarised French public opinion. In a referendum to approve or reject the Maastricht Treaty in September 1992, only a narrow majority of French voters (51/49) were in favour. It might be surmised that this total would have been higher had the referendum not been widely seen as a manoeuvre by Mitterrand to restore his flagging popularity. However we interpret the result, the 1992 referendum illustrated a degree of polarisation over the issue of further European integration which belied official discourse. Detailed analysis revealed that a majority of industrial workers, low-status clerical workers and farmers opposed the Maastricht Treaty. These were the losers – or feared losers – of the modernisation process associated with further European integration. This explained why traditionally left-inclining industrial areas – such as the Nord/Pas-de-Calais – voted against the treaty. To some extent, and in different circumstances, this social division recalled Hoffmann's appreciation of a dynamic France and a static France in the Third Republic. The strongest supporters of the treaty were among the professional middle classes, especially in heavily urbanised areas. The regions with the strongest yes votes were those which had most obviously benefited from closer European integration, but which maintained a distinctive identity within the French nation, such as Alsace-Lorraine and Brittany.

Europe was revealed as an issue which cut across traditional party lines and divided public opinion. Each of the main parties was divided on the issue, some more than others. The PCF came out strongly against the Maastricht Treaty, as creating a Europe of central bankers and capitalists; the PCF was one of the least divided parties on this issue. While rejecting a single European currency, however, PCF leader Hue has given qualified support to the idea of a common European currency. The PS contains the full range of policy positions on the issue of Europe and further European integration (Cole, in Gaffney, 1996). As measured in terms of PS deputies, the Socialists were resolutely favourable to Maastricht. At a 1996 party convention on Europe, however, an amendment criticising a single European currency received strong minority support. The PS electorate was divided between its new middle-class voters, in the main supportive of closer European integration, and its popular electorate, who were far less enthusiastic. The new party leader, Jospin, has moved towards a more qualified stance. Alongside giving official support for the Maastricht Treaty, the 1996 PS convention on Europe urged the need to safeguard the traditional French model of public service, and supported a more assertive social dimension to the European Union. These themes were repeated in the PS campaign for the 1997 National Assembly elections.

The UDF has always contained fervent pro-Europeans within its ranks, notably the inheritors of the Christian-democratic tradition, Force démocrate. Alongside a Christian-democratic vision of Europe, however, the UDF also contained economic liberals in favour of a *laissez-faire* agenda and against a single currency, as well as ultra-conservatives such as de Villiers (cf. Chapter 11). The Gaullist RPR was the most divided of all parties in 1992, with two-thirds of RPR deputies coming out against ratification of the Maastricht Treaty. While premier Juppé was a convinced supporter of the cause of European integration – and determined to push ahead with all necessary measures to meet the Maastricht convergence criteria – many backbench RPR deputies remained unhappy with the Maastricht agenda, including the President of the National Assembly, Philippe Séguin. Finally, while the FN was predictably against the Maastricht Treaty, with its challenge to national sovereignty, Le Pen claimed to be pro-European, insofar as European culture needed to be defended against the threat of invasion from non-European peoples!

15.6 Conclusion and summary

The paradoxical nature of France's relationship with Europe has been explored throughout this chapter. It is probably premature to evoke the Europeanisation of the French political system, though integration has clearly left its mark. This can also be measured by observing the evolution of the French Council of State, the guardian of French administrative traditions. Long resistant to any encroachment from Brussels, the Council of State has increasingly been forced to accept the supremacy of EU law over French law and the need to modify its own practices in order to accommodate this.

The most obvious impact of encroaching Europeanisation is in relation to economic policy and the ramifications of economic choices in all other areas of public policy. Most observers consider French participation to be essential for the success of a single European currency. French governments are also of the view that any single European currency must include France. As stipulated in the Maastricht Treaty of 1992, countries wishing to participate in a single European currency must respect tough economic convergence criteria. In their effort to reach these targets of low inflation, low debt and controlled public expenditure, French governments have been forced to sacrifice several sacred cows: notably, in the form of sweeping cuts in the social security system. The wave of public sector strikes that brought much of France to a standstill in December 1995 was attributed by many to the process of European integration: social security reform had been imposed by the need to rein in public expenditure, in order to qualify for membership of a single European currency. The mass public sector mobilisation against the Juppé plan revealed the extent to which the French public remained attached to their social security system. It also suggested that the French notion of public service appeared out of step with the liberal interpretation of the Maastricht process that prevailed in most other countries. To many, it suddenly became apparent that the logic of Maastricht and the traditional French model were not obviously compatible. To pursue the Maastricht agenda to its conclusion (a single European currency, ultimately a political union) would further modify features of their political, social and economic systems that the French had long taken for granted.

The European debate had never really been posed in these precise terms before. Traditionally expansive French views of Europe depended upon a vision of Europe as an extension of France; hence the emphasis placed on exporting features of the French model for the benefit of others (Harmsen, 1996). But, as Dyson and Featherstone (1996) point out, the paradox of EMU was 'that in order to escape from the constraints of external monetary dependency on Germany, French negotiators were forced to adopt the policy beliefs and institutional arrangements of the country that was being asked to cede power'. In other words, to preserve the illusion of joint leadership within Europe, French governments had to show themselves to be more German than the Germans; hence the creation of central bank independence (1995) and the persistence of higher interest rates than the Germans, in spite of an overvalued currency and record unemployment (12 per cent in 1996).

The process of European integration posed other dilemmas as well. The enlargement of the European Union, combined with the measures agreed for European political and economic union at Maastricht, have increased speculation over a Europe of two or more speeds. The idea of a Europe of variable geometry had been proposed on and off by French and German spokespeople for over a decade. President Mitterrand made several oblique references to the possibility in the 1980s. His proposed European confederation of 1990 was in some senses consistent with this idea, whereby a hard core of closely integrated nations (France, Germany, Benelux, perhaps others) would be surrounded by a looser periphery. In 1994 Chancellor Kohl's party, the CDU, argued that Europe should be composed of a 'core' of five member states (the original six minus Italy), the minimum number feasible for the introduction of a single European currency.

Herewith lies a central dilemma for French policy-makers. It is inconceivable that France could be excluded from an inner core of nations, including by the Germans themselves. This explains the delay in the timetable for the single European currency (1999, not 1997) and the efforts undertaken by French governments to meet the Maastricht convergence criteria. One of the essential objectives of post-war French foreign policy has been to tie the Germans into the western alliance, via the EC and NATO. In a narrow first division of European nations, however, France runs the danger of being submerged in a Germanic sphere of influence. To this extent, closer European integration might appear as less of a positive-sum game than French élites previously supposed.

Indicative bibliography

Cole, A. (1993) 'Looking on: France and the new Germany', *German Politics*, vol. 2, no. 3.

Guoyomarch, A., H. Machin and E. Ritchie (eds.) (1996) *France in the European Union*, Macmillan, London.

Kolodziej, E. (1990) 'De Gaulle, Germany and the superpowers: German unification and the end of the cold war', *French Politics and Society*, vol. 8, no. 4.

Lequesne, C. (1993) *Paris-Bruxelles*, Presses de la FNSP, Paris.

McCarthy, P. (ed.) (1993) *France–Germany, 1983–93: The struggle to cooperate*, Macmillan, London.

Morgan, R. (1991) 'French perspectives on the new Germany', *Government and Opposition*, vol. 26, no. 1.

Tréan, C. (1991) 'La France et le nouvel ordre européen', *Politique étrangère*, no.1.

Yost, D.-S. (1990) 'France in the new Europe', *Foreign Affairs*, vol. 69, no. 5.

Chapter 16

Conclusion

16.1 Introduction and objectives

As its title indicates, Chapter 16 provides a series of concluding judgements on the question of whether French exceptionalism remains the dominant characteristic of the political system. The position is a complex one, since there are countervailing pressures at work. The French political system retains features setting it apart from other European nation-states, but also faces a number of difficulties and challenges which have brought it closer to its European neighbours.

16.2 The end of the French exception?

Most specialists agree that France is a country of paradoxes. It was for long considered an exception to the norm of established western European democracies such as the United Kingdom and Germany, with their stable political systems and their regular alternations in power. The notion of the French exception was briefly introduced in the Preface, and has underpinned analysis in several chapters. The French exception has been employed to describe France's apartness from other European nations.

The concept of the French exception was always a rather ambiguous one. It rarely spelt out in detail why France was exceptional or, if it was exceptional, which nations were non-exceptional. In key senses, each European nation might be considered as exceptional. As Spotts and Weiser recalled in *Italy: A Difficult Democracy* (1986) Italy was always 'a difficult democracy'. In the ensuing decade, it became even more difficult, as the first Italian republic apparently collapsed amidst popular revolt against generalised corruption and political instability, which far surpassed anything witnessed in France. For British premier Margaret Thatcher (1979–90), the whole of the European continent appeared out of step; the powerful coalition of heads of the major European states against the Iron Lady suggested that the UK was really the exceptional power. This was confirmed by John Major's unilateral opt-outs on the Social Chapter and the single currency at the Maastricht summit. Similar judgements could be levelled at other European nations, most notably Germany, which proved exceptional in a rather different sense, to the extent that the German model became a reference for most other countries of the Union, particularly in monetary and economic terms.

While the French exception was nowhere rigorously explained as a model of political behaviour, several central features were held to characterise it:

- A powerful, unified and indivisible central state, a legacy of the process of nation building (Chapters 1 and 2).
- A distrust of intermediary institutions and a suspicion of civil society, justified in terms of the general will (Chapters 9 and 12).
- To borrow Vincent Wright's terminology, if provincial pressures were able to manifest themselves, this was within the context of a Jacobin state.
- A model of Parisian centralisation, producing, in comparative terms, a homogeneous political and administrative élite (Chapter 7).
- A tradition of state intervention (*dirigisme*) in the economic and industrial sphere (Chapter 13).
- An ideologically charged political discourse, the legacy of France's past revolutionary tradition and late industrialisation (Chapter 3).
- The existence of powerful anti-system movements challenging the regime, such as the French Communist Party (Chapter 11).
- An unwillingness of the nation's political élites to engage in face-to-face contact; hence the weakness of a bargaining culture (Chapters 3 and 7).
- An original foreign policy based on preserving national rank (Chapter 2).
- An awkward posture within the European Community, aimed at claiming a leadership role for France within Europe (Chapter 15).

An underlying theme of this book has been that the 'French exception' has been modified in the course of the 1980s and 1990s. This has had an impact upon the nation's political institutions (Part II), its representative forces (Part III) and its role in Europe (Part IV). Each European nation preserves a degree of exceptionality, but each faces common pressures. In the mid-1990s, there are comparable forces provoking change in most European countries. These include global economic change, the impact of European integration, pressures for economic convergence, a calling into question of certain types of political institution and the changing role of the state. It is a central contention of this book that, as a leading European nation with a particular state tradition and historical legacy, these pressures have led to more visible changes in France than elsewhere. The modification of French exceptionalism can be measured in relation to several spheres: the recomposition of the state; the dilution of the left–right cleavages; a weakening of traditional 'anti-system' movements; policy convergence among French élites; and the impact of European integration on domestic French politics.

Reinventing the French state

The history of France is to some extent the history of the French state. In Chapters 1 and 2, we discovered the importance of the state over several centuries in forging national unity. In Dyson's (1980) formulation, a state tradition existed, with the state representing more than its component parts. After the discredit of the wartime Vichy regime, the state discovered new roles in the post-war period as an economic agent and as the provider of social welfare. The state became a first-rank economic actor in its own right. Though the importance of the five-year economic plans was often exaggerated, the state affirmed its presence as a key actor in the sphere of industrial policy, and its control over much financial investment. After de Gaulle's nationalisation programme, the French state owned large tracts of French industry, notably in the sectors of transport, automobiles, steel and energy. The Socialists' nationalisation programme of 1981–2 added a number of leading industrial groups and the bulk of the banking and financial sector to the state's portfolio.

As in other western European nations, the extension of the state's activity went beyond the economic sphere to encompass social protection and welfare. The creation of a comprehensive social security system remains one of the achievements of the post-war tripartite government. The preservation of the social security system, in spite of its permanent chronic deficit, is testament to this. Attempts to reform the social security system have been met invariably with tough opposition and a government climbdown. As the social movement of December 1995 illustrated, this is the one area in which the trade unions still manage to mobilise broad support and to bring the capital to a standstill. In this sphere as in others, there is a widespread positive connotation of the state as an instrument of public service and a guarantee of equality between French citizens. The equality and neutrality of the state forms an important part of the French republican tradition.

Challenges to the French state have come from several directions. As the process of European integration has gathered pace, the role of the French state in economic management has diminished, although French policy-makers remain imbued with an interventionist and voluntaristic vision that sets them apart from Anglo-Saxon liberalism. In the sphere of industrial policy, the interventionist state has ceded ground, notably under the combined pressures of fiscal austerity, European regulation and policy fashion (in the form of the privatisation programmes) (Bauer, 1988; Maclean, 1995). In the domestic arena, the decentralisation and deconcentration reforms of the 1980s and 1990s have substantially altered the nature of centre–periphery relations, having a constraining impact upon the state going beyond that originally envisaged. Finally, the French state has had to cede ground to the supranational appetites of the European Union in a range of policy sectors, where it is no longer able to act alone.

To conclude in the irremediable weakening of the French state would be premature. While the state has sacrificed certain functions, it has jealously guarded others. As was demonstrated in Chapter 8, a hidden motive of the decentralisation reforms was to broaden the financial effort needed for the modernisation of public services to include local taxpayers. This was manifest in a sector such as education, where the new regional authorities undertook a massive financial effort to renovate school buildings that had been left in a state of disrepair by central government. Similar observations might be made in relation to social policy, decentralised to the 96 departmental councils in order to limit escalating central government expenditure in this sphere. The opposition of the *grands corps* to further decentralisation illustrates that the spirit of the state remains very much alive. French policy stances in relation to Europe have tended to favour intergovernmental approaches to European integration which preserve maximum influence with member states. Such characteristic French institutions as the Council of State have pleaded for the preservation of the French identity against encroachments from Brussels. But however much the Council of State might regret diminishing state sovereignty, it cannot by itself reverse this process. Even the powerful French state no longer controls its own destiny in an increasingly interdependent world.

Whatever happened to left and right?

In 1979, Jean Luc Parodi and John Frears published a book entitled *War Will Not Take Place*. The title of this work epitomised the atmosphere of heightened ideological conflict that surrounded the 1978 National Assembly elections, which the left narrowly failed to win. Shortly after that election, Jack Hayward (1978) published an article in *West European Politics* referring to the confrontation of two French cultures throughout French history. This bipolar, partisan political culture, and the mobilising references to socialism, or the defence of freedom it induced, appear archaic as France moves towards the twenty-first century.

Put simply, the left–right cleavage is of less significance in French politics in the mid-1990s than it was in the mid-1970s. The general ideological climate has changed, both in France and elsewhere, as have perceptions of the possibilities of governmental action. The differences separating left and right have become less obvious and less important than previously. In fact, left and right were always broad coalitions. Thus, the historian Réné Rémond referred to the 'three families of the French right' (Rémond, 1982) and the Socialist politician Michel Rocard diagnosed two cultures of the French left. The ambiguity of themes associated with left and right is scarcely new. The early twentieth-century Radical Party was on the left on anti-clerical issues and in defence of the republic, but conservative in terms of preserving the socioeconomic status quo.

In the late 1970s, the left wing of the PS, notably those based around J.-P. Chevènement and CERES faction, complained bitterly of the transfer of values between left and right, protesting notably that the theme of decentralisation was contrary to the left's universalist, republican and egalitarian mission. The cultures of the French left have always been plural: although it was a Socialist government which introduced decentralisation, and heralded it as *la grande affaire du septennat*, this was contrary to a powerful strand of left-wing opinion. In the French republican tradition, centralisation was a guarantor of national, uniform stand-ards, to which majority left-wing opinion remained attached.

The transfer of values gathered pace during the Mitterrand presidency, especially the first term in office (1981–8). The principal policy reversals of the Mitterrand presidency were justified by concepts which were new to the French left, occasionally borrowed from European neighbours, periodically from traditional rivals. The key ideological justification for policy change after 1983 was that of 'modernisation', which owed as much to past Gaullist discourse as any other. In discursive terms, modernisation was interpreted by some as a euphemism for the left abandoning its left-oriented reformist programme of 1981–2. Across a wide range of policy sectors, the left's celestial principles were quietly called into question in the name of moderni-sation and economic efficiency: this occurred notably in relation to economic policy, welfare policy, employment policy, attitude towards the private sector, fiscal policy and industrial policy (Cole, 1994a). The ruling Socialists became obsessed with their new religion of modernisation, with the zeal of the converted.

In a less rigorous manner, the transfer of values also took place on the French right. In reaction to the governmental socialism of the 1980s and 1990s, a series of creeds were adopted. In 1986 the RPR–UDF election manifesto declared its belief in economic liberalism, which, though never quite the same as the Anglo-Saxon variety, marked a clear shift away from Gaullist statism. In 1995 Jacques Chirac reversed this set of priorities and centred his campaign on fighting social injustice and unemployment. Chirac was aware of the political opportunities presented by continuing popular reaction against the previous two governments (1988–93, 1993–5). The key to the success of Chirac's campaign lay in a rather paradoxical alchemy of themes more normally associated with the political left, in conjunction with the desire for an end to 'fourteen years of socialism'. That Chirac placed unemployment at the centre of his campaign proved politically astute, at least for as long as the campaign lasted. In a rather cynical exercise in political marketing, Chirac was able to occupy a pseudo-left niche unavailable to the Socialist Jospin on account of the discredit of governmental socialism after a decade in power.

Despite the plurality within both left and right, until (and including) 1981 each political camp was able to mobilise by referring to distinctive sets of values. Which-ever side one was on, the sense of identity and of belonging to one camp or another was strong. Since the Socialist experience in office (1981–6, 1988–93), the ideologi-cal bearings of left and right have become far more confused. Each side has bor-rowed themes hitherto voiced by others in order to justify its policies. There is an argument that the *mitterrandiste* left appeared most competent when carrying out conservative policies, while the right proved itself more social than the left. Ul-timately, however, values justified changed policies that were to a large extent imposed against the initial will of those concerned. On left and right, ideas served an instrumental function that could not be disassociated from changing political and policy circumstances. This was not necessarily cynical. Difficult political deci-sions imposed themselves on governments of left and right; ideological justifications followed. This was natural, given the nature of the policy problems that each had to face, and the desire to demonstrate legitimacy by governing in the interests of the whole nation, at least symbolically. After a past bathed in an excessively ideological register, values have tended to become more instrumental, elections more prone to the exigencies of political marketing and the circumstances of particular elections.

The decline of traditional anti-system movements

In Chapter 11, the decline of the French Communist Party was appraised at some length. Until the historic setback of 1981, certain observers of French politics had contended that the persistence of a strong Communist Party was proof of French exceptionalism. The concept of polarised pluralism, invented by Sartori to designate Italian politics (one of the two major political forces being permanently in opposition), could be adapted to the French system. The survival of the French Communist Party condemned the left to perpetual opposition. While this proved inaccurate, the decline of the PCF has had an important effect on the operation of the French political system. It is clear that, prior to 1981, the nature of political competition had a constraining effect upon both political discourse and party programmes. The French Socialists were traditionally paralysed by the fear of being labelled as social democratic, the stick with which the PCF regularly beat the PS in order to keep its grip over the left-wing electorate. As leader of the Socialist Party from 1971 to 1981, Mitterrand accepted the PCF's challenge. His determination to break the Communist Party led to the adoption of policy positions apparently more radical than those of European social-democratic parties elsewhere. This explained the radical edge to the Socialists' policies in 1981–2.

The decline of the Communist Party in 1981, accelerated in 1986 and 1988, has weakened the French exception. The Socialist left has, in spite of everything, become managerial; the Communist Party marginal. The Communist bogey is no longer available for the right-wing parties to scare undecided voters away from the left. In conjunction with Jospin's honourable showing in the second round of the 1995 presidential election, and the left–right bipolarity that the 1995 second ballot once again produced, this gave the Socialist left more reason for optimism in the 1997 National Assembly election than in 1993 (see Appendix 2).

At least in some senses, the evolution of the party system during the 1980s and 1990s brought France closer to European norms. The principal political competition is that between a social reformist party on the left and a heterogeneous conservative coalition on the right. This structuring of political space is in line with that of most other European countries, where older party structures (namely social-democratic and Christian-democratic parties) have shown remarkable persistence. The perseverance of a fairly clear-cut bipolarity must also in part be attributed the strong institutional and structural forces that partially shape the nature of French party competition, even in a context where alienation from existing parties has gained ground. The most significant of these forces is the second-ballot electoral system, which penalises minor parties, especially those unable to form alliances.

Even the breakthrough of new movements in French politics found echoes elsewhere in Europe. Existing parties proved incapable in France, as in Italy, Belgium, Germany, Austria and elsewhere, of articulating certain new political issues (notably environmental ones) or of controlling the re-emergence of older issues (those based on national identity and racial intolerance). This led to the growth of new political movements alongside the decline of certain older ones (notably the PCF). The issues of immigration, security and the environment all fell to some extent into this category. The rise and fall of the French Green parties proved a test case not only of the disruptive force of new post-materialist political issues, but also – ultimately – of the resilience of existing party structures. The breakthrough and persistence of the far-right Front national has been altogether more serious. It has been both cause and effect of a changed political agenda which the mainstream parties have been unable to dominate. The potent mixture of immigration, insecurity, national identity and economic deprivation has proved a powerful cocktail, skilfully exploited by the Front's demagogic leader, Le Pen. With the survival and consolidation of the Front national, appraised in Chapter 11, the French polity has ensured continuing attention as an exceptional democracy. As in Italy, the existence of a powerful far-right movement is testament not only to the survival of race-related issues in French politics, but also to a dissatisfaction with the current operation of the political system on behalf of a minority.

Pressurised policy convergence

France was a country rather less different from its European neighbours in 1997 than in 1981, not least in terms of its ideological register, but also in terms of the content of its public policies. Beneath the clash of rival political programmes lay a *de facto* convergence on many areas of public policy. This was particularly acute in relation to economic policy. With the left's abandonment of Keynesian-style reflationary policies in 1982, and its modification of its traditional statism, the dividing line between left and right became blurred, if not extinct as some commentators argued. The monetarist policies engaged by the French Socialists after 1983 were at least as rigorous as those undertaken by conservative administrations in other European countries. Moreover, the strong franc economic policy reduced the room for manoeuvre in other policy sectors throughout the period of Socialist administration, 1983–93.

To some extent all of this was logical. Faced with the heavy task of managing an unreformed economy in the 1980s, as the governing party it was natural for the Socialists to enact the necessary structural reforms to the French economy. Whatever the professed ideological differences between the parties, external constraints weighed increasingly heavily on the freedom of governments of both sides throughout the 1980s and 1990s. In key sectors of domestic policy, difficult choices were imposed upon governments of all political hues.

A pertinent question arising from the study of contemporary French politics is the extent to which external constraints allow room for manoeuvre, notably in relation to economic policy. The belief instilled by all governments since 1983 that there is only one economic policy created its own antibody in the form of Jacques Chirac's presidential campaign of 1995, urging an anti-unemployment strategy and economic growth. His campaign cleverly protested against *la pensée unique*, the notion that there was only one economic path (the strong franc policy) if France was to meet the convergence criteria for a single European currency. This struck a chord with many French electors. But it did not answer the question of whether there was, in fact, only one plausible economic policy. After six months of hesitation, in October 1995 President Chirac strongly supported the creation of the single currency in 1999, and pledged to make the necessary public expenditure cuts to qualify France for membership. In so doing, Chirac answered his own campaign question by a resolute no.

16.3 Forever France?

France has certainly changed. It has not quite become a nation like the others, however. The case for a weakening of the French exception should not be over-stated. In important respects, France retains a highly distinctive place among European nations. Its self-perception as a first-rank power continues to shape foreign policy decisions. No other European nation would unilaterally announce a resumption of nuclear testing, for example, while accusing European partners of a lack of solidarity for expressing opposition, as President Chirac did in 1995. Detailed appraisal of foreign policy (beyond the boundaries of the present study) would provide proof, if proof were needed, of the original role performed by France among the European family of nations. French foreign policy interests in Africa, for instance, are testament to a geopolitical presence that no other European power comes close to matching. A sense of a mission in the world sets France (and the UK) apart from all other European nations, and explains the reluctance of the French to pool sovereignty in the essential sphere of foreign policy.

The French exception appears alive and well in relation to the defence of French language, and in the universalist message of French culture. The French state tradition remains vigorous, as expressed in the continuing control of the *grands corps* over much public policy; and in the pattern of recruitment of political, administrative and economic élites. While altered in some respects, the traditional French model appears to resist better in others. This was illustrated in Chapter 14, for example, with respect to immigration and integration; in Chapter 7, in relation to patterns of recruitment of France's politico-administrative élite; and to a lesser extent in Chapter 12, in relation to the weakness of economic interest groups and the continuing role of the technical *grands corps* in public policy making.

Even in a sphere as quintessentially national as defence policy, however, French policy-makers have been forced to evolve in the new post-cold-war era. Massive defence cuts ordered by President Chirac in 1996 involved a recognition by the Gaullist President of the necessary adaptation to a new world era that his predecessor Mitterrand had been unable to countenance. Most notably, the partial reintegration of France into NATO decision-making machinery in 1996 represented an act of astute political realism that proved beyond former President Mitterrand. This confirmed the paradox noted above that political change often comes from the least expected source. A Socialist President Mitterrand helped to reconcile the French with the market economy; a Gaullist President Chirac helped partially to ease France back into NATO.

Whether or not we are witnessing the end of the French exception, it is clear that the political and policy space has become more complicated, in France as elsewhere. There are a number of common pressures impacting upon European nations, and each European nation interprets these pressures in accordance with its own traditions. The manner in which France has reacted to external and internal pressures for change reveals traits in common with other European nations. As appraised in Chapter 15, trends towards European governance have had at least as much impact upon the functioning of domestic politics in France as anywhere else. However, common pressures manifest themselves in different ways within the cultural context of each individual European nation.

In a range of policy sectors, governments have had to face the unavoidable consequences of policies they have pursued. This is most obvious in the sphere of economic management. Governments in office since the early 1980s have boasted – perhaps rightly – of the healthy economic cure imposed by their tight economic management, in contrast with lax inflationary behaviour of previous French governments. But the human price – in terms of unemployment – is an onerous one, undermining public confidence in the government's ability to manage the economy, to the extent of producing a powerful public reaction against increased insecurity and unemployment.

As the French model becomes challenged from several directions, potential losers have rallied to its defence. Defence of the French model is most obvious in terms of public service. In December 1995, a major social movement appeared to emerge out of nothing in reaction to premier Juppé's proposed reform of the social security system. As is often the case in these circumstances, the strikers articulated a range of contradictory, sectoral demands. The common plea appeared be a defensive one: to preserve features of the French model under threat from a variety of external forces. With the outcome of this particular battle uncertain, it remains a safe bet that the policy responses adopted by French governments will continue to combine particular patterns of governing inherited from French history, with necessarily flexible responses to the changing circumstances of policy making in the twenty-first century.

Appendices

The 1995 French presidential election: a sociological profile of first-round electors

	La	Hu	Jo	Vo	Ba	Chi	de V	Le P	Ch
Sex and age									
Men									
18–24	6	7	19	4	10	32	3	19	0
25–34	6	9	21	3	16	23	4	17	1
35–49	5	10	24	4	16	19	5	17	0
50–64	4	8	21	1	24	20	5	17	0
65+	2	10	19	1	35	16	2	15	0
Women									
18–24	7	6	29	7	14	23	4	10	0
25–34	7	10	29	4	13	17	4	16	0
35–49	7	8	27	5	17	16	7	13	0
50–64	3	8	23	2	25	21	6	12	0
65+	2	8	20	1	37	19	4	9	0
First-time voters	6	7	23	5	13	21	3	21	1
Social class									
Farmers	5	5	13	1	24	29	9	14	0
Artisans, shopkeepers, small business	3	5	8	1	27	28	7	21	0
Senior management, professions	4	5	26	5	21	24	6	6	1
Middle management	7	7	31	5	17	19	4	10	0
Clerical staff	8	10	23	3	15	17	5	19	0
Industrial workers	7	15	21	1	10	15	4	27	0
Unemployed	6	11	24	4	13	20	3	18	1
Housewives	3	6	20	1	24	20	8	16	0
Retired	3	9	20	1	32	19	4	12	0
Religion									
Practising Catholic	4	3	15	2	37	26	5	8	0
Non-practising Catholic	4	7	21	3	21	23	5	16	0
No religion	9	16	32	5	8	12	2	15	1
Total vote	5	9	24	3	19	20	5	15	0

Note: La = Laguiller (Trotskyite); Hu = Hue (Communist); Jo = Jospin (Socialist); Vo = Voynet (Green); Ba = Balladur (Conservative/Gaullist); Chi = Chirac (Gaullist); de V = de Villiers (Ultra-conservative); Le P = Le Pen (National Front); Ch. = Cheminade (Independent).

Source: *Le Monde*/BVA first-round exit poll. Cited in 'L'Election présidentielle, 23 Avril–7 Mai 1995. Special issue of *Le Monde Dossiers et Documents*, May 1995, p. 47.

National Assembly elections, 1958–97 (% of valid votes cast)

	1958	1962	1967	1968	1973	1978	1981	1986	1988	1993	1997[1]
Abstentions and spoilt ballots	24.78	33.33	20.73	21.40	20.42	18.37	30.12	24.9	35.3	34.4	34.99
Extreme left[2]	–	2.02	2.21	3.96	2.20	3.27	1.22	1.5	0.36	1.77	2.52
Communist (PCF)	18.89	21.87	22.51	20.02	21.41	20.61	16.13	9.7	11.32	9.18	9.98
Socialist[3]	15.48	12.43	18.90	16.54	20.82	24.95	39.52	31.6	37.55	20.29	27.65
Ecologists[4]						1.37	1.09		0.35	7.64	6.86
Other non-Communist left[5]	10.87	7.42									
Non–Gaullist 'centre'[6]	11.09	7.88	17.35	12.41	16.67	UDF	UDF	UDF	UDF	UDF	UDF
Other Right[7]	19.97	11.52	with centre	with centre	with centre	UDF	2.66	2.71	2.85	4.72	6.52
UDF + allies						23.89	19.66	42.1 (with RPR)	18.49	19.08	14.34
Gaullists[8]	20.64	36.03	38.45	46.44	36.98	22.84	21.24	42.1 (with UDF)	19.18	20.39	15.59
Extreme right[9]	2.57	0.76	0.56	0.08	0.52	0.75	0.59	10.1	9.74	12.7	15.16

[1] Provisional 1997 Interior ministry figures, pertaining to 566 of 577 constituencies.
[2] Includes PSU, LO, LCR and Trotskyite/Maoist groups.
[3] Includes SFIO (1958, 1962), FGDS (1967, 1968), UGSD (1973), PS-MRG (1978, 1981, 1986, 1988, 1993), PS, PRS MDC (1977).
[4] Includes all ecologists, principally *Les verts* and GE (1993), *les verts*, GE, MEI and fringe groups (1997).
[5] UFD, Radicals, UDSR (1958) Radicals (1962).
6 Includes MRP (1958, 1962), CD, non-Gaullist radicals and *modérés* (1967), CD, PDM, non-Gaullist radicals and *modérés* (1968), Reformist movement and *modérés* (1973).
[7] CNI and *modérés* in 1958 and 1962. Refers to *divers droite* clearly separate from UDF in subsequent elections.
[8] Includes Gaullist allies, notably RI from 1962–73.
[9] Various extreme right, 1958–69; National Front + extreme Right, 1973, 1978, 1981, 1986, 1988, 1993, 1997.
Source: Adapted from Interior Ministry figures for France, including DOM-TOM.

Appendix 3

Presidential elections in the Fifth Republic: first ballot (% of valid votes cast)

	65	69	74	81	88	95
Abstensions and spoilt ballots	16.11	22.81	16.54	20.22	18.62	24.46
Extreme left[1]	–	4.72	2.72	3.41	4.47	5.30
Communist[2]	–	21.52	–	15.35	6.76	8.64
Socialist[3]	–	5.07	–	25.85	34.09	23.30
United left[4]	31.72	–	43.25	–	–	–
Green[5]	–	–	1.32	3.88	3.78	3.32
Centre[6]	15.57	23.42	32.60	–	16.54	18.58
UDF[7]	–	–	–	28.32	–	–
Gaullist[8]	44.65	43.95	15.11	18.00	19.94	20.84
Extreme right[9]	5.20	–	0.75	–	14.39	15.00
Other[10]	2.86	1.28	4.27	6.86	–	3.82

[1] Extreme left: Krivine (LCR) and Rocard (PSU) in 1969; Laguiller (LO) and Krivine in 1974; Laguiller and Bouchardeau (PSU) in 1981; Laguiller, Juquin (ex-PCF) and Boussel (MPPT) in 1988; Laguiller in 1995.
[2] Communist: Duclos in 1969, Marchais in 1981, Lajoinie in 1988, Hue in 1995.
[3] Socialst: Defferre in 1969, Mitterrand in 1981 and 1988, Jospin in 1995.
[4] United left: Mitterrand in 1965 (supported by SFIO, PCF and Radicals) and in 1974 (supported by PS, PCF and MRG).
[5] Green: Dumont in 1974, Lalonde in 1981, Waechter in 1988, Voynet in 1995.
[6] Centre: Lecanuet in 1965, Poher in 1969, Giscard in 1974, Barre in 1988, Balladur in 1995.
[7] UDF behind Giscard d'Estaing in 1981. Divided in 1988 and 1995.
[8] Gaullist: de Gaulle in 1965, Pompidou in 1969, Chaban-Delmas in 1974, Chirac in 1981, 1988 and 1995. Balladur (1995) also a member of RPR, but classed under centre.
[9] Extreme right: Tixier-Vignancour in 1965, Le Pen in 1974, 1988 and 1995.
[10] Mostly a rag-bag of no hopers, the main exceptions being: Royer (3.17%) in 1974 (Conservative); Crépeau (2.21%) in 1981 (MRG); de Villiers (4.74%) in 1995 (Conservative).

Note: For reasons of convenience, certain candidates have been attributed party families they might dispute. Rocard (PSU) and Bouchardeau (PSU) would certainly reject the extreme left etiquette; but both were supported by a radicalised left-wing electorate. Barre and Giscard (1974) were Orleanist conservatives, transformed into 'centrists' because of their opposition to Gaullist candidates. The UDF supported Barre and Balladur in 1988 and 1995 respectively, but neither considered himself the 'UDF' candidate. Barre and Balladur were supported by most of the UDF, especially the CDS, and by some Gaullists. Balladur in 1995 was a member of the Gaullist RPR, but most of his support came from the non-Gaullist centre-right.

Source: Adapted from Interior Ministry figures for France, including DOM-TOM.

Six presidential election run-offs

Year	1965	1969	1974	1981	1988	1995
De Gaulle	55.20					
Mitterrand	44.80		49.19	51.76	54.02	
Pompidou		57.6				
Poher		42.4				
Giscard d'Estang			50.81	48.24		
Chirac					45.98	52.63
Jospin						47.37

Referendums in the Fifth Republic

Date	Object	For	Against	Absten-tions	% of total electorate voting yes
28.9.58	1958 constitution	82.60	17.40	20.16	65.87
8.1.61	Algeria	74.99	25.01	26.24	53.65
8.4.62	Evian agreements	90.81	9.19	24.46	64.78
28.10.62	Presidential election	62.25	37.75	23.03	46.66
27.4.69	Regional/Senate reform	47.59	52.41	19.87	37.09
23.4.72	EEC enlargement	68.32	31.68	39.76	36.38
6.11.88	New Caledonia	79.00	21.00	63.11	26.02
20.9.92	Maastricht Treaty	51.04	48.96	30.30	34.36

Glossary

Atlanticism The belief in and practice of the Atlantic alliance, the military alliance of the USA and western Europe. France has always had a peculiar status within the alliance, particularly since 1965, when General de Gaulle withdrew France from the military command structure of NATO. France has once again participated in NATO meetings since 1995.

Autogestion/*Parti autogestionnaire* *Autogestion* can be translated literally as self-management, but loses something in the translation. It refers to a belief in decentralised management and workers' control, as voiced by students and workers in the events of May 1968. The Socialist Party officially declared itself an 'autogestionnaire' party in the 1970s, but even then the notion appeared highly ambiguous. It was forgotten once the Socialists were in government after 1981.

Deputy-mayor The practice whereby deputies (members of the National Assembly) are often mayors as well.

Dirigiste The process whereby the French state adopted an interventionist and directive approach to the management of the economy and industry in the post-1945 period.

Dreyfus affair The Dreyfus affair polarised French society during the 1890s and early 1900s. *L'Affaire* involved a Jewish lieutenant, wrongly accused by the army high command of selling military secrets to the Germans and exiled to Devil's Island, before finally being recognised as innocent. In the course of the Dreyfus affair, republicans launched a bitter attack against the army and the church, accused of espousing anti-Semitism in order to sabotage the Republic. For their part, opponents of Dreyfus taxed the republicans with treachery to the nation because their attacks called into question the integrity of the church and the army, the two pillars of French national identity.

Enarchie The influence exercised by graduates of the National Administration School (Ecole nationale d'administration), who form a powerful élite in the spheres of politics, the civil service and the economy.

High-tech Colbertism This phrase was coined by Elie Cohen. Colbertism refers to the tradition of central state interventionism in economic and industrial management, after Louis xiv's minister Colbert in the seventeenth century. High-tech Colbertism thus refers to state interventionism in the contemporary context.

Incivisme Literally translated as uncivic behaviour, *incivisme* implies rather more than this in the French, carrying connotations of a tendency in French political culture to challenge those in authority, and to rebel against rules dictated from on high.

Léon Blum Socialist leader of the Popular Front government elected in 1936, the first Socialist-led government in French history. The Popular Front was an alliance between Socialists and Radicals, supported by the Communists, who did not however participate in the government. The Popular Front government pushed through many symbolic social reforms, such as the 40-hour week and paid holidays, but became destabilised by problems of economic management, as well as by the impact of the Spanish Civil War and the ascension of fascism in Europe.

Neo-corporatist A pattern of group–state relations where the state engages in very close co-operation with representatives of labour and capital in making economic policy. This is typified notably by: collective wage agreements negotiated between the state, employers and the trade unions; the representation of capital and labour on key policy-making committees; and the existence of one trade union and one employers' federation.

Présidentiable This refers to an individual who is (or who aspires to be) a credible candidate for the post of President of the Republic.

Poujadist A populist right-wing movement named after Pierre Poujade, elected deputy in 1956 at the head of a movement of small businessmen and shopkeepers. Poujadist became synonymous with reactionary resistance to cosmopolitanism, and to social and economic modernisation.

References and bibliography

Albertini, J.-M. (1978) *L'Economie française*, Seuil, Paris.

Aldreth, M. (1984) *The French Communist Party 1920–84*, Manchester University Press, Manchester.

Almond, G. and N. Verba (1963) *The Civic Culture: Attitudes and democracy in five nations*, Princeton University Press, Princeton, NJ.

Ambler, J.-S. (1985) 'Neocorporatism and the politics of French education', *West European Politics*, vol. 8, no. 3.

Ameller, M. (1994) *L'Assemblée nationale*, PUF, Paris.

Anderson, M. (1970) *Government in France*, Pergamon, Oxford.

Anderson, R.D. (1977) *France 1870–1914*, Routledge and Kegan Paul, London.

Andolfatto, D. (1992) 'Le Débat syndical aujourd'hui', *Regards sur l'actualité*, no. 185.

Andrews, W. (ed.) (1982) *Presidential Government in Gaullist France*, State University of New York Press, Albany, NY.

Andrews, W. and S. Hoffmann (eds.) (1981) *The Fifth Republic at Twenty*, State University of New York Press, Albany, NY.

Appleton, A. (1995) 'Parties under pressure: challenges to established French parties', *West European Politics*, vol. 18, no. 1.

Ardagh, J. (1988) *France Today*, Penguin, Harmondsworth.

Ashby, M.-F.(1982) 'A vision of grandeur: Charles de Gaulle's Fifth Republic foreign policy', *Potomac Review*, no. 22–3.

Ashford, D. (1982) *French Pragmatism and British Dogmatism*, Allen and Unwin, London.

Ashford, D. (1990) 'Decentralising France: how the Socialists discovered pluralism', *West European Politics*, vol. 13, no. 4.

Avril, P. (1982) 'Chaque institution à sa place: le Président, le parti et le groupe', *Pouvoirs*, no. 20.

Avril, P. (1984) 'Les Chefs de l'état et la notion de majorité présidentielle', *Revue française de science politique*, vol. 34, no. 4–5.

Avril, P. (1992) *Le Conseil constitutionnel*, Montchrestien, Paris.

Baguenard, J. (1990) *Le Sénat*, PUF, Paris.

Barsalou, J. (1964) *La Mal-aimée*, Plon, Paris.

Bartolini, S. (1984) 'Institutional constraints and party competition in the French party system', *West European Politics*, vol. 7, no. 4.

Basso, J. (1983) *Les Groupes de pression*, PUF, Paris.

Bauchard, P. (1986) *La Guerre des deux roses*, Grasset, Paris.

Baudouin, J. (1991) 'Le Déclin du PCF', *Regards sur l'actualité*, no. 170.

Bauer, M. (1988) 'The politics of state-directed privatisation: the case of France', *West European Politics*, vol. 11, no. 4.

Baumont, S. (1991) 'Le Régime présidentiel en question', *Cosmopolitiques*, no. 19.

Bell, D.S. and B. Criddle (1988) *The French Socialist Party: The emergence of a party of government*, Clarendon Press, Oxford.

Bell, D.S. and B. Criddle (1994) *The French Communist Party*, Clarendon Press, Oxford.

Bell, D.S., D. Johnson and P. Morris (eds.) (1990) *Biographical Dictionary of French Political Leaders since 1870*, Harvester Wheatsheaf, Hemel Hempstead.

Belorgey, J.-M. (1991) *Le Parlement à refaire*, Gallimard, Paris.

Bénéton, P. and J. Touchard (1970) 'Les Interprétations de la crise de mai– juin 1968', *Revue française de science politique*, vol. 20, no. 3.

Berger, S. (1981) *Organising Interests in western Europe*, Harvard University Press, Cambridge.

Bergonioux, A. and G. Grunberg (1992) *Le Long Remords du pouvoir*, Fayard, Paris.

Bernard, P. (1992) 'La Fonction préfectorale au coeur de la mutation de notre société', *Revue administrative*, vol. 45, no. 2.

Berstein, S., J.-F. Sirinelli and J.-P. Rioux (eds.) (1994) 'La culture politique en France depuis de Gaulle', *Vingtième siècle*, no. 44.

Bevort, A. and D. Labbé (1992) *La CFDT: organisation et audience depuis 1945*, Documentation française, Paris.

Biarez, S. (1989) *Le Pouvoir local*, Economica, Paris.

Biarez, S. and J.-Y. Nevers (eds.) (1994) *Gouvernement local et politiques urbaines*, CERAT, Grenoble.

Bigaut, C. (ed.) (1993) *Le Président de la 5e République*, Documentation française, Paris.

Birenbaum, G. (1992) *Le Front national en politique*, Balland, Paris.

Bloch-Liané, J.-M. and B. Moschetto (1987) *La Politique économique de la France*, PUF, Paris.

Blondel, J. (1987) *Political Leadership*, Sage, London.

Bodiguel, J.-L. (1990) 'Political and administrative traditions and the French senior civil service', *International Journal of Public Administration*, vol. 13, no. 5.

Bodiguel, J.-L. and J.-L. Quermonne (1983) *La Haute Fonction publique*, Presses universitaires de France, Paris.

Bon, F. (ed.) (1969) *Le Communisme en France*, Armand Colin, Paris.

Boudant, J. (1992) 'La Crise identitaire du parlement français', *Revue des sciences morales et politiques*, no. 5.

Boussard, I. (1990) *Les Agriculteurs et la politique*, Economica, Paris.

Brechon, P. (1993) *La France aux urnes*, Documentation française, Paris.

Bréhier, T. (1994) 'Le Conseil général, pierre angulaire de la politique française', *Le Monde*, 19 March.

Brubaker, R. (1992) *Citizenship and Nationhood in France and Germany*, Harvard University Press, Cambridge, MA.

Burin des Roziers, E. (1992) 'De Gaulle et l'Europe', *Tocqueville Review*, vol.13, no 1.

Capdeveille, J. (ed.) (1981) *France de gauche vote à droite*, Presses de la FNSP, Paris.

Carcassonne, G. (1986) 'Typologie des cabinets', *Pouvoirs*, no. 36.

Carrigue, D. (1992) *Le Deputé aujourd'hui*, Assemblée nationale, Paris.

Cerny, P. and M. Schain (1985) *Socialism, the State and Public Policy in France*, Pinter, London.

Cerny, P.G. (1982) *Social Movements and Protest in France*, Pinter, London.

Cerny, P. (1987) 'Public policy and the structural logic of the state: France in comparative perspective', *West European Politics*, vol. 10, no. 1.

Chagnollaud, D. (1988) 'La nomination des hauts fonctionnaires ou les arcanes de la politisation'. Unpublished paper presented to the 3rd National Congress of the French Political Science Association, 5–8 October, Bordeaux.

Chapsal, J. and A. Lancelot (1979) *La Vie Politique en France depuis 1940*, PUF, Paris.

Charlot, J. (1989) 'Les Mutations du système des partis Français', *Pouvoirs*, no. 49.

Charlot, J. (1970) *The Gaullist Phenomenon*, Allen & Unwin, London.

Charlot, J. (1983a) *Les Gaullistes d'opposition*, Seuil, Paris.

Charlot, J. (1983b), 'Le Président et le parti majoritaire', *Revue politique et parlementaire*, vol. 85, no. 905.

Chenot, B. (ed.) (1985) *Le Conseil constitutionnel, 1958–85*, Economica, Paris.

Chenot, B. (1986) *Le Secrétariat Général du Gouvernement*, Economica, Paris.

Cicchillo, R. (1990) 'The Conseil Constitutionnel and Judicial Review', *Tocqueville Review*, vol. 12, no. 1.

Cohen, E. (1995) 'France: National champions in search of a mission', in J. Hayward (ed.), *Industrial Enterprise and European Integration*, Oxford University Press, Oxford.

Cohen, M. (1992) 'The French National Front and immigration: the appeal and the challenge', *Mediterranean Quarterly*, vol. 3, no. 2.

Cohen, S. (1991) 'François le gaullien et Mitterrand l'européen', *Histoire*, no. 143.

Cohen, S. (1986) *La Monarchie nucléaire*, Hachette, Paris.

Cohen, S. (1989) 'La Politique Etrangère entre l'Elysée et Matignon', *Politique Etrangère*, no. 3/89.

Cohen, W. (1990) 'De Gaulle and Europe prior to 1958', *French Politics and Society*, vol. 8, no. 4.

Cohendet, A.-M. (1993) *La Cohabitation*, PUF, Paris.

Cohen-Tangui, L. (1990) 'From one revolution to the next: the late rise of constitutionalism in France', *Tocqueville Review*, vol. 12, no. 1.

Cole, A. (1989) 'Factionalism, the French Socialist Party and the Fifth Republic: an explanation of intra-party divisions', *European Journal of Political Research*, vol. 17, no. 1.

Cole, A. (ed.) (1990) *French Political Parties in Transition*, Dartmouth, Aldershot.

Cole, A. (1993a) 'The presidential party and the Fifth Republic', *West European Politics*, vol. 16, no. 2.

Cole, A. (1993b) 'Looking on: France and the new Germany', *German Politics*, vol. 2, no. 3.

Cole, A. (1994a) *François Mitterrand: A study in political leadership*, Routledge, London.

Cole, A. (1994b) 'Studying political leadership: the case of François Mitterrand', *Political Studies*, vol. 42, no. 3.

Cole, A. (1995) ' *La France pour tous?*, The French presidential election of 23 April and 7 May 1995', *Government and Opposition*, vol. 30, no. 3.

Cole, A. and P. Campbell (1989) *French Electoral Systems and Elections*, Gower, Aldershot.

Cole, A. and P. John (1995) 'Local policy networks in France and Britain: policy coordination in fragmented political sub-systems', *West European Politics*, vol. 18, no. 4.

Collard, S. (1992) 'Franco-German relations since 1945: an overview', *Modern and Contemporary France*, no. 49.

Colliard, J.-C. (1971) *Les Républicans indépendants*, PUF, Paris.

Colombani, J.-M. (1992) 'La Politique et l'argent: toujours plus!', *Le Monde*, 18 January.

Colombani, J.-M. and H. Portelli (1995) *Le Double Septennat de François Mitterrand*, Grasset, Paris.

Costa, J.-P. (1993) *Le Conseil d'état dans la société contemporaine*, Economica, Paris.

Courtier, P. (1994) *La Quatrième République*, PUF, Paris.

Courtois, J. (ed.) (1991) *Les Associations: un monde inconnu*, Crédit coopératif, Nanterre.

Courtois, S. (1992) 'Les Identités multiples du PCF', *Panoramiques*, vol. 4, no. 2.

Crozier, M. (1963) *Le Phénomène bureaucratique*, Seuil, Paris.

Crozier, M. (1970) *La Société bloquée*, Seuil, Paris.

Crozier, M. (ed.) (1974) *Où va l'administration française?*, Editions de l'organisation, Paris.

Crozier, M. and J.-C. Thoenig (1975) 'La Régulation des systèmes organisés complexes', *Revue française de sociologie*, vol. 16, no. 1.

de Baecque, F. (1973) *L'Administration centrale de la France*, Armand Colin, Paris.

de Baecque (1991) 'Sur la Politisation des hautes fonctionnaires', paper presented to the French Political Science Association conference 'Le Modèle français d'administration', 7–8 February.

de Baecque, F. and J.-L. Quermonne (1981) *Administration et politique sous la Ve République*, Presses de la FNSP, Paris.

de Forges, J.-M. (1989) *Les Institutions administratives françaises*, PUF, Paris.

Defrasne, J. (1995) *La Vie associative en France*, PUF, Paris.

de Gaulle, C. and P. de Gaulle (eds.) (1994) *Mémoires d'espoir*, Plon, Paris.

Dely, R. (1995) '887 parlementaires révisent à Versailles', *Libération*, 31 July.

Dion, S. (1986) *La Politisation des mairies*, Economica, Paris.

Dirn, L. (1990) *La Société française en tendances*, PUF, Paris.

Dolez, B. (1995) 'Financement de la vie politique: les lois anti-corruption de 1995', *Regards sur l'actualité*, no. 211.

Donegani, J.-M. (1982) 'The political cultures of French Catholicism', *West European Politics*, vol. 5, no. 2.

Drake, H. (1994) 'François Mitterrand, France and European integration', in G. Raymond (ed.) *France during the Socialist Years*, Dartmouth, Aldershot.

Dreyfus, F. (1990) 'Place et poids de la démocratie chrétienne: le CDS, un parti démocrate chrétien dans l'arène publique', *Revue française de science politique*, vol. 40, no. 6.

Dreyfus, F. (1982) *De Gaulle et le Gaullisme: essai d'interprétation*, PUF, Paris.

Dreyfus, F. (1993) *Les Institutions politiques et administratives de la France,* Economica, Paris.

Dreyfus, F. and F. D' Arcy (1989) *Les Institutions politiques et administratives de la France*, Economica, Paris.

Duhamel, A. (1980) *La République giscardienne*, Grasset, Paris.

Duhamel, A. (1990) *De Gaulle – Mitterrand: la marque et la trace*, Grasset, Paris.

Duhamel, O. (1993) *La Gauche et la cinquième république*, PUF, Paris.

Duhamel, O. and J.-L. Parodi (eds.) (1988) *La Constitution de la cinquième république*, Presses de la FNSP, Paris.

Dumez, H. and A. Jeunemaitre (1993) 'Les Privatisations en France, 1986–1992', in V. Wright (ed.), *Les Privatisations en Europe*, Actes sud, Paris.

Dupeux, G. (1976) *French Society 1789–1970*, Methuen, London.

Dupin, E. (1991) *L'Après-Mitterrand: le Parti socialiste à la dérive*, Calmann-Levy, Paris.

Dupuy, F. and J.-C. Thoenig (1983) *Sociologie de l'administration française*, Armand Colin, Paris.

Dupuy, F. and J.-C. Thoenig (1985), *L'Administration en miettes*, Fayard, Paris.

Duverger, M. (1964) *Political Parties*, Methuen, London.

Duverger, M. (1974) *La Monarchie républicaine*, Laffont, Paris.

Duverger, M. (1977) *L'Echec au roi*, Albin Michel, Paris.

Duverger, M. (1986) *Les Régimes semi-présidentiels*, PUF, Paris.

Duverger, M. (1987) *La Cohabitation des français*, PUF, Paris.

Dyson, K. (1980) *The State Tradition in Western Europe*, Martin Robertson, Oxford.

Dyson, K. and K. Featherstone (1996) 'France, EMU and *construction européenne*: empowering the executive, transforming the state', *Politiques et management public conference*, Paris, 20–1 June.

Ecole nationale d'administration (1992) *Les Corps de fonctionnaires recrutés par la voie d'ENA*, Documentation française, Paris.

Ehrmann, H.W. and M. Schain (1992) *Politics in France*, Harper Collins, New York.

Elgey, G. (1993) *Histoire de la 4e République. 1, La République des illusions: 1945–1951*, Fayard, Paris.

Elgie, R. (1993) *The French Prime Minister*, Macmillan, London.

Elgie, R. and H. Machin (1991) 'France: the limits to prime ministerial government in a semi-presidential system', *West European Politics*, vol. 14, no. 2.

Etienne, B. (1989) *La France et l'Islam*, Hachette, Paris.

Fabius, L. (1992) 'Les Pouvoirs de l'Assemblée nationale', *Revue des sciences morales et politiques*, no. 1.

Fauvet, J. (1963) *La 4e République*, Fayard, Paris.

Favereau, E. (1995) 'Ministères: les clandestins des cabinets', *Libération*, 11 October.

Favier, P. and M. Martin-Roland (1990, 1991) *La Décennie Mitterrand. 1, Les Ruptures 2. Les Épreuves*, Seuil, Paris.

Favoreu, L. (1985) *Le Conseil constitutionnel*, PUF, Paris.

Feigenbaum, H. (1990) 'Recent changes in the French executive', *Governance*, vol. 13, no. 3.

Flockton, C. (1990) 'The French economy and the single European market, *Modern and Contemporary France*, no. 40.

Flockton, C. and E. Kofman (1989) *France*, Paul Chapman, London.

Fontaine, J. (1996) 'Public policy analysis in France: transformation and theory', *Journal of European Public Policy*, vol. 3, no. 3.

Fourastié, J. (1980) *Les Trente glorieuses ou la révolution invisible de 1946–1975*, Fayard, Paris.

Fournier, J. (1987) *Le Travail gouvernemental*, Presses de la FNSP, Paris.

Foyer, J. (1992) 'Les Pouvoirs du Président de la République', *Revue des sciences morales et politiques*, no. 3.

Frears, J. (1981) *France in the Giscard Presidency*, Allen and Unwin, London.

Frears, J. (1988) 'Not sex, the abuse of power: political scandal in France', *Corruption and Reform*, vol. 3, no. 3.

Frears, J. (1990) *Parties and Voters in France*, Hurst, London.

Frears, J. (1991) 'The French parliament: loyal workhorse, poor watchdog', *West European Politics*, vol. 14, no. 1.

Frears, J. and P. Morris (1992) 'La Britannicité de la Ve République', *Espoir*, no. 85.

Frears, J. and J.-L. Parodi (1979) *War Will Not Take Place*, Hurst, London.

Friedberg, E. (1974) 'Administration et entreprises', in M. Crozier (ed.), *Où va l'administration française?*, Editions de l'organisation, Paris.

Friend, J.-W. (1989) *Seven Years in France: François Mitterrand and the unintended revolution*, Westview Press, Boulder, CO.

Friend, J.-W. (1993) 'Mitterrand's legatee: the French Socialist Party in 1993', *French Politics and Society*, vol. 11, no. 3.

Fysh, P. (1993) 'Gaullism today', *Parliamentary Affairs*, vol. 46, no. 3.

Fysh, P. and J. Wolfreys (1992) 'Le Pen, the National Front and the extreme right in France', *Parliamentary Affairs*, vol. 45, no. 3.

Gaffney, J. (ed.) (1988a) *France and Modernisation*, Gower, Aldershot.

Gaffney, J. (1988b) 'French socialism and the Fifth Republic', *West European Politics*, vol. 11, no. 3.

Gaffney, J. (ed.) (1989a) *The French Presidential Election of 1988: Ideology and leadership in contemporary France*, Dartmouth, Aldershot.

Gaffney, J. (1989b) *The Left and the Fifth Republic*, Macmillan, London.

Gaffney, J. (1991) 'Political think tanks in the UK and ministerial cabinets in France', *West European Politics*, vol. 14, no. 1.

Gaffney, J. (ed.) (1996) *Political Parties in the European Union*, Routledge, London.

Gaffney, J. and E. Kolinsky (eds.) (1991) *Political Culture in France and Germany*, Routledge, London.

Gallie, D. (1983) *Social Inequality and Class Radicalism in France and Britain*, Cambridge University Press, Cambridge.

Garraud, P. (1989) *Profession homme politique. La carrière politique des maires urbains*, Harmattan, Paris.

Gélédan, A. (1993) *Le Bilan economique des années Mitterrand*, Le Monde éditions, Paris.

Giesbert, F.-O. (1990) *Le Président*, Seuil, Paris.

Giscard d'Estaing, V. (1976) *La Démocratie française*, Fayard, Paris.

Godt, P. (ed.) (1989) *Policy Making in France*, Pinter, London.

Goguel, F. (1983) *Chroniques electorales*, Presses de la FNSP, Paris.

Grémion, C. (1979) *Profession décideurs: pouvoirs des hauts fonctionnaires et réformes de l'état*, Gauthier-Villars, Paris.

Gremion, P. (1976) *Le Pouvoir périphérique: bureaucrates et notables dans le régime politique français*, Seuil, Paris.

Grosser, A. (1988) 'La Politique européenne du Général de Gaulle', *Espoir*, no. 62.

Groux, G. and R. Mouriaux (1992) *La CGT, crises et alternatives*, Economica, Paris.

Grunberg, G. (1992) 'Les Cadres des partis et la crise de la représentation', *L'Etat de l'opinion 1992*, SOFRES, Paris.

Guettier, C. (1995) *Le Président sous la 5e République*, PUF, Paris.

Guilani, J.-D. (1991) *Marchands d'influence: les lobbies en France*, Seuil, Paris.

Guoyomarch, A. and H. Machin (1992) 'A history of hesitations on the road to Maastricht', *French Politics and Society*, vol. 10, no. 4.

Guoyomarch, A., H. Machin and E. Ritchie (1996) (eds.) *France in the European Union*, Macmillan, London.

Hadas-Lebel, R. (1991) 'François Mitterrand et la fonction présidentielle', *French Politics and Society*, vol. 9, nos. 3–4.

Hall, P. (1983) 'Policy innovation and the structure of the state: the politics—administration nexus in France and Britain', *Annals AAPSS*, no. 466.

Hall, P. (1986) *Governing the Economy: The politics of state intervention in Britain and France*, Oxford University Press, Oxford.

Hall, P., J. Hayward and H. Machin (1990, 1994) *Developments in French Politics*, Macmillan, London.

Hanley, D. (1985) *Keeping Left: CERES and the French Socialist Party*, Manchester University Press, Manchester.

Hanley, D.L. and A.P. Kerr (1989) *May '68: Coming of Age*, Macmillan, London.

Hanley, D.L., A.P. Kerr and N.H. Waites (1984) *Contemporary France: Politics and society since 1945*, Routledge, London.

Hargreaves, A.G. (1995) *Immigration, 'Race' and Ethnicity in Contemporary France*, Routledge, London.

Hargreaves, A.G. and T.G. Stenhouse (1991) 'Islamic beliefs among youths of north African origin in France', *Modern and Contemporary France*, no. 45.

Harmsen, R. (1996) 'The state and European integration: France and the Netherlands', *Political Studies Association conference*, University of Glasgow, 10–12 April.

Hassenteufal, P. (1990) 'Où en est le paradigme corporatiste?', *Politix*, no. 12.

Hayward, J. (1973) *The One and Indivisible French Republic*, Weidenfeld and Nicolson, London.

Hayward, J. (1978) 'Dissentient France: the counter political culture', *West European Politics*, vol. 1, no. 3.

Hayward, J. (1981), 'Surreptitious factionalism in the French Communist Party', *Hull Papers in Politics*, no. 10.

Hayward, J. (1983) *Governing France*, Weidenfeld and Nicolson, London.

Hayward, J. (1986) *The State and the Market Economy*, Harvester Wheatsheaf, Brighton.

Hayward, J. (ed.) (1993) *De Gaulle to Mitterrand: Presidential power in France*, Hurst, London.

Hayward, J. (ed.) (1995) *Industrial Entreprise and European Integration*, Oxford University Press, Oxford.

Hazareesingh, S. (1994) *Political Traditions in Modern France*, Oxford University Press, Oxford.

Helin, J.-P. (1992) 'Le Préfet, les élus et le juge', *Petites Affiches*, vol. 16, no. 151.

Heymann-Doat, A. (1993) 'Les Révisions constitutionnelles de la cinquième république', *Problèmes politiques et sociaux*, vol. 705, no. 28.

Hoffmann, S. (ed.) (1965) *In Search of France*, Harper Torchbooks, New York.

Hoffmann, S. (1994) 'Les Français sont-ils gouvernables?', *Pouvoirs*, no. 68.

Hollifield, J. (ed.) (1991) *Searching for the New France*, Routledge, London.

Horne, A. (1977) *A Savage War of Peace: Algeria, 1954–62*, Macmillan, London.

Huchon, J.-P. (1993) *Jours tranquilles à Matignon*, Grasset, Paris.

Husbands, C. (1993) 'The support for the Front National: analyses and findings', *Ethnic and Racial Studies*, vol. 14, no. 3.

Ignazi, P. and C. Ysmal (1992) 'New and old extreme right parties: the French National Front and the Italian Movimento Sociale', *European Journal of Political Research*, vol. 22, no. 1.

Im, T. (1993) 'L'Administration de l'état face à la décentralisation: l'évolution du système d'action des préfectures', unpublished PhD thesis, Institute of Political Studies, Paris.

Imbert, C. (1989) 'The end of French exceptionalism', *Foreign Affairs*, vol. 68, no. 4.

Institut Charles de Gaulle (1990) *De Gaulle et ses premiers ministres*, Plon, Paris.

Institut français des sciences administratives (1987) *Le Secrétariat général du gouvernement*, Economica, Paris.

Irving, R.E.M. (1973) *Christian Democracy in France*, Allen and Unwin, London.

Isajiw, W. (1974) 'Definitions of ethnicity', *Ethnicity*, no. 1.

Jazouli, A. (1986) *L'Action collective des jeunes Maghrébins de France*, Harmattan, Paris.

Jeannot, G. and M. Peraldi (1991) *L'Envers des métiers: compétences politiques et pratiques professionelles dans les directions départementales de l'Equipment*, Equipement Ministry, Paris.

Jenkins, B. and P. Morris (1993) 'Political scandal in France', *Modern and Contemporary France*, vol. 1, no. 2.

Jenson, J. and G. Ross (1985) *The View from Inside: A French Communist cell in crisis*, University of California Press, Berkeley, CA.

Jobert, B. and P. Muller (1987) *L'Etat en action*, PUF, Paris.

Johnson, R.W. (1981) *The Long March of the French Left*, Macmillan, London.

Judt, T. (1986) *Marxism and the French Left*, Oxford University Press, Oxford.

Jullian, M. (1994) *La France à voix haute: le soldat et le normalien*, Fayard, Paris.

July, S. (1986) *Les Années Mitterrand*, Grasset, Paris.

Kaltenbach, P. (1995) 'Sauver le bébé né en 1901', *Libération*, 24 July.

Keating, M. (1993) 'The politics of economic development: political change and local development policies in the US, Britain and France', *Urban Affairs Quarterly*, no. 28.

Keating M. and P. Hainsworth (1986) *Decentralisation and Change in Contemporary France*, Gower, Aldershot.

Keeler, J. (1987) *The Politics of Neo-corporatism in France*, Oxford University Press, Oxford.

Kessler, M.-C. (1981) 'Le Cabinet du premier ministre et le secrétaire général du gouvernement', in F. de Baecque and J.-L. Quermonne, *Administration et politique sous la Ve République*, Presses de la FNSP, Paris.

Kimmel, A. (1991) *L'Assemblée nationale sous la cinquième république*, Presses de la FNSP, Paris.

Kirchheimer, O. (1966) 'The transformation of west European party systems', in J. LaPalombara and M. Weiner (eds.), *Political Parties and Political Development*, Princeton University Press, Princeton, NJ.

Knapp, A. (1987) 'Proportional but bipolar: France's electoral system in 1986', *West European Politics*, vol. 10, no. 1.

Knapp, A. (1990) 'The Rally for the Republic', in A. Cole (ed.), *French Political Parties in Transition*, Dartmouth, Aldershot.

Knapp, A. (1991) The *cumul des mandats*, local power and political parties in France', *West European Politics*, vol. 14, no. 1.

Knapp, A. (1994) *Gaullism since de Gaulle*, Dartmouth, Aldershot.

Knapp, A. and P. Le Galès (1993) 'Top-down to bottom-up: relations and power structures in France's Gaullist party', *West European Politics*, vol. 16, no. 3.

Koenig, P. (1994) 'Le Financement des partis politiques en France', *Revue d'Allemagne*, vol. 26, no. 2.

Kolodziej, E. (1990) 'De Gaulle, Germany and the superpowers: German unification and the end of the cold war', *French Politics and Society*, vol. 8, no. 4.

Kriegel, A. (1985) *Les Communistes français dans leur premier demi-siècle*, Seuil, Paris.

Kriegel, B. (1992) 'L' Idée républicaine', *Revue politique et parlementaire*, vol. 94, no. 962.

Kuhn, R. (1995) *The Media in France*, Routledge, London.

Kuisel, R. (1979) *Capitalism and the State in Modern France*, Cambridge University Press, Cambridge.

Kuisel, R. (1991) 'De Gaulle, le défi américain et la Communauté européenne', *Espoir*, no. 76.

Labbé, D. (1992) 'Elections aux comités d'entreprise: le déclin des syndicats', *Travail et Emploi*, vol. 53, no. 3.

Labbé, D. and M. Croisat (1992) *La Fin des syndicats*, Harmattan, Paris.

Lachaise, B. (1994) 'Le RPR et le gaullisme: les infortunes d'une fidelité', *Vingtième siècle*, no. 44.

Lacouture, J. (1965) *De Gaulle*, Seuil, Paris.

Lacouture, J. (1981) *Pierre Mendès-France*, Seuil, Paris.

Lacouture, J. (1991) *De Gaulle, 2. The Ruler*, Harper Collins, London.

Lacroix, B. (1992) *Le Président de la République: usages et genèses d'une institution*, Presses de la FNSP, Paris.

Ladrech, R. (1989) 'Social movements and party systems: the French Socialist Party and new social movements', *West European Politics*, vol. 12, no. 2.

Ladrech, R. (1994) 'Europeanisation of domestic politics and institutions: the case of France', *Journal of Common Market Studies*, vol. 32, no. 1.

Lagroye, J. and V. Wright (eds.) (1979) *Local Government in Britain and France*, Allen and Unwin, London.

Lancelot, A. (1983) *Les Elections sous la Ve République*, PUF, Paris.

Lapeyronnie, D. (1992) *Les Immigrés en Europe*, Documentation française, Paris.

Larkin, M. (1988) *France since the Popular Front: Government and People, 1936–1986*, Clarendon Press, Oxford.

Lasserre, H. (1985) 'La Crise du syndicalisme aujourd'hui', *Les Temps modernes*.

Laughland, J. (1994) *The Death of Politics: France under Mitterrand*, Joseph, London.

Lavau, G. (1981) *A quoi sert le Parti communiste français?*, Fayard, Paris.

Lazar, M. (1990) 'Les Partis communistes italien et français et l'après-Staline', *Vingtième siècle*, no. 28.

Le Bras, H. (1995) *Les Trois France*, Odile Jacob, Paris.

Le Cacheux, J. and L. Tourjanski (1992) 'The French decentralisation ten years on: local government finances', *Local Government Studies*, vol. 18, no. 4.

Lefeburé, T. (1991) *Lobby or Not to Be*, Plume, Paris.

Le Galès, P. (1992) 'New directions in decentralisation and urban policy in France: the search for a post-decentralisation state', *Environment and Planning C: Government and Policy*, no. 10.

Le Galès, P. (1993) *Politique urbaine et développement local*, Harmattan, Paris.

Le Galès, P. (1995) 'Du gouvernement local à la gouvernance urbaine', *Revue française de science politique*, vol. 45, no. 1.

Le Galès, P. and J. Mawson (1994) *Management Innovations in Urban Policy: Lessons from France*, Local Government Management Board, Luton.

Le Galès, P. and M. Thatcher (eds.) (1995) *Les Réseaux de politique publique: le débat autour des 'policy networks'*, Harmattan, Paris.

Lemaire-Prosche, G. (1990) *Le PS et l'Europe*, Editions universitaires, Paris.

Le Monde (1995a) *François Mitterrand: 14 ans de pouvoir*, Le Monde dossiers et documents, Paris.

Le Monde (1995b) *L'Election présidentielle de 1995*, Le Monde dossiers et documents, Paris.

Le Net, M. (1991) 'Les Lobbies et le pouvoir', *Problèmes politiques et sociaux*, no. 662.

Le Pourhiet, A. (1987) 'Les Emplois à la discrétion', *Pouvoirs*, no. 40.

Lequesne, C. (1993) *Paris-Bruxelles*, Presses de la FNSP, Paris.

Le Spectacle du monde (1989), *Les Affaires*, no. 323.

L'Express (1987) 'La Corruption en France', *L'Express*, 10–16 April.

Lipset, S.M. and S. Rokkan (eds.) (1967) *Party Systems and Voters' Alignments: Cross-national perspectives*, Free Press, New York.

Lochak, D. and J. Chevallier (1986) *La Haute Administration et la politique*, PUF, Paris.

Long, M. (1981) *Les Services du premier ministre*, Presses universitaires d'Aix, Aix-en-Provence.

Long, M. (1992) 'Le Conseil d'état et la fonction consultative: de la consultation à la décision', *Revue française de droit administratif*, vol. 8, no. 5.

Long, M. (1995) 'Le Conseil d'état: rouage au coeur de l'administration et le juge administratif suprême', *Revue administrative*, vol. 48, no. 283.

Lorrain, D. (1993) 'Après la décentralisation: l'action publique flexible', *Sociologie du travail*, vol. 35, no. 3.

Lorrain, D. and G. Stoker (1995) (eds.) *La Privatisation des services urbains en Europe*, La Découverte, Paris.

Lorwin, V. (1972) *The French Labor Movement*, Harvard University Press, Cambridge, MA.

Loughlin, J. and S. Mazey (1994) 'The end of the French unitary state? Ten years of regionalization in France', *Regional Politics and Policy*, vol. 4, no. 3.

Mabileau, A. (1991) *Le Système local en France*, Montchrestien, Paris.

Mabileau, A., P. Garraud and G. Parry (1989) *Local Politics and Participation in Britain and France*, Cambridge University Press, Cambridge.

Machin, H. and V. Wright (eds.) (1985) *Economic Policy and Policy-Making under the Mitterrand Presidency: 1981–84*, Pinter, London.

Machin, H. (1989) 'Stages and dynamics in the evolution of the French party system', *West European Politics*, vol. 12, no. 4.

Maclean, M. (1993) 'Dirty dealings: business and politics in France', *Modern and Contemporary France*, vol. 1, no. 2.

Maclean, M. (1995) 'Privatisation in France 1993–94: new departures, or a case of *plus ça change?*', *West European Politics*, vol. 18, no. 2.

Marcou, G. (1992) 'Les Collectivités territoriales et l'éducation nationale', *Savoir*, vol. 4, no. 2.

Marcou, G., J.-P. Costa and C. Durand-Prinborgne (eds.) (1992) *La Décision dans l'éducation nationale*, Presses universitaires de Lille, Lille.

Marcus, J. (1995) *The National Front and French Politics: The resistible rise of Jean-Marie Le Pen*, Macmillan, London.

Massot, J. (1986) *La Présidence de la République en France*, Documentation française, Paris.

Massot, J. (1987) *L'Arbitre et le capitaine*, Flammarion, Paris.

Massot, J. (1993) 'Chef de l'état et chef du gouvernement: dyarchie et hiérarchie', *Notes et études documentaires*, no. 4983.

Massot, J. and O. Fouquet (1993) *Le Conseil d'état: juge de cassation*, Berger-Levrault, Paris.

Maus, D. (1991) 'Parlement et politiques publics: l'exemple de la Ve République', *Politiques et Management Public*, vol. 9, no. 2.

Maus, D. (ed.) (1992) *Les Grands Textes de la pratique institutionnelle de la Ve République*, Documentation française, Paris.

Maus, D., L. Favoreu and J.-L. Parodi (eds.) (1992) *L'Ecriture de la constitution de 1958: actes du colloque du 30ème anniversaire*, Economica, Paris.

Mayer, N. (1996) 'Le FN est d'extrême droite: ce sont ses électeurs qui le disent', *Libération*, 22 July.

Mayer, N. and P. Perrineau (eds.) (1989) *Le Front national à découvert*, Presses de la FNSP, Paris.

Mayer, N. and P. Perrineau (1992) 'Why do they vote for Le Pen?', *European Journal of Political Research*, vol. 22, no. 1.

Mazey, S. (1986) 'Public policy-making in France: the art of the possible', *West European Politics*, vol. 9, no. 3.

Mazey, S. and M. Newman (1987) *Mitterrand's France*, Croom Helm, London.

Mazey, S. and J. Richardson (eds.) (1993) *Lobbying in the European Community*, Oxford University Press, Oxford.

McCarthy, P. (ed.) (1987) *The French Socialists in Power*, Greenwood Press, Westport, CT.

McCarthy, P. (ed.) (1993) *France–Germany, 1983–93: The struggle to cooperate*, Macmillan, London.

McMillan, J. (1985) *Dreyfus to de Gaulle: Politics and society in France 1889–1969*, Edward Arnold, London.

Mendras, H. (1989) *La Seconde Révolution française*, Gallimard, Paris.

Mendras, H. and A. Cole (1991) *Social Change in Modern France*, Cambridge University Press, Cambridge.

Menon, A. (1994) 'Defence policy in the Fifth Republic: politics by any other means', *West European Politics*, vol. 17, no.4.

Mény, Y. (1987) 'France: the construction and reconstruction of centres', *West European Politics*, vol. 10, no. 4.

Mény, Y. (ed.) (1989) *Idéologies, partis politiques et groupes sociaux*, Presses de la FNSP, Paris.

Mény, Y. (1992) *La Corruption de la république*, Fayard, Paris.

Mény, Y. (1993) 'La Décennie de la corruption', *Le Débat*, no. 77.

Michelat, G. and M. Simon (1977) *Classe, religion et comportement politique*, Presses de la FNSP, Paris.

Milner, S. (1992) 'French trade unions and the single European market', *Modern and Contemporary France*, no. 51.

Milza, P. (1994) 'Le Front national crée-t-il une culture politique?', *Vingtième siècle*, no. 44.

Mitra, S. (1988) 'The National Front in France: a single-issue movement?', *West European Politics*, vol. 11, no. 2.

Mitterrand, F. and E. Weisel (1995) *Mémoire à deux voix*, Odile Jacob, Paris.

Mitterrand, F. (1964) *Le Coup d'état permanent*, Plon, Paris.

Montaldo, J. (1994) *Mitterrand et les quarante voleurs*, Grasset, Paris.

Moon, J. (1995) 'Innovatory leadership and policy change: lessons from Thatcher', *Governance*, vol. 8, no. 1.

Moravscik, A. (1993) 'Idealism and interest in the European Community: the case of the French referendum', *French Politics and Society*, vol. 11, no. 1.

Moreau-Defarges, P. (1985) 'J'ai fait une rêve . . . Le président Mitterrand, artisan de l'union européenne', *Politique étrangère*, no. 2/85.

Morgan, R. (1991) 'French perspectives on the new Germany', *Government and Opposition*, vol. 26, no. 1.

Morizet, J. (1990) 'Le Problème allemand vu de France', *Défense nationale*, vol. 46, no. 1.

Morris, P. (1994) *French Politics Today*, Manchester University Press, Manchester.

Morris, P. and B. Jenkins (1993) 'Political scandal in France', *Modern and Contemporary France*, vol. 1, no. 2.

Mouriaux, R. (1993) 'Les Syndicats', *Politiques*, no. 5.

Mouriaux, R. and G. Bibès (1990) *Les Syndicats européens à l'épreuve*, Presses de la FNSP, Paris.

Muller, P. (1989) *Airbus, l'ambition européenne. Logique de l'état, logique de marché*, Harmattan, Paris.

Muller, P. (1990a) *Les Politiques publiques*, Paris, PUF.

Muller, P. (1990b) 'Les Politiques publiques entre secteurs et territoires', *Politiques et management public*, vol. 8, no. 3.

Muller, P. (1992) 'Entre le local et l'Europe: la crise du modèle français des politiques publiques', *Revue française de science politique*, vol. 42, no. 2.

Muron, L. (1994) *Pompidou: le Président oublié*, Flammarion, Paris.

Newman, M. (1987) 'Conflict and cohesion in the British Labour Party and the PCF', *West European Politics*, vol.10, no. 3.

Northcutt, W. (1992) *Mitterrand: A political biography*, Holmes and Meier, New York.

Padgett, S. and W.E. Patterson (1991) *A History of Social-Democracy in Post-War Europe*, Longman, London.

Parodi, J.-L. (1978) 'Les Règles du scrutin majoritaire', *Revue française de science politique*, vol. 28, no. 1.

Parodi, M. (1981) *L'Economie et la société française depuis 1945*, Armand Colin, Paris.

Passerron, A. (1987) 'Comment ils ont placé leurs amis', *Pouvoirs*, no. 40.

Paxton, R. (1972) *Vichy France: Old guard and new order*, Columbia University Press, New York.

Paxton, R. (1973) *La France de Vichy: 1940–1944*, Seuil, Paris.

Péan, P. (1994) *Une Jeunesse Française*, Fayard, Paris.

Percheron, A. (1982) 'Religious acculturation and political socialisation in France', *West European Politics*, vol. 5, no. 2.

Perrineau, P. and N. Mayer (1992) *Le Front national à découvert*,Presses de la FNSP, Paris.

Pfister, T. (1986) *Dans les coulisses du pouvoir*, Albin Michel, Paris.

Pierré-Caps, S. (1991) 'L'Adaptation du parlement français au système communautaire', *Revue française du droit constitutionnel*, no. 6.

Pitts, J. (1981) 'Les Français et l'autorité', in J.-D. Reynaud and Y. Grafmeyer (eds.), *Français, qui êtes-vous?*, Documentation française, Paris.

Politis (1989) 'Les Années fric', *Politis*, 10–16 February.

Portelli, H. (1992) *Le Parti socialiste*, Montchrestien, Paris.

Portelli, H. (1994) *La Ve République*, Grasset, Paris.

Pouvoirs (1993) Special issue on 'Le Parlement', no. 64.

Py, R. (1985) *Le Secrétariat général du gouvernement*, Documentation française, Paris.

Quermonne, J.-L. (1987) 'La Présidence de la République et le système de partis', *Pouvoirs*, no. 41.

Quermonne, J.-L. and D. Chagnollaud (1991) *Le Gouvernement de la France sous la cinquième république*, Dalloz, Paris.

Racine, P. (1973) 'L'ENA et son évolution', *Revue administrative*, no. 26.

Rails. S. (ed.) (1987) *Textes constitutionnels français*, PUF, Paris.

Ranger, J. (1981) 'Le Déclin du Parti communiste', *Revue française de science politique*, vol. 36, no. 1.

Ravitch, N. (1990) *The Catholic Church and the French Nation, 1589–1989*, Routledge, London.

Raymond, G. (ed.) (1994) *France during the Socialist Years*, Dartmouth, Aldershot.

Regan, M.-C. and F.L. Wilson (1986) 'Interest group politics in France and Ireland: comparative perspectives on neo-corporatism', *West European Politics*, vol. 9, no. 3.

Rémond, R. (1982) *Les Droites en France*, Aubier, Paris.

Revue française de science politique (1990) *Naissance de la cinquième république*, Presses de la FNSP, Paris.

Revue politique et parlementaire (1992) 'Les Valeurs de la république', *Revue politique et parlementaire*, vol. 94, no. 962.

Rey, H. and F. Subileau (1991) 'PS: structures et organisation', *Regards sur l'actualité*, no. 171.

Richardson, D. and C. Rootes (eds.) (1995) *The Green Political Challenge*, Routledge, London.

Richardson, J. (1982) *Policy Styles in Western Europe*, Allen and Unwin, London.

Ridley, F. (1970) *Revolutionary Syndicalism in France*, Cambridge University Press, Cambridge.

Rioux, J.-P. (1987) *The Fourth Republic 1944–1958*, Cambridge University Press, Cambridge.

Robert, J. (1988) 'De l'indépendance des juges', *Revue du droit public*, no.1.

Rolin, F. (1990) 'Risques et chances: la décentralisation et les associations', *Territoires*, October.

Rondin, J. (1986) *Le Sacre des notables*, Fayard, Paris.

Rosanvallon, P. (1993) 'La Décentralisation', *Pouvoirs locaux*, no. 18.

Ross, G., S. Hoffmann and S. Malzacher (1987) *The Mitterrand Experiment*, Polity Press, Oxford.

Rousellier, N. (1994) 'La Ligne de fuite: l'idée d'Europe dans la culture politique française', *Vingtième siècle*, no. 44.

Roussel, E. (1984) *Georges Pompidou*, Lattès, Paris.

Safran, W. (1991, 1994) *The French Polity*, Longman, London.

Sartori, G. (1966) 'European political parties: the case of polarised pluralism', in G. La Palombara and M. Weiner (eds.) *Political Parties and Political Development*, Princeton University Press, Princeton, NJ.

Sartori, G. (1976) *Parties and Party Systems*, Cambridge University Press, Cambridge.

Schain, M. (1987) 'Racial politics in France: the National Front and the construction of political legitimacy', *West European Politics*, vol. 10, no. 2.

Schmidt, V. (1990a) *Democratising France*, Cambridge University Press, Cambridge.

Schmidt, V. (1990b) 'Engineering a critical realignment of the electorate: the case of the Socialists in France', *West European Politics*, vol. 13, no. 2.

Schmidt, V. (1996) *From State to Market*, Cambridge University Press, Cambridge.

Schmitter, P. and G. Lehmbruch (eds.) (1979) *Trends toward Corporatist Intermediation*, Sage, London.

Schneider, R. (1994) *Les Dernières Années*, Seuil, Paris.

Seurin, J.-L. (1986) *La Présidence de la République en France et aux Etats-Unis*, Economica, Paris.

Shennan, A. (1993) *De Gaulle*, Longman, London.

Shields, J. (1990) 'A new chapter in the history of the French extreme right: the National Front', in A. Cole (ed.), *French Political Parties in Transition*, Dartmouth, Aldershot.

Shields, J. (1991) 'The politics of disaffection: France in the 1980s', in J. Gaffney and E. Kolinsky (eds.), *Political Culture in France and Germany*, Routledge, London.

Shields, J. (1995) 'Le Pen, and the progression of the extreme-right in France', *French Politics and Society*, vol. 13, no. 2.

Simon, J. (1992) 'La Décentralisation du système éducatif – six ans après', *Savoir*, vol. 4, no. 2.

Singer, D. (1991) 'The resistible rise of Jean-Marie Le Pen', *Ethnic and Racial Studies*, vol. 14, no. 3.

Stenhouse, T.G. (1996) *La Participation politique des Maghrébins de France*, Harmattan, Paris.

Stevens, A. (1991) 'Culture and public policy: the case of environment policy in France', *Modern and Contemporary France*, no. 44.

Stevens, A. (1992, 1995) *The Government and Politics of France*, Macmillan, London.

Stirn, B. (1991) *Le Conseil d'état: son rôle, sa jurisprudence*, Hachette, Paris.

Stone, A. (1989) 'In the shadow of the Constitutional Council: the "juridicisation" of the legislative process in France', *West European Politics*, vol. 12, no. 2.

Stone, A. (1992) 'Where judicial politics are legislative politics: the French Constitutional Council', *West European Politics*, vol. 15, no. 3.

Suleiman, E. (1974) *Politics, Power and Bureaucracy in France*, Princeton University Press, Princeton, NJ.

Suleiman, E. (1978) *Elites in French Society: The politics of survival*, Princeton University Press, Princeton, NJ.

Suleiman, E. (1991) 'The politics of corruption and the corruption of politics', *French Politics and Society*, vol. 9, no. 1.

Tacet, D. (1992) *Un Monde sans paysans*, Hachette, Paris.

Thiebault, J.-L. (1989) 'Jalons pour une analyse des conflits gouvernementaux sous la Vème République', *Les Cahiers du CRAPS*, no. 7.

Thiebault, J.-L. (1993) 'Party leadership selection in France', *European Journal of Political Research*, vol. 24, no. 2.

Thoenig, J.-C. (1973) *L'Ere des technocrates*, Editions de l'organisation, Paris.

Thomson, D. (1969) *Democracy in France since 1870*, Oxford University Press, Oxford.

Thullier, G. (1985) *Les Cabinets ministériels*, PUF, Paris.

Tiersky, R. (1974) *French Communism, 1920–72*, Columbia University Press, New York.

Tiersky, R. (1994) *France in the New Europe*, Westview Press, Boulder, CO.

Tiersky, R. (1995) 'Mitterrand's legacies', *Foreign Affairs*, vol. 74, no. 1.

Todd, E. (1995) 'Aux origines du malaise politique français. Les classes sociales et leur représentation', *Le Débat*, no. 83.

Todd, O. (1988) *La Nouvelle France*, Paris, Seuil.

Tréan, C. (1991) 'La France et le nouvel ordre européen', *Politique étrangère*, no. 1/91.

Tuppen, J. (1988) *Chirac's France*, Macmillan, London.

Valence, G. (1990) *France–Allemagne. Le retour de Bismarck*, Flammarion, Paris.

Vernardakis, G. (1992) 'Inside perceptions of public policy making in France: preliminary analysis', *International Journal of Public Administration*, vol. 15, no. 9.

Vesperini, J.-P. (1993) *L'Economie de la France sous la cinquième république*, Economica, Paris.

Viansson-Ponté, P. (1994) *Histoire de la république gaullienne. 1, La Fin d'une époque: mai 1958–juillet 1962. 2, Le Temps des orphelins: août 1962–avril 1969*, Fayard, Paris.

Vincent, G. and V. Aubert (1977) *Les Français, 1945–1975: chroniques et structures d'une société*, Masson, Paris.

Vincent, G. and A. Gournay (1980) *Les Français, 1976–1979: chronologie et structures d'une société*, Masson, Paris.

Weber, E. (1979) *Peasants into Frenchmen: The modernisation of rural France*, Chatto and Windus, London.

Weber, H. (1986) *Le Parti des patrons*, Seuil, Paris.

Weil, P. (1991) 'Immigration and the rise of racism in France: the contradictions in Mitterrand's policies', *French Politics and Society*, vol. 9, no. 3–4.

Williams, P.M. (1964) *Crisis and Compromise: Politics in the Fourth Republic*, Longman, London.

Williams, P.M. (1970) *Wars, Plots and Scandals*, Longman, London.

Williams, P.M. and M. Harrison (1965) *De Gaulle's Republic*, Longman, London.

Williams, P.M. and M. Harrison (1969) *French Politicians and Elections*, Cambridge University Press, Cambridge.

Wilson, F.L. (1985) 'Socialism in France: a failure of politics not a failure of policy', *Parliamentary Affairs*, vol. 38, no. 2.

Wilson, F.L. (1987) *Interest Group Politics in France*, Cambridge University Press, Cambridge.

Winchester, H. (1993) *Contemporary France*, Longman, Harlow.

Withol de Wenden, K. (1991) 'Immigration policy and the issue of nationality', *Ethnic and Racial Studies*, vol. 14, no. 3.

Worms, J.-P. (1966) 'Le Préfet et ses notables', *Sociologie du travail*, vol. 8, no. 3.

Wright, G. (1987) *France in Modern Times*, Longman, London.

Wright, V. (1974) 'Politics and administration under the French Fifth Republic', *Political Studies*, vol. 22, no. 1.

Wright, V. (ed.) (1979) *Conflict and Consensus in France*, Frank Cass, London.

Wright, V. (1989) *The Government and Politics of France*, Unwin Hyman, London.

Wright, V. (ed.) (1993) *Les Privatisations en Europe*, Actes sud, Paris.

Yost, D.-S. (1990) 'France in the new Europe', *Foreign Affairs*, vol. 69, no. 5.

Ysmal, C. (1989) *Les Partis politiques sous la Ve République*, Montchrestien, Paris.

Ysmal, C. (1990) 'La Crise électorale du Front national', *Revue française de science politique*, vol. 40, no. 6.

Zarka, J.-C. (1994) *Le Président de la 5e République*, Ellipses, Paris.

Index